OUR TEAM

OUR TEAM

The Epic Story of Four Men and the World Series
That Changed Baseball

Luke Epplin

FLATIRON
BOOKS
NEW YORK

www.flatironbooks.com

Designed by Omar Chapa

Library of Congress Cataloging-in-Publication Data

Names: Epplin, Luke, author.
Title: Our team : the epic story of four men and the World Series that
    changed baseball / Luke Epplin.
Description: First edition. | New York : Flatiron Books, 2021. | Includes
    bibliographical references and index.
Identifiers: LCCN 2020047458 | ISBN 9781250313799 (hardcover) |
    ISBN 9781250313805 (ebook)
Subjects: LCSH: Cleveland Indians (Baseball team)—History. |
    Doby, Larry. | Veeck, Bill. | Feller, Bob, 1918–2010. | Paige, Satchel,
    1906–1982. | World Series (Baseball) (1948) | Baseball players—
    United States—Biography.
Classification: LCC GV875.C7 E77 2021 | DDC 796.357/640977132—dc23
LC record available at https://lccn.loc.gov/2020047458

Our books may be purchased in bulk for promotional, educational, or business use. Please contact your local bookseller or the Macmillan Corporate and Premium Sales Department at 1-800-221-7945, extension 5442, or by email at MacmillanSpecialMarkets@macmillan.com.

First Edition: 2021

10 9 8 7 6 5 4 3 2 1

For my parents
and for Beth

CONTENTS

OUR TEAM

INTRODUCTION

There had seemingly never been a better night for baseball in Cleveland than on August 20, 1948. The hometown Indians, a hard-luck franchise that hadn't sniffed the postseason in more than a quarter-century, sat atop the standings in the American League with six weeks left in the regular season. It'd been more than a week since the team had lost a game. Each of the Indians' last three wins had been a shutout, putting them one shy of the American League record for consecutive scoreless contests. Even though experience had conditioned fans not to set their expectations too high when it came to the Indians, there was a budding sense all around northern Ohio that this summer would play out differently, that the neck-and-neck pennant race finally would break their way, that the club's cobbled-together roster of underdogs and oddly shaped pieces that resembled no other's somehow would power them past the more conventional lineups fielded by the New York Yankees and Boston Red Sox.

In the fevered hours before game time on that muggy Friday evening, swarms of cars and pedestrians clogged the streets and walkways leading to the Indians' mammoth stadium on the southern shore of Lake Erie. Inside, according to the Associated Press, fans "sat, stood, stooped, crouched, and literally hung from the railings," spilling into whatever empty spaces they could find. More than 78,000 spectators turned out, a new attendance record for a night game in Major League Baseball. Everywhere around them, the changes sweeping through professional baseball in the wake of World War II would've been evident. Beyond the fences in left field were more than twenty green-and-white-striped tents, inside of which hundreds of mayors from across Ohio were being feted by the Indians' front office. Festively attired musicians blew their horns while parading through the stands. A vaudeville act and a fireworks show were soon to start.

Most significantly, warming up to start for the Indians that night was Leroy "Satchel" Paige, the lone Black pitcher on the lone integrated club in the American League, someone who was incongruously both a major-league rookie and a baseball legend.

The entirety of the scene—the raucous pregame entertainment, the integrated roster, the fan-friendly stadium flooding over with spectators—was enough to stop members of the opposing Chicago White Sox on the steps of the visitors' dugout. "Baseball sure has changed," muttered White Sox catcher Aaron Robinson while scanning the field in disbelief.

At the forefront of this postwar sports revolution was Bill Veeck, the most eccentric and forward-thinking executive of his era. Only thirty-two years old when he'd purchased the Indians in 1946, nursing a leg injury he'd suffered while serving in the South Pacific, Veeck wasted no time in turning Indians games into the hottest ticket in baseball. Fireworks exploded, outlandish gate prizes were dispersed, contortionists clowned around on the sidelines, and Veeck, his head bare and his sports shirt unbuttoned at the neck, limped through the stands, shaking hands and gabbing with fans on how to make home games even more entertaining. Unbound by decorum and convention, disdainful of prejudices and formalities, Veeck was, as Cleveland sportswriter Gordon Cobbledick proclaimed, "a phenomenon the like of which hasn't been seen since some ancient Roman hawked the first ticket of admission to the Colosseum." While attendance exploded across the major leagues in the latter half of the 1940s as returning servicemen eased back into American life at the ballpark, in Cleveland Veeck's irresistible mix of winning baseball and diverting sideshows would smash audience records across the board. Some days, Cleveland's Municipal Stadium, a ballpark so enormous that one writer claimed "the customers at the end of each foul line need radios to follow the games," seemed too cramped.

To show his gratitude to the Indians fans who had been turning out in jaw-dropping numbers throughout the summer of 1948, Veeck invited hundreds of mayors from every corner of the state, from the biggest cities to the smallest towns, to serve as stand ins for their citizens on the night of August 20. In the tents that he'd erected between the bleachers and the left-field fences, Veeck threw them a pregame garden party, complete with linen-covered tables, potted plants, a four-tier cake topped with baseballs, and roving entertainment by clowns, troubadours, and vaudeville performers.

Traditionally, during a game when the symbolic eyes of the entire state were on the home team, efforts would have been made to ensure that Bob Feller, the longtime ace of the pitching staff, started for the Indians. Ever since he'd crashed the majors cold as a seventeen-year-old fireballer straight out of the Iowa cornfields, Feller had resonated among wide swathes of white America. He possessed the uncanny ability to embody whatever the public craved at a particular moment: homespun values during the Depression, selfless patriotism during the Second World War, entrepreneurial drive during the postwar consumer boom. In his years since returning home from the war, where he'd served aboard a naval battleship, Feller had dedicated himself as much to striking out batters on the field as to cashing in on his name and persona off it, setting the template for the athlete as businessman. By 1948, however, Feller had begun to falter, both on the mound and in fan affection. Not only was he uncharacteristically struggling to tally more wins than losses, but he found himself overshadowed for the first time since donning a major-league uniform by another pitcher on his own team, the same one he'd squared off against over the past dozen years on the off-season barnstorming trail.

Instead of Feller, it was Satchel Paige who strolled to the mound for the Indians at game time. Over more than twenty seasons in the Negro Leagues, Paige had built himself into a cultural icon whose pitching lore crossed racial lines during an era when he himself couldn't. By the time Major League Baseball took its first tentative steps toward integration, Paige was already easing into his forties, a generation removed from the Black players being scouted as pioneers. It was partly through his duels with Feller on the off-season barnstorming circuit, where cobbled-together squads of major- and minor-league players often faced off against their counterparts in the Negro Leagues, that Paige would exhibit his undiminished mastery over batters, no matter their race. For three consecutive Octobers after the war, Paige and Feller, the premier Black and white pitchers of their time, would duel against each other, likely never imagining that they'd soon join forces in Cleveland.

In July 1948, Veeck had shocked the sporting world by bringing Paige to Cleveland to bolster the Indians' pitching ranks during the stretch run of a pennant race destined to go down to the wire. The blowback had been swift and ferocious, with certain members of the traditionalist baseball establishment accusing Veeck of making a mockery of the sport by signing someone of Paige's advanced age. It didn't take long for Paige to silence his doubters. During his first month with the Indians, he'd surrendered a mere seven runs over thirty-eight and a third innings. His initial three starts in the majors attracted more than 200,000 fans, which led sportswriter Ed McAuley of the *Cleveland News* to dub Paige "the greatest drawing card in the history of baseball."

That much was clear to Veeck as he gazed out from the press

box at Municipal Stadium on August 20 to a packed house of fans who could barely contain their excitement at watching Paige ply his trade. "This thing has gone beyond me," he mumbled in wonder. When reporters asked him how the Indians had managed to shatter the nighttime attendance record while playing the White Sox, the last-place team in the American League, Veeck didn't hesitate in asserting: "It's Paige. The guy is spectacular."

For all the widespread publicity his first month in the majors had generated, Paige hadn't been the player whom Veeck had chosen to integrate the Indians. Starting in center field that evening was Larry Doby, a hard-hitting, soft-spoken former infielder who just now was finding his footing on the Indians. In July 1947, eleven weeks after Jackie Robinson had debuted on the Brooklyn Dodgers, snapping the color line that had segregated Major League Baseball since the late nineteenth century, Veeck had signed Doby, a twenty-three-year-old rising star on the Newark Eagles of the Negro National League, and rushed him onto the Indians' roster. Unlike Robinson, whose pit stop in the minor leagues had eased his transition to the Dodgers, Doby would journey literally overnight from the Negro to the major leagues, suiting up for the Eagles one day and then the Indians the next.

The second Black player in the majors, Doby found himself wholly unprepared for the trials that awaited him. For the remainder of the 1947 season, he'd barely made a mark amid clubhouse dissension, scant playing time, and persistent racial abuse. Critics of integration labeled him a bust, proof positive of the unpreparedness of players from the Negro Leagues. Doby's subsequent turnaround in 1948, from dejected benchwarmer to indispensable catalyst of the Indians' improbable charge to the pennant, was shaping up to be one of the most meaningful sports stories of the postwar era.

Together, on August 20, Paige and Doby would almost single-handedly propel the Indians to victory. Right from the start, Paige came out cool and in control, needing just eleven pitches—only two of which missed the strike zone—to send down White Sox batters in the opening frame. On the mound he resembled, in one columnist's eyes, "the most serious of workmen, a fine old craftsman calling upon the artistry, the control and the cunning which some 30 years of pitching have given him." The jubilant masses never broke his concentration. Paige pitched around a leadoff single in the second inning, then retired the side again in the third, this time on a mere nine pitches. He'd wade into trouble an inning later, when he walked White Sox first baseman Tony Lupien at the start of the fourth, then surrendered a single to Luke Appling. Doby, however, was there to bail him out. Fielding Appling's single on a dead run in center field, Doby rifled a throw to third that beat the sliding Lupien to the bag by inches. Having snuffed out the White Sox rally with his arm in the top half of the inning, Doby would boost Paige's odds of winning with his bat in the bottom half. With two on and two out, Doby drilled the second pitch he saw into center for a single, driving in the game's lone run.

Only once more would the White Sox mount an offensive attack. Leading off the seventh inning, White Sox slugger Pat Seerey lofted a soaring fly to center off Paige that looked certain to clear the fence. Breaking back on contact, Doby raced to the wall, stretched his glove high over his head, and made a leaping grab that robbed Seerey of a game-tying home run. Paige would take it from there, not allowing a single batter to reach base in the final three innings. The game ended in less than two hours with a 1-0 win for Paige, who threw just ninety-two pitches while going the distance.

It was a victory that was as much his as it was Doby's. "This was undoubtedly the first time in major league history," one columnist wrote afterward, "that two Negroes have combined their talents so effectively to produce an important victory, the one pitching and the other by his hitting and fielding." During a nail-biting pennant race in which every game mattered, Paige and Doby salvaged one that might have sunk the franchise in any other season. Paige would later call it the biggest start of his decades-long career. An editorial in Cleveland's largest newspaper, *The Plain Dealer,* dubbed the contest a "triumph of racial tolerance."

It is perhaps inevitable that the second team in Major League Baseball to integrate in the twentieth century would be overshadowed by the first. Many decades later, the popular narrative about baseball integration often doubles as one about the Brooklyn Dodgers and Jackie Robinson, whose gutsy play and trailblazing path in the face of rank bigotry would rightfully secure him a permanent place in the nation's collective imagination, one that has since swollen to mythic proportions. But there was another meaningful and dramatic narrative unfolding at the same time in Cleveland, where the hometown Indians would whip fans across northern Ohio into a state of delirium during the summer of 1948, the season after the franchise had desegregated its roster.

This is the story of how that team came to be as told through four of its key participants: Bill Veeck, Bob Feller, Satchel Paige, and Larry Doby. These men, two white and two Black, diverged in temperament, background, and outlook. Each in his own way represented a different facet of the emerging integration saga that had just begun to play out across professional baseball. Their unlikely union would elevate new athletic idols and lead to the reevaluation of old ones, would remake sports as a business and the individual athlete as a brand, and would help puncture long-standing stereotypes that so much of white America harbored toward Black ballplayers. As the backbone of a team that epitomized the postwar American spirit in all its hopes and contradictions, Veeck, Feller, Paige, and Doby would captivate the nation during their thrilling run to the World Series in 1948, all the while shining a light forward for a country on the verge of a civil rights revolution.

PART I

BEGINNINGS

1

The Duel

On October 5, 1936, thousands of people packed the unpaved roads of Van Meter, Iowa. Farmers interrupted their harvesting, schools across Dallas County closed, even Iowa governor Clyde L. Herring made the trip from Des Moines. They descended in droves on a nondescript farm town smack in the middle of the state to pay tribute to a native son whose legend had sprouted suddenly that summer.

Bob Feller's ascent from the cow pastures of Iowa to national prominence had been as breathtaking as it was baffling. No player had ever stormed into Major League Baseball with such startling force. How could someone who'd never apprenticed in the minors throw a fastball that some major leaguers deemed the swiftest they'd ever encountered? The sound of the pitch smacking into a catcher's mitt was enough to make baseball veterans—some of whom were more than twice Feller's age—gape at the round-cheeked wunderkind on the mound.

He was a figure straight out of a dime-store novel, an adolescent dream come to life. In his very first start with the Cleveland Indians, he'd tied the American League record of fifteen strikeouts in a single game. Columnist Gordon Cobbledick of *The Plain Dealer* called it probably "the greatest major league pitching debut in all history." Four starts later, he'd tied the major-league record of seventeen strikeouts. Feller was seventeen years old.

Now he was back in his hometown, roughly five months after he'd departed for Cleveland. On a hastily erected stage, a string of dignitaries took turns singing Feller's praises. The mayor awarded him a key to the city, others gifted him a trunk for his travels. Later, Feller suited up for an exhibition game on the rain-drenched field of the high school he'd yet to graduate from. He fanned eleven of thirteen batters to dig in against him.

His next turn on the mound, however, wouldn't be such a breeze. Crossing the heartland that October was a barnstorming squad fronted by Rogers Hornsby, a seven-time National League batting champion who now was the aging player-manager for the St. Louis Browns. In the decades before television had penetrated American households, barnstorming took players to places farther afield than the Midwestern and Northeastern cities where all sixteen major-league clubs were clustered, to fans who otherwise wouldn't have been able to see them. Feller himself, who'd grown up hundreds of miles from the nearest major-league city, had watched Babe Ruth and Lou Gehrig play in Des Moines on a barnstorming tour years earlier. These tours were mostly slapdash ventures, stitched together by promoters and headed by superstars like Hornsby and St. Louis Cardinals pitching ace Dizzy Dean. For players, they offered one final payday before the cold weather settled in—a means of augmenting salaries kept in check by organized baseball's reserve clause, which tied players to the clubs that had originally signed them. The style of baseball was often loose and flashy, with room for vaudevillian interludes. Sometimes, to ramp up attendance and heighten the drama, all-white teams competed against rosters of players from the Negro Leagues—a rare spectacle during an era when baseball and segregation went hand in hand.

Hornsby's barnstorming squad was scheduled to pass through

Des Moines on October 7. Ray Doan, the tour's coordinator, knew just who to call to guarantee a packed house. The announcement that Bob Feller would start that evening triggered a scrum for tickets. His father, Bill, snatched up four hundred of them—enough for the entire town of Van Meter. More than an exhibition game, this would be a matchup with stakes, one that would pit the local white prodigy against a Black pitcher already shrouded in myth.

Squaring off against Feller in Des Moines would be Leroy "Satchel" Paige.

From spring training to the World Series, an entrenched color line separated Feller and Paige. That had been the case since the end of the nineteenth century, when white players like Adrian "Cap" Anson, an Iowa native who starred on the Chicago White Stockings, objected to playing against interracial competition, and Black players like Moses Fleetwood Walker and John "Bud" Fowler were released or drummed out of organized baseball. Eventually, owners in the major and minor leagues forged a so-called gentlemen's agreement not to sign players of Black African descent. Though never formalized, the agreement kept rosters all-white for decades.

This Jim Crow system spurred the development of professional Black baseball circuits across the country. Even the most successful of these Negro Leagues were long on talent but short on funds, and thriving in them required both endurance and improvisation by players and clubs alike. In between league games, cash-strapped teams often competed anywhere they could make a buck. Sometimes, players would sweat through a doubleheader, pile into a beaten-down bus, drive through the night, and awaken sore and stiff in a distant town for nine more frames on fields that were frequently rock-strewn and hard as brick. "It was just a continuous scuffle," remembered Johnny Davis, an outfielder for the Newark Eagles. "Play here this afternoon, another game tonight, ride six hundred miles, play somewhere else. Sometimes you put on the uniform, it was still

wet." Black boardinghouses offered temporary but unreliable relief. In some, bedbugs, scratchy sheets, and firm mattresses robbed
players of essential rest. Often, no restaurants would serve them,
so players passed around sleeves of crackers and tins of sardines, or
searched for diners that would sneak them sandwiches through the
back door.

The grinding pace of life in the Negro Leagues could be a strain
on players' muscles and minds, but they competed on the diamond
with hunger and creativity, developing a more kinetic style of baseball than their major-league contemporaries. During the Depression, when the unemployment rate for Black workers periodically
hovered at 50 percent, playing in the Negro Leagues, veteran player
Ted Page would assert, was "the way I had to keep from washing
the windows in a downtown store or sweeping the floor." Not only
did baseball lift some players, at least temporarily, out of backbreak-
ing or menial labor, but it turned them into idols in their communities and beyond. Negro League teams formed the beating hearts
of metropolitan Black districts across the country; their games were
places where fans, often decked out in their finest garments, reveled
in rooting collectively for players whose talents and feats sparked
ardent communal pride. Through regular write-ups in Black newspapers, figures like Josh Gibson, James "Cool Papa" Bell, and Buck
Leonard became familiar names among Black Americans in the
1930s. And there was one star who outshone them all.

On days Satchel Paige pitched, Negro League fans rushed to
their seats early. They didn't want to miss perhaps the most curiously
electrifying spectacle in sports: that first glimpse of Paige, tall and
lean and stoic, walking measuredly toward the mound. Toeing the
rubber, he stood as straight as a weather vane on a windless afternoon. His arms were long and sinewy, his calves so slender Paige
padded them with multiple pairs of socks. When the leadoff batter
dug in, Paige would windmill his right arm, hike his left leg skyward, and let go a fastball that some opponents swore would hum as

it zipped past. His pitching was athleticism blended with theater—the complementary poles of every Paige performance, though Paige made it clear he favored one over the other. "I ain't no clown. I ain't no end man in no vaudeville show," he avowed time and again. "I'm a baseball pitcher, and winning baseball games is serious business."

By the time he was to face Feller in October 1936, Paige had become the go-to player for white barnstormers seeking a formidable foe on the mound and a reliable crowd magnet whose name alone attracted thousands of Black fans to the ballpark. The appeal of a Feller-Paige matchup, however, extended beyond simple gate receipts. In addition to speed, charisma, and self-confidence, each had a narrative and a persona wholly attuned to the times. As deeply as Bob Feller's story was beginning to resonate with white Americans during the Depression, so too had Satchel Paige's fed the imagination of millions of Black Americans.

The roots of Feller's legend took hold a decade earlier alongside his family's barn, an archetypal dark-red wooden structure a few miles northeast of Van Meter. Baseball and farm work were the knotted strands of Feller's childhood. From an early age, he helped his father, Bill, milk the cows, muck the barn, and lug water from the nearby Raccoon River. At lunchtime and "almost every night after chores were done, they would be out playing catch in the barnyard," remembered Bob's younger sister, Marguerite Goodson.

Bill Feller had taken over the family farm as an adolescent. As a result, Goodson said of her father, "He didn't get to do the fun things like playing baseball and all that. So he was going to be sure that his son didn't have to miss out on that, too." Just as he stocked the farm with cutting-edge machinery, he sought out top-line gear for Bob: spiked shoes, major-league-caliber gloves, a pinstriped uniform. To aid his son's development, he hung a wire loop on a tree for Bob to use as a throwing target. He hammered together a batting cage and squatted behind a sawed-off board to catch Bob's tosses.

In winter, when snow piled high in the pasture, Bill strung lights through the rafters of the barn so that his son could continue throwing indoors.

As his son came of age, Bill could sense a rare ability in his form, rhythm, and follow-through—even in the way Bob stood on the mound and glared into the mitt. So in the spring of 1932, when Bob was thirteen, Bill leveled a patch of rutted terrain at the western edge of the farm. With his son's help, he sawed down some trees and with the lumber erected a backstop, a scoreboard, outhouses, a concession stand, and a chicken-wire fence. From home plate, one could see a grove of oak trees in the distance, so they dubbed the field "Oak View Park." Building the baseball diamond was as much a grand gesture of confidence in Bob's potential as a gift to fast-track his son's development.

Recruiting some local players, Bill outfitted them in baggy gray uniforms with "Oak View" emblazoned across their chests. At that time, nearly every town and many industries across Iowa fielded baseball teams. Entire communities would turn out for weekend games, no matter that they were staged on diamonds carved into farmland. "People would drive their cars up and park and watch from their cars," Goodson recalled. To continue to make money on the land he sacrificed, Bill charged a quarter for admission, thirty-five cents for a doubleheader.

At first, Bob played mostly at shortstop and in the outfield for the Oak Views and local American Legion teams. It wasn't until 1934 that Bob first took the mound. Even though he was only fifteen years old, his blazing speed proved too much for grown men. He struck out fifteen batters in his first start, twenty in his second, and fifteen more in his third. Just like that, Bob was the talk of the central Iowa baseball circuit.

In October, Bill and Bob drove to St. Louis to attend the middle games of the 1934 World Series, which pitted the Detroit Tigers against a down-and-dirty Cardinals squad known as the Gashouse

Gang. Bill had worried that seeing major-league pitching at its finest would intimidate his son, but as they watched from the stands, a different thought flashed through Bob's mind: "I can do that."

That winter, Bob shot up several inches. Years of hauling water and tossing hay bales had thickened his shoulders and thighs. When he stood on the mound in 1935, he no longer looked like a kid playing dress-up. His speed was so overwhelming—and his control so unreliable—that, according to his high school catcher, "it got so the high school teams wouldn't schedule [Van Meter]. Said to wait till Bob graduated." In addition to the Oak Views, Feller suited up for a club organized by the farmers' union in Des Moines. While leading the team to the Iowa state championship, he allegedly struck out 361 batters over 157 innings that summer. Other semiprofessional teams clamored for his services, which he doled out for gas money and a hefty fee on the side.

At some point, word of Bob's feats reached Cleveland Indians executive Cy Slapnicka, who also hailed from Iowa. Arriving unannounced at Oak View Park one day in July, Slapnicka perched on the bumper of a car parked behind the backstop. After watching a few of Bob's pitches, he sensed that this was the sort of prospect scouts spent their lives trying to unearth. "His fastball," Slapnicka remembered, "was fast and fuzzy; it didn't go in a straight line; it wiggled and shot around." Afterward, Slapnicka and Bill Feller hashed out a modest contract that would ship Bob to a Class-D club in Fargo-Moorhead the next season, setting him on a traditional path to the Indians through the minor leagues.

Months later, Slapnicka attended a luncheon in Cleveland with his fellow Indians executives. When asked about the signing, Slapnicka, who was not usually prone to embellishment, announced: "Gentlemen, I've found the greatest young pitcher I ever saw . . . I suppose this sounds like the same old stuff to you, but I want you to believe me. This boy that I found out in Iowa will be the greatest pitcher the world has ever known."

In the spring of 1936, however, Bob strained his pitching arm. Because of the injury, Slapnicka instructed Bob to skip Fargo-Moorhead and report to Cleveland for rehabilitation after his junior year of high school concluded. On the day of his departure, Bob and his father strolled past the barn and over to dormant Oak View Park, where they paced around the bases in silence. The field had been built partly on a dream they'd shared, and now that it was on the verge of coming true, there seemed to be little more to say.

In Cleveland, Bob rehabbed quickly. Soon he was starting for a local amateur club, then was given a three-inning assignment with the Indians during an exhibition game against the St. Louis Cardinals over the All-Star break. These were still the Gashouse Gang Cardinals, the same core group of players that Bob had watched in the World Series two years earlier. He'd thought then that he could've held his own on the mound. Now, improbably, he was about to find out.

More than 10,000 spectators filed into Cleveland's League Park on July 6, 1936. Before the game, Frankie Frisch, the Cardinals player-manager whose dashing feats in college athletics had earned him the nickname the "Fordham Flash," was shooting the breeze with sportswriter Harry Grayson when the sound of a ball smacking into a catcher's mitt jolted them both upright. "Who in the hell is that fireballer?" Frisch reportedly asked, peering out of the dugout at the fresh-faced pitcher warming up on the sidelines.

Grayson, repeating an untrue rumor, explained that he was some prospect Slapnicka had signed who hawked peanuts in the stands during his downtime.

"Peanuts," Frisch bellowed. "That kid's the fastest pitcher I ever saw." Frisch motioned to rookie infielder Stu Martin. "Stu, how'd you like to play second base tonight?" he asked with mock innocence. Turning back to Grayson, Frisch quipped, "They're not gonna get the old Flash out there against that kid."

Feller entered the game in the fourth inning, with the score deadlocked at 1-all. His first throw thumped into the catcher's mitt with such a loud crack that the batter, Bruce Ogrodowski, backed off the plate in disbelief. Seemingly wanting nothing to do with the unknown pitcher, the slow-footed Ogrodowski bunted weakly to third for the out. Cardinals shortstop Leo Durocher approached the plate next. Feller greeted him with a bewildering mix of fastballs down the middle and well outside the zone. Durocher swung through a third strike far off the plate, then nearly burst out laughing. It was absurd, this supposed peanut vendor showing up the first-place club in the National League.

Feller struck out two in the fourth, then three more in the fifth. Coming to bat once again in the sixth, Durocher told the umpire, "I feel like a clay pigeon in a shooting gallery," as he went down on strikes. In the end, Feller struck out eight batters over three innings.

In the clubhouse afterward, Cardinals pitcher Dizzy Dean, rarely at a loss for words, seemed tongue-tied at what he'd just witnessed. "The kid's a natural," he declared, "he can't miss." Emmet Ormsby, the home plate umpire, echoed Dean's praise: "The best pitcher I have ever seen come into the American League in all my experience," he said, adding: "I don't care if [Feller] is only 17. He showed me more speed than I have ever seen uncorked by an American League slabster."

Any plans that the Indians might have had for delaying Feller's entrance into the majors no longer seemed reasonable. So, on July 14, Feller boarded an overnight train to Philadelphia, where the Indians would play the Athletics. From his Pullman berth that evening, Feller gazed out at the Allegheny Plateau. A faint sliver of moon hung in the sky, and the dim lights of small farming communities blinked in the distance. As he lowered his head to the pillow, the pulsing clackety-clack of the train wheels blurred into an echoing refrain: "You're on your way, you're on your way, you're on your way."

A month of mop-up duty in the Indians' bullpen ensued. It wasn't until August 23, after the club had fallen out of pennant contention, that

Feller got the call for his first start against the St. Louis Browns. On that scorching Sunday afternoon in Cleveland, with the players' flannel uniforms clinging to their skin like damp washrags, Feller set a fittingly scorching pace, striking out ten batters through five innings. His fastball looked "like a white streak," his curveball "broke over the plate like a rabbit turning a sudden corner." In the dugout he wolfed down salt tablets while the trainer fanned him with a bath towel—whatever it took to find relief from the late-summer sun. While he did surrender a run, Feller managed to close out the contest with fifteen strikeouts, equaling the American League record in his first ever complete game.

Word of the outing rocketed across the country. It was unprecedented, astonishing, impossible. Reporters wasted no time in hailing Feller as the sport's next icon. "Feller's magical feat of fanning 15 St. Louis Browns Sunday caused more ebullition among baseball followers than any happening since [Babe] Ruth's withdrawal from the big time [in 1935]," crowed Franklin Lewis of the *Cleveland Press*.

Rival clubs jammed the Indians' phone lines, begging them not only to start Feller the next time they came to town, but to announce it in advance to boost attendance. On their subsequent five-city road trip, the Indians obliged in Boston and New York, but fans there witnessed a different pitcher altogether. Against the Red Sox, Bob surrendered four runs in five innings. Four days later, the Yankees knocked him out of the box after just one inning. For a precocious adolescent, the sting of those defeats must have been largely unfamiliar.

When the team's train pulled into the station in Cleveland after two weeks on the road, Bill Feller was waiting on the platform. "Thought I'd come in and see a ball game," he told his dumbfounded son in greeting. Bob later wrote that he "was as happy as a kid to see him."

The following day, on September 7, Bob mowed down ten St. Louis Browns in a complete-game victory. Bill also stuck around for his son's next start, on September 13 against the Philadelphia Athletics. That overcast afternoon, Bob hurled one of the most unusual games in baseball history. His fastball was feral, bordering on reckless. According to one writer, "a picture of their wives wearing black" likely flashed through batters' minds each time Feller's heater buzzed in. He piled up strikeouts and yielded a mere two singles, but he also walked nine batters, hit one, and threw one pitch over the umpire's head. Those who managed to reach first realized they could almost jog to the next base in the time it took Feller to execute his high-kick windup. Seven men stole bases off him, including a swipe of home. In the end, however, enough pitches crossed the plate for Bob to tally seventeen strikeouts, snapping the single-game American League record and tying Dizzy Dean for the major-league mark. It was an easy 5-2 win for the Indians.

To the mystified reporters who asked him how it felt to break a record that had stood for twenty-eight years, Feller answered with a bluntness that belied his inexperience: "What are you going to do if you pitch the ball and they can't hit it?"

It was that simple. He had five major-league starts under his belt, and already his name was etched in American folklore.

For white audiences, Feller's sudden rise from farm-field diamonds to major-league ballparks was the American Dream writ large. For Black audiences, it must have confirmed something they already knew: that major-league clubs would rather roll the dice on a white adolescent with no professional experience than sign a Black star.

For decades, major-league organizations had sunk significant resources into combing the sandlots for white prospects. They poured funds into farm systems; they hired slews of ex-players to drill fundamentals into rookies with minuscule chances of ever blossoming into stars; they dispatched bird-dog scouts on days-long treks to the middle of nowhere to file reports on the sons of farmers, coal miners, and factory workers whose feats on the diamond had prompted county-spanning chatter. A player like Feller was the prize, the needle in the nation's haystack of white talent. All the while, scores of Black players capable of upending pennant races toiled in the shadows.

Leroy "Satchel" Paige was one of them. By 1936, his nomadic baseball odyssey had swept him from the depths of the Deep South to the heights of the Negro Leagues. He'd been born thirty years earlier in a tumbledown district of Mobile, Alabama, during an era marked by intimidation, violence, disenfranchisement, and unyielding Jim Crow laws. Unlike Feller, Paige wasn't afforded time to learn baseball through his father, an itinerant landscaper and dockworker who was a sporadic presence in his impoverished childhood. Instead, from an early age, he'd had to earn his keep at the L&N Depot in downtown Mobile. When trains clattered in, Paige and his fellow porters collected the bags of the passengers, who would flip them up to a dime per satchel. One day, Paige showed up with some rope and wooden poles. While other porters snatched one satchel at a time, Paige hung several together along the poles, tying them tight with rope. "I carried so many satchels that all you could see was satchels. You couldn't see no Leroy Paige at all," he later claimed. Forever after, Leroy became "Satchel," his coin-stuffed pockets a testament to his budding business sense.

Paige's path to professional baseball was markedly different from Feller's. In the absence of a father who showered him with attention and top-notch equipment, Paige first learned the game on the muddy streets of Mobile, sometimes using branches for bats and bottle caps for balls, and on the sandlots with his older brother Wilson. He also built up his arm and honed his aim by chucking stones at squirrels, birds, and even his fellow students. At the Alabama Reform School for Juvenile Negro Lawbreakers, where he'd been sent at age twelve for shoplifting and other delinquent acts, Paige recalled that officials told him that "all that wild-a'-loose feelin' I put in rock throwin', I ought to put in throwin' baseball."

Paige trained at the school under baseball instructor Moses

Davis, who taught the gawky teenager—all skin and bones at six-foot-three, 140 pounds—how to leverage his slender frame in his pitching windup and how to study batters' knees to discern their weaknesses. During his five-year stint there, Paige dedicated himself to refining his newfound craft. Shortly after his release in 1923, at age seventeen, Paige tagged along with Wilson for a tryout with the Mobile Tigers, a Black semiprofessional club that passed a hat through the stands to cover expenses and sometimes resorted to paying its players in kegs of lemonade.

Paige enjoyed a fruitful apprenticeship with the Tigers, practicing and studying the game for hours on end, doing whatever it took to improve. As word of his speed and stellar outings spread across southern Alabama, other teams vied for his services, which Paige was happy to provide on a game-by-game basis for the right price.

Paige pitched in his hometown until 1926, when he was signed by Alex Herman, a Black Mobile native himself and the manager of the Chattanooga White Sox in the Negro Southern League, a minor-league circuit for Black ballplayers with franchises spread across Southern states. Paige already had speed, so Herman took it upon himself to preach the gospel of control to his top prospect. At practice, he'd command Paige to knock down rows of soda bottles carnival-style, or toss baseballs through a knothole in a wooden fence. Soon, home plate became too wide for Paige. He'd fold a handkerchief in four and instruct his catcher to place it anywhere on the plate. Taking the mound, Paige would hurl pitch after pitch over the cotton square. To up the ante, he'd sometimes replace the handkerchief with a dime or a gum wrapper.

As his skills blossomed, so too did his awareness of what he could do with them. "I said to myself," he later stated, "'Satch, ole boy, you've got something. You can make plenty of greenbacks in pro baseball. There ain't nothin' to it. All you gotta do is stand out there on a mound and blow 'em past those hitters and you can get rich.'" Over the following decade, Paige became a man on the run, jumping from Chattanooga to Birmingham to Cleveland to Pittsburgh to North Dakota and wherever else he could boost his bottom line. For several seasons in the mid-1930s, he anchored the rotation of the famed Pittsburgh Crawfords, a Negro League squad that could've stood toe-to-toe with any major-league club. Though the roster was studded with equally skilled stars—future Hall of Famers like Josh Gibson, James "Cool Papa" Bell, and Judy Johnson—no one could match Paige's pull and charisma.

During starts, Paige had one eye on the batters and the other on the fans. If the game was in hand, he would rely on bluster and bravado to keep spectators engaged, hollering out exactly what the next pitch would be and then snickering when batters skulked away red-faced and flustered. He had strong, agile wrists and long fingers that wound his pitches tight with backspin, making them appear to rise and shrink as they sailed plateward. His fastball became so notorious that Paige conjured up colorful nicknames for its many different iterations: bee ball, long Tom, jump ball. "You know how sometimes you see lights flicker before your eyes?" Newark Eagles shortstop Monte Irvin once asked. "Well, that's what Paige's pitches looked like." Occasionally, against bush-league rosters, Paige would wave his fielders to the bench and handle the hitters by himself, the lone man on the field. Despite these bits of showmanship, perfecting his craft remained Paige's driving concern. "You gotta live pitchin' to be a good one—think pitchin', eat pitchin', sleep pitchin', work on it," he asserted.

On off-days, the Crawfords would lease Paige's services to semiprofessional clubs struggling to stay afloat—which in the Depression was nearly all of them. He'd blow into whistle-stop towns guaranteeing to send down the first nine batters on strikes. Paige pitched in back lots and cow pastures and dirt patches with skinned infields. When the weather cooled, he pushed south into the Caribbean and Latin America, playing through the winter as many Negro Leaguers did to make a living. "If there was a place where baseball was played," wrote columnist A. S. "Doc" Young, "Satchel Paige was known there and probably had been there."

Against major leaguers on the barnstorming trail, Paige's outings carried meaning beyond the box score. Baseball officials were aware that contests that pitted all-white against all-Black squads could rattle the foundations of the sport's color line. If Negro League players routinely routed their competition, segregation would become harder to justify.

No one understood this better than Kenesaw Mountain Landis. A longtime federal judge whose furrowed face and tuft of white hair gave him the appearance of an industry titan crossed with a revivalist preacher, Landis had assumed the commissionership of Major League Baseball in 1920 with a mandate to clean up a sport rocked by gambling scandals. Under a lifetime appointment during which he presided theatrically over the league with near unchecked powers, Landis enforced the racial status quo by practicing a form of public denial and private enforcement of the color line. For off-season barnstorming games, Landis laid down strict regulations: He restricted the number of days major-league players could barnstorm (ten), disallowed the use of league apparel, prevented three or more teammates from joining forces on one team, and demanded that all matchups be characterized as "exhibitions." These rules signaled that barnstorming contests were to be thought of more as diversions than as serious sporting events. That attitude, in turn, helped shape the perception of Black players among white fans and players. In their eyes, even when Black barnstorming squads beat white ones, as often happened, the casual competition was no match for the supposed rigors of the major leagues. "Most of us didn't believe [Negro League players] were equal to us players or that so many would become superstars," Pittsburgh Pirates slugger Ralph Kiner later wrote. "There was a myth that they were primarily entertainers and that if they played for all the marbles, they wouldn't be nearly as competitive as we were."

It was Satchel Paige who most vividly exposed the absurdity of that attitude. As historian Jules Tygiel argued, "The well-publicized exploits of Paige versus the major league stars, perhaps more than anything else, awakened fans, sportswriters, and baseball officials to the potential of Black ballplayers." Some of the league's biggest names, everyone from Lou Gehrig to Carl Hubbell, affirmed that Paige belonged in the majors. Before he'd logged a single at-bat in the majors, Joe DiMaggio scratched out an infield single against Paige in an off-season contest. New York Yankees scouts were ecstatic: "DiMaggio All We Hoped He'd Be—Hit Satch One for Four," they gushed in a telegraph to Yankees officials. There was no better way, Negro League pitcher William "Sug" Cornelius claimed, for white prospects to test their readiness than to face Paige. "If they could hit Satchel," he said, "they were big-league material."

In the mid-1930s, Paige barnstormed across the country with Dizzy Dean, perhaps the only pitcher who could match him as much athletically as performatively. Their rivalry culminated in 1934 with a thirteen-inning face-off in Los Angeles, which Paige won 1-0. A twenty-year-old office boy for the Chicago Cubs named Bill Veeck happened to be in the stands, and while decades of baseball-viewing lay ahead of him, he would insist that this was the greatest pitching showdown he ever witnessed. Dean, who'd grown up hard in backwater Southern communities steeped in segregation, made clear that he'd share a rotation with Paige in a heartbeat. "Satchel and me," he stated, "would be worth a quarter of a million to any major-league club. We'd clinch the pennant mathematically by the Fourth of July and go fishin' until the World Series. Between us, we'd win 60 games."

When Paige caught wind of Dean's prediction, he scoffed. "Heck," he asserted, "*I'd* win 60."

Dean's words underscored a reality as fundamental to that era as gravity: If Satchel Paige were white, major-league owners would have mortgaged their ballparks to sign him. But he wasn't. So they didn't.

Now, on October 7, 1936, Paige was set to duel in Des Moines with an adolescent twelve years his junior. Against white barnstormers Paige always buckled down, taking pride in dispatching the best the major leagues had to offer. No doubt he was ready to do the same with Bob Feller.

It was an eight o'clock start. The game would be played under the lights at Western League Park, a snug stadium that hosted the Class-A Des Moines Demons during the regular season. Desperate for crowds during the Depression, the minor leagues had been at the forefront of what was then known as "night baseball." By 1935, as many as sixty-five minor-league franchises had installed permanent lighting in their ballparks. Derided by purists, night baseball had yet to catch on in the major leagues. Only one franchise, the Cincinnati Reds, had scheduled games after dark. In the Negro Leagues, it was a different story. Forced to innovate and experiment to make ends meet, farsighted owners like J. L. Wilkinson of the Kansas City Monarchs lugged portable lighting systems from town to town so that they could stage night games on whichever fields their teams played.

If hurling post-sundown was new to Bob Feller, sharing the field with Black athletes was not. On several occasions, Bill Feller had welcomed racially diverse teams to Oak View Park, though none of them were anywhere near as talented as the one his son was about to face. As columnist Sec Taylor of *The Des Moines Register* put it, these were players "who undoubtedly would be in the National or American league if they were white instead of black."

By the time Feller strutted to the rubber that evening, 5,000 fans were shivering in the stands. Leading off was Pittsburgh Crawfords center fielder Cool Papa Bell, perhaps the fastest man in baseball, an especially dangerous figure for a pitcher who struggled to hold runners on base. Fortunately for him, Feller dispatched Bell without much hassle.

The next batter up, Sammy Hughes of the Washington Elite Giants, popped a weak fly between Feller and first baseman Johnny Mize. As Mize charged the ball, fielding it on a bounce, Feller neglected to cover the bag, and the speedy Hughes streaked down the line for an infield single.

No other batter would make it that far. Over three innings Feller set down eight of ten batters on strikes. It was another awe-inspiring performance. This time, however, it wouldn't be enough for the win.

Satchel Paige also surrendered a first-inning single, when third baseman Heinie Mueller laced an offering through the infield. Unruffled as always, Paige proceeded to strike out seven of the next nine batters.

For three frames, Paige and Feller were reverse images of each other: Black and white, lanky and stocky, smooth and jerky, precise and wild, composed and fussy. It was only after they exited in the fourth, with the score knotted at zero, that batters on both sides relaxed. According to *The Des Moines Register,* "The pitches served up by the [relief] hurlers seemed to have strings tied to them, so slow were they in comparison to the hard ones thrown by Bob and Satchel." In the end, Paige's squad edged Feller's by a 4-2 margin.

For his short stint, Feller walked away with three hundred dollars, a full sixth of what he'd grossed in three months with the Indians. (It's unknown how much Paige pocketed, though Black barnstormers generally earned less than their white counterparts.) He'd also battled to a draw with his renowned opponent. With Feller on the rise and Paige in his prime, it must've seemed certain that their paths would cross again.

2

Learning to Be Alone

Like Bob Feller, Larry Doby was born into a baseball family. His father, David, had staked a reputation during the early decades of the twentieth century as one of the top players on the Black semiprofessional circuits across central South Carolina. His mother, Etta Doby, carried a memory of David and Larry together. It took place on a dusty baseball diamond sometime around 1929, when Larry was five years old. After a game in which David had starred, Larry ran onto the field. He was, Etta recalled, "looking for his daddy." It was an image that seemingly summed up their relationship. Unlike Feller, whose father was a steadfast and animating presence in his athletic development, Larry Doby would experience his father during his formative years more as an absence, as someone whose circumstances as a Black man in the Jim Crow South never afforded him the luxury of pouring time and money into his son's passion.

Decades earlier, in 1895, a new state constitution had been ratified that entrenched white supremacy across South Carolina. Through such means as poll taxes and literacy tests it effectively disenfranchised the vast majority of Black residents, and also barred white and Black students from attending the same schools. In the years after the Supreme

Court's *Plessy v. Ferguson* ruling in 1896 that upheld the "separate but equal" doctrine, South Carolina lawmakers passed numerous Jim Crow ordinances that mandated race-based segregation in a wide variety of facilities, from restaurants to waiting rooms to public transportation. At the same time, employment-based discrimination severely restricted the occupational opportunities of Black workers, relegating many to sharecropping and other forms of low-wage labor. Even as Black citizens practiced various forms of resistance and subversion in their everyday lives, threats of violence and lynching by white mobs upheld the state's strict racial hierarchy.

David Doby, whose own father had been born into slavery, found work in an industry unique to his inland hometown of Camden. In the late nineteenth and early twentieth century, white socialites from the north, seduced by Camden's temperate winters and lush countryside, began flocking to its opulent seasonal resorts. The town's miles of bridle paths and sand roads that wended through cotton fields and thickets of longleaf pines made it a horse lover's paradise. Guests would ship their prized Thoroughbreds and show ponies alongside them via rail for the winter.

With the influx of visitors and horses came an influx of jobs. Karl P. Abbott, the owner of the Kirkwood Hotel, a sprawling resort distinguished by its white-columned façade, wrote that he staffed "the establishment with trained Negro servants who smiled and bowed and rendered perfect service, albeit with much amusement and secret disdain." As bellboys, groundskeepers, chambermaids, and caddies, Black workers were expected to maintain a pose of sunny servility among the white guests. Their roles were in keeping with the romanticized antebellum atmosphere that white Southerners cultivated in Camden for wintering Northerners, complete with race relations that appeared less severe on the surface than in other parts of South Carolina, but were in practice no less demeaning, patronizing, and restrictive.

David Doby toiled as a stable hand and horse groomer for visiting white families. When not working, he pursued his passion for baseball. Once, while playing a pickup game on the dirt roads of Camden's Black Bottom district, he caught the eye of Etta Brooks. They married and, in 1923, Etta gave birth to their son, Lawrence Eugene.

The marriage never found its footing. During the summer David followed the horses he groomed north to the racing hotspot of Saratoga Springs, New York. After a while, his prolonged absences must have felt more like desertion. To support herself, Etta joined the multitudes of Black migrants flocking to the industrial cities above the Mason-Dixon line, settling in Paterson, New Jersey, where she was hired as a live-in domestic worker for a wealthy white family. She left her son behind in Camden in the care of his grandmother, Augusta Brooks. Years later, in 1934, David Doby fell into a lake and drowned while fishing in upstate New York.

Though it was only a stone's throw away, the exclusive world of polo grounds and golf courses was far from the one that Larry Doby grew up in. The Black Bottom district on the south side of Camden was another world altogether, flood-prone and mosquito-ridden, an area dense with tin-roofed shacks lacking basic services like plumbing and electricity. Even as more and more Black families crowded into Camden from the countryside, roads remained unpaved, calls for improvement unheeded. On occasion during Doby's boyhood, horse-drawn carriages would trot down the muddy streets, out of which white passengers would flip coins to the Black children playing nearby and then beckon the youngsters over so that they could tousle their hair. Even as a child, Doby had gained enough of a racial consciousness to steer clear of any outstretched hands.

To survive in the Depression, Augusta Brooks scrubbed clothes for white families while Larry took on a series of odd jobs: delivering ice, picking cotton, chopping wood. She also forged a pact with her athletically inclined grandson during his downtime: So long as he swept the dirt that collected around their modest frame house on Market Street, he had permission to put the broom to better use in the streets.

Stickball was the game of choice for the children of Black Bottom. Doby would join his neighbors whenever possible, standing barefoot next to a pie pan that served as home plate, his curled fingers squeezing a broom handle. A slugger even then, he wore out two brooms a month taking vicious cuts at rubber balls.

As he grew, Doby's hitting prowess grabbed the attention of Richard DuBose, a Black baseball instructor and promoter who'd managed a semiprofessional team on which David Doby had starred. DuBose remembered David's son from those days, toddling after his father, a glove already in hand. "That kid was just a natural player," DuBose recalled. "He was a thin kid and you would never know the power those skinny arms carried until you saw him throw the ball or swing a bat. He just lived and breathed baseball." During his preteen years, Doby sometimes would ride with DuBose's teams to adjoining towns, where he'd compete against men many years his senior.

As he inched toward adolescence, Doby's home life took a turn. Little by little, his grandmother had succumbed to dementia, and Doby soon was forced to move a few blocks away to his aunt and uncle's house on Lyttleton Street. There, his boyhood stabilized. His skills on the ball field were developing, and he'd enrolled in the Mather Academy, a renowned school for Black students that boasted extensive extracurricular and cultural opportunities and a curriculum that instilled pride in Black history and achievement.

It was, Doby would later recall, an uncommonly tranquil period. But like many such periods early in his life, it was fleeting.

The change came by request of his mother, who summoned him to Paterson so that he could start his freshman year in New Jersey's integrated high school system. In 1938, Doby packed his belongings and headed north, trading the rural backcountry of inland South Carolina for the smoky factory-scapes of northern New Jersey, as many Black natives from mid-Southern states had done over the past few decades, clustering in Paterson in hope of gaining a foothold in the booming textile industry that had earned Paterson the nickname "The Silk City," even if, as author Anita Flynn documented, jobs beyond the menial level for these migrants were often few and far between.

In some ways, Doby's years at Paterson's Eastside High School foreshadowed the larger struggles he would face as a baseball pioneer. Of the roughly three hundred students in his incoming class, only a handful were Black. Through sports—football in autumn, basketball in winter, baseball in spring—this quiet transplant from the South would forge a toehold in an overwhelmingly white world.

During the 1930s, high school football games in New Jersey were freighted with meaning. Many student-athletes were the sons of immigrant laborers, first-generation adolescents caught between cultures. Strapping on a brown leather helmet and plowing into their peers from rival high schools while fans roared from the bleachers was a community-building spectacle that knitted together the diverse ethnic strands spooled through the area's industrial cities.

Though Doby's superior athletic ability enabled him to blossom into an all-state star, as the lone Black athlete on the football team he had to shoulder burdens that didn't weigh down his teammates. Often, opposing players would purposefully pile on Doby, digging their knees into his back while chants of "Amos 'n' Andy!" rippled through the stands. Al Kachadurian, the quarterback at Eastside High, would grow angry when he suspected other clubs of rough-housing, but Doby never appeared to, or at least he didn't show it. Instead, he'd scramble back to the huddle as if he hadn't felt or heard a thing. "I never saw him lose his cool. Never," Kachadurian recalled.

Still, Doby seemed to feel these racial injustices deeply. Sometimes, in the locker room or on the practice field, a mood would wash over him all at once. He'd burrow deep within himself, lapsing into silence for reasons his teammates couldn't understand. "He'd withdraw," Kachadurian said. "He wouldn't talk. He wasn't belligerent. He just wouldn't say anything."

It wasn't necessarily that he felt unaccepted. On the contrary,

Doby later said that his athletic exceptionalism turned him into a sort of "school hero, always one of the crowd, going everywhere with my white schoolmates—parties, dances, shows, whatnot." But even when they went to the movies, Doby would have to climb two flights of stairs to the upper balcony—the only section where Black patrons were allowed to sit (though not as rigidly codified, segregation was the norm in the North as much as in the South)—while his teammates found seats on the ground floor. Afterward, they'd wait for him to descend before departing. According to Doby, "The important thing is that we all walked together, and we all walked back home together." It was this camaraderie that Doby reveled in, even if at times he erected emotional guardrails that his teammates could neither penetrate nor fully comprehend.

Part of the reason had to do with his unstable home life. Because of her work as a live-in domestic maid, Etta Doby was away for days at a time. "My mother would take the bus and come visit me every Thursday and Sunday," Larry remembered. "But it was always a little bit awkward. I didn't really know her very well, and I missed being able to play stickball with my friends." Rather than living with her consistently, Larry spent years shuttling between his mother's acquaintances, rarely staying long enough in one place to feel comfortable. To his biographer, Joseph Thomas Moore, Doby said of his high school years, "I had been alone most of my life. I had gotten accustomed to that. Not that I wanted to be alone. You learn to live with being alone."

One person, however, managed to penetrate his defenses. During his sophomore year, Doby eyed a Black freshman student strolling by his house on her way to school. Her name was Helyn Curvy. Soon, Doby began timing his departure to coincide with hers. At first, she was wary of his status as the alpha jock of Eastside High. "Everybody looked at him with some kind of reverence," Curvy told sportswriter Sam Lacy. "Almost every move he made in those days, I interpreted as a mark of egoism," she continued. "And gradually I formed the opinion he was little more than a 'big swellhead.'" But Doby kept wooing her, and eventually she saw beyond the accolades. By the time he graduated, in June of 1942, they'd become inseparable.

His senior year, Doby was nothing short of a sensation, someone whose name in New Jersey was "known from Cape May to Hoboken." On the gridiron he juked tacklers and barreled downfield all the way to Eastside High's first-ever state football championship. On the basketball hardwood, as Al Kachadurian remembered, "he was pure speed. He was the only one who had moves. No one could touch him." Once, he faked out a defender so completely that, as one reporter quipped, the player required "a St. Bernard and a searching expedition" just to relocate Doby. Disbelief was a common postgame reaction. "We thought we were playing five Doby's," a player from Passaic Valley High School said after his squad had been drubbed by Eastside. "He was all over the floor."

During the spring Doby doubled his workload, hustling back and forth between the track and baseball teams in an effort to become the only graduate of Eastside High School to letter in four sports. Despite having never attempted the broad jump before, Doby broke the conference record in his first track meet, soaring nearly twenty-one feet. Eventually, his long leaps would earn him a fifth-place medal in the state.

But Doby's ability to thrive in unfamiliar athletic scenarios was perhaps most evident on the baseball diamond. Competing on both the Eastside High squad and the Paterson Smart Sets—a Black semiprofessional club managed by Pat Wilson, a mentor who one writer claimed "saw in Larry a devotion to baseball equal to his own"—he adapted to wherever he was stationed in the field. "Doby, who has played everything but the Hut Hut Song on a piccolo, is no stranger to shifts," wrote Doc Goldstein of the *Paterson Evening News*. "With the local Smart Sets he has played first, second, third, short, second [*sic*] and the outfield. In each position he has been more than competent, often turning in the impression that he was born for that particular berth."

At one point Eastside High manager Al Livingstone even toyed with the idea of sending him to the mound before deciding it was better for Doby to focus on what he did best: roping line drives into the outfield grass. "When ever that ball rode within socking distance of the platter," Goldstein asserted, "Doby would lash out with his wrists and send the sphere on an excursion." Even when he slapped grounders that should have been easy outs, his blazing speed often propelled him to first faster than high school infielders could throw to the bag.

Doby's local celebrity grew to such an extent that a testimonial dinner was convened in his honor in February of 1942. At a packed church in downtown Paterson, poems about his athletic feats were recited, speeches delivered, musical arrangements performed. The school faculty presented Doby with a gold wristwatch while his coaches dubbed him "the greatest athlete to ever represent Eastside High School, bar none." Doby, who had spent the evening "nervously fidgeting in his chair, modestly embarrassed as the compliments came thick and fast," murmured a few words of thanks when called upon to speak, which struck one reporter as consistent with his reputation of being "one of the most level-headed, modest athletes around."

Still, despite the ceremonies and Doby's all-state standing in football, basketball, and baseball, there was an uneasy subtext that cast a shadow over everything. "You could see the potential," Kachadurian told sportswriter Hank Gola. "He'd get four hits in a row or something, and the kids would go home and say, 'Too bad he's Black . . . Too bad for Larry.' We felt sorry for him."

What his teammates likely didn't understand was that Doby's dreams of athletic stardom differed from their own. Doby knew little of the major leagues. While he recognized names from the newspapers he hawked in his downtime, he later said that he never aspired to emulate those players because there was no one in Major League Baseball who looked like him. There was, however, another league that piqued his interest. Before long, the attraction would be mutual.

At some point, during the spring of 1942, an umpire from Paterson tipped off Abe and Effa Manley—co-owners of the Newark Eagles in the Negro National League—about a raw eighteen-year-old phenom tearing through the high school and semiprofessional baseball circuits. Intrigued, the Manleys arranged for a hush-hush tryout, which Doby aced. Soon, Doby found himself inking his first professional contract.

Abe and Effa Manley were a husband-wife duo who ran the Eagles jointly, their strengths and weaknesses in harmony with each other. Abe was reserved yet passionate, equipped with an unerring eye for promising players; Effa was hard-nosed yet bighearted, skilled equally at keeping the Eagles afloat financially and pushing back at those who questioned a woman's place in the traditionally masculine realm of professional sports. They'd purchased the franchise in 1935 and brought the Eagles from Brooklyn to Newark the following year. Over the next few seasons, as the Homestead Grays dominated the six-team Negro National League, the Eagles held their own with players such as pitcher Leon Day and the so-called Million Dollar Infield—a quartet of players (Ray Dandridge, Willie Wells, George "Mule" Suttles, and Dick Seay) so indispensable that if they were paid what they were worth, their collective value would supposedly reach seven figures.

This was a rarefied, cutthroat world that Doby was entering, one where veterans clinging to precious roster spots greeted rookies with suspicion, if not hostility. Unsure of his place in it, Doby struck a guarded pose. "The first two or three days [Doby] came to the ball club, most of the guys he didn't know," Max Manning, an Eagles pitcher, told historian John Holway. "But once he saw he was going to be accepted with open arms, he blossomed."

It didn't take long for writers to hail the Eagles' new recruit as an "overnight sensation," another gem unearthed by the Manleys. But they didn't call him Larry Doby. To maintain his amateur status, Doby played under an alias: Larry Walker, from Los Angeles, California. Rather than committing himself fully to the itinerant, year-round grind of professional Black baseball, Doby planned to attend Long

Island University on a basketball scholarship in the fall of 1942. Under visionary head coach Clair Bee, the Brooklyn-based college had transformed into a hardwood juggernaut, amassing an astonishing record of 93-9 over the past four seasons while clinching two NIT championships. It seemed a perfect fit for Doby. He could hone his skills in a sport that some considered his best, study to become a physical education teacher, stick close to Helyn, and return incognito to the Eagles each summer.

A path forward, safe and unswerving, had opened up before him. And then the war changed everything.

3

The Storybook Ballplayers

If Larry Doby had paid attention to major-league players during high school, there was one name that would've been unmissable. Bob Feller blew into Major League Baseball the year after Babe Ruth, at age forty, had washed out of it. His timing couldn't have been better. By 1936, the year Feller stunned the baseball establishment with his record-breaking debut, the majors had begun casting about for a new idol. Dizzy Dean had filled the role for a while, but Feller was soon established as the likely successor to the throne. As *Time* magazine asserted, "Babe Ruth made his big-league debut in 1914. The character who, 23 years later, seemed highly likely to develop into an even more prodigious figure upon the U.S. scene is Cleveland's Robert William Feller." Indians executive Cy Slapnicka agreed: "[Feller] has captured the imagination of the youngsters in a way no one else, with the possible exception of Ruth, ever approached."

Just as Ruth, with his towering home runs and unquenchable appetites, had epitomized the excesses of the Jazz Age, Feller struck a chord with a nation still clawing its way out of the Great Depression. In the 1930s, white Americans, disillusioned with modernity and gripped with nostalgia, began looking to the preindustrial past

for comfort. Romanticized stories of small towns and the plainspo-
ken, prudent folks who dwelled there once again seized the collective
imagination. Feller—disciplined, earnest, and rural—came across as
a peach-fuzzed personification of that nativist sensibility. *The Saturday Evening Post* dubbed him "the storybook ball player of the generation." That magazine's profile, written by J. Roy Stockton in the
winter of 1937, unfolded like a fable about a no-nonsense farmer
who'd reared a professional baseball player as surely as he would've a
prized hog. "I never knew of another case," Stockton stated, "where
a man, starting from cradle scratch, manufactured his son into a
$100,000 pitcher."

Mythmaking was second nature to many sportswriters in the
opening decades of the twentieth century. Since there was no need
to embellish Feller's on-field feats, the task instead was to cast the
father-son duo as timeless emblems of "real America"—heartland-
reared farmers who swore by the tried-and-true values on which
the country had supposedly been built: hard work, self-reliance, and
durable family bonds. Bob's instant success reaffirmed myths that
white America liked—perhaps needed—to tell about itself. "Other
boys in their teens dreamed of walking right out of the cornfields to
the major leagues and standing the heavy hitters on their burning
ears," one reporter wrote. "Bob Feller actually did it. Which proves
that America is still America, and a country boy can make good
overnight in the 'big time' if he has the heart."

At a time when Shirley Temple reigned as Hollywood's top box-
office draw, Feller became her athletic counterpart—"the American
boy in the American game," as *Baseball Magazine* later put it. Like
Temple, Feller contained multitudes: he was both a prodigy and a
hayseed, a self-effacing adolescent and a self-confident performer.
Journalists played up Feller's agrarian roots, his supposed impervi-
ousness to fame, his very ordinariness as he returned to Van Meter
for his senior year of high school following his three-month stint on
the Indians. "He hasn't acquired any air of false sophistication and

isn't trying to," one Cleveland sportswriter asserted. "He could go back behind that plow tomorrow and feel at home." Slipping into his new persona, Feller gamely attributed his success to his wholesome upbringing. "I don't smoke or drink. I don't even drink coffee. I drink plenty of milk," he told a troop of Boy Scouts, adding: "Use your head. Use your common sense. Live a good clean life."

Before the start of the 1937 season, Feller, with the aid of a ghostwriter, penned a weeks-long autobiographical series that ran in newspapers nationwide. Everything the public craved was there: the farm, the diamond carved into the pasture, the breakthrough. His life story, a narrative tailor-made for a nation whose faith in its core principles had been shaken, was turning into a currency as valuable as his right arm, and as historian David Vaught argued in *The Farmers' Game,* Bill and Bob Feller proved expert at shaping and commodifying a homespun version of it.

They proved equally adept at maximizing his earnings, drawing a hard line with the Indians in contract negotiations and hiring an agent to drum up sponsorships and endorsements. "Barring misfortunes which I cannot foresce, the boy has a good chance to take a cool million from baseball and its by-products," Cy Slapnicka asserted after he'd signed Feller to a $10,000 contract, the richest ever for a rookie.

Feller's high school graduation in the spring of 1937 was a nationwide sensation. Upward of one thousand curiosity seekers wedged into Van Meter's high school gymnasium for the occasion. Newsreel cameras whirred in the bleachers; floodlights illuminated the stage. For the graduating class of nineteen, the superintendent plucked diplomas from a papier-mâché baseball, and then unveiled a gold-toned portrait of the school's most famous alumnus from underneath an American flag. NBC Radio aired the entire ceremony live from coast to coast.

Regardless, it took a while for the storybook version of Feller to line up with the one who actually toed the rubber for the Indians.

He battled injuries in 1937, then had problems locating home plate in 1938, a season in which he became the first major-league pitcher since the 1890s to walk more than two hundred batters. When in trouble, Feller leaned on the trick that had punched his ticket off the farm: "hiking his left leg high, pulling back an arm tied together with Iowa farm sinews, and letting go (toward the general direction of the plate) with a fast ball pitch that sang a song of sorrow as it pounded into the catcher's glove."

His single-minded devotion to physical fitness and his craft, however, sharply reduced his learning curve. Feller stocked a file cabinet with information on the strengths and weaknesses of hitters across the American League, and sometimes sequestered himself in his hotel room to hone his form, flinging baseballs into pillows propped up on the bed frame. "When he first came up to the Indians," sportswriter Bob Dolgan said, "the older guys who'd led the hard life of older ballplayers, drinking too much, roughhousing . . . used to make fun of him. 'Here's the calisthenics kid again,'" they joked, as Feller ran wind sprints on the field or chinned himself up on the dugout ledge.

Feller continued to rely on the guidance of his father, but Bill Feller could no longer swoop in every time his son hit a rough patch. Toward the end of 1936 Bill had come down with a debilitating illness, which was eventually diagnosed as a terminal brain tumor. His physical deterioration over the next few years coincided with the fulfillment of Bob's potential.

By the time Feller turned twenty, going into the 1939 season, skeptics no longer could dismiss him as a one-trick pony. Alongside his famed fastball, he'd perfected an equally devastating curveball, which New York Yankees outfielder Charlie Keller claimed behaved like "an epileptic snake." Each season from 1939 through 1941, Feller paced the American League in wins, strikeouts, and innings pitched. Records began to fall: eighteen strikeouts in a single game; the only no-hitter ever hurled on Opening Day; the youngest player, at age twenty-two, to log one hundred wins and one thousand strikeouts that century. He had a princely salary, sponsorships with the likes of Wheaties and Wilson (to preserve his all-American image, Feller refused to endorse cigarettes), and even a candy bar that bore his likeness.

Though a rising crop of superstars, led by Joe DiMaggio and Ted Williams, had sprouted in the majors, it was Feller, according to *Life* magazine, who remained "unquestionably the idol of several generations of Americans, ranging in age from 7 to 70. They represent every city, town and village in the land, speak of him familiarly as 'Bob' and talk about him by the hour, with enthusiasm." There was no reason to assume he wouldn't retire with several all-time pitching records to his credit.

As the forties got under way, Feller found himself largely peerless among major-league pitchers. His closest match in speed and symbolism toiled on the opposite end of the color line.

Mythmaking similarly subsumed Satchel Paige in the mid-1930s and early 1940s. Paige noticed the trend especially among sportswriters: "They started talking about me like I wasn't even a real guy, like I was something out of a book." As *Pittsburgh Courier* columnist Wendell Smith put it: "[Paige] is the subject of a baseball saga which reads like fantastic fiction. No author has ever been able to create a tale that equals the feats of this human beanpole."

In an era when racial oppression hardened across the South and families who'd fled north frequently found themselves entrapped in hard labor and segregated ghettos, Paige was freewheeling and footloose, burnishing his legend in sandlots and stadiums across the country. If Feller stood for rootedness, stability, and comfort, Paige resonated as a representation of mobility, self-determination, and defiance. "I was living," Paige later said. "I was playing all over the

U.S. then, while Ted [Williams] and Joe [DiMaggio] were playing only in big-league cities. I don't believe there is a place I didn't play, every little town, in coal mines and penitentiaries."

Tales of Paige's exploits and persona—his blurry fastball and pinpoint control, his showmanship and bravado, his knack for creating drama and holding audiences' attention even in blowouts—filled the pages of Black newspapers and spread through communities across the country, growing taller with each retelling, transforming Paige into a fabled figure. Like Feller, he too contained multitudes: He was at once droll yet deadly serious, sociable yet aloof, a quick-witted fabulist who could wax philosophical on topics ranging from fishing to photography to antiques. "He was terminally unpredictable," said Pittsburgh Crawfords teammate Jimmie Crutchfield, "the prize inside the Cracker Jack box of baseball."

The blurring of man and myth, of Paige the pitcher and Paige the legend, came to occupy the heart of his mystique, and he knew just how to leverage his talent and celebrity to his own considerable economic benefit during a time when Black baseball mostly was in dire financial straits. Unlike Feller, Paige couldn't rely on income from endorsements because companies at that time neglected Black consumers and didn't believe Black athletes could market products to white Americans. Instead, he worked tirelessly to build himself into an individual enterprise. Barely a decade into his professional career, the man who once pitched for lemonade had evolved into baseball's foremost headliner, no matter if he was throwing in league games or wherever his travels on the barnstorming trail took him.

Paige's legend proved so compelling that mainstream publications that otherwise turned a blind eye to the Negro Leagues began to take notice. Especially with his languorous gait and deadpan demeanor, many white writers and spectators detected in Paige traces of the shuffling, drawling character of Stepin Fetchit, who was played in movies and on stage by popular Black actor Lincoln Perry. It was a comparison that Paige seemed to play up when it suited him as he navigated through segregated spaces across the country. "Paige was a very intelligent man, and he played to the hype," historian Larry Lester said. "He did a little step-n-fetch for the white folks" before barnstorming contests. As Mel Watkins wrote in his biography of Perry, "many whites saw Fetchit's screen character as a comforting reaffirmation of prevailing stereotypes. The persona on some level provided a way for Paige to disarm racist fans unaccustomed to seeing a Black man square off against white competition. For predisposed viewers, the craven, trifling character he brought to the screen offered superficial support for claims of across-the-board Negro inferiority and justification for a continued paternalistic policy toward blacks." But then, as the first batter dug in, Paige would turn the tables. White spectators who expected sideshow-like entertainment from what they initially might have perceived as a "clown pitcher" instead witnessed a studious, dead-serious moundsman calling upon his hard-earned craftsmanship and cunning to baffle batters. It was a subtly subversive performance, one that won over—or at least neutralized—fans at the start without also compromising Paige's dignity or dominance in the end.

All through the Depression, Paige remained on the move. Pittsburgh Crawfords owner Gus Greenlee surrounded Paige with seemingly everything he could want: a stadium built solely for the team, a stacked lineup, sufficient leeway to make a mint on the side, and a buzzing nightclub, the Crawford Grill, where players could unwind after games. "Highest salaried man on his team and on a good many teams, his own car from the management, [Paige] can ride comfortably while the rest of the team goes by bus. Anything he wants is his and he takes it," asserted one columnist for the *Philadelphia Tribune*. It wasn't enough to convince Paige to settle. Always on the chase for more—money, exposure, freedom, acclaim—he jumped to places as disparate as North Dakota and the Dominican Republic during the mid-1930s.

Exasperated, Greenlee sold Paige's contract to the Newark

Eagles in 1938, four years before Larry Doby would sign with the Eagles. Rather than reporting to New Jersey, Paige headed south of the border, where he injured his arm experimenting with curveballs in Mexico City. Back in the States, Paige searched for a doctor with a miracle cure. One specialist poked and prodded his numb limb, then informed him that his pitching days might be done.

For weeks, Paige holed up by himself, sleepless and sick with self-pity. The only Negro League executive to reach out was J. L. Wilkinson, the white co-owner of the Kansas City Monarchs, who was never one to let a promotional opportunity slip away. Aware of his injury, Wilkinson beckoned Paige to Kansas City to front a barnstorming squad of lesser talent. The subsequent tour was an exercise in humiliation. Paige was a shell of himself, a broken-down fighter stumbling through the sticks. Pitching two innings at a time, he lobbed the ball underhand and sidearm and any other way he could, setting it on a tee for bush-leaguers to crush. His fastball was gone, and with it went his identity. At night, while dunking his arm in hot water, Paige thought of returning to Mobile. His world, once so expansive, was constricting.

And then it all came back. Before one outing, Paige heaved a pitch to his catcher and, for the first time in a while, felt nothing. He tried a few more throws. Still pain-free. His dormant confidence kicked in like a reflex. Assuming his usual stance, Paige froze at the peak of his windup, then sidestepped off the mound, massaged the ball, slipped his glove on and off. Finally, rearing back, he blazed the ball across the plate. His fastball had returned. Somehow, he'd been granted what he called a "second childhood."

Joining the Monarchs in Kansas City as the thirties gave way to the forties, Paige soon picked up where he'd left off, a headliner again. His legend loomed so large that during the 1941 season *The Chicago Defender* worried that fans might not turn out "to see a Negro baseball game UNLESS Paige is in it." Articles went out across

the wire with such headlines as: NEGRO HURLER EARNS MORE MONEY
YEARLY THAN FELLER. Paige's strikeouts, *The Saturday Evening Post*
gushed, were positively "Fellerian."

For mainstream publications, at least, it seemed that the lone
yardstick with which to gauge Paige's clout and accomplishments
was through his storybook counterpart in the league that barred
him. Since the last time they'd faced each other, in 1936, Feller had
blossomed into a full-fledged ace, while Paige had wandered lame
through the wilderness, only to return no worse for the wear. In
1941, their rivalry would resume.

Their first face-off in 1941 took place on October 5 in front of a
mixed-race crowd of 10,000 at St. Louis's Sportsman's Park. Paige
was reportedly racked with fever but chose to compete anyway—an
unwise decision, it turned out. By the fourth inning, he'd dug his
Kansas City Monarchs into a 4-1 hole against Feller and his roster
of major- and minor-league players. Feller, for his part, hardly broke
a sweat. "I thought they would be harder than that," he said of the
Monarchs. "I just loafed through for the most part."

Afterward, both pitchers scurried to Dayton, Ohio. His fever
broken, Paige emerged the following evening in customary form.
For three frames at Ducks park the duel was on: Paige struck out
five; Feller did the same. Paige yielded four scratch singles; Feller
held the Monarchs hitless. Neither allowed a run. Eventually, with
the Monarchs leading 5-2 in the eighth, the game was called so that
the players could catch an overnight train to Kansas City.

Before they departed, an enterprising reporter popped into both
clubhouses to ask the two aces what each thought of the other. Paige
showered his opponent with praise: "Whadda you expect me to say,
that [Feller] isn't any good? Listen, that there boy is just about the
best. That curve ball of his cracks when it breaks . . . [Feller] just
pulls back and fires that ball and there it is in the catcher's glove. But
he's gotta be good or he wouldn't go in that American League like

he does." Smiling mischievously, Paige added: "He's gotta be good. Struck me out, didn't he?"

Feller was more equivocal. "[Paige] can really throw that ball when he wants to. His only trouble is that he doesn't want to very often," he said. "Satch is one of the few Negro baseball players I think could make the major league grade and stick. I've seen just about all of them, and there are only a few who I think could make good up there. Satchel is one of them. You know, Paige is pretty old for a pitcher. He's 33 [he was actually 35], and most pitchers that old in the National and American leagues are depending on their head to do their pitching. But not this Paige. He can still throw a fast ball that smokes—when he wants to. His biggest trouble is that he doesn't want to really bear down often enough. I wouldn't say that he'd be great in the major leagues if he were up there. You've got to remember that conditions are a lot different from this barnstorming business once you're up there in the majors."

Perhaps aware of the harshness of his assessment, Feller back-tracked a bit: "I'll tell you one thing, [Paige] could make good in the majors, and I know it, because he's better than a lot of pitchers who are in the majors today . . . Oh, you can't take it away from him. He's a great pitcher all right. And when he wants to he can really throw that apple. He's got a terrific fast ball when he really wants to use it, but his curve ball isn't much. It's still good enough, though. That lazy change of pace he throws, which gets a big laugh out of the crowd, wouldn't work in the majors. They'd be dragging and bunting it constantly and he'd get worn out."

It was a long-winded, looping response, larded with boilerplate prejudices shared by many major leaguers. Paige, Feller seemed to suggest, fell short of the threshold for major-league excellence not because of systemic discrimination that left him reliant on year-round barnstorming but because of his own supposed moral defects: He favored playing to the rafters over bearing down on batters, he'd neglected to reinforce his pitching arsenal, his work ethic paled in comparison to

Feller's. His response reinforced the ways that Feller's own personal narrative, along with the mythology that had built up around it and the values embedded within it—self-reliance, rugged individualism, the power of the will to overcome obstacles and circumstances—appeared to blind him to the barriers that Black stars couldn't simply bootstrap away.

While Paige never directly responded to Feller's comments, he'd provided an answer of sorts two months earlier. "I ain't had three days' rest since I started playin' baseball and I been playin' since I was 15," Paige told a reporter in August 1941. "Boy, I sure laughs when I see in the papers where some major league pitcher says his arm is sore because he's overworked and pitches every four days. Man, that'd be a vacation for me." Of Negro Leaguers in general, Paige asserted: "We don't get no babying. We work, drive in a car all night, and work the next day. And [we] play more baseball in two days than those big league fellows play in a month." To achieve the same degree of renown among Black fans that Feller enjoyed from the get-go among white ones—not to mention similar financial gains—Paige had had to wring thousands of innings out of his right arm, learning to pace himself by not wasting his best pitches on subpar batters. What Feller interpreted as a reluctance to bear down was more likely road-tested savvy that enabled Paige to pitch as frequently as necessary without sacrificing his effectiveness. In an era when the mainstream media hailed Feller as an avatar of archetypal American values, Paige embodied them equally, even if so much of white America remained oblivious to it.

The two pitchers would duel one more time, on October 7 in Kansas City. Feller tossed three innings, ceded three bunt singles, and fanned six; Paige threw two frames, gave up one run on two hits, and struck out five. Feller had bested Paige in the first game, but they'd battled to a standstill the next two. More rounds would surely follow, perhaps as early as the next off-season. The money was too good, the crowds too thick, and the rivalry too balanced to leave it at that.

4

The Gingerbread Man

In late June of 1941, Bill Veeck boarded a train from Chicago to Milwaukee. Only twenty-seven years old, he'd resigned his position as treasurer of the Chicago Cubs to embark on what some might have considered a hopeless venture: He'd just purchased the Milwaukee Brewers, a minor-league club that was no one's idea of a prize. The previous decade, Milwaukee had been among the best drawing cities in the minors, but in recent years, the Brewers had sunk deep into debt and mediocrity. Two months into the 1941 season, the team was buried in the cellar of the American Association. The roster was starless, the fans had lost faith, and derelict Borchert Field, the Brewers' misshapen cigar box of a ballpark, looked as if it might collapse into a heap of scrap lumber at any moment. It was a bleak proposition—a bankrupt club that could easily bankrupt its new owner.

But that's not how Bill Veeck saw it. For weeks, he'd scrambled to raise enough funds to cover the $100,000 price set by the Brewers' previous owner. Not only did Veeck agree to shoulder the team's existing debt, but he also talked the City National Bank into loaning him $50,000 to refurbish the rotting ballpark. He steamed into Milwaukee with a handful of dollars in his pocket—several of which he blew straightaway in a tavern—a swirl of ideas in his head, and the brash optimism of a born hustler. Hank Greenberg, the Detroit Tigers slugger, would later say that if he ever were marooned on a desert island, he'd pick Veeck as his companion, because within no time Veeck would convince him of how lucky they were to be stranded there. Even in the direst of circumstances, he possessed the innate ability, according to sportswriter Ed Linn, "to carry everybody along on his own enthusiasm, to make them feel that they were living in historic times, that great things were in the air, that ultimate triumph was inevitable."

Since childhood, the refrain from a nursery rhyme had echoed in Veeck's mind like a mantra: *Run, run as fast as you can. You can't catch me, I'm the Gingerbread Man.* Starting from behind seemed to suit him. It heightened the drama, set the stakes high.

Veeck would either make good in Milwaukee or go broke trying.

Ever since Veeck was a boy, baseball had run in his blood. His father, Bill Veeck, Sr., had made his way as a young man from rural Indiana to Chicago, where he wrote evenhanded sports columns for the *Chicago Evening American* that caught the eye of William Wrigley, the chewing gum magnate who'd acquired a controlling stake in the Chicago Cubs in 1918. During spring training of that same year, Wrigley invited several writers to dinner, and there, according to legend, he asked Veeck, Sr., if he thought he could run the Cubs any better than the current regime. "I certainly couldn't do any worse," Veeck, Sr., quipped. And soon thereafter he made the improbable leap from critiquing the club to running it.

What the elder Veeck lacked in experience he made up for in ingenuity. Both he and Wrigley were self-made men with a knack for promotion, a willingness to challenge tradition, and an ability to breed loyalty in customers. During an era when owners mostly expected the sport to sell itself and ballparks generally were rough around the edges, Veeck and Wrigley went to great lengths to convince legions of

Chicagoans to spend their summer afternoons sunning themselves at Cubs Park. They renovated and scrubbed the stadium, trained a contingent of nattily attired ushers to clamp down on gambling and boorish behavior, and courted women through aggressive Ladies' Day sweepstakes. While many owners feared that radio broadcasts, a novel phenomenon at the time, would take away the reason to attend games, Veeck and Wrigley intuited they were an essential part of cultivating a broader fan base.

In 1919, when the elder Veeck had assumed his position as team president, nearly 425,000 paid customers passed through the gates at Cubs Park, seventh among sixteen teams in the majors. Eight years later, that number had soared to 1,159,168, making the Cubs the first National League club to cross the seven-figure mark in attendance. In 1929, they shattered the single-season attendance record in the majors, drawing a shade under 1.5 million fans. That same season, the Cubs stormed into the World Series on the strength of a lineup that Veeck and Wrigley had meticulously assembled.

These were lessons the younger Veeck would take to heart. His father hadn't simply thrown open the ballpark gates and waited for fans to flock in. He'd wooed them, he'd fussed over their comfort, he'd made it easier for them to track the team's progress away from the stadium. He'd invested time and Wrigley's considerable bankroll on roster and game-day enhancements and was rewarded with more spectators than the sport had ever known.

There was another, more direct lesson that he would impart. One Sunday afternoon, he beckoned his son to the desk of the club secretary, where ticket vendors had stacked the gate receipts from that day's game. The piles of crisp green bills were more money than the younger Veeck had ever seen.

"You look at that money and it all looks exactly the same, doesn't it?" the elder Veeck asked. "You can't tell who put it into your box office. It's all exactly the same color, the same size, and the same shape. You remember that." His son never forgot it.

* * *

The Wrigley-Veeck era came to an abrupt end when Wrigley died of heart disease in 1932 and Veeck, Sr., succumbed to leukemia a year later. All at once, at age nineteen, Veeck, Jr., faced an unforeseen reckoning. It was the depths of the Depression. Veeck felt like a burden on his mother at Kenyon College, which had admitted him on a football scholarship. "The joy ride was over, then," Veeck later said. "I had to get out and earn a few bobs on my own." So midway through his sophomore year, he dropped out and, upon returning to Chicago, knocked on the one door that had been open to him his entire life: the Cubs' front office.

William Wrigley's son Philip had since taken over the franchise. As withdrawn as his father had been sociable, Philip wore his inheritance like a yoke. Despite their opposing temperaments, Wrigley was willing to add Veeck to the Cubs' payroll in 1933 as an office boy.

True to form, Veeck plunged into his position with boundless energy, trying his hand at nearly every off-field task imaginable, no matter how mundane. He worked concessions, counted ticket stubs, manned the switchboard, edited a magazine entitled *Fan and Family*, and resodded the field. He even oversaw the planting of the iconic ivy along the redbrick outfield wall at Wrigley Field, as Cubs Park had been renamed in 1927. It was an inside-out crash course on ballpark operations, supplemented by night classes in accounting and business law at Northwestern University. Soon, Veeck worked his way into the Cubs' front office, first as assistant secretary and later as treasurer.

By 1941, Veeck had a plum post among the Cubs' executive ranks; a lifetime's worth of baseball knowledge; a wife, Eleanor, who'd once dropped out of college to ride horses and elephants in the circus; and two young sons. Still only in his mid-twenties, he likely could have coasted through adulthood working for the Cubs in his home city. But there was a restive and rebellious way about

Veeck that precluded him from ever being satisfied with settling. Veeck was, former Cubs first baseman and manager Charlie Grimm observed, "a restless young man who wanted to be more than a figure-man in the front office," someone who harbored radical ideas for injecting fun and excitement into the game-day experience that went beyond what Philip Wrigley could stomach. Whenever Veeck brought up one of his promotional schemes, Wrigley wouldn't even hear him out, cutting off his spirited junior employee before he could finish his thought.

Early in the 1941 season, Milwaukee Brewers owner Henry Bendinger made it known he was seeking someone to take the debt-ridden club off his hands. Veeck sensed an opportunity to break loose. In Milwaukee, a mere ninety miles to the north but far from the glare of the major-league spotlight, he'd have his own laboratory in which to experiment. Veeck didn't hesitate. He started running.

To woo disaffected Brewers fans, Veeck first placed himself in the thick of them. Before games, he stood at the entrance to Borchert Field like a "parson telling the faithful how glad he is to see them out for the services." Athletically built, with curly hair the color of sawdust, Veeck wore no hat, no tie, and no suit. In contrast to his father, who never would've shown up to work in attire unbefitting an executive, Veeck broke every sartorial norm of that buttoned-up era, bustling about in sports shirts unbuttoned generously at the neck, lightweight gabardine jackets, and slip-on moccasins. The casualness of his dress heralded his posture as a man of the people, which was reinforced by his insistence that incoming customers call him "Bill."

Once the game got under way, Veeck rambled from one end of the ballpark to the other, covering more ground over nine innings than his center fielder, as one writer put it. Incapable of sitting still, he was forever plopping in and out of vacant seats, gabbing with fans and angling for ideas on boosting their comfort and pleasure. He roared encouragement to Brewers batters and spewed venom at the umpires. After the final out, Veeck hustled to the main exit to wave goodbye to anyone he might not have come into contact with during the game, staying put until the last attendee passed by. Once, as fans were shuffling toward the gates, a custodian switched off the field lights. Enraged, Veeck charged back into the ballpark. "What's the idea?" he exclaimed. "The people are still in the park. I don't want this to happen again. Keep the lights on until you are sure every person has left the park."

Veeck's promotional philosophy could be summed up in one sentence: "The meat always looks better with a garnish of greens." It was an organization-wide undertaking. As owner, Veeck burned through every penny of his loans, scrubbing the stadium, wheeling in new hot dog carts, and dressing ushers in snazzy outfits. Charlie Grimm, who'd followed Veeck from Chicago to Milwaukee, assumed dual roles with the Brewers: manager of the team and banjo-plucking centerpiece of an all-Brewers band, which entertained crowds before games and between innings. Any employee with musical aptitude, no matter how questionable, could join— Veeck himself did, on the sliding whistle. He later claimed to have retained a washed-up pitcher solely because he played a mean violin.

Bands at ballparks weren't novel, but the sensibility was. Baseball front offices generally frowned on promotions that veered into spectacle. Ladies' Days, stadium enhancements, pregame commemorations—those were all fine. But executives drew the line at stunts that threatened to sully the alleged dignity of the national pastime. True, there had been coaches like Al Schacht and Nick Altrock of the Washington Senators who had performed clownish comedy routines for hometown crowds, but Senators owner Clark Griffith was quick to assert that baseball would never "go in for any Hippodrome stuff." Anything that smacked of the big top was suspect.

Veeck threw it all out the window. He wanted to win as much as any owner; he also wanted audiences to have fun even when the Brewers lost. High-minded principles contributed nothing to his bottom line. The ballpark experience he envisioned was a type of theater that had room for competitive play *and* diverting sideshows. "Curiosity is the spice of life," Veeck explained. "If you give the fans nothing else except a ball game, they'll come out in certain numbers. But arouse their curiosity and they'll come out in droves."

From 1942 onward, "Veeck's Varieties" were in full swing at Borchert Field. There were quiz shows, footraces, glow-in-the-dark yo-yo exhibitions, tightrope walkers, and marriage ceremonies at home plate. Sometimes, a beer keg stuffed with torn tickets would be rolled onto the field, out of which employees would read stub numbers into a microphone while a band blared behind them. Customers with the corresponding tickets were awarded absurd items like bushels of peaches, live lobsters, blocks of ice, greased pigs, kegs of nails, or squabs tied to a string. Watching flabbergasted winners wrestle with their unruly prizes provided belly laughs for innings on end. Veeck rarely announced these promotions in advance. He thought it better to surprise fans, to make them think they'd miss out if they stayed home. "What we are trying to do," he wrote, "is to get the whole city in a frame of mind where they are asking, 'What's that screwball going to do next?'"

Once he set foot in Milwaukee, Veeck didn't stop running. Twenty-hour days weren't uncommon. One minute he was tossing batting practice, the next tearing across town toward his latest speaking engagement to plug the Brewers. "He has no patience with delay and formality," observed John C. Hoffman of *Esquire*. "He goes from one place to another with the quickest possible speed." With rival owners Veeck wheeled and dealed at a blistering rate, remaking the roster on the fly through shrewd negotiating tactics and exceptional baseball instincts. Veeck peddled so many players that manager Charlie Grimm used to ask him periodically, "Who is on the team today?" The only time Veeck seemed to stand still was in the hours following a particularly tough loss, when he stewed in bed alone, refusing to eat dinner. The press found him irresistible, the players bighearted, the umpires combative, the other owners in the American Association confounding. Fans who'd long ago soured on the club took to him from the start. "We're going to be in the race next year," they recited like true believers. "Bill Veeck won't let us down."

Somehow, he didn't. Dead on arrival in 1941, the Brewers inched within one game of the American Association pennant in 1942. Attendance skyrocketed along the way. Through invention, persuasion, eccentricity, and tireless devotion to fans and winning, Veeck converted a flatlining franchise into a baseball moneymaker.

As if that weren't enough, there were larger plans that Veeck was chasing. One of them involved Satchel Paige.

5

Two Sides of the Navy

On December 7, 1941, two months after barnstorming with Satchel
Paige, Bob Feller was driving along Route 6 from Iowa to Chicago,
where he planned to hammer out the following season's contract
with Indians executives. It was a crisp, cloudless Sunday afternoon. Through the windshield of his Buick Century, flat prairieland
stretched for miles.

Davenport came into view around midday. As Feller crossed
the Mississippi River into Illinois, a news flash interrupted the pro-
gramming on his dashboard radio: Japanese planes had bombed
Pearl Harbor.

Feller's mind went blank. He motored along in a daze. With
each passing mile his resolve hardened. He knew what he had to do.

That past summer, as young men registered for the nation's
first-ever peacetime draft and as players like Hank Greenberg were
inducted into the armed services, Feller had mulled over whether
he should enlist, going so far as to chat with former heavyweight
boxing champion Gene Tunney about the physical fitness program
he now spearheaded for the Navy. Tunney reportedly had told Feller

that "his fame would attract many boys to the Navy and that he would thus serve his country better than by waiting for his draft call." But family concerns had stopped Feller short. His father's illness continued to ravage his body, rendering him too weak to tend to the farm. As the sole provider for the family, Feller had deferred to his mother's pleas to stick close to home. After the attack on Pearl Harbor, however, everything changed.

From his hotel room, Feller phoned Tunney, who flew out to Chicago straightaway. They met a few days later at the Federal Building on South Clark Street. Feller, his hair slicked back, wore a black pinstriped suit with a white handkerchief in the breast pocket. His enlistment ceremony was broadcast live nationwide in what turned out to be a recruitment bonanza for the armed forces. "With all the kids in the country wondering what they ought to do, it was the only thing I could do," Feller dutifully said.

Enlisting in the Navy didn't require Feller to venture far from the public eye. In 1942, he joined the baseball team at the naval base in Norfolk, Virginia. It made no difference that he mostly faced off against callow draftees and lifelong minor leaguers in service-league games—curious fans turned out all the same. That summer, it was said that Feller "couldn't pitch in an empty lot in a blackout without the news getting around."

With Feller anchoring the pitching rotation, the Norfolk squad flattened their opponents, allegedly winning ninety-two of one hundred contests. From time to time Feller also jetted to benefit games to sell war bonds. At Wrigley Field in late May, nearly 30,000 spectators showed up to witness Feller, Dizzy Dean, and several white service players square off against Satchel Paige's Kansas City Monarchs. At the last minute, Feller received orders to return to his naval station, and Paige took advantage of his absence, leading the Monarchs to a 3-1 victory. Later, in Cleveland, more than 60,000 fans welcomed back the Indians ace for an exhibition match that pitted top military players against the American League All-Star team. There, Feller's major-league sabbatical caught up to him, as AL sluggers knocked him out of the box in the second inning.

His military tenure could've continued far from the front lines of combat. But Feller wouldn't stand for being what one writer called an "animated recruiting poster" for the Navy, more symbol than sailor. He'd enlisted with the intention to fight, not to hurl fastballs past starstruck seamen. So he volunteered for gunnery school and then accepted an assignment as a chief petty officer and commander of an antiaircraft battery of 40-mm guns on the USS *Alabama*, a newly commissioned 35,000-ton battleship. It would set sail for the North Atlantic at some point after Christmas.

In the meantime, he made tentative plans to wed his girlfriend, Virginia Winther. They'd met years earlier in Florida while Feller was visiting a friend at Rollins College, where Virginia was enrolled as an art student. Throughout their long-distance courtship, he'd yet to bring her back to Van Meter, preferring to hold off until his father recovered.

That day never came. On January 11, 1943, while the USS *Alabama* was cruising south along the East Coast, the ship's chaplain summoned Feller into his quarters. Feller instinctively knew the bad news was about his father. The next day, he boarded a coast guard cutter en route to Norfolk, where he would hop a flight to central Iowa to attend his father's funeral. But first he phoned his fiancée to break two bits of news: She would finally get to see his hometown, and they would wed immediately after the wake. It'd been his father's wish that they marry despite his illness, and Feller, a devoted son till the end, followed through.

During his leave in Van Meter, Feller broke away from his family at some point to stroll out to the muddy pasture where Oak View Park had once been. Even though few visible markers of the ball field remained, for a moment it all came back to him: he and his father carving out the diamond, the teams motoring in to take a crack at the teenage phenom, the batters watching helplessly as his fastball zipped by. Not even eight years had passed since his last game there, but that period must've seemed like a dispatch from another life. Nothing, he sensed, could ever be the same.

In the fall of 1942, when he enrolled at Long Island University on a basketball scholarship, Larry Doby had more to worry about than racking up points and rebounds. The military draft had gone into effect, and college athletes were prime candidates for selection. Hoping to delay the inevitable, Doby transferred in the spring semester to Virginia Union University, a historically Black institution in Richmond, but his time there wouldn't be long. A draft notice soon arrived at Doby's residence in Paterson. So in the summer of 1943, midway through his second season playing baseball for the Newark Eagles of the Negro National League, he embarked on a journey from Newark's Penn Station to the Great Lakes Naval Training Station outside Chicago. Five years after his arrival in New Jersey from South Carolina, Doby was once again steaming toward an uncertain future.

This time he wasn't alone. Scattered through the railcars were some recognizable faces—amateur athletes, Black and white alike, whom Doby had played with or against during high school in Paterson. Doby took comfort in their presence. "We were all on the same train," he reflected. "So I'm thinking that we're all going to be together," like a sports team traveling communally to an away game.

When the train rolled into Chicago and the passengers disembarked, however, military officials brusquely divided the white recruits from the Black ones. As Doby marched away from his white acquaintances, the blunt force of government-enforced discrimination struck him like never before. "This was the first time that segregation really stung me like this," Doby later stated. "I wasn't expecting it in the military. I had no idea. It hurt a lot."

The separation was abrupt and humiliating. The same country

that was compelling Doby to put aside his future to fight on its be-
half had reduced him to second-class citizenship before his basic
training had even begun. "It was a shock," Doby recalled. "If you've
never been exposed to [segregation] from the outside and it suddenly
hits you, you can't take it. I didn't crack up; I just went into my shell."

It was a familiar feeling for many Black recruits arriving at
Great Lakes. For decades, no branch of the armed services practiced segregation as rigidly as the Navy. Almost immediately after the
battleships docked in the wake of World War I, the Navy closed its
ranks to Black Americans. They were allowed to enlist again in 1933,
but solely as stewards and mess attendants, tending to white troops
during the day and retiring to separate quarters at night. The bombing
of Pearl Harbor spurred change, but only to a degree. Though Black
recruits soon would be admitted as apprentice seamen, they were
not treated equally. Clark Clifford, who acted as President Harry
Truman's naval adviser during World War II, looked back on the
compulsory segregation of that period with disgust. "I thought the
Navy at times resembled a Southern plantation that had somehow
escaped the Civil War," he wrote in his memoirs. "Blacks swabbed
the decks, shined shoes, did the cooking, washed the dishes, and
served the food. Virtually no other jobs were open to them." In turn,
many Black sailors came to see themselves, in the words of military
historian Bernard C. Nalty, "as outsiders, excluded from the real
Navy, serving as workers rather than fighters."

Boot camp training for Black naval recruits took place at a segregated section of Great Lakes named after Robert Smalls, an enslaved
Black man from Doby's home state of South Carolina who'd gained
his freedom during the Civil War by commandeering a Confederate
steamship and steering it to the Union side. The white officer in charge
of Camp Robert Smalls, Lieutenant Commander Daniel W. Armstrong, told the *Chicago Tribune* in 1942: "Camp Smalls' duty is to
toughen the Negro recruits to navy life, but very little we put these
boys thru can be considered tough when you understand the life they

have been used to." In addition to the separate and unequal accommodations, certain directives, such as having to sing spirituals on Sunday evenings in an effort to cultivate what white officers considered to be Black culture, struck many as demeaning. Doby responded to this unfamiliar environment in a way that his high school teammates from Paterson likely would've recognized: Characteristically quiet and guarded, he retreated further inward. "I don't ever recall his leaving [the base] with the boys," one acquaintance remembered, "although he did leave by himself once or twice."

Once more, it was through sports that Doby would find his footing. By the time he arrived in 1943, the Great Lakes Naval Station was crawling with athletes. Even though nearly 100,000 men trained on its grounds at any given time, it was said that "you could throw a baseball anywhere on the station and at least two big leaguers will try to catch it."

The baseball Bluejackets, as the Great Lakes service team was called, was helmed by Mickey Cochrane, a retired catcher who twice had been named the most valuable player in the American League. His presence triggered a scrum of major-league talent to the base. Sluggers Johnny Mize and Barney McCosky turned out, pitchers Virgil Trucks and Schoolboy Rowe followed. During wartime, the baseball Bluejackets steadily crushed whatever competition crossed their paths, whether industrial, military, or even major-league clubs, racking up an astonishing 188-32 record overall. They were youthful and sound, expert at boosting morale and raising funds, and, like every team packed with major-league players, uniformly white.

Because the mass recruitment of Black men into the Navy was still new, there were no sports teams for Doby to join during his first few months at Great Lakes. That would change early in 1944, when he began lacing up on what was quickly deemed "one of the best— and most unheralded—basketball teams in the midwest area." That winter, the all-Black sailor squad trounced its hardwood opposition by an average of twenty points, with Doby netting close to fourteen points per contest. The familiar rhythms of sports enabled Doby to settle into a familiar routine on the base. To his hometown newspaper, he described his schedule as such: "We hit the deck at 5:30 o'clock every morning, go to chow at 7, clean the rooms for inspection at 8, I take my two classes until 11:30, then chow again, basketball practice from 1 to 4, then take care of the games. My day is over at 7."

Once the weather warmed, Doby, at age twenty, became one of the youngest players to earn a spot on the newly organized Black Bluejackets, a baseball club studded with Negro League standouts. In the summer of 1944, as part of the Midwestern Serviceman's Baseball League, they cut across the northern heartland, competing against military bases and technical schools and company clubs in industrial cities like Fort Wayne, Battle Creek, and Urbana.

All season long, the two baseball teams at Great Lakes ran parallel to each other. With a 48-2 record, the white Bluejackets were the toast of the armed services. Wherever they went, waves of publicity washed over them. The Black Bluejackets, in comparison, played to less fanfare. Though they rolled to a league championship and a respectable 32-10 mark, press coverage was sparser, and players resented not being able to compete with or against their white counterparts. "I wanted to find out how good I was in their company—and couldn't," Doby asserted years later. "That made me think."

A proposed exhibition game between the two clubs in April 1944 was rained out and never rescheduled. Then, on June 17, seven members of the Black Bluejackets, including Doby, were chosen to compete on a Black all-star team against the white Bluejackets. For nine innings, veteran Negro League hurler Herbert "Doc" Bracken held the potent white lineup to one hit, but an untimely series of walks, grounders, and passed balls saddled him with a 3-0 loss. Doby walked away convinced that several Black players could've cracked the white Bluejackets' roster. That he hadn't even been granted a tryout grated on him. "I thought: 'This is a crying shame when I'm here to protect my country,'" Doby recalled. "But I couldn't do anything about it—I was under Navy rules and regulations and had to abide by them or face the consequences."

Doby would have to settle for affirmation elsewhere. Once, after Mickey Cochrane watched a Black Bluejackets' game, he sought out Doby. "Larry," Doby remembered him saying, "if I was still managing in the big leagues, I'd want you on my side."

In August 1944, Doby hung up his spikes for the season—his last, it turned out, with the Black Bluejackets. Because of his athletic prowess, he'd been able to bypass the messman duty into which so many Black sailors had been funneled, securing instead a coveted role as a physical education instructor. As the naval skirmishes in the South Pacific escalated, Doby soon would be sent to lead drills and exercises on the other side of the world.

6

No Gentleman

As Bob Feller and Larry Doby began prepping for war, Bill Veeck turned his sights toward Satchel Paige. Success had come quick for Veeck as owner of the Milwaukee Brewers, but his ambitions were greater still. A covert operation late in 1942 foreshadowed his road forward.

That off-season, the Philadelphia Phillies of baseball's National League had come onto the market. No club in the majors was more down on its luck. In each of the last five seasons the team had lost more than one hundred games. In 1942, the Phillies had finished nearly twenty games behind the next-worse team in the National League. Not a single pitcher from that season's roster had sported a winning record, and no batter had reached double figures in home runs. For years Phillies owner Gerry Nugent had dealt away promising players to cover operational costs. By the end, he could no longer make ends meet.

It was, in short, the exact sort of challenge that Veeck embraced.

The timing was particularly intriguing. Already the military draft had claimed numerous major-league players. Owners were forced to patch up their depleted rosters with spare parts salvaged from baseball's scrap heap: creaky veterans, high schoolers, and career minor leaguers. If the Phillies were to take advantage of a wartime scramble that had the potential of upending pennant races, they'd need to retool their lineup fast. But with talent in short supply and with fifteen other franchises all picking from the same diminishing pool of players, it seemed a steep task. So Veeck made a radical decision: If he were to purchase the Phillies, he'd pick from a different pool altogether, one that the major leagues had snubbed since its inception.

He'd sign players from the Negro Leagues.

Veeck had come of age at exactly the right moment in exactly the right city to gain awareness of the richness of the Negro Leagues. Ever since Rube Foster—the pioneering player-executive who organized the Negro National League in 1920—built the Chicago American Giants into the dominant club of its era, the Windy City had been at the crossroads of Black baseball. In 1933, Comiskey Park on Chicago's South Side began hosting the East-West Game, a heavily attended all-star contest that drew both the country's top Black athletes and luminaries annually to the city. Growing up in Chicago, where he'd attended his share of American Giants and East-West games, Veeck developed a deeper knowledge of Black baseball than most white fans had. Cleveland Jackson, a writer for the *Call & Post*, the leading Black newspaper in Cleveland, would later marvel not only at Veeck's "surprising knowledge of outstanding Negro baseball players," but also at his ability to quote "individual players' names, their positions, and teams."

While Veeck hadn't made an attempt to integrate the Milwaukee Brewers, he'd fought prejudice in other ways. In Ocala, Florida, where the Brewers had conducted spring training in 1942, Veeck wandered into the colored section of the bleachers one afternoon to chat with some spectators. The sheriff hustled over to inform him that only Black fans were permitted there. When Veeck refused to budge, the sheriff phoned the Ocala mayor, who rushed to the ball-park and pleaded with Veeck to respect the city ordinances on seg-regation. Rather than back down, Veeck informed them that if they continued to pester him, he'd pull the Brewers out of Ocala on the spot and make a stink about it in the press.

After that, Veeck made an effort to sit, daring security to do something about it.

"I have always had a strong feeling for minority groups," he later wrote in his autobiography, adding: "It seems to me that all my life I have been fighting against the status quo, against the tyranny of fossilized majority rule. I would suppose that whatever impels me to battle the old fossils of baseball also draws me to the side of the underdog. I would prefer to think of it as an essential decency."

Veeck had been tracking Satchel Paige's career in particular at least since 1934, when he'd sat in the stands at Los Angeles's Wrigley Field during Paige's thirteen-inning face-off with Dizzy Dean. Not even two months after he'd purchased the Brewers, in August 1941, Veeck had hosted Paige and the Kansas City Monarchs at Borchert Field for an exhibition game against the Birmingham Black Barons.

Paige's appearances were sometimes booked through Abe Saperstein, a promoter for the Negro American League. Like Veeck, Saperstein was a scrappy hustler from Chicago who knew how to make a buck and amuse a crowd. At five-foot-three, he appeared not to have an athletic bone in his rotund body, but what he lacked in physique he made up for in imagination. Since the late 1920s, he'd owned and managed the Harlem Globetrotters, an all-Black basketball squad whose fast-paced, razzle-dazzle style wowed spec-tators and left earthbound opponents in the lurch. "Negro athletes are supposed to be strictly front runners," Saperstein said in 1942. "You know—great when they're ahead but inclined to fold when the white boys put the pressure on them. In short, they lack the mashed potatoes. The Globe-Trotters have done as much as Joe Louis to show that idea is cockeyed."

Even though several writers and Negro League executives accused Saperstein of exploiting Black players for profit, certain clubs, including the Kansas City Monarchs, continued to rely on him for bookings. Just because a venue booked the Monarchs, however, did not guarantee Paige's participation. Paige, Saperstein made clear, was strictly "an individual proposition," someone who generated enough publicity and ticket sales on his own to merit separate financial arrangements. For Paige to play, in other words, venues would have to pay.

In his pursuit of the Phillies in 1942, Veeck relied on Saperstein and Black sportswriters from *The Chicago Defender* and other publications to help him identify top players from the Negro Leagues who would be able to transform a last-place team into a contender. Paige, of course, was chief among them. Undoubtedly there would be blowback, but Veeck was prepared to weather it. "The only thing blocking [integration] was no law, it was just a gentlemen's agreement," he later said. "And I was no gentleman."

Besides, during a time when Black soldiers were risking their lives overseas, Veeck believed that any attempt among members of the baseball establishment to thwart his efforts by codifying its discriminatory practices would trigger a firestorm of criticism. America's entry into a global conflict against overtly racist adversaries had prompted renewed rounds of national soul-searching. Black newspapers led the charge in calling out the disparity between the democratic principles for which the country was fighting abroad and the segregationist policies it enforced on the home front. The "Double V Campaign," first touted in *The Pittsburgh Courier,* called for the simultaneous defeat of international fascism and domestic racism. Taking their cue from this movement, Black sportswriters over the following years would champion integration in baseball with renewed and righteous urgency. Intrepid columnists like Wendell Smith of *The Pittsburgh Courier* and Fay Young and Sam Lacy of *The Chicago Defender* grilled major-league executives, helped arrange tryouts for Negro League players with major-league clubs, and called for boycotts of major-league games.

Concerned with the newfound vulnerability of the color line, *The Sporting News*, a weekly publication so influential among white professional baseball circles that it came to be known as "the bible of baseball," saw fit to rally the league's conservative ranks in the summer of 1942 with an editorial entitled "No Good from Raising Race Issue." Its opening line was unequivocal: "There is no law against Negroes playing with white teams, nor whites with colored clubs, but neither has invited the other for the obvious reason they prefer to draw their talent from their own ranks and because the leaders of both groups know their crowd psychology and do not care to run the risk of damaging their own game."

The pressure ran all the way to the top. In July 1942, as Paul Dickson recounts in his biography of Veeck, an old quote from Leo Durocher resurfaced in the press in which the Brooklyn Dodgers manager had indicated that he knew of several managers who would welcome Black players but major-league owners wouldn't stand for it. Per usual, Landis's public and private responses to the possibility of major-league integration diverged. Away from the press, in his Chicago office, Landis berated Durocher, then turned around and reiterated to reporters afterward that "Negroes are not barred from organized baseball by the commissioner and never have been during the 21 years I have served. There is no rule in organized baseball prohibiting their participation and never has been to my knowledge. If Durocher, any other manager, or all of them, want to sign one, or 25, Negro players, it is all right with me."

Writers like Fay Young saw these statements for what they were: hot air. No owner, he knew, would dare to "take up Landis' challenge." But that all might change if Veeck were to buy the Phillies.

At some point after the 1942 season had concluded, Veeck supposedly made an offer to Phillies owner Gerry Nugent, who responded favorably. While in Chicago to firm up his financial support, Veeck paid a courtesy visit to the commissioner's office to inform Landis, whom he'd known since childhood, of his intentions. It proved to be a ruinous mistake.

Landis, Veeck recalled, reacted with neither shock nor assent to Veeck's stated plan of integrating the Phillies. Though the commissioner's own impressions of the meeting remain unknown, it's not a stretch to assume that Veeck's burgeoning reputation as someone who took pleasure in bucking the consensus wouldn't have been lost on Landis.

After the meeting, Veeck hopped an overnight train to Philadelphia. Soon thereafter, he caught word that the National League had assumed control of the Phillies. Under the guidance of Ford Frick, the league president, the team was soon sold to William Cox, a thirty-three-year-old lumber magnate and baseball novice (who would be banned for life a mere year later for gambling on his own club). In an instant, Veeck's plan crumbled to dust.

Decades later, some historians would cast doubt on Veeck's intention of purchasing and integrating the Phillies, pointing to a lack of contemporaneous evidence and Veeck's lifelong habit of embellishing and revising his memories in service of more entertaining stories. Veeck, however, stuck to his account. "I always will believe Landis leaked our plans to Frick," he later stated, adding: "We'd have had Satchel Paige pitching for us and winning 30 games a year . . . I don't blame the other club owners [for opposing the sale]. We'd have walked away with the pennant."

After his bid to buy the Phillies fell through, Veeck redoubled his efforts to woo fans and win pennants with the Milwaukee Brewers during wartime. Since purchasing the team, Veeck had made a point of seeking out potential customers on their own turf. Sometimes he gave multiple speeches in the same day, plugging the Brewers before every civic group, church dinner, Kiwanis luncheon, or industrial plant within driving distance of Milwaukee.

In the early 1940s, Milwaukee clanked and thundered with ramped-up industry to aid the war effort. Almost 40 percent of the labor force toiled in the factories that had earned the city the moniker of "The Machine Shop of the World." While promoting his club and answering letters, Veeck heard workers complain about being unable to catch the Brewers in action because of their wartime shifts. These were men and women breaking their backs to supply weapons for the battlefield while being deprived of pleasures on the home front. A solution both practical and progressive came to him: morning baseball.

In 1943, Veeck shuffled the Brewers' schedule so that select games would start at 10:30 A.M., after the graveyard shifts had let out. "We're bringing baseball into tune with the times," he explained, adding: "Hours don't mean a thing any more since people are working around the clock everywhere." Before the start of the season's first morning game, on May 8, 1943, swing-shift workers were greeted at the gates by a seven-piece swing band belting out peppy tunes. Instead of hot dogs and beer, ushers clad in garish pajamas and nightcaps handed them doughnuts, coffee, and cornflakes.

It was a flawless promotion, at once heartfelt and attention-grabbing. "Billy Veeck," Esquire crowed, "is running the greatest baseball show on earth and making it pay dividends." That summer, neither gasoline rationing nor austerity measures kept the turnstiles from clicking. What once had been "one of the loneliest stretches of uninhabited chairs anywhere in the entertainment world" was now the buzziest ballpark in the minor leagues. While clinching their first American Association pennant in seven years, the Brewers shattered the team attendance record by drawing more than 332,000 fans, better than a few major-league clubs in 1943.

Shortly after the season ended, Veeck met up in New York City with former boxing champion Barney Ross, who mesmerized him with tales of his South Pacific skirmishes while serving in the Marine Corps. By then, Veeck himself had begun to think deeply about the war. "I'm the guy who has to look at my face every morning when I shave," he told the *Milwaukee Sentinel*, "and when they started drafting fathers I knew there was only one thing to do."

In November of 1943, he trooped to the Marine recruiting station in Milwaukee with Brewers manager Charlie Grimm and treasurer Rudie Schaffer in tow. Neither expected the recruiters to express much interest in their boss, who was pushing thirty with flat feet, a checkered history of leg injuries, and a wife and three kids to support. To Grimm and Schaffer's surprise, however, Veeck bounded out, gave a sharp salute, and exclaimed: "I'm in!" His decision to join the Marines, one columnist wrote, "seemed sudden—it was a shock, in fact—but it was characteristic. He figured it was time for him to go, so he went."

Like other prominent figures who'd enlisted, Veeck could've coasted through the war in a mostly promotional capacity, but the very notion of special treatment cut against his everyman leanings. Declining all commissions, Veeck was sworn in as a private and eventually shipped out to Bougainville Island in the South Pacific the following year.

He wouldn't last there long.

7

Tales from the South Pacific

In the spring of 1943, Bob Feller and his fellow sailors aboard the USS *Alabama* steamed north toward Iceland. Their first assignment, a chilly and taxing one, was to shadow Allied convoys transporting supplies to the port of Murmansk in northwestern Russia, keeping an eye out for German U-boats lurking along those northerly routes.

For someone who'd grown up landlocked, Feller found his sea legs fast, but others weren't so lucky. Turbulent ocean currents pitched and rolled the battleship from side to side. Some sailors became so seasick they could neither shave nor eat. Loitering on deck amid stormy weather was especially treacherous. Men talked of waves as big as mountains that splashed seawater over the rails and coated the topside with ice, which crews had to scrape off continually. Feller knew of the damage such weather could do. One blustery night, an enlisted man stopped by the chief petty officers' lounge to ask Feller for an autograph. After a brief chat, he left to dump some trash into the ocean. It'd be the last anyone would see of him. He was swept overboard into the cold waters.

At night in the lower Arctic Circle, temperatures plummeted, leaving seamen on watch duty feeling as if they were trapped in an icebox. They downed cup after cup of coffee but still retreated to their quarters with wind-burned faces and numb limbs. To pass the time, some pressed pennies into the bulkhead, where they froze instantly against the steel.

Mercifully, the *Alabama*'s stint in the North Atlantic was short and free of conflict. In August of 1943, the ship plowed back to Norfolk, Virginia, and then continued on through the Panama Canal en route to the South Pacific. There, the days were balmy and the crystalline waters gentler. When at fleet anchorages, the *Alabama* functioned like a miniature floating city, more populous than Feller's hometown of Van Meter and loaded with amenities. There were doctors, barbers, dentists, welders, pharmacists, chaplains, tailors, and postal workers. A printing press churned out a ship newspaper, bakers rose before dawn to prepare hundreds of loaves of bread for breakfast, and a twenty-piece, Glenn Miller–style dance band performed periodically in the mess hall. Movies sometimes were screened on the fantail after sundown. *Casablanca* was shown so many times that crew members sitting on the turrets could yell out lines in unison with Humphrey Bogart.

In his downtime, Feller kept in shape by socking a punching bag in the boiler room, skipping rope, and running laps around an improvised jogging path on deck. He also found catchers to squat for him on deck while he pumped fastballs and worked on his slider. "I was lucky," Feller later said, "being on a battleship big enough to allow me a regular chance to throw and catch, skip rope, swim and take systematic exercise." Some afternoons, he and his crewmates sailed to nearby islands to match up against sailors from other ships on baseball diamonds carved out of palm groves and littered with coral. Improvising with the materials on hand, they sometimes used blocks of wood for home plate and sacks as bases. Once, a game was disrupted when a pack of sailors on a hunt for wild boars burst onto the field with knives held high. Afterward, aboard the *Alabama*, Feller kicked back in the chief petty officers' lounge on the stern side of the second deck. At night he slept on a coiled iron bunk hinged to the back wall of a room behind the lounge.

If life was more comfortable during downtime in the South Pacific, it was no less dangerous when the battleship went on the offensive. One crew member remembered that Japanese planes attacked the *Alabama* whenever it helped wrest occupied islands from their control. Once, a plane on a suicide mission barely missed striking the *Alabama*, splashing ocean water onto the battleship's gun crews as it fell. In June 1944, the *Alabama* faced its gravest test while it was anchored near the Mariana Islands alongside a sizable portion of the American fleet, preparing for an invasion of Saipan. The Japanese military, as historian Harold J. Goldberg wrote in *D-Day in the Pacific*, "saw an opportunity for a decisive battle that would turn the war's momentum in its favor." Its plan called for a risky surprise attack on the gathered fleet in a desperate attempt to halt the advancement of the United States across the Pacific.

On June 19, 1944, shortly after dawn, the first wave of Japanese aircraft took to the sky. Shortly thereafter, technicians monitoring the long-range SK radar on the *Alabama* and other vessels sounded the alarm. U.S. pilots dashed to their own fighter aircraft and zoomed full throttle toward the approaching planes. The Japanese, who'd hoped to catch their opponents flat-footed, found themselves entangled in a surprise counterattack.

As the director of a 40-mm antiaircraft battery on the *Alabama*, Feller would've climbed into his gun mount alongside his fellow crew members. That day, whenever enemy aircraft came within range, the fleet unleashed a barrage of gunfire. The Japanese planes charged headlong into the action. One dropped a bomb on a neighboring vessel, the USS *South Dakota*, that killed two-dozen sailors on impact. A little while later, another plane swooped down and emptied a whistling bomb from overhead that splashed down just wide of the *Alabama*.

Feller and his crewmates manned their positions until sundown, spraying rounds at descending planes. Amid the billowing smoke and earsplitting racket, they watched numerous Japanese aircraft burst into flames and spiral down, blackening the surrounding sea with oil and wreckage. It was, Feller later wrote, "the most exciting 13 hours of my life. After that, the dangers of Yankee Stadium seemed trivial."

The Japanese lost more than four hundred aircraft; the United States, in comparison, suffered minimal losses. U.S. pilots had picked off so many Japanese planes that they would eventually dub it the Great Marianas Turkey Shoot. Reeling from the humiliating defeat and the subsequent loss of Saipan to U.S. forces, Hideki Tojo, the prime minister of Japan, tendered his resignation in July—a signal, even as the war raged on, of just how significant those battles in which Feller had taken part were for the United States' eventual victory.

Months later, in October 1944, Feller listened to the World Series from his bunk via shortwave radio. He could've been excused for not recognizing many of the players involved. That year, more than 60 percent of major-league starters from 1941, Feller's last season, had enrolled in the armed services. Their absence had scrambled up professional baseball, enabling the St. Louis Browns, the perennial laughingstock of the majors, to seize its only American League pennant. Opposing them were the St. Louis Cardinals, whose star slugger, Stan Musial, had yet to be called to duty. An all–St. Louis World Series would've been unthinkable before the war, but these were far from normal times.

Tuning in to the World Series no doubt reinforced in Feller the sense of all he was giving up in his years away. Three seasons were lost and a fourth would soon follow. Along with them went any realistic chance of making a run at some of baseball's lifetime pitching records. Without those years of his prime, the lofty goals Feller had once set for himself no longer seemed within reach.

Monetary concerns similarly weighed on him. So far, the war had cost Feller upward of two hundred thousand dollars, and there was no way to recover those earnings through contracts and endorsements alone. He needed to think big, to come up with plans that were grander and more ambitious than anything he'd ever conceived of before.

During those long days at sea, Feller thought of his off-season barnstorming tours. He thought, too, of Satchel Paige. And soon he had an inkling of what he wanted to do.

In late April of 1944, Bill Veeck washed ashore on Bougainville Island, a violin-shaped block of volcanic earth along the western edge of the Solomon Islands. Steamy, damp, and crawling with insects, Bougainville wreaked havoc on the men who patrolled its perimeters. In the middle of the island ran a steep ridge that sloped downward into dense, swampy jungles swarming with mosquitoes. Not even the coasts offered relief. The sandy beaches thickened without warning into muddy marshes. It was, as one Marine remembered, "like running across thirty feet of the Sahara and suddenly dropping off into the Everglades." Heat and humidity saturated the air, coating troops' skin in a slick, ever-present layer of sweat. After a while, many Marines broke out in swollen abscesses, fungal infections, and blisters. "Jungle rot," it was called, as if the landscape itself was slowly chewing through their bodies.

Veeck proved especially susceptible to these tropical maladies. In the months that he served on Bougainville as part of a Marine defense battalion, according to biographer Paul Dickson, Veeck shuttled in and out of sick wards to have sores drained and infections treated. When not preoccupied with his health, Veeck had to stay alert for Japanese planes overhead and snipers on the ground. At night he shone searchlights into the pitch-black sky to spot the incoming bombers that rained shells down on the U.S.-controlled territory. As soon as a plane flashed across the beams, members of his antiaircraft unit would holler: "Get that Imperial son of a so-and-so!" Veeck slept in a tent in the evening and brewed coffee over a blowtorch in the morning. Still the owner of the Milwaukee Brewers, he tracked the team's progress through clips and letters sent to him by associates.

In addition to operating searchlights, Veeck was responsible for loading heavy shells into 90-mm antiaircraft guns. One day, he suffered a grave injury when a misfiring artillery piece kicked back onto his lower right leg, slicing deep. The subsequent wound, compounded by ulcers and an earlier injury he'd suffered to the same leg during college, failed to heal, so in September of 1944, roughly five months after he'd landed there, Veeck was forced to leave Bougainville to embark on a new, more sedentary journey through hospital beds, first in Guadalcanal and later in California. "I was," Veeck would write of his brief stint in the Marines, "an albatross around Uncle Sam's neck."

Granted medical leave in November, Veeck traveled to Milwaukee the following month to attend a dinner thrown in his honor. One by one, baseball executives and writers took to the podium to praise the wounded veteran who'd unleashed such freewheeling, mischievous fun in their city. At the end, Veeck hobbled to the stage. According to *The Sporting News*, "tears filled his eyes" as he stood before the admiring friends from his prewar life, aware perhaps for the first time that his stint as owner of the Brewers—what Veeck would call "the great time of my life," a period of "all light, all laughter"—never could be the same. The attendees gathered there witnessed a rare event: The man who'd spoken before seemingly every civic group in Milwaukee found himself too choked up to say anything.

His right foot was no more on the mend than when he'd left Bougainville. Veeck would spend most of the following year laid out in hospitals, racked with pain and pumped with penicillin, wheeled into amputation wards but stubbornly refusing to ponder the loss of a leg despite a worsening bone infection that made such a procedure seemingly inevitable.

Veeck's wartime absence had also stretched his increasingly strained marriage to its breaking point. His wife, Eleanor, did not share in his passions. He reveled in stadiums packed with fans;

she preferred open spaces dotted with animals. While he'd looped through the Wisconsin speaking circuit as owner of the Brewers, she'd tended to their children on the 160-acre farm they'd moved to outside the town of West Bend, twenty-five miles northwest of Milwaukee. The winters, when roads became impassable and water pumps froze, were hard. Eleanor had to nail rugs over cracks in the walls to keep the snow out. Slowly, the distance between them had grown, even before Veeck was shipped halfway across the world.

In October 1945, shortly after the Brewers clinched their third American Association pennant in as many years, Veeck sold the team for a significant profit. With the earnings, he purchased a ranch for his family outside of Tucson, Arizona, far removed from the nearest city with a major-league club. Before he'd enlisted, Veeck had seemed to some like the future of baseball. As his dashed plans for integrating the Philadelphia Phillies suggested, he harbored grander ambitions that were as yet unfulfilled. But now, for the first time since he'd dropped out of college, Veeck was out of the game entirely. And it was uncertain when, if ever, he'd find his way back.

Early in 1945, months after Veeck's life-altering injury, Larry Doby shoved off for the Ulithi Atoll, a remote ringlet of South Pacific islands midway between Guam and the Philippines. In the lagoon that the islands encircled, the United States Navy had established one of its largest fleet anchorages. Roughly one thousand vessels—battleships, aircraft carriers, dry docks, and destroyers—bobbed in its clear-blue waters. To the idle sailors, it resembled a bustling aquatic parking lot. There were water taxis, ships that doubled as post offices and hospitals, and even a barge that delivered ice cream to neighboring vessels.

The islands of the Ulithi Atoll were unremarkable—sandy discs of palm-dotted earth scarcely peeking above the tide. After herding the native residents together on a southern islet far from the fleet, the military proceeded to erect officer quarters, Quonset huts, mess halls, and airstrips barely long enough for planes to land on.

But the only bit of land that most sailors anchored there would come to know was the sixty-acre, helmet-shaped island of Mogmog.

By the time Doby arrived in January 1945, Mogmog had already been transformed from a nondescript sandbar to the recreational capital of the South Pacific. From early afternoon to early evening, ferries transported thousands of sailors, desperate to escape the monotony of their ship-bound lives, to its southern landing strip. There, some batted softballs and spiked volleyballs on bulldozed fields of coarse sand; others shed everything but their shoes and skinny-dipped in the reef-lined beaches. Pretty much everyone sipped their allotment of diluted beers while lounging beneath groves of coconut trees. The island was a boozy oasis in a vast desert of water. It was said that if you linked together all the empty beer bottles discarded on Mogmog, the line could've stretched from New York City to Pearl Harbor.

In many ways, whether he was leading calisthenics for the Black Seabees on Mogmog, organizing athletic events for disembarking seamen, or hauling cargo from ships, his service in the Ulithi Atoll must've seemed the best Doby could've hoped for. Because of Mogmog's unique role as a social gathering spot, the loneliness that afflicted many sailors in the Pacific likely didn't cut as deep there. Sometimes there was music in the open-air bandstand, followed by movies when the sun set. In the lagoon Doby would've gazed out at a hive of maritime activity, with small boats buzzing about like so many worker bees. To author Samuel Hynes, who served on a nearby island, the Ulithi Atoll "seemed a pastoral, innocent place, a long way from the real war." Only once while Doby was stationed there did Japanese planes pierce their safe harbor, dive-bombing Mogmog in a raid that inflicted minimal damage.

On special occasions, entertainers were flown in to perform for the fleet. The spring of 1945 brought in two teams of white professional ballplayers on an island-hopping tour of the Pacific. Competing on Mogmog was a challenge. Sharp-edged coral was scattered across the playing field. Because home plate was a mere 255 feet from the shoreline, long fly balls dunked right into the ocean. Regardless, starved for the sport that reminded them of home, servicemen clustered onto the island for the contest, which featured such major-league notables as Virgil Trucks and Mickey Vernon.

When the tour ended, the teams were dissolved and the players fanned out across the Pacific. Vernon, a first baseman for the Washington Senators, wound up back at the Ulithi Atoll. Though Black and white sailors slept in different camps at night, the relatively relaxed attitude toward segregation during the day permitted Doby and Vernon to share the same playing fields. Soon, they struck up a friendship. "Many nights," Vernon told his biographer, "[Doby] would stop by my tent, and we would talk or go to a movie together." It didn't take long for Vernon to recognize Doby as the best athlete on the island. His respect for Doby ran so deep that later on Vernon would pen a letter to Clark Griffith, the elderly owner of the Senators. He would inform his boss of the Black sailor he'd served with who had clear-cut major-league potential.

Griffith never followed up on the tip.

Shortly after Christmas, in 1944, the USS *Alabama* reversed course and embarked on a long journey to the United States. Weeks later, when the battleship docked in Seattle, Bob Feller took liberty along with his crewmates, but he wouldn't follow them back to the Pacific. It was finally time for Feller, who would receive eight battle stars for his service, to return to baseball.

In his years away, the public had tracked Feller's whereabouts through periodic newspaper dispatches. Now the pitching icon was home, and while no one yet knew whether maritime life had robbed Feller of his fastball, he slipped effortlessly back into the persona he'd cultivated before the war. When asked about Major League Baseball's decision not to suspend the sport during wartime, Feller said: "Baseball and malted milks and a duck hunting trip are the things the fellows want to come back to when this thing is over."

Feller soon reported to the Great Lakes Naval Station outside of Chicago, months after Doby had left it. His assignment was to manage the baseball Bluejackets. Though he wasn't slated to join the roster, within weeks he was penciling himself in for regular trips to the mound. By early August 1945, when U.S. forces dropped atomic bombs on Hiroshima and Nagasaki, he'd worked himself into playing shape.

The end of the war galvanized Feller to hurry back to the majors. He begged for an immediate release so that he could salvage the final month of the season, but his admiral wouldn't hasten the bureaucratic process. As Feller later informed writer William B. Mead, the admiral told him, "Oh, young man. Take your time and don't worry about getting out. Things don't move very fast in the Navy." It was an answer Feller couldn't accept. Every additional day was costing him wins and money. So he broke protocol and put in a direct call to the secretary of the Navy. By August 22, exactly a week after the Japanese announced their surrender, he was a civilian again.

The same day he was discharged, Feller and his now-pregnant wife boarded a midnight plane to Cleveland. The next afternoon, he hashed out a contract with the Indians; the following evening, he was slated to start. There was little reason to rush back. In his absence, the Indians had muddled through a series of pedestrian seasons, and 1945 was no different. But Feller was determined to make up for lost time regardless of the Indians' dim pennant hopes.

According to *The Sporting News*, the Cleveland press covered his arrival "almost as if it were another V-Day." A print ad placed by Higbee's, a large department store in Cleveland, put it best: "In welcoming Bob Feller home, we welcome all the fine, young returning Cleveland manhood that he so ably represents." The city's sportswriters—a mostly tough-minded, sharp-elbowed lot—dropped their defenses and took turns fawning over the ace. Feller, one reporter proclaimed, "had out-grown his role of hero to small boys and to the followers of the game of baseball. He is a hero to everybody, in the old, accepted sense of the term."

Still, they could tell that something had changed. It wasn't physical, per se, although his sunken cheeks had shed their prewar pudginess. What these journalists sensed was deeper, a sort of psychic layer he hadn't worn before. It was clear from looking at him that Feller "has been places—dangerous places—and has seen things. It shows in his face and in his eyes." His perceived innocence—for so long a key part of his appeal—was gone.

In the days leading up to his return, so many fans phoned the Indians' front office for tickets that the switchboard crashed. In a downtown hotel the Cleveland mayor convened a luncheon for Feller that filled to capacity while numerous others failed to gain entry. A while back, the Indians' ownership had suspended broadcasts of games for fear of fans choosing the radio over the ballpark, but as a goodwill gesture they allowed multiple stations in northern Ohio to carry Feller's first start live.

Before the game, the Indians staged a ceremony shaded with civic pride and patriotism. It featured a military marching band leading a procession of World War I veterans, the Cleveland mayor, and players from the Indians and the visiting Detroit Tigers. As the national anthem played, the American flag was slowly lowered into the hands of uniformed soldiers. Watching Feller stand at attention before the troops, a writer for *The Plain Dealer* meditated on "how splendid it was of a young man to volunteer his services to his country, forswearing a fabulous salary, to keep the Germans from pulling down our flag—to keep the Japs from raising the Rising Sun emblem over the White House."

When Feller finally took the mound, the crowd buzzed with anticipation, and perhaps a bit of dread that he wouldn't live up to his prewar standards. Feller broke the suspense early, blowing a first-pitch fastball by Jimmy Outlaw, the Tigers' leadoff hitter. Unsurprisingly for a pitcher with less-than-stellar control, he proceeded to fire a few offerings wide of the mark. Finally, with the count full and the tension at a breaking point, Feller fooled Outlaw with a curve that dipped just inside the strike zone.

Indians fans cheered themselves hoarse, seemingly with relief. The Axis powers had yielded; Bob Feller had struck out a major-league batter. The war was over.

Feller picked up the win that night, along with four others over the next month, but in some ways what he accomplished off the field mattered more. In September, he lobbied the new commissioner of Major League Baseball, Albert "Happy" Chandler—a former Kentucky governor and senator who'd taken over the post following Kenesaw Mountain Landis's death late in 1944—to expand the window for off-season barnstorming. Rather than the customary ten days, Feller requested thirty, a full month's worth of extracurricular baseball. As he argued, "We lost several years of competition, of making money, and unlike people in most business we never can make up those years because our business is based on youth. I certainly can use some extra money this fall to pay my bills. And I can make this extra money barnstorming." To woo the commissioner, Feller volunteered to organize and run an off-season Florida camp for servicemen who hoped to break into professional baseball.

As soon as the season ended, Feller set off to barnstorm along the West Coast, where he would face off against Satchel Paige for the first time in four years. Both were reminded anew of the public appetite for their duels. On October 2, 1945, more than 22,000 fans—reportedly the largest crowd ever to watch a baseball game in Los Angeles, with thousands more turned away at the gates—squeezed into that city's Wrigley Field to see Feller and his roster of major and minor leaguers match up against Paige and the Kansas City Royals, an all-Black squad led by Negro League veteran Chet

Brewer that played along the Pacific Coast in the off-season. Each pitcher threw five innings. Feller was dominant, but somehow Paige was better, striking out ten to Feller's six.

Playing shortstop that night for Paige's squad was a fellow teammate from the Kansas City Monarchs who'd garnered national acclaim before the war as a star halfback on UCLA's football team. Neither Paige nor Feller could've guessed then that twenty-six-year-old Jackie Robinson had already committed in secret to crossing over into the Brooklyn Dodgers organization the following season.

Weeks later, after the Dodgers announced that Robinson would integrate their Montreal farm club in 1946, reporters asked Feller, one of the few major-league pitchers to have faced him, to assess Robinson's chances of making the cut. He didn't sugarcoat his answer. Robinson, Feller asserted, was "a typical football player—they're all alike. They're tied up in the shoulders—can't hit an inside pitch to save their necks." He went on to praise Robinson's character, calling him "well-educated and a very high-type fellow." But he would need more, in Feller's estimation, to flourish in the major leagues. "Honestly," Feller concluded, "I can't see any chance at all for Robinson. And I'll say this—if he were a white man I doubt if they'd even consider him as big league material."

Whereas other major leaguers might have opted for a more diplomatic tone given the sensitive nature of the signing, Feller once again evinced little hesitation about expressing his opinions directly, a tendency that only increased once he'd returned from the war. "He let you know where he stood," Marguerite Goodson said of her brother. "And I said about him before, there were two sides of it: his side and the wrong side." In his own defense for these particular statements, Feller said, "All of the Negro ball players know me, and I'm sure they'll tell you I'm not prejudiced in the least. But if anybody asks, there's no sense in kidding. I'll tell them what I actually believe."

It was true that Feller's years on the October barnstorming

circuit had revealed an open-mindedness about sharing the field with Black players. Nevertheless, his snap judgment of Robinson's abilities, similar to his assessment of Paige's four years earlier, reinforced prejudicial beliefs that Black ballplayers lacked the capacity to overcome apparent flaws in their techniques, which placed them outside the realm of major-league worthiness. It hardly seemed to matter that Feller himself had come to the majors loaded with talent yet less than fully formed, with an undependable curve and a tendency to walk batters by the dozen. His subsequent storybook narrative of accomplishment and acclaim seemingly led him to look for individual faults and deficiencies in players who'd faced structural barriers and prejudices that precluded them from ever experiencing arcs similar to the one Feller had undergone.

Feller's persona had been ideally suited to a nation reeling from the worst financial crisis it'd ever faced. But, along with the country, baseball was now changing, and it was uncertain how Feller would adjust to the coming postwar era.

One evening late in October 1945, Larry Doby was lounging in a recreation center on Mogmog. A radio blared in the background. The war had ended, but Doby's service there had yet to conclude.

At some point, as Doby later told *Sport* magazine, a sailor sprinted up to him in a state of euphoria, hollering about the news he'd just heard.

"Are we going home?" Doby asked, seemingly unable to think of anything else that would prompt such excitement.

No, the sailor declared. "But when we do, maybe you can get into the big leagues. The Dodgers have just signed Jackie Robinson!"

A tingling sensation rippled through Doby's body. The announcement altered his postwar plans on the spot. "I forgot about going back to college," he later told his biographer. Baseball now would be his path forward.

PART II

BREAKTHROUGHS

8

The Crossroads

After the war, Satchel Paige was at a crossroads.

For years, as the military draft had claimed numerous Black ballplayers like Larry Doby, Paige had carried on as before on the home front, leading a Kansas City Monarchs squad loaded with stars like Hilton Smith, Willard Brown, and John "Buck" O'Neil to a Negro League World Series championship in 1942. As more and more Black families from the South streamed north to take advantage of booming wartime industries, the Negro Leagues prospered like never before. Swing-shift workers with cash to spare sought comfort and relief in their unfamiliar new settings at the ballpark, never more so than when one particular player swung through town.

With the support of Monarchs co-owner J. L. Wilkinson, Paige once again became a man on the run, tossing a handful of innings in as many games as possible, trying to be everywhere at once. This time, however, it was different. In the Depression, he'd busted contracts and crisscrossed across the continent. "Any club that offered me a little more dough, I was Johnny-on-the-spot," Paige said of those footloose years. But he'd begun to feel the effects of those years as he aged. "Bangin' around the way I was, playing for guarantees on one team after another that I never heard of, in towns I never seen before, with players I didn't know and never saw again, I got lonesome," Paige later said.

Now, in Kansas City, he laid down roots for the first time since leaving Mobile. He took up photography; collected antiques, shotguns, tailored suits, and Spanish guitars; and, in a drugstore where he went to purchase film, met the woman who would become his third wife, Lahoma. Paige still tore through back roads when semiprofessional clubs came calling, but there was never any doubt he'd return to the Monarchs. "Once a baseball gypsy," Wendell Smith of *The Pittsburgh Courier* wrote, "Satchel is now a 'home boy.'"

Inching toward forty, Paige reinvented himself on the mound. He was soon relying as much on cunning as on speed, mixing in curves and changeups with his heater. To bewilder eager opponents, he'd sometimes freeze for a split second mid-windup before completing his pitching motion. This hesitation pitch threw batters off-balance and amused fans to no end. Between starts, he fussed over his right arm and conserved his energy to an almost comical degree, rarely getting up even for a drink of water. In his athletic old age he'd become, as Paige described himself, like a bullfighter "who can tell what the bull is going to do by watching his knees. When the batter swings and I see his knees move, I know just what his weaknesses are. Then I just puts the ball where I knows he can't hit it."

An entire generation of fans—Black and, increasingly, white—had come of age hearing of his exploits, and all this time later Paige was still the biggest name in the circuit. Wendell Smith hailed him as "Mr. It" in sports, "the gem that comes along once in a hundred lifetimes." His earnings attested to that. The thirty to forty thousand dollars Paige raked in annually exceeded what many marginal major leaguers earned over their entire careers.

Then, all at once, the bottom dropped out. In 1946, for the first time that century, a handful of Black players suited up for minor-league organizations affiliated with the Brooklyn Dodgers. And Paige wasn't among them.

Amid the flurry of wartime activism that had tested the strength of the color line, Paige had seemed almost an afterthought. The reasons were varied. Part of it was his age, part his own professed concerns about integration, and part his long-standing reputation as a maverick. In 1942, when asked if he'd ever sign with a major-league club, Paige had asserted, "They'd have to offer me what I made last year—$37,000." Even then, he voiced grave reservations: "You might as well be honest about it . . . There would be plenty of problems, not only in the South where the colored boys wouldn't be able to stay and travel with the teams in spring training, but in the North where they couldn't stay or eat with them in many places.

"All the nice statements in the world from both sides aren't going to knock out Jim Crow," he concluded.

These were statements out of step with the activists and writers on the front lines of the fight for integration, but they meshed with his own experiences. Paige knew the toll that travel in a segregated society took on Black athletes. With his star power, he'd been able to take aim at segregationist laws and practices in his own way over the years, notably by making it known he'd compete only in places that could guarantee accommodations for himself and his squad. He'd come to believe that it'd be better and more practical for an all-Black team to push for entry into the majors first. In a 1945 letter to Wendell Smith, Paige wrote: "I see in *The Courier* where the major leagues are trying out some colored players. Please listen to me—the Negro will never break into the majors like that. You see, the owners and managers will always have a way to find fault with our very best players. The only way I see we can make it is to pick an All-Star club of our own to play their best club and let the whole world see it."

What's more, it couldn't have been lost on Paige that as he neared his fortieth birthday (some believed he was roughly a decade older than that), he seemed to many baseball insiders a likelier candidate for retirement than for breaking the color line. Smith wrote as early as 1941 that "the sun is setting on Paige's spectacular, incomparable career. Before many more moons they'll put him on the shelf which harbors the great antiquities of baseball." He also later admitted that he hadn't advocated for Paige for fear that major-league executives would laugh him off the premises.

The honor of being the first player from the Negro Leagues to sign with a major-league organization instead went to Jackie Robinson, who'd come to Kansas City in 1945, shortly after being discharged from the Army. Paige had mostly steered clear of the opinionated and strong-willed twenty-six-year-old in the lone season they'd played together on the Monarchs, treating him like any other rookie. Even so, when the announcement went public, Paige, in his role as the most recognizable figure from the Negro Leagues, put his best spin on the milestone. "They didn't make a mistake by signing Robinson," he said while barnstorming in late October 1945 against Bob Feller. "He's a No. 1 professional player. They couldn't have picked a better man." Wistfully, with what one reporter detected as a "touch of mist" in his voice, Paige declared: "Robinson's opportunity is one of the greatest breaks of all time for colored athletes."

In private, he lamented that it hadn't come for him. "I'd been the guy who'd started all that big talk about letting us in the big time," Paige wrote in his autobiography. To his fiancée, Lahoma, Paige was even more blunt. "They took that kid off our team and didn't even look at me." When she reasoned that it was probably because Robinson was young, Paige cut straight to the heart: "He's no Satchel Paige."

That Jackie Robinson was no Satchel Paige was likely a point in his favor as far as Brooklyn Dodgers president Branch Rickey was concerned. By and large, Rickey viewed the Negro Leagues as a racket run by gamblers and booking agents, rife with flimsy contracts, er-

ratic scheduling, and scattered leadership. Rickey hadn't even bothered to seek permission to sign Robinson from Monarchs co-owners
J. L. Wilkinson and Tom Baird, let alone offer them any compensation.

For a quarter-century, Rickey had kept the baseball establishment off-balance. At his core was a tangle of contradictions. He was a
radical and a conservative, a scamp and a saint, a profoundly religious
man who picked the pockets of his players. Sweeping into a room, he
would confound listeners with baroque sermons that swirled about
like smoke from his ubiquitous stogie. He had the verbal dexterity of
a seasoned orator and the owl-like visage of an absentminded profes-
sor, complete with mussed hair, round glasses, and bow ties affixed
to rumpled suits. The minor-league farm system Rickey pioneered as
president of the St. Louis Cardinals led to a string of pennants and
regular summonses to the commissioner's office to discuss its legality.
Though respectful of his front-office skills, sportswriters skewered
Rickey every chance they could, calling him "The Mahatma" and "El
Cheapo," and his office the "Cave of the Winds."

Rickey's push for integration was as complicated as his own
personality. Personal experience and Christian principles had per-
suaded him of the injustice of the color line. In interviews, Rickey
sometimes reminisced about a trip the college baseball team he once
coached had taken to South Bend, Indiana, where a hotel refused to
accommodate Charles Thomas, a Black catcher. After coaxing the
clerks to let Thomas sleep in his room, Rickey looked on as a tear-
ful Thomas, staring at his hands as he rubbed them together, murmured, "Black skin . . . black skin. If I could only make 'em white."

But Rickey was not motivated solely by altruistic concerns. The
potent Dodgers club he'd taken over late in 1942 carried scads of
players on the wrong side of thirty. That season they'd faded in October, squandering the pennant to the youthful St. Louis Cardinals.
Rickey, who'd assembled that same Cardinals' roster, doubtlessly
knew that if the Dodgers stood pat, the Cardinals would continue

to lap them. One evening, while playing bridge with Harold Parrott, the team's traveling secretary, Rickey made his purposes clear.
"Son," he told Parrott, "the greatest untapped reservoir of raw material in the history of the game is the black race! The Negro will make
us winners for years to come. And for that I will happily bear being
a bleeding heart, and a do-gooder, and all that humanitarian rot."

Bill Veeck's plan for desegregating the Philadelphia Phillies'
roster had been to stockpile top Negro League players and toss
them straightaway into the major-league fire. Rickey, by contrast,
tiptoed toward the color line, fussily analyzing the ramifications of
each step forward. "Branch Rickey was innovative," historian Jules
Tygiel wrote, "but he was not impulsive." Rickey consulted academ-
ics, sportswriters, civic leaders, and scouts. He studied volumes on
race relations, compiled binders of information on promising Negro
Leaguers, even helped form another Black league, the United States
League, to scout players and pocket gate receipts in the meantime.
Whichever players he selected would move deliberately through the
Dodgers system, giving all parties time to adjust and iron out their
differences. In Jackie Robinson, he identified a model candidate:
young but not callow, sensitive but hard-edged, college-educated
and a veteran of interracial competition, someone who was self-
assured enough presumably to weather whatever abuse fans and the
media hurled his way.

Paige never had a chance. There were three separate strikes
against him: his advanced age, his price tag, and his maverick tendencies. In his history, in his style, in his very being, Paige seemed
to represent the Negro Leagues in full: the pride, flash, defiance,
and creativity. All of which would get him nowhere with Rickey.

Since no other team in the majors seemed inclined to follow
Rickey's lead, Paige opened the 1946 season as he would any other:
by carrying on, one outing at a time, moving ever forward across the
country's lonesome back roads.

9

Effa Manley's Dilemma

In January 1946, Larry Doby returned home from the South Pacific. Immediately in demand, he soon was leaping for rebounds and diving for loose balls as a member of the Orange Triangles, a Black semiprofessional basketball club in northern New Jersey. It was an encouraging sign for Effa Manley, the co-owner of the Newark Eagles, who was no doubt eager to know whether twenty-eight months in the armed services had compromised the skills of her promising young second baseman. "He is some basketball player," Manley wrote to Eagles shortstop Monte Irvin, marveling anew at Doby's athleticism.

The Newark Eagles had toiled through the war years with rosters drained of stars, but now that players like Irvin and Doby had been discharged from the service, the team seemed poised to make a run at the franchise's first-ever Negro National League pennant—so long as Effa Manley and her husband, Abe, could hold the roster together. Their efforts to re-sign Irvin and Doby would show just how difficult that would be.

Irvin, like Doby, had been a four-letter athletic phenom at an integrated high school in northern New Jersey who'd transitioned to the Eagles shortly after graduation. Many believed that Irvin's all-around game and even-tempered manner rendered him a prime candidate to bust baseball's color line. Unbeknownst to the Manleys, a scout had approached Irvin earlier that off-season to gauge his interest in following Jackie Robinson into the Brooklyn Dodgers organization in 1946. The timing, however, was all wrong. While in the Army, Irvin had developed an inner-ear imbalance, which threw off his rhythm at the plate. He would need time to regain his form before considering such an offer.

In February, Doby, freshly committed to baseball in the wake of Robinson's signing, ditched the basketball court to team up with Irvin in the Puerto Rican Winter League. There, Irvin was approached about playing baseball that upcoming season in the Mexican League. For years, officials from the Mexican League had lured Black players, including Irvin, south of the border with promises of fatter paychecks than the Negro Leagues could offer. After word trickled back to Effa Manley, she made a shrewd calculation.

In a letter to Irvin dated February 9, 1946, she used integration as a means of drawing him back to the Eagles. "I believe more Major League teams will take Negro's [sic]," she wrote, adding: "This is one of the important reasons why you should play in America this year, so you can be seen for one thing. If the experiment with Negro's in the Majors is successful, all the teams will be ready to take you, and almost all of them pay better salaries than Brooklyn." Underscoring her aversion to the predatory means through which the Dodgers had poached Jackie Robinson from the Kansas City Monarchs, Manley added: "There are several teams I would wrather [sic] see have you than Brooklyn."

With Doby, who was five years Irvin's junior and not yet as established, Manley favored a different negotiating tactic. When Doby refused to sign his contract for the upcoming season, presumably choosing to hold out for better terms, Manley reacted not with flattery but with fury. "To date," she wrote to Doby in March, "I have not had the courtesy of a reply from you. Having met your mother

I know you were not raised this badly. There is only one conclusion to reach, that is you are being very poorly advised by someone both stupid and ignorant of baseball conditions."

It was a characteristically forceful response from Effa Manley, who, as a woman in a sport run by men, had always held her own by confronting her challenges head-on, brashly and unapologetically. Knowing not to cross Manley further, Doby agreed to the contract before the Eagles bus departed for spring training.

When it came to Effa Manley, looks were deceiving. In photos she appeared in her patterned dresses and fashionable hats a paragon of style and refinement—a poised, striking woman with olive skin, hazel eyes, and bobbed hair. But beneath this polished surface was a fearless, strong-willed, acid-tongued crusader for civil rights and Black baseball, someone who, as one writer declared, "runs a man's business better than most of the men who are engaged in it and commands respect everywhere in the sphere of big league baseball."

There was another way her appearance wasn't all it seemed. Throughout her life, questions about her background persisted. Her mother, Bertha Brooks, was a white seamstress whose two marriages had both been to Black men. Effa, however, later claimed that she'd been born of an illicit affair her mother had carried on with a white stockbroker. Raised in Philadelphia in an interracial household, Effa learned to negotiate her way through Black and white spaces. After moving to New York City as a young adult, she made her home in Harlem, but her fair skin enabled her to find employment in jobs available only to white applicants in lower Manhattan. As author Shakeia Taylor wrote: "[Effa] would take the subway downtown as a white woman, and return to Harlem as a Black one."

She met Abraham Manley at some point around 1932. He was more than a decade older than her, a stout, sharply dressed Black man of leisure and reserve who had banked a small fortune in Camden, New Jersey, running the numbers racket, a form of illegal gambling prevalent in Black communities. They married and years later, before the 1935 season, purchased a Negro League franchise in Brooklyn. Following a sparsely attended summer at Ebbets Field, the Manleys merged their club with one in Newark and left Brooklyn behind for good. The Newark Eagles debuted in 1936 at Ruppert Stadium, a ballpark tucked into an immigrant-heavy industrial district called The Ironbound.

A committed activist already celebrated for organizing boycotts against discriminatory businesses around New York City, Effa Manley recognized the pride that Newark's swelling Black population took in the Eagles. Many had migrated in waves from the South. With housing scarce and largely segregated, most residents crammed into tenement buildings in a blighted sector of the Third Ward, which bordered downtown Newark. Theaters shuttled Black customers to the balcony; department stores barred them from dressing rooms.

Despite the restrictions, a thriving Black cultural scene took hold in Newark, with Eagles games at the heart of it. On certain summer Sundays, Black worshippers would attend morning services and then strike out for Ruppert Stadium still dressed in their church clothes, spending the afternoon basking both in the sun and the togetherness while rooting for homegrown idols who looked like and lived among them. Newark native LeRoi Jones, who later became the poet Amiri Baraka, thought of the Eagles as "something *we* possessed. It was not us as George Washington Carver or Marian Anderson, some figment of white people's lack of imagination, it was us as we wanted to be and how we wanted to be seen being looked at by ourselves in some kind of loud communion."

To foster that communal pride, Effa Manley held her players to exacting standards. If she spotted something she disapproved of—muddied socks, frayed clothes, lackadaisical fielding—she summoned the offending party to her redbrick residence on Crawford Street and tore into him. As Eagles outfielder Johnny Davis told historian John Holway, Effa would remind them: "You are my ball players, and you're going to look like my ball players."

While Abe Manley reveled in the perks of owning a club—the travel, the camaraderie, the late-night bull sessions—he entrusted his wife with the more mundane tasks of budgets, promotions, schedules, and daily operations. "My husband manages and travels around with the team," Effa once stated. "That is his hobby, but when it comes to real business, that is, baseball business, I have, I think, the final say-so." Just like in the major leagues, the executive ranks of the Negro Leagues largely were an insular gentleman's club that regarded women as intruding presences. When Effa started to attend league meetings alongside her husband, who served as treasurer of the Negro National League, several officials balked. Gus Greenlee, owner of the Pittsburgh Crawfords, was said to have griped that "the proper place for women is by the fireside, not functioning in positions to which their husbands have been elected."

But Manley stood her ground. Speaking fast and forcefully, she stumped for improvements in contracts, scheduling, and leadership that might steer the Negro Leagues on a steadier course. When pressed, it was said, she could spew profanity "in seven languages."

As she grew into her role, Manley became bolder about injecting civil rights advocacy into game-day festivities. In between innings, she often raised awareness and funds for organizations like the NAACP, for which she served as treasurer of the Newark chapter at one point. Appalled at reports of violence from the South, Manley staged anti-lynching campaigns at Ruppert Stadium. As the war raged on, she invited Black military regiments to the ballpark as distinguished guests.

Integration presented new challenges for the Manleys. Throughout the winter of 1946, rumors had been flying about which Black players Branch Rickey was targeting. By early April, Effa Manley's phone was ringing off the hook. She wrote to Abe, who'd already left for spring training in Jacksonville, Florida, that she must have fielded a million calls in his absence. Reporters were all sniffing for the same scoop: Had the Dodgers organization signed Don Newcombe, a nineteen-year-old pitcher for the Eagles? Effa Manley put them off as best she could, but would soon have to confirm that Rickey had indeed raided their club.

Stewing with anger one month before the season opener, Manley took stock of her options. Dragging the Dodgers to court for seizing Newcombe was certain to backfire. Even if she succeeded in retaining Newcombe, she knew that Black fans and sportswriters, eager to see Negro League players make good in white baseball, would've accused her of "racial treachery of the rankest sort."

But neither could she simply bite her tongue. "I think we look positively stupid sitting still and letting Rickey get away with this grand larceny," she fumed in a letter to Ed Gottlieb, the booking agent for the Philadelphia Stars of the Negro National League. In addition to Newcombe and Jackie Robinson, Rickey poached Roy Campanella from the Baltimore Elite Giants and John Wright from the Homestead Grays without compensating the owners. There was no telling how many more players the Dodgers president had in his sights.

As Manley wrote to her husband: "We have so many boys [on the Eagles] who are Major League material we may wake up any morning and not have a ballclub, if this keeps on." And if that were to happen because of the unilateral precedent set forth by Rickey in terms of signing players from the Negro Leagues, then it would mean the loss not only of a business the Manleys had invested heavily in but of a community touchstone they'd worked hard to foster and enrich.

Quitting, however, was not an option. Effa Manley would fight, as she always had, not merely because of her dedication to her team, but because of the larger significance that the Eagles carried. "In continuing in the baseball," she wrote before the start of the 1946 season to Raleigh "Biz" Mackey, the Eagles player-manager, "I feel I am doing something for the whole race."

10

The Deal Is Closed

Early in 1946, Bill Veeck was laid up on his 11,000-acre ranch on the lower slopes of the Rincon Mountains, twenty-five miles southeast of Tucson. He'd come to Arizona after selling his stake in the Milwaukee Brewers to save his legs and his marriage. Neither result seemed likely.

On Valentine's Day, Veeck went under the knife once more. This time, a piece of bone was sliced from his hip and grafted onto his shattered right foot. Amputation was an idea Veeck still refused to consider. From childhood onward, he'd labored in an occupation that measured men by their physical prowess. When their legs gave out, they were done. "I felt there was something shameful about [becoming physically disabled]," Veeck wrote in his autobiography, "as if the loss of a leg would make me less of a man." Instead, having been rendered effectively immobile from surgeries and lingering infections, he lounged around and watched the desert bloom, day by excruciating day.

As March turned to April, a quartet of major-league clubs swung through Tucson for some spring-training exhibition games. Afterward, Veeck invited a handful of team officials and journalists to his ranch. Energized by an evening of sports banter, Veeck realized there was no use fooling himself any longer: Baseball was where he belonged. A few weeks later, before the start of the 1946 season, he tossed some outfits into a battered suitcase and hopped a plane to the Midwest.

He enlisted help in his pursuit. For months Veeck had swapped phone calls with Harry Grabiner, another baseball lifer who'd retired as vice president of the Chicago White Sox in 1945. At first, they gabbed weekly about the pleasures of pastoral life, as if trying to talk themselves into it. But neither was convinced. As soon as Veeck resolved to jump back into baseball, he rang Grabiner and asked if he would join him. A reliable backstage operator with decades of experience keeping a cash-strapped club in the black was exactly the sort of right-hand man Veeck would need.

In mid-April, Veeck and Grabiner huddled over lunch at Chicago's Blackstone Hotel to consider their options. Veeck would have loved nothing more than to purchase the White Sox and reestablish his roots in the Windy City, but the club wasn't on the market. It seemed, however, that two other franchises could be snagged for the right price: the Pittsburgh Pirates and the Cleveland Indians. Before making his decision, Veeck set out to gauge the mood of each city himself.

Pittsburgh was a bust. Something in Veeck's gut warned him that the setup wasn't right. The price tag was steep, the roster punchless, the regional economy at the mercy of the steel industry. If Veeck were to make a splash in the majors, this wasn't the club for him.

Along the banks of Lake Erie in northeastern Ohio, Veeck caught a different vibe. In 1946, Cleveland was a smoky, bustling city firing on all cylinders. The war had brought its sputtering industry roaring back to life. If Veeck had peered out from one of the bridges that traversed the Cuyahoga River, he'd have seen, as *The New York Times Magazine* documented, a boundless industrial landscape of "ore mountains, towering smokestacks, blast furnaces and giant cranes, busy making steel." There were also oil refineries above whose roofs rose "vent pipes with orange flames playing around their tops day and night: torches lighting a scene." That year, more than 550,000 Cleveland workers toiled in industries that churned out such goods as iron, transportation equipment, and electrical machinery. Production boomed, the labor force held steady in the peacetime transition, and the city's proximity to waterways, raw materials, and other major metropolitan centers led some to dub it the "best location in the nation."

Despite it all, the mood on the street was anxious. Clevelanders had spent nearly two decades in a defensive crouch. First there'd been the Depression, during which the city had bled population after a half-century of runaway growth. Then came the war and its attendant traumas, followed by servicemen streaming back to find housing shortages and a scarcity of mass produced consumer goods. Workers had deferred their desires for so long by then that they hardly knew what to do with the money and time that some now had to burn.

Cleveland, it was clear, was in need of a release, some sort of spark to ignite the emotions the city had bottled up for a generation. The Indians seemed unlikely to provide it. For days Veeck sidled into the front seat of taxis and popped into taverns to shoot the breeze about the hometown baseball club. A damning picture emerged. The team's current ownership group, conservative to its core, exerted minimal effort to draw fans to the ballpark, and even less to entertain them once they'd shown up. Often, their promotional strategy seemed to consist of rejiggering the rotation to ensure Bob Feller took the mound on weekends and holidays. Apathy had settled in. To Veeck's astonishment, some cabdrivers didn't even know if the Indians were playing at home on any given afternoon.

Far from being discouraged, Veeck couldn't believe his good

fortune. "It occurred to me," he later wrote, "that if the [Indians] could show a profit while playing its games in secrecy, it might be a gold mine if we demolished the iron curtain and gave the citizens to understand that we would welcome them at the ball park." The conditions were ripe for an all-out Veeckian blitz of salesmanship and bravado. Cleveland had everything he was looking for: diversified industry, passionate if disillusioned fans, and a solid roster foundation on which to build. And then there was the Indians' enormous lakefront stadium, an ovular colisseum of concrete and steel that was bigger than any ballpark in the major leagues. No executive would've been foolish enough to believe its 78,000 seats could be filled on a regular basis, but Veeck was raring to try.

As Veeck descended on the city, Alva Bradley, the president of the Indians, was conducting business as usual from the Marion Building in downtown Cleveland. Trim and handsome with a sweep of silver hair, the sixty-two-year-old Bradley wore his blue-blooded gentility like a well-tailored suit. Born into a shipping and real estate dynasty and groomed since birth for the executive ranks, Bradley projected an air of gentlemanly reserve at all times. From early in his business career he established himself as a fixture of Cleveland high society, leading the local chamber of commerce and serving on the boards of various foundations and charities. In 1927, Bradley teamed up with a syndicate of his peers—local titans of industry and commerce whom columnist Franklin Lewis dubbed "The Millionaires"—to acquire one of the few assets in Cleveland they didn't currently own: the Indians. Despite not being a majority stakeholder, Bradley was chosen as president.

The late 1920s were a heady, optimistic time in Cleveland. The cranes and scaffolding that dotted the rapidly changing urban landscape attested to the city's economic might. In 1928, the year after Bradley's syndicate bought the Indians, voters approved financing for a stadium that would be constructed on a landfill bordering Lake

Erie. Upon completion, it would be able to seat roughly 78,000 people, more than any other outdoor arena in the world, and it would be nearly four times as large as League Park, the cozy ballpark that the Indians had called home since their founding at the turn of the twentieth century.

But by the time the Indians moved from the smallest ballpark in the majors to the biggest, midway through the 1932 season, conditions had changed. The collapse of the stock market three years earlier had ushered in the Great Depression. Walloped by job losses and economic stagnation, many workers no longer could cover the cost of a bleacher seat. In 1933, Indians games drew an average of 5,000 fans in an arena built for fifteen times that number. No one was satisfied. Fans missed the intimacy of the previous park; owners lost money; players groused about the acres of outfield turf. By season's end, Bradley dragged the team back to League Park. Years later, the Indians would settle on an arrangement of playing in Municipal Stadium for certain night and weekend games and in League Park the rest of the time. A stadium intended to showcase municipal strength now stood vacant on the lakefront most days, a cavernous symbol of overreach.

It was during Bradley's tenure especially that fatalism became entwined with Indians fandom. Since the formation of the eight-team American League in 1901, the Indians, through a series of name and ownership changes, had followed a familiar pattern: charging from the gates in April before staggering in the summer homestretch. "Always in Cleveland," columnist Shirley Povich asserted, "the standing of the clubs in the American League can serve as a calendar. If the Indians have a long winning streak, it's spring surer'n heck. Somehow, spring never seems to last in Cleveland. The Indians begin to lose ball games, the wolves start singing in the stands, and the manager wants to leap in the lake."

The first and only time the Indians had advanced to the postseason was in 1920, when a roster led by player-manager Tris Speaker defeated the Brooklyn Robins to clinch the World Series title. For the next quarter-century, the club invariably settled somewhere in the middle, never first, never last. The emergence of Bob Feller in 1936 seemed to presage another championship, and it'd nearly happened four years later, when Feller racked up twenty-seven wins and the Indians fended off their rivals for much of the summer. But a mutiny against manager Ossie Vitt, whose caustic coaching style had tried players' patience, coupled with a September swoon left the team a game behind the pennant-winning Detroit Tigers when the 1940 season ended. A year afterward, the team lost Feller for nearly four seasons to the service.

Through it all, Bradley hungered for a pennant that never materialized. As the postwar era dawned, there was discontent among the team's stockholders. Two majority holders in particular, brothers John and Francis Sherwin, were itching to unload their shares. Quietly, they'd put out feelers behind Bradley's back. Early in the season, Bill Veeck answered their call.

Bradley had little warning of what was about to hit him.

From the start, the negotiations were cloaked in secrecy. Veeck clammed up around reporters sniffing for details. When one asked him in late May if he'd put forth a seven-figure offer to buy the Indians, Veeck threw up his hands. "Where would I get that kind of money?" he protested. "The day before yesterday I was supposed to be buying the Pittsburgh Pirates. Tomorrow, they may have me buying the Phillies. I better get back to Tucson, Arizona, right quick and end all this speculation." Behind the scenes, Veeck hustled up a backing syndicate and made significant headway with the Sherwin brothers' attorney, hammering out an option to purchase the Indians within thirty days. His future with the Indians seemed to hinge on keeping the current team president in the dark as long as possible, since there was always the possibility that someone as well-connected and deep-pocketed as Alva Bradley might put together his own competing offer.

In mid-June, Veeck braced himself for the final stretch. To stave off attention, he shacked up downtown at the Hotel Cleveland under a pseudonym. The whirlwind schedule he'd endured for the past two months had left him drained and disheveled. His infected right foot was wrapped in a cast and stabilized by steel braces, his bare toes poking out of the end. The open wounds reeked so strongly that he had to pour capsules of cologne down his cast just to mask the stench. When he hobbled into banks to secure funds, some clerks found it hard to believe the man before them—sporting neither a hat nor a tie; smelling of pus and smoke and perfume—was a serious customer.

Despite his pain and secrecy, Veeck continued to prowl the streets every chance he could, limping into taverns to talk baseball, showing up at a golf tournament, even slipping undetected into an Indians game to scout the club. At one point he stopped by the law offices of J. J. Klein, a prominent Cleveland attorney, for some legal advice. Upon learning that Veeck was angling to buy the Indians, Klein indicated that a client of his might be interested in joining the syndicate, then rang up Bob Hope out in Hollywood. Hope, who'd grown up in Cleveland, leapt at the chance to own a stake in his hometown club, giving Veeck a coveted local investor, and star power to boot.

The backroom dealings were effective. Once Bradley finally caught on, it was already too late. On June 22, 1946, the team shareholders met one last time and approved the sale of the club for slightly less than $1.6 million. Immediately afterward, Veeck and Harry Grabiner were summoned.

Veeck, one reporter claimed, "made a strange appearance in the sedate office," hobbling in with his head bare, his white shirt unbuttoned at the collar, and a thick sock covering the foot of his cast. Exhaustion and the worsening infection on his right leg had drained the color from his face.

Bradley and Veeck eyed each other from across a generational and philosophical divide. Bradley was the consummate establish-mentarian, Veeck the eccentric maverick. Bradley, *The Sporting News* contended, believed "baseball is baseball" and that was enough for owners to sell; Veeck was burning to upend that mind-set. Baseball, he declared that afternoon, "has got to be fun. That's the only way to have it. There must be something gala or festive about it. Every-body has to have a good time. There can't be any standoffish dignity. There's no dignity in my makeup. I'm Bill. There is no 'Mr.' If there's a job to be done, I'll do it."

Setting aside their differences, the two men signed papers and posed for photos, then Veeck emerged from the offices and said simply: "Gentlemen, the deal is closed." A "visibly shaken" Bradley trailed him.

There was no time to reflect on what had just happened. The afternoon game between the Indians and the Boston Red Sox was about to start. Bradley arrived at League Park in the second inning, making his way to the owners' box. His entrance elicited hardly a murmur from the sparse crowd.

Veeck and Grabiner hitched a ride from Ed McAuley, a cigar-chomping sportswriter for the *Cleveland News*. Awaiting them at the gate was Robert Goldstein, one of the new stockholders, and Frank Kohlbecker, the team's business manager. "I suppose you gen-tlemen want to go up to the office," Kohlbecker said, expecting to lead his bosses on a tour of the facilities. Veeck, however, couldn't bear to miss an inning of action. So McAuley guided them toward the entrance to the owners' box near the Indians' dugout. But the mere thought of walling himself off in the owners' box appalled Veeck. "Box?" he reportedly exclaimed when reporters asked which box he'd occupy. "Hell, I never sat in a box in my life. I'm no rich boy." Instead, he scrambled for the nearest stairwell and burst forth into the open air.

It was the third inning. The Indians were up a run. Veeck limped through the aisles along the first-base side of the grandstand.

Goldstein and Grabiner followed, along with a troupe of photographers snapping rolls of pictures. Little by little, the crowd shifted its gaze toward the new owner, whose name and likeness had been a mainstay in the press. Indians players clambered to the top step of the dugout, craning their necks to catch a glimpse. Between pitches, even the umpires stole quick glances. When it became apparent that Veeck was seeking to watch the game among the masses, waves of applause rippled through the ballpark. Roaming from one end of the grandstand to the other, Veeck plopped down in empty seats and chatted up fans. By the time the game ended with a narrow Indians victory, crowd sentiment was unreservedly on his side.

The next day, an astonishing total of 52,720 fans turned out for a Sunday doubleheader at Municipal Stadium. Armed with a notepad and pencil, hobbling from row to row, Veeck tried to reach them all. Starting in the upper reaches behind home plate, he wound down to the lower tier and then shoved off toward the bleachers, where he stayed through the second game. He shook hands, fished around for ideas, and scribbled page after page of suggestions. After walking about for hours, Veeck was forced to call in a doctor around midnight to treat his ailing leg.

For months Veeck had run himself ragged. Soon, he'd have to reckon with his right leg. But not yet. Another race had begun. There was no time to slow down.

11

Exploding the Fireworks

One of the first things to go was the door to Bill Veeck's office—a signal that nothing would happen behind closed doors during his tenure as owner of the Indians. Veeck also lifted the previous administration's radio embargo of Indians games and installed a battery of phones at League Park. When customers rang, he'd sometimes pick up himself. When they wrote, he'd respond. To newspaper editors across Ohio, Veeck penned personal letters. "We know how many of those fans from nearby cities used to come to games here," he said. "We want them all back." Columnist Franklin Lewis opined that "Veeck's immediate and close contacts with the common man . . . is a studied pose, albeit a refreshing one." But it was no act. He was courting fans and selling the Indians the only way he knew how: personally, vigorously, and with radical transparency.

The fruits of his labor were apparent on July 23, 1946. Hours before game time, thousands of fans already had begun streaming toward the Cleveland lakefront. There was nothing remarkable about that night's contest. It was a Tuesday, and the Indians were back home after an unexceptional 6-5 road trip. Bob Feller wasn't scheduled to start, and the Indians' opponent, the Philadelphia

Athletics, had burrowed deep into the American League cellar. The mood, however, was expectant. In the previous day's papers, Veeck had teased a revival of the pregame sideshows that had catapulted him to acclaim in Milwaukee. "I shouldn't want anybody to get the wrong idea," he told the *Cleveland News*. "We're not trying to substitute vaudeville for victory. No one can do that. We just thought that the fans who come to the game might enjoy themselves more if we put on a little show."

Emerging through Municipal Stadium's shadowy passageways, fans would have spotted, on the track in center field, a canvas tepee crowned with a kitschy feather headdress. Seated inside was a fifteen-piece band whose members ripped through peppy swing numbers during batting practice. To top off the festivities, Veeck had custom-ordered fireworks from a company that had guaranteed a "nice half-hour show." That wasn't what he had in mind. "I want the whole works," Veeck told them, "but I don't want a half-hour show. I want you to shoot off the whole business in 10 minutes."

At 8:20 P.M., as the stadium lights dimmed, "a scattering of aerial bombs exploded with a staccato roar, and the darkness was pierced by a frantic sky show that had everything in it but the kitchen sink," the *Plain Dealer* reported. Over the next ten minutes colorful bursts of fire erupted at lightning speed, climaxing with a mock battle between "three brilliantly lighted airplanes, whose fiery propellers whirled as they shot streams of tracers into each other." The barrage of noise and light was so intense that veterans groups later would caution Veeck about triggering battlefield flashbacks in men freshly discharged from the armed services.

In many ways, the spectacle epitomized Veeck's approach to the 1946 season. The mediocre Indians team he'd inherited had as realistic a shot of snatching the pennant as his crushed right foot did of healing. Instead, to rouse the city's fan base from its stupor and to signal that the old ways of doing business no longer applied, Veeck aimed to squeeze in all the stunts and promotions he could think up. He would tear down the walls between fans and the front office. He would bring fun back to the ballpark. He would explode the fireworks all at once.

Bob Feller, too, returned to baseball in a rush. Throughout the winter and into the spring of 1946, his wife, Virginia, found him restless and bursting at the seams with nervous energy. "To me," she later wrote, "it appeared as though he continuously was trying to make up for lost time." His stint overseas ingrained in Feller a sense of how short athletic careers could be. He came back racing against the clock, not just as a pitcher gunning for whatever records were still within reach, but as a businessman whose window for raking in swollen paychecks would close as soon as his right arm wore out.

Feller entered the season in perhaps the best shape of his life, thanks in part to the training camp he ran in January for return-ing veterans hoping to break into professional baseball. In only his fourth start, on April 30 in Yankee Stadium, he tossed a no-hitter that cut short any lingering questions about whether, as the Asso-ciated Press put it, "blazing Bobby Feller, with that whip-lash for a right arm, had not left some of his vaunted speed on the high seas." On May 17, he whiffed fourteen Washington Senators, bumping his strikeout total to eighty-five, an average of 10.5 per game, higher than in any of his prewar seasons. No pitcher since Walter Johnson in 1912 had tallied more than three hundred strikeouts in a season. If his brisk pace held, not only was that number within his reach, but there were murmurs that Feller might even have a shot at the single-season mark: 343 by Philadelphia Athletics ace Rube Wad-dell in 1904.*

Still a headstrong perfectionist and a stickler for conditioning, Feller continued to subject himself daily to rigorous workouts that

---

* Baseball historians, after a careful inspection of box scores from the 1904 sea-son, would later revise Waddell's strikeout total to 349.

he mapped out with the precision of a military operation. On game days, he began warming up exactly seventeen minutes before taking the mound if the weather was cold, thirteen minutes if it was warm. Between starts he was right back on the field: falling to his knees for push-ups, sprinting along the outfield track, squatting and stretching and kicking his legs high. Even in his hotel room Feller was forever squeezing handgrips and doing biceps curls with the dumbbells he stashed in his luggage.

Off the diamond he was just as busy pitching his business ventures. Money was of utmost concern to him that season, as it was for many servicemen who'd sacrificed years of their prime and then reentered the majors in competition with a rising crop of younger players. Even though Major League Baseball expanded team rosters early in 1946 to give veterans extra job security, there was still no minimum salary requirement and no pension plan. Careers were fleeting enough as it was, and if players washed out of the majors, many had little to fall back on. The need for greater leverage to maximize player earnings took on newfound urgency, but owners, accustomed to dictating salaries with unimpeded authority, were reluctant to cede an inch.

The time was ripe for disruption. While workers walked off the job by the millions across the country, union organizers began nosing around baseball clubhouses, as did figures like Jorge Pasquel, the loaded president of the Mexican League, who dangled fat contracts in front of desperate players. Fed up with their flat wages, several major leaguers did the unthinkable, jumping across the border to Mexico.

Hoping to make a bigger splash, Pasquel wired a three-year offer reportedly worth $300,000 to Feller one Saturday afternoon during spring training. Feller responded the next Monday: "Sorry I cannot accept your generous offer due to present obligations." When asked why he'd taken a day to think it over, Feller quipped, "Because I don't do business on Sunday." The steep bump in pay hadn't tempted him. "What good would [Pasquel's] money be to me?" Feller mused. "I am making as much as any player can right now." His contract with the Indians, which clocked in at around $50,000, was indeed richer than any that had ever been given to a major-league pitcher. Besides, Feller wasn't seeking a simple boost in salary; he was seeking to become a mogul himself, not in a front office, but in the peddling of his own name, story, and abilities.

Every moment Feller could spare that season was dedicated to drumming up outside interests: a radio show, a syndicated newspaper column, a memoir, even franchise ownership in the minor leagues (which ultimately fell through). But none of those ventures consumed him like the barnstorming extravaganza he'd pondered since his service in the South Pacific. The previous year he'd pulled in more than $20,000 for his hastily arranged jaunt to the West Coast. This time, Feller began planning a country-spanning, airborne spectacular that would be more sweeping and professional than any domestic tour ever attempted. Rather than partnering with agents and promoters to handle the finances and logistics—plotting the transcontinental route, recruiting the players, chartering the airplanes, leasing the stadiums, booking the hotels—Feller made the unusual decision to serve as the tour's sole creative and executive force. His go-it-alone stance was inseparable from what he perceived as its central purpose: making money. Barnstorming was the sport's most lucrative off-season activity, and by fashioning himself, in one writer's words, as the Orson Welles of roving October baseball, Feller aimed to corner the market for his own personal benefit.

He sunk a sizable share of his nest egg into the tour, upward of $50,000. The investment left him exposed, operating without a net. Setbacks of any sort—meager crowds, bad weather, plane malfunctions—could devastate him. Virginia Feller feared they might wind up bankrupt by year's end. "I had a lot of faith in him," she recalled, "but I thought this time he was getting in too deep."

Undaunted, Feller bet big on himself. He already knew how to sell the tour. In interviews he laid out his vision of pitting the country's best white players against a lineup of top Black stars. In essence, Feller would double down on what he called "racial rivalry" at the exact moment that the color line was falling. But that alone wouldn't be enough. For this risky endeavor to pay off, and for the tour to live up to its billing, he would need to rekindle a racial rivalry of his own against the only pitcher whose drawing power with Black fans was equal to Feller's own with white fans.

Bob Feller needed Satchel Paige.

Feller wasn't the only one with Paige on his mind. Shortly after buying the Indians, Bill Veeck rang Abe Saperstein. His question to the Negro Leagues' promoter was straightforward: Does Satchel Paige still have it?

Even though Saperstein no doubt answered affirmatively, Veeck hesitated to bring Paige—or any other Black player, for that matter—to Cleveland in 1946. The reason had more to do with timing than his own principles. He sensed that such a signing would have struck many as just another gimmick during a season when promotions ostensibly took precedence over wins. Unlike when Veeck had attempted to purchase the Philadelphia Phillies and pack its war-depleted roster with Negro League stars, rapid-fire integration wouldn't have been enough to propel the Indians into contention, not when the team trailed the Boston Red Sox by nearly twenty games in the American League standings.

Instead of plunging into uncharted territory, Veeck kept doing what had worked before: running like there was no tomorrow. "The only way I know how to run a ball club is the hard way," he later wrote. "Among other things, the hard way requires that you sign your life over to the customers." Ten days into his tenure, the *Cleveland News* documented Veeck's around-the-clock schedule: showing up with the dawn at the team offices, fielding one phone call after another while shopping for new players, dashing out to give speeches, scurrying back for the game, holding court in the pressroom, tying up loose ends until only the ballpark's night watchman remained, then chatting up fans at nearby taverns past midnight.

The ceaseless activity took a toll on his injured leg. "Only a few of Veeck's close friends knew," wrote columnist Franklin Lewis, "that many evenings he slipped into his hotel room, threw off the shoe with the built-in brace and clinched his fists and rolled on the bed in agony." The next morning, he'd be right back at it. One afternoon in July, Veeck plopped down among a pool of reporters in the Indians' pressroom. Hitching his pants, he removed the brace and sock from his right leg and stared down at his foot. It was purple and swollen. "I'm going to lose this thing," he told them, "sure as I'm sitting here."

But there was little time to dwell on his leg during a season when fans were flocking to ballparks in record numbers. As Detroit Tigers third baseman George Kell later told writer Danny Peary, it was as if the entire country were saying, "We've all been through this terrible war and now here's baseball, the one great constant in our lives." Thanks to Veeck, that trend was especially pronounced in Cleveland. Every Indians home game promised something novel and diverting. Music blared, fireworks lit up the sky, and Jackie Price, a baseball stuntman and bit player, entertained incoming crowds with outlandish tricks: standing on his head while playing catch; unfastening his belt and catching fly balls in his pants; tooling around the outfield in a jeep while shagging fungoes; hanging upside down by his heels in a makeshift trapeze while swatting fastballs around the field. As he'd done in Milwaukee, Veeck marketed to women and families by reviving Ladies' Days, sprucing up the ballparks, and handing out orchids and nylons, which had been in short supply during the war due to military restrictions.

Once, Veeck set up a 100-yard dash across the field between George Case, the fastest member of the Indians' roster, and Jesse Owens, a longtime Cleveland resident. The four-time Olympic gold medalist, clad in a major-league uniform, won the race with ease. Another time, Veeck arranged for a parade of fire trucks to circle the stadium. When asked what fire trucks had to do with baseball, Veeck told reporters simply that people like fire trucks.

During the games themselves, the Indians sometimes stationed Max Patkin, a clown and contortionist whom Veeck had added to the team's coaching staff, along the first-base line. Rail-thin and double-jointed, Patkin would bend down until his face nearly scraped the ground, pretend to swipe the catcher's signs, then flash a flurry of nonsensical gestures to the batter. If the action lagged, Patkin would pull a folded-up newspaper from his back pocket. Before games and between innings, he'd dance the jitterbug with fans.

For some, Veeck's antics were a step too far. One New York sportswriter groused that they were "a travesty on serious baseball." Red Sox slugger Ted Williams quipped: "There are times when you don't know whether you are opposing another major league ball club or a travelling circus." The criticism could sting. One day, Patkin brought some scathing newspaper clippings into Veeck's office. "Max," Veeck asked, brushing them aside, "did they spell your name right?"

The results, nevertheless, spoke for themselves. During the week of July 28, the Indians attracted close to a quarter-million spectators over seven dates (including two doubleheaders)—almost half the home attendance total from the entire previous year. Clevelanders, columnist Gordon Cobbledick observed, began speaking of Veeck "as if he were a magician, possessor of a secret not revealed to other men." Bob Feller agreed: "It is doubtful," he wrote, "that any city ever responded as quickly and deeply to the promotion of one baseball figure" as Cleveland did to Veeck. If the team's torrid home attendance pace continued into September, the Indians had a realistic shot at drawing more than a million fans in a season for the first time in its history.

Just six months earlier, Veeck had been marooned on his ranch in Arizona, dreaming of ballparks brimming with people. Before a Sunday afternoon game on August 4, he found himself gazing out from the press box at that very sight—nearly 75,000 spectators in total, the largest crowd at Cleveland's lakefront stadium since it'd opened. Stopped momentarily by the sight, Veeck could do nothing more than shake his head in wonder.

By the beginning of August, Bob Feller had racked up 239 strike-outs, 104 short of Rube Waddell's mark. Of the fifty-three remaining Indians games, Feller aimed to start seventeen of them. If he struck out a shade more than six batters per contest, the single-season record would be his. "I'm going to pitch all I can—days, nights, Sundays, and whenever it looks as if I might do the club some good," he vowed. Veeck, for one, embraced the proposal, recognizing that Feller's run at the record could only aid his goal of crossing the seven-figure mark in attendance.

Over the next two months, Feller took the mound whenever possible, whether as a starter or a reliever. In between, there were stadiums and airplanes to book, promoters and players to line up, and travel logistics to hammer out for his upcoming barnstorming tour. The frantic pace wore him down. In mid-August, Sec Taylor, a sports columnist for *The Des Moines Register* who'd known Feller for more than a decade, paid the pitcher a visit. He could hardly believe his eyes. "Feller does not look quite well," Taylor wrote. "His face appears drawn and thin, but he insists he still weighs 180 pounds . . . I have an idea he has too many irons in the fire for his own good."

Even on days he started, there were engagements that piled up, some of which Feller wasn't given the opportunity to refuse. One such incident took place on August 20, an hour or so before game time at Griffith Stadium in Washington, D.C. In an era before radar guns, no one could say for certain the precise speed of a Feller fastball. There had been several crude attempts to measure his velocity, most notably in 1940 when, on a blocked-off street in Chicago, Feller had thrown at a paper bull's-eye at the exact second a Harley-Davidson zoomed past him at eighty-six miles per hour. The ball punctured the red center well ahead of the motorcycle.

That evening, Senators owner Clark Griffith cooked up a wholly original pregame promotion that would approach the question through scientific means. He'd shipped in a lumiline chronograph, an instrument which the U.S. military used to calculate the velocity of speeding artillery shells. That night, Griffith hoped to give the crowd a thrill by having Feller pump some fastballs through its boxy wooden frame. In a manner that typified the owners' proprietary arrogance toward players at the time, Griffith at no point sought Feller's consent in the stunt.

Feller saw the speed test for what it was: a way for Griffith to draw fans to his park—more than 30,000 in total on a Tuesday evening, Washington's largest turnout since Opening Day—by exploiting Feller's talents. Decades of team ownership had likely conditioned Griffith to expect player deference in the face of front-office directives. It was that very attitude that Feller now was hell-bent on contesting. If Griffith wanted him to perform beyond his contractual obligations, he'd have to deal with Feller not as a pitcher but as a peer, businessman to businessman. When Griffith came to the Indians clubhouse to fetch that evening's pregame attraction, Feller refused to budge until the Senators owner forked over one thousand dollars.

The demand caught Griffith flat-footed. Unable to cancel a promotion he'd spent a week plugging, Griffith found himself in an unfamiliar position: negotiating with a weak hand. Eventually, the two men settled on seven hundred dollars. Only then did Feller emerge onto the field and fire some fastballs into the heart of the chronograph, the swiftest one blowing by at 98.6 miles per hour.

A little more than a month later, on September 28, Feller outdid himself by taking an enormous leap in his business dealings, becoming the first professional player to incorporate himself. Dubbed Ro-Fel, Inc., his corporation consisted of three stockholders: Feller as president, his father-in-law, M. P. Winther, as vice president, and his wife, Virginia, as secretary-treasurer. "The main reason I incorporated," Feller later explained, "was to protect my family against liabilities which might grow out of [my] sideline deals. If one of my barnstormers were hurt, for example, there would be plenty of money in the corporation to discharge my responsibility. I wouldn't have to worry about anyone slapping claims against my personal property."

Beyond the legal reasoning, Feller's incorporation sent a clear signal that he was becoming more than just a star player bound to a major-league club. He was now a one-man enterprise, someone whom columnist Shirley Povich would call "the personification of [the] businessman ball player."

As the season rushed to a close, Feller was running out of time. Coming into the final week, he found himself twenty-three strike-outs shy of the single-season record of 343. To reach it, he threw three complete games and recorded a five-inning save over the Indians' final six games, striking out twenty-eight batters over thirty-two innings. In total, Feller tallied 348 strikeouts over 371.1 innings—the most innings pitched in the majors since 1917, nearly eighty more than anyone else that season. Of the forty-two games he started, Feller completed thirty-six, which no pitcher had done since 1916 and no pitcher has matched since.

Twenty-six of the Indians' sixty-eight wins in 1946 came from Feller, a number which might've been higher had he not flagged down the stretch. On August 8, Feller had sported a record of 21-6; the rest of the way, as his right arm tired out, he went 5-9. "I don't think I could [break the record] again," Feller told reporters immediately after having done so, "and I wouldn't want to if I could."

Instead of resting, Feller departed straightaway to Pittsburgh. There, the day after starting the closing game of the Indians' season, he took to the mound at Forbes Field for the opening game of the barnstorming tour he'd spent the summer planning. His fortune was tied up in filling stadiums through daily duels with Satchel Paige in October, and there was no backing out now.

12

Opposite Directions

After home games in 1946, the Newark Eagles migrated from Ruppert Stadium to the Grand Hotel, a squat two-story structure in the heart of the city's Third Ward district. Amid drinks and dancing, Eagles players and everyone around them—workers and owners, fans and luminaries—exulted in one another's company. "At the Grand Hotel, the ballplayers and the slick people could meet," wrote poet Amiri Baraka. "Everybody super-clean and highlifin', glasses jingling with ice, black people's eyes sparklin' and showin' their teeth in the hippest way possible." For Baraka, those midsummer nights represented "black life that was celebrated by being itself at its most unencumbered."

At times, groups would peel off for home-cooked, Southern-style meals at the Bill and James' restaurant around the corner. In the streets they might've heard the muffled rhythms of jazz and big bands pulsing from the smoky nightclubs nearby. As Newark's Black population grew and formed vibrant communities through the 1940s, the Third Ward became a compulsory stopover for touring Black musicians and entertainers, a compact version of Harlem across the Hudson. Even though much of Newark remained restricted to Eagles players, this slice of the city was theirs. "Those were special times," Monte Irvin recalled, "mainly because we were young and we knew we could play."

They were special for Larry Doby, too, who found in his first uninterrupted season in the Negro Leagues what he'd been seeking since high school: respect, comfort, acceptance. The Eagles, he recalled, were a close-knit club, both on the field and off it. The players lodged in the same hotels, ate in the same restaurants, and lifted one another's spirits after losses. And it was this solidarity and support that fueled the twenty-two-year-old Doby's ascension into the league's superstar ranks.

His appearance alone set scouts' imaginations on fire. At six-foot-one, Doby was solidly built yet lean for someone with fence-clearing power. He stood stiff and deep in the batter's box, his stance open, his bat hoisted high and perpendicular to the ground. Trusting his snap reflexes, Doby chased pitches below the knees and above the belt, inside and out—anything he could get a piece of. His swings were whirring blurs, as sudden and vicious as roundhouse punches. Sometimes their unrestrained force twisted him around entirely. But when he hit balls square, they shot skyward like jets to flight.

On the base paths, his strength gave way to speed. Tearing around with the "high knee-action gallop of a football halfback," Doby often flopped headfirst and arms forward onto his belly to beat throws. If he had a weakness, it was in the field, where he seemed caged as a second baseman, unable to roam free.

Doby romped through the season's first half with a batting average well north of .300. "I think Larry is the best prospect in baseball," Effa Manley asserted that summer, "and can do all the things Jackie Robinson has done [in the minor leagues]." His fast start turned heads among baseball bigwigs. It was rumored that Clyde Sukeforth, a scout for the Brooklyn Dodgers, attended every Eagles game around New York City that summer. Once, during an Independence Day contest at Yankee Stadium between the Eagles and the New York Black Yankees, Branch Rickey himself turned up in the stands. Manley later was quoted in the *Paterson Evening News* as saying that "Larry was the reason for the visit of the Brooklyn boss." She herself took this as an opportunity to confront the man who'd poached Don Newcombe from her club months earlier—and to stave off further raids.

Dan Parker, a columnist for the *New York Daily Mirror,* overheard her prickly exchange with the Dodgers president. "Mr. Rickey, I hope you're not going to grab any more of our players," she said, adding: "You know, Mr. Rickey, we could make trouble for you on the Newcombe transaction if we wanted to." Manley went on to inform Rickey, according to a letter she wrote to Chicago American Giants owner J. B. Martin, that "there were several men on my team [who were] potential Major League material. [Rickey] could put them right on The Dodgers team, and not have to send them to the sticks for training. I told him I would gladly let him have them, but I did feel they were worth an amount of cash in view of my investment in them."

It wasn't that Manley objected to Eagles players crossing over to the majors. What she wanted was for Negro League owners to retain a voice and a financial stake in the process. Perhaps because Manley already had to surrender 20 percent of her gross receipts to the New York Yankees for use of Ruppert Stadium (the Yankees' Triple-A club, the Newark Bears, also played there), she attempted to forge such a relationship with Yankees officials, urging them that summer to consider Doby for their farm system.

The money that major-league franchises raked in by renting their ballparks to Negro League clubs was a key reason they remained reluctant to change the segregated status quo. The Yankees were no different. Though happy to accept Manley's checks, they had no interest in her players. And until a franchise other than the Dodgers did, Manley would have to remain vigilant.

On the same afternoon that Effa Manley dressed down Branch Rickey in the Bronx, the Newark Eagles smothered the Black Yankees 3-1, then raced across state lines to Trenton for a night game against a white all-star squad from New Jersey's semiprofessional Industrial League. The result was lopsided, to say the least. "Adding machines, comptometers, and various other devices were required to compute the score," the *Trenton Evening Times* quipped after the Eagles hung thirty-one runs on their hapless opponents, fourteen in the final inning alone. They were as exuberant as they were merciless—an attitude that served them well all summer long.

The generational tide in Black baseball was turning. For eight of the last nine years, the Homestead Grays had laid claim to the Negro National League title, but now their weatherworn stars— Buck Leonard, Josh Gibson, James "Cool Papa" Bell—had slowed a step. In contrast, the Eagles were fresh-legged and championship-starved, armed with a youthful lineup that gave opposing pitchers fits. Shortstop Monte Irvin was flirting with a .400 average; first baseman Lennie Pearson had shot up the leaderboard in hits; and Doby was neck and neck with slugger Josh Gibson in home runs. Their dominance extended to the mound, where the team trotted out a trio of aces: Max Manning, Rufus Lewis, and Leon Day, who'd set the tone for the season by tossing a no-hitter on Opening Day. Eagles fans packed the grandstands from May to September in numbers unseen before the war.

The Eagles wrapped up the season's first half with a 25-9 record, tops in the Negro National League. If they won both halves of the split season, as seemed likely, the team would advance automatically to the Negro League World Series in September. There was little doubt about which club they'd face there. With a 27-8 first-half mark, the Kansas City Monarchs were coasting through the Negro American League. In Ted Strong and Willard Brown, the Monarchs sported stars of their own in their athletic prime. And in Paige they had a player whose prime seemed to have extended indefinitely.

* * *

On August 6, a warm and sticky Tuesday evening in northern New Jersey, spectators turned out by the thousands at Ruppert Stadium to see both a probable World Series preview and what one *Asbury Park Press* writer called the "greatest attraction in Negro baseball." It was Satchel Paige's first appearance in Newark that summer, and he put on a typical show, "whipping his throwing arm around his head in the old familiar fashion." No amount of windmilling, however, could fool the Eagles batters. They tagged Paige for two runs over three innings, ultimately downing the Kansas City Monarchs 7-4. Paige, as always, shrugged and moved on.

Even though demand for his services hadn't waned, Paige couldn't simply brush aside the broader changes taking root that summer. In the Brooklyn Dodgers' farm system, there were several former Negro League players who were more than holding their own—Jackie Robinson on the Montreal Royals; Roy Campanella and Don Newcombe on the Nashua Dodgers in New Hampshire. At the same time, there was a budding crop of current Negro League players who invited speculation about when they, too, might cross over to the minors. They were young men like Larry Doby who had come of age amid war, budding civil rights activism, and tentative integration, and who more and more were taking over the reins from members of Paige's generation, those men at the tail end of their playing careers who'd been born too early seemingly to factor into this speculation.

Regardless, Paige remained optimistic—defiant, even. An Associated Press article claimed that Paige continued "to nurse a hope that his smoke-ball will win him a chance to pitch baseball in the major leagues." As he insisted, "Don't let 'em tell you I'm too old to pitch baseball . . . I'm not too old . . . only 40 come September 25. And 40—even 50—isn't old if your arms and legs are only 20."

Whether because of age or the endless barnstorming offers that continued to pour in, Paige had turned almost exclusively into a three-to-five-inning specialist, someone who threw long enough to whet audiences' appetites without tiring himself out in the process. On days Paige pitched, Monarchs hurlers readied themselves for the thankless task of relieving the one player everyone had turned out to see. Through the season's first half, Paige had yet to toss a complete game. Whether he was still capable of doing so became an open topic of debate.

Despite these abbreviated outings, Paige was far from a nostalgia act. The season's second half found him in top form. During an East Coast swing in early July, Paige pitched sixteen scoreless innings across four games, drawing more than 50,000 spectators in the process. Doubts persisted nonetheless about his stamina. His chance to assuage them arose on August 30 at Sportsman's Park in St. Louis, where the Monarchs could clinch the Negro American League pennant with a win over the Indianapolis Clowns. After Kansas City dropped the first game of the doubleheader, Paige closed out the season himself in the second, retiring the first nine batters on just twenty-five pitches, then cruising to a complete-game victory.

In the days afterward, Paige uttered two revealing comments. "Eighteen thousand in the stands . . . just wanted to let 'em know old Satch still had it," he asserted with customary bravado. But when asked how he felt going the distance, he said that he was building himself up for "Bob Feller and that [barnstorming] series which is coming up." The statements pointed to Paige's dual reality that summer: He had one eye on shoring up his place in the Negro Leagues' pecking order, and the other looking beyond that.

On August 10, Larry Doby married Helyn Curvy in Paterson, New Jersey. He'd slipped an engagement ring on her finger years earlier, before departing for basic training. Despite his desire to wed before he shipped out to the Pacific, Curvy elected to wait until after the war. Upon his discharge, however, it was Doby who held out for months in the face of Curvy's pleas, as if, in sportswriter Sam Lacy's words, to "show that he too could be obstinate." When they finally tied the knot, it was a rushed affair. They exchanged vows in the early afternoon, then hustled to Trenton for a night game. Too much was at stake to miss a game that season, even on his wedding day.

Less than a month later, on September 4, the Eagles drubbed the New York Cubans 17-5 to clinch the Negro National League pennant. As a team, they'd batted a tick above .300, the best in Black baseball. Monte Irvin and Doby, the two players Effa Manley had taken such pains to re-sign, rewarded her efforts by pacing the offensive attack, with Irvin batting .394 and Doby .342. As expected, their opponent would be the Kansas City Monarchs.

Before the start of the Negro League World Series, Satchel Paige buzzed in and out of New York City, "bragging about what he was going to do to the Eagles." Whatever damage he might inflict, he would do it out of the bullpen, where he could pitch as often as necessary for the Monarchs over the seven-game series.

An opportunity arose immediately in the opening contest, on September 17 at the Polo Grounds in Manhattan, when the Monarchs, clinging to a 1-0 lead, called on Paige in the sixth inning to snuff out an Eagles rally. Though he ended up blowing the lead, Paige recovered it at the plate the following inning by singling and eventually crossing home as the go-ahead run. Then, calmly and efficiently, he shut out the Eagles the rest of the way, striking out the side to end the game. Once again, Dan Burley of the *New York Amsterdam News* proclaimed, Paige "proved his right to the distinction of being 'Baseball's Man of the Hour.'"

In the second game, two days later at Newark's Ruppert Stadium, it was Larry Doby who played the savior's role, pulling his team out of a 4-1 hole with a two-run shot deep into the left-field bleachers in the seventh inning. Once more, Paige trudged to the mound to preserve the Monarchs' precarious 4-3 advantage. This time, however, his magic deserted him. The Eagles knocked in four runs against Paige, tying the series with a 7-4 win.

After the teams split the next two games in Kansas City, the Monarchs pushed the Eagles to the brink of elimination with a victory in the fifth game. When they returned to Newark to try to close out the series, however, Paige wasn't among them. He didn't show up for the sixth game, which the Monarchs subsequently lost, nor for the final contest. Several of his teammates also went missing. The Monarchs' shorthanded roster proved an obstacle too great to overcome in the seventh game, allowing the Eagles to edge past their depleted rivals by a 3-2 margin to clinch the franchise's first championship.

While the series had commenced in a swirl of excitement before 20,000 fans at the Polo Grounds, it concluded less than two weeks later with the stands at Ruppert Stadium half full. Only 7,200 people had shown up for the decisive contest, fewer than had seen Paige pitch in Newark in early August. Fan interest, fervent at the beginning, had drifted elsewhere by the end.

So, too, had some of the Monarchs. "At that point," wrote Monarchs first baseman Buck O'Neil in his autobiography, "even though the Negro leagues had had their best season—clearing two million dollars in profit for the first time that year—it was true that most guys had their sights set on other things than black baseball." For Paige, the exposure and paychecks he could garner while barnstorming with Bob Feller apparently took precedence over another Negro League World Series title, which his Monarchs had won four years earlier. Rather than finishing the job in Newark, he'd gone to Pittsburgh, where Feller's tour soon would kick off. An aged star like Paige, it seemed, had more to gain from a month of matchups against major leaguers than from two more days of bullpen work against the Eagles.

For Doby, the opposite was true. Undoubtedly, he was hungry not only to claim his first championship but to solidify his place among his youthful peers. What's more, there was reason to believe that major-league front offices would be monitoring the postseason. Roy Campanella, who'd just wrapped up his first season on the Nashua Dodgers, later revealed that Branch Rickey paid him $500 to scout the Negro League World Series. In his subsequent report to Rickey, Campanella recommended two players above all: Monte Irvin and Larry Doby.

Another distraction from the Negro League World Series was a minor-league championship taking place at the same time, hundreds of miles away. The aptly named Little World Series pitted the Louisville Colonels against the Montreal Royals. The Royals' star attraction was Jackie Robinson, who'd led the International League in batting average and runs that summer while spurring his team to a 100-54 record. Black newspapers covered the series with rapt attention as Robinson spearheaded the Royals to victory in six games.

These worrisome trends didn't dampen the Eagles' jubilation. In the hours after clinching the championship, Doby and his teammates celebrated with their fans in Newark. For Effa and Abe Manley, it must have been an evening to savor. They'd drawn a record 120,000 fans to Ruppert Stadium that season. Their players were young, their profits ample, their community admiring.

But there were warning signs everywhere that massive changes were soon coming to the Negro Leagues.

13

Head-to-Head

The first game in Bob Feller's 1946 barnstorming tour laid bare the many ways the undertaking could go wrong. It was September 30, and Pittsburgh was in the midst of a strike by the city's power utility workers. Streetcars and buses had stopped running; many downtown businesses were shuttered. With power plants operating well below capacity, newspaper ads urged residents to turn on only one light at a time and to unplug household appliances. On top of that, a cold front was sweeping through the region, coating the outfield grass at Forbes Field with the autumn's first frost.

Feller was forced to scramble. Unable to play under the lights, he rescheduled the game for midday. By the time Satchel Paige took the mound that afternoon, a mere 4,600 spectators were scattered through the stands, not even a fourth of what Feller had banked on. While the game itself lived up to Feller's expectations, with the aces matching each other pitch for pitch over three innings (Paige's squad ultimately eked out a 3-1 victory), it was a worrisome start to a tour already swamped with pitfalls.

Throughout the past summer, sportswriters had scoffed at the idea of the onetime Iowa farmboy pulling off the most elaborate barnstorming tour in baseball history. For them, the whole thing seemed "uproariously funny." Even Bill Veeck, though supportive in public, whispered in private that he expected Feller to lose $50,000 on the venture.

Major-league front offices were also skeptical, though for different reasons. At a time when overnight train travel was the norm, when no team journeyed regularly by air, Feller had arranged for some two dozen flights in a month. The specter of grisly injuries to their star players, whether on the diamond or in plane-related mishaps, haunted some baseball officials. The owners of the Boston Red Sox and Detroit Tigers went so far as to pay outfielder Ted Williams and pitcher Hal Newhouser $10,000 apiece—one-fourth of each man's salary in 1946—to lounge around at home in the off-season instead.

Feller still managed to cobble together a balanced roster for his side that featured the batting champions from the American and National Leagues (Mickey Vernon and Stan Musial, who would join the tour as soon as the World Series concluded), a slew of participants from the 1946 All-Star Game (including Ken Keltner, Sam Chapman, Spud Chandler, and Charlie Keller), and a mix of young talent (Johnny Sain, Phil Rizzuto, Jim Hegan, and Bob Lemon, among others).

For help in assembling an opposing squad of top Black stars, Feller had reached out to Kansas City Monarchs co-owners Tom Baird and J. L. Wilkinson. In a letter to Effa Manley dated September 2, 1946, Baird wrote, "We want the best players on the Paige All stars we can get, at least players that look best to the colored owners and fans for we want to win as many games as we can from Bob Feller." But it was easier said than done. Jackie Robinson, for instance, eschewed the tour for one of his own, recruiting such luminaries as Buck Leonard and Roy Campanella to his side.

For Larry Doby, the choice came down to finances. After signing a contract to play for Paige's squad, he quickly changed his mind. "The deal gives Feller and his team 60 percent [of the gate receipts] and Paige 40 with the players on our team getting half of [Paige's] percentage," Doby explained to the *Paterson Evening News*. "I decided that wasn't so good and so I tied up with Jackie Robinson for his all-star trip. I have a better deal with him because he is giving the players a guarantee and a percentage privilege."

Regardless, the lineup pieced together for Paige's squad was capable of running up the score on their white opponents wherever they played. Flanking Paige on the mound were Hilton Smith, Barney Brown, and Max Manning; surrounding him on the field were Sam Jethroe, Hank Thompson, Willard Brown, Quincy Trouppe, Lennie Pearson, Gene Benson, and Buck O'Neil, among others. Most important, there was Paige himself. Feller had conceived of the tour with him in mind, and now he would count on Paige's drawing power to save him from financial ruin.

The day after their opening matchup in Pittsburgh, the two teams traveled northeast to Youngstown for an afternoon game, and then on to Cleveland for a night game. There, the atmosphere in Municipal Stadium was unusually charged for an exhibition contest. Even though it would be the tour's only stopover on Feller's home turf, many of the 10,000 fans in the stands—an estimated two-thirds of whom were Black—hadn't braved the night's bitter winds to see him. They'd come for Paige. To the *Call & Post*'s Cleveland Jackson, the turnout and enthusiasm were evidence that "Negro fans will support a sport wholeheartedly, if some attempt is made to attract their attention. They also indicate to baseball team owners how many Negro fans will come out to see baseball when they have Negro players performing in [the] big time circuit."

The moment Paige walked onto the field, "a roar of pride rose from the partisan crowd." His first pitch to leadoff hitter Phil Rizzuto dipped outside the zone. The second darted down the middle, bringing fans to their feet. When a languorous curve froze Rizzuto as it broke across the plate, cheers echoed through the aisles even though Paige had yet to throw a third strike.

He never did. Unfazed, Rizzuto induced a rare walk from Paige, then dashed home two batters later on a throwing error by Buck O'Neil. The major leaguers went on to hang four more runs on Paige's team. For perhaps the first time, a Cleveland crowd walked away disappointed in a contest that ended in a Feller victory.

Thanks to the surge in Black fans, the tour found its footing. Throngs of people began to turn out at every stop: 22,000 in Chicago, 10,000 in Cincinnati, 13,000 in Newark, 22,000 in New York City. On Sunday, October 6, a massive crowd, allegedly the largest ever to turn out in New York City for a game that featured an all-Black lineup, streamed into Yankee Stadium for the tour's second contest there in two days. According to Dan Burley of the *New York Amsterdam News,* the stands that afternoon "were loaded to such an extent that the third deck in the spacious Yankee Stadium was for the first time, thrown open to fans at a Negro ball game." Of the 27,462 fans—many believed the actual attendance was closer to 35,000—Burley estimated that a little more than 20 percent were white.

The two headliners rewarded the faithful by going five innings apiece. Feller, who'd taken only one day off since breaking the single-season strikeout record a week earlier, came out flat and fatigued. Paige turned back the clock. Alone on center stage in baseball's biggest arena, in front of a mob of adoring fans in the media capital of the country, he stymied batters with an age-old array of bee balls and long Toms, hesitation pitches and wrinkled curves. No runner so much as touched third base in the five frames Paige threw. "The duel between Paige and Feller was definitely one-sided, all in the former's favor," declared *The New York Times* after Paige's 4-0 victory.

The exposure was invaluable. Unable to turn heads as often as he once had in the regular season, Paige forced the attention of the baseball world on the barnstorming trail. It was in these matchups against Feller, Buck O'Neil would argue, that "Satchel made his case for being a big-leaguer."

The tour mirrored Feller's life in 1946: saturated, enterprising, exhausting. There were thirty-five contests over twenty-seven days, from Connecticut to California and everywhere in between. (Concerned with Jim Crow restrictions in the South, Feller restricted the tour to the country's northern half except for a few games in Kentucky, where his squad faced off not against Paige's team but rosters of local players.) Every day was accounted for, sometimes with day-night doubleheaders in cities hundreds of miles apart. As soon as the last out was made, the players shuttled from the showers to the pair of DC-3 planes Feller had contracted at $2,000 a day, one for the Bob Feller All-Stars, the other for the Satchel Paige All-Stars. A week or so in, even the most travel-seasoned athlete was buckling.

Fans and executives fretted over whether Feller was risking injury and exhaustion, especially after his innings-heavy season. He shrugged off their concerns. "You can bet on one thing: I'm not going to do anything to injure my salary wing," he said in reference to his arm. Besides, he had larger aims to strive for. "It's nice to collect those greenbacks," Feller told reporters during the tour, "but I sure could use some sleep."

While money certainly was foremost in Feller's mind, he also seemed to be chasing something deeper, an independence that none of his major-league peers could claim, one that more closely resembled what Paige had carved out for himself. Impressive as Feller's coast-to-coast tour was, it paled in comparison to Paige's own feat of building himself into the country's premier barnstorming attraction without any of the advantages Feller's race afforded him.

Even Feller's principal innovation—traveling via airplane—was one that Paige had gotten to first. Earlier that season, to enable Paige to meet more of the one-game barnstorming offers that flooded in,

Monarchs co-owner J. L. Wilkinson had leased a two-passenger Cessna plane with "Satchel Paige" scrawled on both sides of the fuselage. Even though the experiment was cut short after a few turbulent flights, it underscored the extent to which Paige matched Feller as much in business as on the field.

On some level, each pitcher used the tour to strive toward what the other had. Feller could count on the stability of the major leagues; now he wanted the economic freedom of the road—or the air, in his case. Paige, in contrast, could always hit the highway to draw crowds and pocket gate receipts; now, more than ever, he sought a path into the majors, before it was too late.

Two incidents during the tour's West Coast swing cast a shadow over the enterprise. Once the teams had completed their cross-country journey upon reaching California, Paige and his all-star squad disbanded, and Paige joined forces with Chet Brewer and his Kansas City Royals, playing against Feller's team to packed houses in Los Angeles and San Diego. At some point, Brewer, while scrutinizing the ticket sales, noticed that Feller had paid Paige 15 percent of the net receipts, not the gross receipts that their agreement had called for. After confronting Feller, Paige eventually filed suit against his adversary in early November for the $1,711.58 that he was still owed.

The second incident took place in Sacramento on October 21. Feller, per usual, had cut his time razor-thin. He was to start a game at 8 P.M. against a team of Pacific Coast League players, catch an overnight flight forty minutes later to New Jersey, distribute autographed baseball-bat pencils at a milk convention in Atlantic City the following day while collecting two thousand dollars for his services, then jet back across the country so that he could pitch the next afternoon in Bakersfield, California.

After two rapid-fire innings in Sacramento, Feller bolted into the clubhouse. Chasing after him, sportswriter Steve George squeezed in some questions as Feller undressed: "I'd like to ask you what your impressions are of Negro ball players. You've been playing against Satchel Paige and his team and other colored teams as well. Do you think they'll make the big league grade?"

Feller didn't hold back in his response. "Haven't seen one—not one," he said. "Maybe Paige when he was young. When you name him, you're done. Some are good hitters. Some can field pretty good. Most of them are fast. But I have seen none who combine the qualities of a big league ball player."

"Not even Jackie Robinson?" George asked.

"Not even Jackie Robinson," confirmed Feller.

The words ricocheted through the Black press. Cleveland Jackson deemed them "the most astonishing [comments] made by a nationally known sports figure within the past twenty years." Jackson took particular umbrage at Feller's willingness to disparage the same players whose drawing power and competitive play had enabled his risky financial gamble to pay off. What's more, Feller's statements gifted a go-to excuse to major-league executives hesitant to follow Branch Rickey's lead on integration. After all, if the pitcher who'd just spent weeks facing what he deemed the best in Black baseball didn't find any players major-league worthy, then who were they to argue?

Never mind that Monarchs third baseman Hank Thompson had battered Feller the entire tour, taking him deep a handful of times. Or that Feller supposedly told Philadelphia Stars center fielder Gene Benson: "You have to be a relative in my family, as hard as you hit me." Or that Paige had been everything Feller could've hoped for— still the perfect rival for Feller a decade after their first duel.

As demeaning as they were, Feller's opinions were wholly in keeping with mainline beliefs among white athletes. Still, from a modern perspective, it seems jarring that Feller would be so dismissive of the major-league potential of Black players when his actions at the time could reasonably have been construed as broad-minded on racial matters. Feller, *The Baltimore Afro-American* reported, "was criticized by the Dixie riff-raff for choosing a colored team for exhibition games, but he stuck to his guns." He exposed himself to defeat every time he faced off against Satchel Paige. These high-profile matchups, in turn, helped introduce many white fans, reporters, and executives to Negro League players they might not otherwise have seen.

Buck O'Neil believed that "even though it was black against white, this tour was an event that could have a real effect on big-league integration, because it took place after Jackie had proven himself [in the minors], and if a lot of us weren't that lucky, we could at least prove ourselves against big-leaguers in these games." And despite the problems before and during the tour with regard to disparities in pay, several participants felt that Feller's compensation was generous enough. Newark Eagles pitcher Max Manning claimed afterward, "I had more money in my pocket than I ever saw in my life."

The tour, like Feller himself, was complicated: It advanced the cause of integration while selling itself on the separation of the races; it exposed white fans to the talents of Negro League players while undercutting them through its organizer's statements; it opened with Paige sharing the national spotlight with Feller and ended with one filing a lawsuit against the other. Here, similar to the previous times they'd faced each other, the two headliners maintained an uneasy and unspoken awareness of the barriers that separated them. "[Paige and I] never talked about the fact that [Paige] couldn't play in the major leagues," Feller stated decades afterward. "It was all under the surface. That's just the way it was. Nothing you could do about it."

Despite it all, the entire undertaking ended up being an unequivocal triumph for Feller. He'd logged 13,000 miles in the air, performed in front of 250,000 fans, and walked away with nearly $80,000 in profits, more than his salary with the Indians in 1946. Baseball officials who'd smirked at Feller's overreach no longer were laughing.

His lucrative, player-empowered barnstorming put front offices in an awkward spot. The opening weeks of his tour had coincided with the Major League World Series, a seven-game nail-biter between the St. Louis Cardinals and the Boston Red Sox. Because the games had alternated between two of the league's smaller ballparks, which limited the number of tickets sold, the players' postseason bonuses clocked in lower than usual: $3,742.23 for each of the victorious Cardinals, $2,059.99 for each Red Sox player. Any member of the Red Sox could've pocketed more cash by barnstorming with Feller. Had Cardinals superstar Stan Musial been able to fly around on Feller's tour for its entirety, he would've pulled in nearly double what he'd cleared for winning a championship. "If the magnates do not make the [World Series] prizes worth while," *The Sporting News* warned, "they may be confronted with the strange spectacle of players trying to stay out of the classic so they can go barnstorming."

In the end, Feller's earnings for 1946 totaled $150,000, the most profitable year ever for a professional baseball player. In the fifteen months since his release from the armed services, the all-American boy of the Great Depression had built himself into a commanding postwar entrepreneur. He was a barnstorming impresario, a multimedia brand, a one-man syndicate, and a force that owners and executives would have to reckon with.

14

Hands and Knees

The off-season came, but Bill Veeck didn't slow down. His October schedule was booked solid. He attended the 1946 World Series, jetted to Tucson for a quick visit with his family, and tore around northern Ohio speaking before as many groups and organizations as he could reach. Given the pain in his right foot, it was unsustainable.

On October 22, Veeck stepped from the elevator of the Cleveland hotel where he lived and crumpled to the ground. Unable to stand, he crawled to his suite on his hands and knees. His itinerary called for him to give a talk at a Rotary club the next day and then host a charity football game in Massillon, a town about sixty miles south of Cleveland. He wouldn't think of canceling these engagements. Instead, he asked his secretary to set up a doctor's appointment upon his return.

In the examination room, as soon as he glimpsed Veeck's swollen foot, the doctor sent him away to the Cleveland Clinic. There, a bedside phone line was installed; associates briefed him daily on all Indians matters. From early in the morning until late at night, a steady stream of visitors traipsed through his room. Every corner was littered with baskets of flowers, fruit, and cigarettes.

Even though Veeck, as columnist Franklin Lewis put it, had

been "in more hospitals than a rented wheelchair" over the past few years, it was different this time. The orthopedist laid down an ultimatum: The foot would have to come off.

At ten minutes past noon on November 1, 1946, Veeck was wheeled into an operating room, where surgeons sliced off his right leg seven inches below the knee. At 4:30 that same afternoon, a call came into the sports department of the *Cleveland Press*. The voice on the other end was faint and sluggish. "This is Bill Veeck . . . How did those picks go today at Cincy?" the Indians owner, still groggy from the effects of anesthesia, asked about that morning's minor-league draft.

Mere hours after the amputation, Veeck was already back to work.

By all accounts, Veeck took the loss of his foot in stride. When sportswriter Hal Lebovitz first visited the clinic after the operation, he found a bedridden Veeck playing with a Slinky. More than a thousand letters and three hundred telegrams were piled up next to him. So many bouquets of flowers had poured in that Cleveland florists had started to discourage callers from placing orders. Veeck shrugged at the attention. "I said there would be changes made and players cut right and left when I bought the Indians last summer. And what happens? I'm the one who winds up getting cut! But it could have been worse, Bob Feller's right arm, for instance. I'd rather give a leg to the Indians than have anything happen to Bob's pitching arm!"

Seventeen days after his surgery, Veeck was discharged from the hospital. A truck was needed to haul away the mounds of gifts that had accumulated in his room. Two months later, he was fitted for an artificial leg at the J. E. Hanger Company in downtown Pittsburgh. The one he chose was carved from English willow and fastened on with brown leather straps. After attaching the wooden limb, Veeck took a few uncertain strides forward. Then, according to the *Pittsburgh Post-Gazette*, a "cocky grin" spread over Veeck's face. Soon, he began strutting up and down the store corridors.

"Take it easy, Bill," one of the clerks pleaded. "A fellow shouldn't bite off more than he can chew at first."

"Depends on how big his mouth is," Veeck shot back, and with a flourish he swung his new leg high like a dancer in a chorus line.

Being rid of the crutches on which he'd hobbled about for the better part of two years was cause for celebration. His custom-tailored wooden leg was slated to arrive in Cleveland in late January. Veeck sent out invitations to a "Back on My Feet" dance scheduled for the day of its arrival.

On the evening of January 28, more than three hundred guests filled the glamorous Vogue Ballroom in Cleveland's Hollenden Hotel. Veeck didn't hold back. He danced waltzes and rumbas, fox-trots and sambas—whatever the Sammy Watkins Orchestra threw at him. After a while, blood started to trickle down the wooden appendage that had been delivered only hours earlier, leaking onto the dance floor.

If he was in pain, Veeck didn't let on until the last guest had retired. Then he limped to the elevator and collapsed upon reaching his floor. Just as he'd done three months earlier, he crawled on his hands and knees to his room. There, as Veeck later wrote in his autobiography, he discovered that the strain of dancing had rubbed his tender stump raw, "and the blood, in drying, had glued it solidly to the wooden leg." He had to soak for hours in a hot bath before the prosthetic unstuck itself. Afterward, according to Franklin Lewis, he writhed in bed while "ripping pains tore at the flesh of his stump."

Of the many concerns Veeck had in the winter of 1946–47, the Indians pitching ace wasn't one of them. "I'm very happy Bob Feller took that barnstorming trip after the season," Veeck said in February 1947. "Now we know he can pitch every day."

Contract negotiations between the two began almost as soon as Feller's tour ended. They huddled together first in November, shortly after Veeck's discharge from the Cleveland Clinic, then again at the start of the new year. While other major-league executives steeled themselves for knock-down, drag-out contract battles with their stars, Veeck and Feller were navigating something wholly different: an agreement between two corporations.

Feller came to the talks armed with meticulously calculated estimates of how much the Indians had made on days he'd pitched versus on days he hadn't. Veeck countered by pointing out that because of the surge in fans his promotions had elicited, Feller's attendance-based bonus clauses enabled him to collect "something like $25,000 more [in 1946] than he expected to get."

The way forward was through a mutually enriching partnership based on trust. The deal they inched toward would include a base salary similar to the one from the previous season, but with enhanced bonus clauses. If the Indians duplicated their home attendance numbers from 1946, then the contract would amount to the richest in baseball history, eclipsing the $80,000 deal Babe Ruth had inked in 1930. Since Veeck had already announced his intention of moving all Indians home games to Municipal Stadium for the 1947 season, severing the club's link to League Park and its measly seating capacity, it seemed a cinch that the team's home attendance would continue its upward trajectory. Feller was on board. "I'm willing to gamble on attendance, an improved team and on Veeck's proven ability to draw big crowds," he stated after his second sit-down with Veeck.

On January 20, 1947, Feller drove to Cleveland from his winter home in Waukegan, Illinois. The next morning at ten, he stomped into League Park in a snowstorm. He wore a blue pinstriped suit and a tan topcoat with matching fedora. Veeck, hatless and jacketless, whisked the pitcher into his office and asked the gathered reporters and photographers to "give us five minutes, please."

Twenty minutes passed, then twenty more. Finally, the door swung open and the press scuttled in. A ceremonial signing ensued, after which Veeck declared, "[This contract] is the biggest ever signed by me, by Bob and to my knowledge, the largest ever signed by anybody. I understand Babe Ruth's biggest was $80,000 . . . Well, this is bigger."

Flashbulbs lit up the room. Feller, seated confidently at the owner's desk, pretended to calculate his astronomical bonuses on an adding machine while Veeck clutched his head in mock distress. At one point, a photographer asked Feller to pose in the same chair again. Veeck quipped, "Well, he owns it. Why not?" Later, Veeck gestured out the window at the snow-dusted infield. "I think [Feller's] part of the ball club stops just at that point," he joked, pointing to the first-base stands.

The punch lines persisted past that day. What Veeck lost in funds he gained in material, which was an even trade-off for someone who relied on the speaking circuit to drum up business. From then on, at luncheons or dinners, Veeck often opened with some variation of the line "I come to you through the courtesy of my employer, Bob Feller."

More so than Feller, the issues that preoccupied Veeck that off-season revolved around building a go-nowhere club into a championship contender as quickly as possible. Despite having more than doubled the size of the Indians' minor-league farm system during his first year as owner, Veeck had little patience for multiyear rebuilding projects or incremental progress. "I'm not the kind of fellow who can sit around and wait while minor leaguers are growing into major leaguers," he asserted. "I want the best team I can get right now."

There was a ravenous hunger for a pennant among Indians fans, which no number of fireworks displays or coaching-box clowns could satiate. Wall-to-wall promotions were fine for one season, but offering more of the same risked inciting a backlash if the team continued to stagnate in sixth place.

True, the Indians had ridden the postwar baseball boom to the seven-figure mark in attendance in 1946, but so had nine other clubs.

Attendance at major-league games overall almost doubled, shooting from 10,841,123 total paid attendees in 1945 to 18,523,289 in 1946, the most in baseball history to that point. The Yankees ended up as the first franchise to draw more than two million fans, shattering the single-season record Veeck's father had helped establish decades earlier as president of the Chicago Cubs. If Veeck hoped to match the Yankees' success at the gate—and ensure that last summer's fan surge wasn't a fluke—he'd have to contend with them in the standings as well.

Much to his frustration, Veeck had his hands tied on who would lead the team. Over the decades, Cleveland had gained a reputation as a place that chewed up managers raw. Some alleged that Indians owners hired managers "for the exclusive and unholy purpose of firing them." From 1933 to 1941, the team cycled through five skippers (including one manager twice).

After the 1941 season, Lou Boudreau, the Indians shortstop, let team president Alva Bradley know of his interest in the vacant manager spot. The idea of an untested twenty-four-year-old a mere two full seasons into his playing career piling managerial responsibilities on top of his on-field duties might have seemed laughable, but Indians executives were desperate enough to give it a go. While player-managers were common in that era, they were generally aging veterans easing their way out of the league. Only one player-manager— Roger Peckinpaugh, who at the age of twenty-three helmed the New York Yankees for the final three weeks of the 1914 season—had been younger than Boudreau.

Classified as 4-F during the war because of his arthritic ankles, Boudreau learned the managerial ropes amid depleted rosters and low expectations. For the most part, Indians fans cut the kid some slack because his brilliant play on the field counterbalanced his debatable decisions on the sidelines.

Increasingly as the war dragged on, it was Boudreau who filled the Feller-shaped hole in Cleveland's heart, though in a slightly different way. Fans admired Feller as they would a Greek god. His gifts appeared otherworldly, unobtainable to commoners. They expected dominance from Feller and walked away puzzled when he failed to deliver it. With Boudreau the opposite was true. Little about him suggested excellence. As one writer put it, Boudreau "runs like a dray, has a batting stance that may only be termed ludicrous and seems to lack every ingredient that would make a star. Yet he daily makes plays that can only be explained by necromancy . . . Since he moves no faster than a largo it can only be held that he has the intuition of a bird dog and the persistence of a bill collector." Boudreau's struggles were earthly, relatable. That he managed not only to overcome them but to become a perennial MVP candidate seemed nothing short of extraordinary. Fans cheered him as they would an overachieving son. It didn't hurt that, with his coal-black hair and soft features, Boudreau was a hit with the city's female fans.

Immediately after purchasing the Indians, Veeck had summoned Boudreau, along with Harry Grabiner and stockholder Bob Goldstein, to his downtown hotel suite. They ordered room-service steaks and got right down to business. Veeck made it clear that he thought the world of Boudreau as a player but not as a manager. Too often, in Veeck's mind, Boudreau managed from his gut, his decision-making devoid of any underlying strategy or philosophy.

None of this surprised Boudreau. For days he'd heard rumors that the new ownership group intended to replace him. Far from being ambushed, Boudreau was poised for a counterattack. After Veeck said his piece, Boudreau launched into a detailed defense of his managerial tenure. Then he threw down his trump card: "If I am relieved as manager," he told Veeck, "I will have to be traded. I will not play ball for Cleveland under another manager."

Veeck had no choice but to fold, aware of the resentment he'd stir up by ousting a fan favorite during his first weeks in Cleveland. An uneasy truce was forged. Boudreau would stay at the helm until his contract ran out after the 1947 season. Then the matter would be revisited.

* * *

For now, Veeck rolled up his sleeves to revamp the Indians' roster. Right away he found a like-minded trading partner in New York Yankees co-owner Larry MacPhail, a promoter and character nearly as outsized and creative as Veeck himself. During the 1946 World Series, MacPhail had approached Veeck at Fenway Park to gauge his interest in Joe Gordon, an acrobatic second baseman who'd fallen out of favor with the front office in the Bronx. In his first season back after two years in the service, Gordon had wound up with a piddling .210 average and a chip on his shoulder as large as the bald spot on his head. Where other owners might have shied away from a disgruntled player on the wrong side of thirty, Veeck bet that a change of scenery could help Gordon, the Most Valuable Player in the American League a mere four years earlier, regain his prewar form. Together, Veeck and MacPhail scribbled out the parameters of a deal that would ship Gordon to Cleveland for pitcher Allie Reynolds.

On the heels of that blockbuster trade, the two men huddled for another. The Indians had a spare second baseman to peddle (Ray Mack) and the Yankees had a reserve outfielder Veeck coveted (Hal Peck). Years earlier, as a member of the Milwaukee Brewers, Peck had tripped while carrying a shotgun and blasted two of his toes off. He'd managed to make a full recovery, and Veeck, admiring his gumption, came to consider Peck a good-luck charm. As part of a larger deal, MacPhail compiled a list of fifteen minor-league pitchers for Veeck to choose from. One name stood out: a knuckleballer for the Oakland Oaks of the Pacific Coast League named Gene Bearden.

Like Peck, Bearden was damaged goods. While serving in the Navy during the war, he'd shipped out to the South Pacific aboard the USS *Helena*. During a skirmish with Japanese forces in the Solomon Islands in 1943, three torpedoes struck the ship, flooding its interior and throwing Bearden from a ladder. An officer, slinging the unconscious Bearden over his shoulder, lugged him onto a rubber life raft. There, they bobbed about before being saved by a rescue team. Bearden had a fractured skull and a crushed right knee. Aluminum plates were slotted into both.

Some doctors told him that his pitching days were done. But Bearden was persistent. Unable to lift his right leg high during his windup, the southpaw compensated by learning to throw his own peculiar version of a knuckleball. As *Sporting News* editor J. G. Taylor Spink later explained, "Bearden holds [the ball] with three fingers, instead of two, pays no attention to where he grips the ball and throws with a full follow-through motion that makes it look and travel like a fast ball without a spin."

Veeck couldn't have known then that his pursuit of a good-luck charm would result in perhaps the most significant trade he'd complete as the Indians owner.

As the winter wore on, a sense of urgency gripped Veeck. Despite the many changes he'd made, the Indians couldn't yet be considered a championship contender. Their pitching rotation beyond Feller was thin, and they were in need of outfielders who could patrol the bountiful grass in the spacious stadium where the Indians now would play all of their home games.

With a dearth of top-line starting pitchers on the trading block, Veeck improvised with the resources on hand. He'd always reveled in player reclamation projects, and the team's rotation was unusually rife with them. The most extreme case was Don Black, a longtime drunk who'd been known to stagger onto the field with whiskey on his breath. In September 1946, Veeck had urged the right-hander to give Alcoholics Anonymous a shot. If Black stuck with the twelve-step program, Veeck would agree to write off his debts and secure him an off-season job at a Cleveland manufacturer. The effort paid off. By the time of his departure for spring training in 1947, Black was newly sober.

Then there was Bob Lemon, the most unlikely pitcher in baseball.

Originally an infielder in the Indians' farm system, Lemon had enlisted in the Navy in 1943 and ended up stationed just outside Pearl
Harbor, where he patrolled third base for a local service team. Because
the team played several games per week, its roster was perpetually
short on pitchers. In desperation, manager Billy Herman, taking note
of the movement on Lemon's tosses across the infield, pushed him
into emergency mound duty. It was an inspired decision, as Lemon
seemed incapable of throwing a ball that didn't have something extra
on it, whether spin, drop, or curve. "Any pitch of mine," Lemon later
wrote, "has more natural wrinkles than a washboard."

Because he'd appeared briefly in the majors before the war,
Lemon was entitled to a thirty-day trial with the Indians upon his
return in 1946. Nobody, sportswriter Tom Meany claimed, would
have "bet a nickel that he would remain with the club one day after
that." Boudreau parked him in center field but lost patience as Lemon
struggled to boost his batting average above .200.

When the Indians rolled into New York City in early May,
Yankees manager Bill Dickey pulled Boudreau aside and, pointing at Lemon, reportedly asked, "How about pitching that kid? He
showed me the best curve of anybody in Hawaii during the war."
It seemed far-fetched. Few players outside of Bucky Walters of
the Cincinnati Reds had successfully converted from a fielder to a
pitcher once they'd landed in the major leagues, and as Lemon himself would state: "I knew as much about pitching when I joined the
Indians as Bill Veeck knows about knotting a tie." Regardless, the
choice before him was clear: the mound or the minors.

Veeck endorsed the experiment. After Lemon acquitted himself reasonably well in the bullpen in 1946, Veeck phoned him and
declared, "From now on you're a pitcher, so forget everything else.
We may start you next season."

If the starting rotation concerned Veeck, the Indians' lack of
depth in the outfield panicked him. All winter long he'd inundated
Washington Senators owner Clark Griffith with trade offers for his

center fielder, Stan Spence. Once, in late January, Veeck impulsively canceled all engagements and caught a flight to Orlando. Ambushing Griffith at the team's spring training digs, he fired off every sales tactic in his arsenal, but to no avail. Veeck, Ed McAuley reported, "not only failed to get Spence, he failed to get a hotel room. He was able to snatch a few hours' sleep in a conference room before the conferees went into session, but landed in Cleveland early January 27, a weary and disappointed commuter."

The season was approaching; the roster was still incomplete. In February 1947, Veeck opened a guest address to the Ohio General Assembly in Columbus with a joking plea that hinted at actual desperation: "I would like for you to enact a law providing that anyone in the state of Ohio who can play centerfield must report immediately to the Cleveland Indians."

Nothing had worked. He'd have to explore other options. As always, Veeck had one in mind.

Despite his aversion to backseats of any kind, Veeck took one to Branch Rickey on integration. As players like Jackie Robinson, Roy Campanella, and Don Newcombe worked their way through the Dodgers' farm system, Veeck proceeded, in his own words, "slowly and carefully, perhaps even timidly," waiting with uncharacteristic patience for the preliminary results to emerge in Brooklyn before making his move, at times sending out mixed signals in the process.

In July 1946, for example, Veeck insisted to Cleveland Jackson that he had "absolutely no objections" to desegregating the Indians' roster. But, Veeck added, he would only "purchase a qualified Negro player if it meant the difference between a mediocre and a championship team for Cleveland. However, in my opinion," he concluded, "none of the present crop of Negro players measure up to big league standards." Jackson, who would excoriate Bob Feller months later for uttering a similar statement, held his fire on the Indians owner, likely because Veeck's forward-looking manner, familiarity with the

Negro Leagues, and accommodation of the Black press suggested a greater openness to integration than his executive peers.

That same month, a joint steering committee was established by officials from the Amerian and National Leagues to look into various baseball-related issues that had cropped up since the end of the war, the so-called Race Question among them. A draft of the ensuing report advanced several arguments for maintaining baseball's segregated status quo: Black players hadn't received what they deemed the requisite training to develop the "technique, the coordination, the competitive attitude, and the discipline" needed to thrive in the majors; a dramatic increase in Black spectatorship might dissuade white fans from attending games and thus cause profit margins to plunge; and owners' bottom lines would also suffer from losing revenue derived from renting their ballparks to Negro League clubs. Even though the section on race was excised from the final report, Branch Rickey would later claim that no other major-league executive had joined him in objecting to its conclusions.

Veeck's caginess on the color line masked the preparatory steps he'd begun to take behind the scenes. In January 1947, he poached Bill Killefer, a baseball lifer, from the Dodgers in part to serve as the Indians' scout for the Negro Leagues. The following month, a Black man named Louis Jones marched unannounced into the Indians' offices and asked if he could assist the club. Jones was a Pittsburgh native who'd gained notoriety as the husband of singer Lena Horne, though the couple had divorced in 1944. Jones, Horne later wrote, "had two special strikes against him—he was a college man and he was a minister's son. Both led him to expect more of the world than it was prepared to give a Negro—any Negro—then."

Taken with Jones's assured manner, Veeck hired him as the Indians assistant director of public relations, making him the first Black executive in Major League Baseball. Among other duties, Jones was tasked with forging inroads with the city's Black civic leaders and communities, whose support Veeck believed would be crucial in defusing whatever racial tensions might arise should the Indians' roster become desegregated. There was an unfounded fear at the time, shared by Veeck and Branch Rickey alike, that exuberant enthusiasm among Black fans for whichever pioneering players broke the major-league color line could possibly enflame teams' traditionally white fan bases, resulting in a host of problems that, if unaddressed, might put the larger project of integration at risk. "If Jackie Robinson *does* come up to the Dodgers," Rickey told an audience of Black civic leaders in February 1947, "the biggest threat to his success—the *one* enemy most likely to ruin that success—is the Negro people themselves." Rickey as much as Veeck encouraged these leaders to preach a message of "self-policing" to Black fans attending games.

What's more, Veeck believed that Brooklyn, with its history of multicultural accommodation, seemed a far better setting than Cleveland for the integration process to unfold. But in reality, there was reason to believe that Cleveland was just as suitable a staging ground. Over the past few decades the city's Black population had shot up considerably, from roughly 8,400 residents in 1910 to more than 84,000 in 1940. While no official Jim Crow laws awaited the Southern Black migrants who sought greater freedom and opportunity along the smoky southern shores of Lake Erie, segregation and inequality persisted all the same. The Cuyahoga River, which split Cleveland in two, served as a de facto racial barrier; establishing residency west of its banks was a near impossibility for incoming Black families. A huge percentage ended up in the same place: sealed off in certain jam-packed East Side neighborhoods and restricted in the employment available to them.

The Second World War was a turning point. Black residents gained a greater foothold in expanded wartime industries and, more important, a platform for calling attention to the ongoing discrimination they faced. In 1945, the city council convened the Cleveland Community Relations Board, making Cleveland, according to *Ebony* magazine, "the first American city to promote inter-racial understanding with public funds." With the passage of the Fair Employment

Practices ordinance a few years later, the same board was granted the authority to investigate cases of work-related discrimination. Because of such strides forward, *Ebony* dubbed Cleveland at mid-century "the most democratic city in [the] U.S.," one that had "better race relations than any other big city in America."

As Black migrants from the South laid down roots in Cleveland, Black athletes blossomed there. Foremost among them was Jesse Owens, an Alabama transplant whose four gold medals in the 1936 Olympics in Berlin undercut the host country's belief in Aryan supremacy. Following in his footsteps was Harrison Dillard, a sprinter who would collect a total of four golds of his own in the 1948 and 1952 Olympics.

Since the early 1920s, the Negro Leagues had stumbled in their efforts to establish a Black baseball franchise in Cleveland, with a parade of clubs coming and going. But the arrival of the Buckeyes in 1942 heralded a new era. The team would split their games between various cities that first season before settling for good in Cleveland in 1943. Led by player-manager Quincy Trouppe and outfielder Sam Jethroe, the Cleveland Buckeyes would clinch the city's first Negro League World Series championship a mere two years later, in 1945. Improbably, the Buckeyes beat the Indians to integration when a white pitcher named Eddie Klep briefly donned their uniform in June 1946.

Months later, the Cleveland Browns of the newly formed All-America Football Conference charged onto the gridiron for their debut season with a pair of Black players, Marion Motley and Bill Willis, in tow. Far from being hampered by their integrated roster, the Browns romped to the championship while leading the league in attendance.

By the time the Indians returned to action in the spring of 1947, integration in Cleveland sports was no longer hypothetical. The Indians were the ones that lagged behind.

15

The Promise

In his autobiography, *I Never Had It Made,* Jackie Robinson wrote that in the weeks after he broke the major-league color line in April 1947, he often felt like "a black Don Quixote tilting at a lot of white windmills." The abuse nearly broke him. Bench jockeys demanded he go back to the cotton fields, the jungle, the bushes. Some hotels refused to accommodate him. Letters poured in with threats to him and his family. Players on the St. Louis Cardinals allegedly plotted to walk out of their first game against the Brooklyn Dodgers.

When he first signed Robinson, Branch Rickey had laid out a series of directives for the rookie to follow. Most important, Robinson was to hold his temper at all times, absorbing the blows without lashing out or fighting back. Pioneers like Robinson, sportswriter A. S. "Doc" Young later asserted, "had to walk a straight path, narrower than for any previous performer, and live as straight-laced as religious servants dressed in the cloth." His teammates, a few of whom had circulated a petition in spring training calling for his removal, were wary and distant at first. "In the clubhouse Robinson is a stranger," journalist Jimmy Cannon wrote in mid-May. "The Dodgers are polite and courteous with him but it is obvious he is isolated by those with whom he plays . . . He is the loneliest man I have ever seen in sports."

It didn't help that Robinson opened the season in a slump. But as the weather warmed, so did his bat. He raised his average by forty points in May, then by fifty in June. The kinetic and gutsy play that had won hearts and changed minds in Montreal came into view. Spurred on by Robinson, the Dodgers surged to the top of the National League standings in late June and never relinquished the lead. Everywhere he'd played—the minors, spring training, and now the majors—he'd excelled, which helped convince certain skeptical fans and teammates that Robinson had earned his spot in the league.

On May 3, as Robinson was fighting for his place in Brooklyn, the Newark Eagles opened their 1947 season against the New York Black Yankees in Stamford, Connecticut. On that cold, misty Saturday afternoon, the team picked up where it had left off. While Monte Irvin and Lennie Pearson clubbed two homers apiece, it was Larry Doby who stole the show. Setting a single-game Negro National League record, he lofted three balls beyond the outfield fence at Mitchell Field. The Eagles ran away with a 24-0 victory.

Twenty-three years old and fresh from a winter stint in Puerto Rico during which he'd batted .358 with fourteen home runs, Doby stood poised for a breakout summer. In the Eagles' first eight games he smashed seven home runs. His batting average was a preposterous .517. The Eagles, in turn, romped through the season's first month with what Effa Manley deemed "a vigor that fairly oozed confidence."

The threat of fans shifting their allegiance from the Eagles to an integrated major-league team nearby didn't deter the Manleys from pouring money into their club. In the off-season, they'd upgraded the team's rickety bus with a sleek Stratoliner, across whose sides was painted "Negro World Champions." Air-conditioned and roomy, the bus had set the Manleys back $15,000, which Effa Manley brushed off. "The personal health and comfort of my boys are my chief concern and I will leave no stone unturned in order to keep them happy," she told the *New York Amsterdam News*.

While attendance at Eagles games in Newark's Ruppert Stadium started out strong in 1947, it leveled off gradually as Jackie Robinson more and more commanded the attention of Black fans. As during the previous season, Dodgers scouts remained steadfast presences in the stands. Their interest in Doby, already strong, intensified as the temperature ticked up.

Soon, they had company.

On May 27, Bill Veeck placed a midnight call to Lou Boudreau. The Indians had just lost to the Tigers in Detroit, dropping them to fourth place in the American League with a 13-13 record. The 1947 season, not yet a quarter completed, was already slipping away.

Both men knew what was missing. Boudreau begged his boss for a hard-hitting outfielder; Veeck reportedly told him he was willing to "separate the club coffers from a very large bundle of currency to obtain the same." But being willing to spend wasn't all it took. If Veeck hadn't been able to land a premium outfielder during the winter, what chance did he have of doing so now, weeks before the major-league trading deadline?

Unbeknownst to Boudreau, Veeck wasn't looking only at the trade market. At some point in the off-season, he'd reached out to Ray Dandridge, a former third baseman for the Newark Eagles who now was burning up the Mexican League. But Dandridge, according to Veeck biographer Paul Dickson, was reluctant to sacrifice his stability and five-figure salary for the uncertainty of the Indians' offer. Veeck also reached out to Abe Saperstein along with a handful of Black sportswriters, Cleveland Jackson and Wendell Smith among them, for advice and guidance about which players in the Negro Leagues had the best futures in baseball. Like Rickey, Veeck hoped to desegregate his club with young players who had experience enough to handle the burdens of being racial pioneers but whose best seasons were still on the horizon.

Their search soon narrowed to Larry Doby. He seemed to possess everything that major-league executives were searching for in a Negro League player. He was a married war veteran who'd competed on integrated teams in high school and college, and he was demolishing Negro League pitching like no one else. The scouting report that Bill Killefer filed on Doby affirmed the choice: "[Doby] can play in this league . . . I don't know whether he belongs in the infield or the outfield, but he can play."

Brooklyn Dodgers scouts were slightly cooler on Doby. One argued that he "is a fine prospect but he hasn't learned where the strike zone is. He's two years away from the majors." Clyde Sukeforth, who'd scouted Doby the previous summer, would assert that there "are many excellent athletes in the Negro loops and Doby was one of the very best but the jump immediately to the majors is too great—almost unfair to the players themselves." Instead, as they'd done with Jackie Robinson, the Dodgers preferred to ship their signees to the minors to fine-tune their fundamentals and help them acclimate to all-white dugouts.*

Veeck favored a different tactic. "I'm not going to sign a Negro player and then send him to a farm club," he asserted to *The Pittsburgh Courier*. "I'm going to get one I think can play with Cleveland without having to go to the minors first. And, when I do find him he's going to join the club right away." Part of his rationale was practical. With the top clubs in the Indians' farm system spread through the South and in Baltimore, a city notoriously hostile to Black play-

---

* Eager for pitching reinforcements in late 1947, Branch Rickey would add Dan Bankhead directly from the Negro Leagues to the Dodgers' roster in late August. The following two seasons, Bankhead would be shipped to minor-league clubs in New Hampshire and Minnesota before spending his lone full season in the majors with Brooklyn in 1950.

ers, his options were limited. Veeck also believed that Jackie Robinson's protracted entry into the majors and the eighteen-month media storm it'd fomented had put "too much pressure" on him. More than anything, Veeck desired a pennant as soon as possible, and his vision for rapid-fire integration was wholly in keeping with his go-for-broke, whatever-works approach to achieving it.

"One afternoon when the team trots on the field," Veeck predicted, "a Negro player will be out there with them."

One night in June 1947, Roy Campanella rang Larry Doby. Since the season before, when he'd been the starting catcher for the Dodgers' Class-B farm club in Nashua, New Hampshire, Campanella had moved up to the Triple-A Montreal Royals. He was a step away from the major leagues, the lone Black player who could say as much—but not, he sensed, for long. Somewhere along the line, Campanella had caught wind that the Dodgers planned to sign Doby and send him to Montreal for seasoning. Over the phone, he told Doby that they could expect to become Royals teammates imminently.

Before they put forth an offer, however, Dodgers officials learned of the Indians' interest in Doby. For the first time, two major-league clubs were jockeying for the same player in the Negro Leagues. Rather than swooping in before the Indians could act, Branch Rickey backed off. He seemed to understand that as long as the Dodgers were the only major-league franchise that had crossed the color line, integration would remain precarious. But if another joined them—especially one in the American League—integration would inch closer to being an irreversible reality.

As Rickey told Wendell Smith, "It certainly would be good if some other club signed a Negro player. It would help us a lot. You know, there are a lot of people in baseball who haven't gotten over the fact that we went ahead and put Robinson on our club. If someone else signs a Negro player, we'll at least have some one on our side."

* * *

Late in June, Louis Jones, the Indians assistant director of public relations, paid Doby an unexpected visit in Paterson, New Jersey. The two, who had never met before, attended a Yankees game against the Indians in New York City on the 25th. Frank "Spec" Shea, a right-handed rookie, was pitching for the Yankees. Jones likely didn't know that Doby had rapped a double off Shea months earlier in Puerto Rico, where his winter team, the San Juan Senadores, had played an exhibition series against the Yankees. So when Jones asked Doby if he could play the kind of baseball they were watching, Doby didn't hesitate in responding: "There's nothing down there I can't do."

The following evening Jones traveled to Trenton to watch the Eagles clash with the Baltimore Elite Giants, a surging divisional rival. The Eagles racked up five quick runs in the first but then squandered their momentum and, eventually, the lead. Doby tallied three hits in the losing effort, which was presumably enough to satisfy Jones.

Before leaving, Jones pulled Doby aside and let him know that he'd likely be back in a week or so. There was reason for Doby to be skeptical. Ever since Jackie Robinson had signed with the Dodgers in late 1945, rumors had flown about numerous other Negro League players being on the verge of signing with this or that major-league organization, none of which had come to pass.

Jones, however, kept his word.

16

A New and Strange World

On July 1, 1947, the phone rang in the Eagles' team office in Newark. Days earlier, Abe Manley had warned his wife that the owner of the Cleveland Indians might call at any time, so it was hardly a surprise to Effa when she found herself in conversation with Bill Veeck.

Never one to indulge in small talk, Veeck cut right to the chase, asking Manley how much she expected in a deal for Larry Doby. This was a welcome question for someone who'd been so outspoken about the need for Negro League owners to be compensated for finding and cultivating their players. Veeck, for his part, had already told sportswriter Cleveland Jackson that, unlike Branch Rickey, he hoped to sign Black players through standard procedures, not by means of raids.

Before Manley could respond, Veeck put forth an offer of $10,000.

Manley fell silent. In her estimation, it was an insultingly low sum, and, true to form, she let him know as much. "Mr. Veeck, you know if Larry Doby were white and a free agent, you'd give him $100,000 to sign with you merely as a bonus." She paused to collect herself, then acknowledged that she had limited leverage in these negotiations.

While holding firm on $10,000, Veeck promised to wire an

additional $5,000 if Doby stuck with the Indians for more than thirty days. Before agreeing, Manley phoned her husband for his approval. Abe, upon hearing the figure, had the same knee-jerk reaction. "Oh, Effa, we can't let Doby go for that small amount of money. Besides, that would wreck our entire ball club. What about the morale of our other players when they hear that we've sold Doby to the major leagues?" Ultimately, mindful of the criticism that would blow their way should they let money block Doby's path, the Manleys chose to accept the offer.

That same day, the Eagles squared off against the Philadelphia Stars in Trenton. It was just another game for Doby, who knocked in three runs on as many hits, sparking his team to a 6-4 victory. He knew nothing of what had transpired between Veeck and the Manleys.

Rumors swirled regardless. The following evening, on July 2, the two clubs played again in Wilmington, Delaware. After the Stars beat the Eagles with a walk-off sacrifice fly, reporters chased down Doby and asked if they could expect to see him in an Indians uniform soon. "It may be," he answered uncertainly, "but I don't know until I get back to Newark."

That night, the Eagles' bus cut north through New Jersey. It was 5:30 in the morning on July 3 when Doby finally stumbled home to his Paterson residence and plopped into bed.

The ringing of the phone interrupted his much-needed sleep. Doby peeked at a nearby clock: a few minutes before seven. Irritated, he fumbled for the receiver. On the other end was Effa Manley. "Larry," she reportedly said, "you have been bought by the Cleveland Indians of the American League and you are to join the team in Chicago on Sunday."

Doby was speechless. Hanging up, he shuffled to the center of the bedroom, where he gazed at himself in a mirror. Except for a sock he'd absentmindedly pulled on, Doby, according to sportswriter Sam Lacy, "wore nothing more than what he had on when the family doctor slapped him."

He stood naked before the journey ahead of him.

As the press raced to Paterson to interview Doby, Veeck assembled his own group of reporters in Cleveland to announce the signing. The quotes that circulated in newspapers over the following days laid out Veeck's personal take on the milestone. "I don't think any man who has the ability should be barred from major league baseball on account of his color," Veeck declared. "The entrance of Negroes into both major leagues is not only inevitable . . . it is here." It was his belief that the war had "advanced us in regard to racial tolerance . . . I probably will catch hell for a while, but it is my hope it will work out." Amid these high-minded ideals, Veeck offered another, more pragmatic reason for nabbing Doby: "[Jackie] Robinson has proved to be a real big leaguer, so I wanted to get the best of the available Negro boys while the grabbing was good. Why wait?"

Originally, Veeck had intended for Doby to make his debut in Cleveland, but now that the word was out, he instructed Louis Jones to escort the Eagles star from Newark to Chicago, where the Indians would face the White Sox in a weekend series starting on July 5. In the meantime, Veeck convened an Indians team meeting. Aware of grumblings among some players, he didn't mince words, telling the Indians in no uncertain terms that Doby was going to be a star some day, so either they shut their mouths and go along with his plan, or they spend the rest of their careers on farm clubs.

Publicly, Boudreau supported the move. He issued a statement calling the acquisition "a routine baseball purchase," promising to give Doby every chance to "prove that he has the ability to make good with us." Privately, however, Boudreau harbored deep skepticism. He'd begged Veeck for help in the outfield, which Doby, a second baseman, presumably couldn't provide. Besides, Joe Gordon, Veeck's major off-season acquisition, had just been voted the starting second baseman in the upcoming All-Star Game, so there was little chance that Boudreau would bench a newly invigorated Gordon to give Doby playing time at second. It led the Indians manager to wonder if signing Doby was just another means of drawing fans during a season in which the Indians once again would fall well short of the postseason.

Boudreau was fighting for his managerial life as it was. His contract ran out at the end of the season; there was no guarantee another would be extended. He had three months to turn around a team that by then had sunk to fifth place and would now be dealing with something as novel and sensitive as integration.

On Independence Day, a boisterous holiday crowd, more than 4,000 strong, turned out for the afternoon doubleheader at Newark's Ruppert Stadium. Doby's mother, Etta, and his wife, Helyn, milled about the stands, as did Louis Jones, who'd ridden an overnight train from Cleveland.

Because the Newark Bears, the white minor-league affiliate of the New York Yankees, had decided to dress at Ruppert Stadium before departing for their own afternoon doubleheader in Jersey City, the Eagles players were forced to suit up elsewhere, then ride the team bus to their home turf. Soon after Doby stepped off the bus, photographers swarmed him. Stiff and uneasy, he squeezed the handle of his bat so tightly while posing that "his knuckles seemed to pop." Later, during fielding drills, Eagles manager Biz Mackey slapped one grounder after another his way. Racked with emotion, Doby booted some, bobbled others.

Before the opening pitch, Eagles players and civic leaders gathered at home plate for an impromptu ceremony. The gifts they presented to Doby were practical and heartfelt: a shaving kit, a travel case, a check for fifty dollars. Amid sustained applause, the public-address announcer reminded the crowd of an upcoming anti-lynching meeting in Newark.

The opening game was a runaway for the Eagles, punctuated by a moon-shot home run that Doby launched into the left-field stands in the sixth inning. It would have been a fitting farewell had he not followed it up by fumbling a ground ball in the eighth, then another in the ninth. Effa Manley had seen enough. "Larry's so nervous he's not himself," she reportedly muttered. "He has a train to make, so I'm sending word for him to get dressed."

As the second game got under way, Doby stepped sopping wet from the showers into a scrum of program-waving kids who'd snuck into the clubhouse for autographs. In between scribbling his name, he buttoned his gray sports shirt to the throat and slipped on a tan jacket with a folded handkerchief in the front pocket. Then he set off with a group of friends and family for Newark's Penn Station.

While Louis Jones bustled about the terminal, Doby took a seat on a wooden bench, flanked by Helyn and his mother. He spoke faintly to the assembled reporters, almost in a whisper, clasping and unclasping his hands all the while. At one point Doby turned to Helyn and murmured: "I feel—well, more than nervous. I feel almost like I was going into a new and strange world."

Four years before, when he was reporting for the Navy, Doby had waited at the same station for an overnight train to the same city. That journey had exposed him to racial prejudice like he'd never known before. And now here he was again, on the brink of another passage to somewhere far away and foreign. In the eyes of *New York Amsterdam News* columnist Dan Burley, Doby appeared in those moments before boarding the train stunned by "the strangeness of his position and deeply afflicted by the role he was so unexpectedly called upon to play . . . He seemed like a boy going off forever from all the things that had been familiar to him."

Away from the phone calls and photographers, Doby slept soundly for the first time in days. It was a quarter to eleven the next morning when the train screeched to a halt in Chicago's Union Station. Menacing gray clouds hung low over the steely skyline. In mere hours the Indians would square off against the White Sox. Doby hadn't even signed a contract yet. There was little time to waste.

A taxi whisked Doby and Jones to the Congress Hotel. There, Doby came face-to-face with the man who'd brought him to Chicago. As Doby would later tell interviewer William J. Marshall, the Indians owner stuck out his hand in greeting and said, "Lawrence, I'm Bill Veeck."

"Nice to meet you, Mr. Veeck," Doby responded.

Immediately Veeck shot back, "You don't have to call me Mr. Veeck. Call me Bill."

Doby was dumbfounded. Like any Black man who'd grown up in the South, he'd learned to refer to white elders by their last names, if not out of respect then out of fear of retaliation. But everything about Veeck was different: how he called Doby by his full name, how he sported an open-necked collared shirt with holes in the sleeves to such an historic occasion, how he looked his new recruit directly in the eyes with discernible sincerity.

Soon, they were speeding south toward Comiskey Park. From the taxi and in the hallways of the ballpark, Veeck gave Doby a rushed version of the directives Branch Rickey had laid out for Jackie Robinson: no arguing with umpires, not even to contest balls and strikes; no fighting or mouthing off to opposing players; and no associating with white women in the stands. Veeck concluded with a promise that stuck with the rookie through the turbulent times ahead: "We're in this together, kid."

The reassurance helped. "It made me relax a lot," Doby later stated.

In a cramped office at Comiskey Park, Doby signed the contract laid out before him while seemingly "half the news photographers in the Midwest" smashed together to snap pictures. Unlike the upbeat Veeck, Doby wore the apprehensive look of a human test subject. According to one reporter, "His voice was so low during an attempt at [an] interview that it was scarcely audible." At one point, trying to ease the tension, Veeck patted Doby on the back and said, "Just remember you're only another baseball player."

When the press conference ended, Jones and Marsh Samuel, the Indians publicity director, guided Doby down into the clubhouse, where the Indians players, fully suited up, sat in front of their lockers, waiting. Gordon Cobbledick later claimed that as soon as Doby appeared, "an electric tension charged the steaming air. The wordless hostility seemed to crackle and spark. No one spoke a tentative 'Hello.' No one said, 'Relax, kid, you're all tightened up.'" Some cast their gazes to the floor, others watched as Doby threaded his way through the stuffy room, not making eye contact with anyone. "Not even the scuffle of a solitary spike on the bottom of a shoe broke the horrible, tomblike muteness," Franklin Lewis wrote.

Boudreau instructed Doby to change into the uniform that trainer Lefty Weisman had set aside for him. Then Doby huddled with his new manager for a quick rundown of the team signs, just enough to get him through the afternoon game. As seemingly bewildered as everyone else, Boudreau peppered Doby with a series of elementary questions: What positions could he play? Where did he think he could help the Indians? What style of baseball did they play in the Negro Leagues? Afterward, he escorted Doby around the clubhouse, introducing him to his lined-up teammates. Some, like Joe Gordon, Bob Lemon, and Jim Hegan, gripped Doby's hand in welcome; others barely clasped it at all. A few refused to shake his hand altogether.

There was little time to dwell on the frosty reception. The game would start soon, and the players hustled onto the diamond, where groundskeepers were rolling up the tarpaulin blanketing the soggy infield. Doby was the last to emerge, and the spectators, a significant portion of whom were Black, began applauding upon their first glimpse of him. "With each step the chorus swelled until, as [Doby] approached the first base dugout, it had attained the proportions of an ovation," Cobbledick reported. With batting practice canceled because of the rain, Indians players instead doubled up to toss baseballs back and forth. Doby waited for a partner. One minute passed, then another. No one glanced his way.

Over the past three hours, he'd met scores of people, shaken dozens of hands, and had his picture snapped hundreds of times. Now, Doby stood before 15,000 fans in a major-league ballpark, yet he felt all alone. The humiliation was swift and public, much as his introduction to military life had been years earlier. Both were new, devastating experiences for him, ones Doby couldn't put into perspective in the moment. All he could process was the pain.

Finally, after several minutes Joe Gordon tossed Doby a baseball. A while later, he took infield practice alongside Gordon at second base, appearing "stiff and not sure of himself on ground balls" to some reporters. Boudreau watched him intently during these drills. He hadn't penciled the newly arrived rookie into the starting lineup that afternoon, instead waiting to see if an opportunity might arise over the course of the game.

It was another lackluster effort from the Indians, who scratched out three hits over six innings while falling behind 5-1. Then, in the seventh, the stirrings of a rally started. The first two Indians batters walked, the next grounded out to the shortstop. Bryan Stephens, a pitcher with one career major-league hit to his name, was due up next. Realizing a change was needed for the Indians to have any shot at victory, Boudreau hollered for Doby to grab a bat.

Once again, the crowd cheered as Doby emerged from the dugout. "It took but a few short minutes [for Doby] to walk up to that plate," wrote Cleveland Jackson. "But for 13 million American Negroes that simple action was the successful climax of a long uphill fight whose annals are like the saga of the race." As Doby assumed his usual stiff stance, his teeth were chattering. "I didn't hear a sound," he later recalled. "It was like I was dreaming."

Earl Harrist, a husky reliever from rural Louisiana, hurled

his first pitch over the plate, and Doby, swinging with everything he had, lunged fruitlessly at the ball. Harrist then tried to sneak a similar offering past him, but this time Doby connected, drilling a line drive that streaked "like a bullet" past the third-base umpire, landing mere inches outside the foul line. Harrist was officially on notice: Doby may have been green and nervous, but he was no push-over. Cautiously, Harrist tossed the next two pitches low. With the count even, he pressed his luck with another fastball, and Doby, eager to make contact, swung straight through it.

Despite the strikeout, it was far from a disastrous debut. His swing was wild and his plate discipline suspect, but the foul, so close to being a stand-up double, hinted at his potential.

After the game, the Indians players decamped for the Del Prado Hotel—all except Doby. He and Jones were driven to separate accommodations at the DuSable Hotel, a storied Black institution on the city's South Side. Having not eaten since breakfast on the train, Doby joined Jones and sportswriters Cleveland Jackson and Fay Young for dinner at the nearby Palm Tavern, another Black establishment.

Afterward, Doby reflected on his first day in the majors. He told interviewer William J. Marshall years later that the Indians players who'd refused to shake his hand in the clubhouse "didn't bother me at the moment because I don't think I was thinking too much about it. I was somewhat wrapped up in the game itself in terms of being able to play." It was only once he returned to his hotel and sat there by himself that "it dawned on me that that kind of situation had happened."

For two years Doby had spent numerous summer nights on the road with his Eagles teammates, taking the edge off whatever miscues and strikeouts had occurred during that day's game through their companionship. But there were no players to talk to that evening, no one to help him process everything that he'd been through over the past twenty-four hours.

The lights went out across Chicago. Larry Doby was alone.

17

Closed Ranks

Rain fell hard in Chicago all night. When Doby awoke on July 6, the skies were smudged charcoal. It was only after he arrived at Comiskey Park hours later that the sun broke through the gloom.

Across the city's South Side, pastors rushed through their Sunday services so that worshippers could make their way to the ballpark in time to watch Doby warm up before that afternoon's doubleheader between the Indians and the White Sox. They had no idea whether he would see any action, and for that matter, neither did Doby.

He didn't play in the first game, but before the next, Boudreau opted to test him out at first base, a position Doby hadn't manned since high school. It was a decision that would haunt Doby for the rest of the season.

In 1947, the Indians sported a pair of sturdy but unestablished Texans, Les Fleming and Eddie Robinson, both of whom were auditioning for the role of starting first baseman. Boudreau had opened the season with Robinson at first base only to bench him for Fleming two games in. Robinson cracked the lineup again in mid-May but then found himself riding the pine once more in mid-June. His confidence plummeted alongside his batting average. Finally, in early July, Robinson marched into the manager's office to plead his case. "Don't worry about it," Boudreau assured him. "You're my first baseman, and you're going to be our first baseman for the future." Robinson's life story had already rendered him a sympathetic figure in the Indians' clubhouse. In 1946, while beating out Jackie Robinson for Most Valuable Player in the International League as a member of the Triple-A Baltimore Orioles, he'd overcome career-threatening nerve damage to his right leg and suffered through the death of his two-year-old daughter from a terminal brain tumor. Heartened by his pep talk with Boudreau, Eddie Robinson knocked two pitches over the fences on the Fourth of July.

One day later, Doby would step into the Indians' clubhouse in Chicago. He was an infielder with seemingly nowhere to break in. Shortstop Lou Boudreau and second baseman Joe Gordon constituted perhaps the best double-play combination in baseball. Ken Keltner was a six-time all-star who'd patrolled third base for the Indians for nearly a decade. As urgently as the team needed outfield reinforcements, Doby had minimal experience there. Only at first base, it seemed, could the Indians test out their newest member.

For Eddie Robinson, who'd spent five years in the minors and three in the Navy and now was hanging on in the majors by his fingernails, Doby's sudden appearance registered as an acute danger. For many struggling major leaguers, integration triggered historically rooted fears and prejudices that equality for Black players would lead to a loss of jobs and standing for white players. In Robinson's mind it boiled down to this: "Well, we're going to get Black players, and some of us are going to lose our jobs." At that time, there were more than twelve thousand men playing professional baseball, only about four hundred of whom were in the major leagues, nearly all on one-year contracts. Unestablished players who'd clawed their way up feared they were one batting slump or roster change away from being cast back to the minors, playing for scraps in wooden stadiums linked by bus routes.

While Robinson would later insist that his misgivings about

Doby's arrival in Cleveland were based solely on playing time, integration also forced him and his teammates to grapple with numerous other factors. As he stated nearly seven decades later, "I'm a Texan boy and I was raised in the South. And I can say that none of the guys were too happy to have the first black player [in the American League] on the team." Robinson reportedly told Boudreau that he worried about adverse reactions from his neighbors in Baltimore, where he resided in the off-season.

His concern was common, especially among white Southern ballplayers. Monte Irvin later told author Anthony J. Connor that even those players "who might've wanted to be friendly had to be careful or they'd be criticized as 'nigger-lovers' by the folks back home." For others, it came down to prejudice. "We were Southerners who had never lived or played with Negroes, and we didn't see any reason to start then," wrote Kirby Higbe, a starting pitcher for the Brooklyn Dodgers who'd demanded a trade when Jackie Robinson joined the team.

Even players from Northern states who supported or were indifferent to integration had to take their teammates' reactions into consideration. Indians catcher Jim Hegan, a Massachusetts native, said that for many of those who hailed from the North, integration "didn't make any difference. But you didn't know if you were going to hurt the feelings of the fellas from the south, who were your friends at the time, if you went over and welcomed Larry [Doby] too strongly."

As Bill Greason, a Black pitcher who played for the St. Louis Cardinals in 1954, explained decades afterward: "Any white guy who might have wanted to be friendly to a black ballplayer was in a spot; he had to worry about being ostracized by his own."

Upon learning that Doby would replace him at first base in the second game of the doubleheader against the White Sox, Eddie Robinson chipped some mud off his spikes but said nothing. When Harold "Spud" Goldstein, the Indians traveling secretary, approached him to ask if Doby could borrow his first baseman's mitt, Robinson flatly refused. After some prodding, Robinson finally surrendered his glove—and then announced he was quitting the club. Earlier, he'd sought out Les Fleming and suggested that they both walk off the team in protest. Fleming, five years older than Robinson, wasn't tempted. "You can quit," he said, "but I ain't."

As the game started, Robinson sat alone in the clubhouse, half-dressed, crying despite himself. Sometime in the early innings, Bill McKechnie wandered down from the dugout. Silver-haired and bespectacled, McKechnie looked more like a scholar than a former manager who'd twice steered his clubs to World Series championships. In the off-season, Veeck had signed the sixty-year-old McKechnie, known as "Deacon" for his ability to restore faith in ballplayers who'd lost their way, to the richest coaching contract in baseball to assist Boudreau in precisely this type of situation.

McKechnie came right to the point: "I understand why you quit, and your teammates understand as well," McKechnie said according to Robinson's recollections. "But the public isn't going to understand it that way. They're going to say you didn't want Doby to play because he's black. I think you're making a big mistake, and I don't want to see you play the rest of your career with that stigma on you."

After McKechnie left, Robinson mulled over his words, then changed back into his uniform. Boudreau said nothing when Robinson stepped into the dugout in the sixth inning. As he walked by, several teammates patted him on the back.

The incident fizzled out in a matter of hours, with no consequences for Robinson. Doby, however, would feel its aftereffects for the remainder of the season.

In the following days, players and sportswriters closed ranks around Eddie Robinson. "The unfortunate aspect of Boudreau's first inspection of his newest player (Doby)," Gordon Cobbledick wrote, "was the fact that to use him he had to bench Eddie Robinson, who must be about ready to believe that the cards are stacked against him in base-ball and in life." Ed McAuley reported that some players were upset that Doby had been introduced "at the expense of Eddie Robinson," regarding Veeck's new acquisition "as a publicity stunt for which the prospects of some other members of the squad will be sacrificed."

It didn't help that during the broadcast of the doubleheader, an announcer had stated that Veeck planned to hire another player from the Negro Leagues to keep Doby company. The studio and switch-board soon were bombarded with callers demanding to know why "a big league baseball player needed any other company than the team-mates already on the list." Reports trickled in that Indians scouts had trained their sights on Sam Jethroe, a speedy center fielder for the Cleveland Buckeyes. Jethroe, the *Cleveland Press* predicted, "likely will be in major league baseball before the week is out." There had been room on the Indians' roster for Veeck to add Doby without de-moting anyone, but if Jethroe were signed, someone would be sent down. The very thought of it, columnist Jim Schlemmer of the *Akron Beacon Journal* asserted, had players "snorting and claiming they are being discriminated against, and some of them are threatening every-thing from refusal to play *with* Doby to refusal to play *for* the Indians."

At the Major League All-Star Game a few days later, one par-ticipant anonymously gave voice to the fears and biases rippling through clubhouses across the league: "The Negroes holler 'dis-crimination.' Well, [Jackie] Robinson moves right into the National League after only one year in the AAA minors, and Doby gets a job in the American League without previous schooling in white base-ball. I fought my way through the minors for five years. I rode buses all night for three of those five years, so that I could get a chance in the majors. If we are to have Negroes in the majors, let them go through the long preparation the white player is forced to un-dergo. Let us not discriminate against the white player because he is white." Pointing out that Doby had endured similar trials in the Ne-gro Leagues, and that he'd been barred from the same preparation as white players not because of ability but because of a segregated system, likely would've meant little to those who believed the Negro Leagues to be inferior to the minors.

Boudreau found himself in a tough spot. Despite Eddie Robinson's outburst, Doby's first start had been encouraging. He'd legged out a run-scoring single—his first hit in the majors—while fielding his unfamiliar position flawlessly. "[Doby's] going to get his chance to prove what he can do," Boudreau had told reporters afterward. "No, this doesn't mean he's our first string first baseman. Let's say he will share the work there." But by the time Boudreau returned to Cleveland, two days after competing in the All-Star Game, he was spouting a new line. "I intended to play [Doby] on first base tonight [July 10], but I don't believe I will," he said. "However, he will be among the first line of pinch-hitters, or runners, and might play a few innings."

For his part, Veeck had expressed misgivings with Boudreau's handling of Doby in Chicago. "We don't like to take the boy right off the train and stick [him] right in the lineup," he said. "It's not fair to him because he probably is very nervous and if he doesn't get three for five in his first game, he'll be a bum. We don't want to hurt his chances." It was later revealed that Boudreau and Veeck jointly decided to slow Doby's transition, believing that his skills were ultimately better suited to the outfield. But on some level they also must have intuited the backlash that continuing to start Doby at first base might trigger. "You would have to be an idiot to overlook the animosity among the Indians toward Doby," columnist Franklin Lewis asserted. And the Indians' brass, most assuredly, were not idiots.

Doby never played at first base again that season. Nor did he start another game.

In Cleveland, Doby lodged in the Majestic Hotel, a Black-owned institution which served as a hub of the city's Black political and social life as well as a haven for travelers and visiting performers. His welcoming party consisted of several prominent athletes and community figures, including members of the Cleveland Buckeyes and Marion Motley and Bill Willis of the Browns. Even with this positive reception, Doby confided to his wife during their nightly phone calls that amid the stress, isolation, and rancor of his first week, he'd shed seven pounds.

Having a fellow Black teammate might have eased Doby's burden, but whatever plans the Indians once had for signing Sam Jethroe stalled, perhaps out of fear of further dissension. In late July, Veeck claimed his scouts had informed him that there "aren't a half-dozen promising players in the Negro leagues." As a result, he saw "no possibility of a large-scale migration of Negro League players into the majors" until another generation had passed. In the weeks after Doby's debut, Veeck himself had to contend with the blowback. He received thousands of letters from disgruntled fans, many with racist sentiments. One package contained mounds of human feces. Rather than stuffing them in the trash, Veeck responded to nearly all of them.

At the same time, Veeck was dealing with an equally pressing issue. After his amputation, the Indians owner didn't give himself time to recover. During the season's first few months, he'd taken to joining the Indians for batting practice before games at the lakefront stadium. Often shirtless, he'd swat balls clear to the warning track or challenge players to footraces, surprising them with how swiftly he could barrel across the field on his prosthetic limb.

The endless activity aggravated his still-tender leg. Doctors soon informed him that another two inches would need to be shaved off. On July 24, nineteen days after signing Doby, Veeck once again was wheeled into an operating room at the Cleveland Clinic. "I've got no one but myself to blame for this," he remarked. "When I get out of here this time I'll be a good boy."

It wasn't until the end of August that the clinic cleared Veeck for release. "This one was rougher than the first, and they're not going to get me back," he vowed afterward. "No dances, no foolishness and no leg for about two months."

* * *

Of all his teammates, it might have been reasonable to assume that Bob Feller would have most empathized with Doby's plight. Like Doby, Feller had never played an inning of minor-league baseball, skipping straight to the Indians' roster. He'd been his own kind of curiosity: an unknown adolescent among men.

But Feller had been lauded for his potential and given time to work through his mechanical flaws on the mound. Perhaps because of his personal narrative of acceptance, or perhaps because of his own skepticism about Black players' readiness for the major leagues, there was no indication that Feller made a concerted effort to help Doby navigate his uncertain situation. "Feller was sort of in his own world," Doby would state decades later, "really only concerned with what affected Bob." Feller himself admitted as much. "I paid very little attention," he said about Doby's introduction to the Indians. "Shook hands, said hello, welcome to the wigwam or some comment such as that and went about my own business."

In 1947, Feller was preoccupied with thorny problems of his own, an injury foremost among them. On June 13, during a start against the Philadelphia Athletics, he logged two strikeouts in the opening inning, then struck out the side in each of the next two frames. To Indians coach Oscar "Ski" Melillo, Athletics batters that night "looked as if they were swinging at a flea." Twenty strikeouts, a previously unthinkable number for a single game, seemed within reach.

Leading off the fourth inning was left fielder Barney McCosky. Feller fired two quick strikes past him. Unexpectedly, catcher Jim Hegan signaled for a curve. As Feller strode forward in his delivery, his left foot landed in a patch of loose dirt he'd kicked up from throwing so many fastballs. Losing his balance, Feller tumbled headlong down the mound, breaking the fall with his knees and pitching hand. For a minute or so he lay there on his back, then he stubbornly got up, tossed a few warm-up pitches, and announced he was all right. But he wasn't.

It was later discovered that Feller had torn a muscle in his right shoulder, wrenched his left knee, and cracked one of his ribs. The injuries dogged him all season. While completing his pitching motion, he often felt tiny "ice pick stabs" ripple across his body. Years later, Feller would claim he was never the same pitcher again. "If I lost it on any one day," Feller stated, "that was it."

In addition to his injury, Feller was contending with a building fan backlash in Cleveland. It'd been apparent as early as May 23, when Feller had surrendered three runs (two earned) in two innings to the lowly St. Louis Browns. "The All-American Boy got himself booed last night in the smog within Soot Stadium," columnist Franklin Lewis wrote afterward, adding: "The All-American Boy has been throwing a few home run balls of late and the habit is not being excused by local audiences."

The boos—strange sounds during a Feller outing—were evidence of the sharper, less forgiving stance Indians fans took toward the team's ace that season. Some of it had to do with Feller's on-field performance, which was nowhere near as spectacular as in 1946. True, his name continued to top the leaderboard in wins and strikeouts, but statistics didn't tell the entire story. He just didn't look the same. His signature pitch no longer sent an awed hum through the stands. Especially after the injury, one writer opined that Feller "seemed to be protecting his speed as though there were just so many fast balls in his muscular arm and he was not going to squander them uselessly." Even in games Feller won, mild disappointment hung in the air, as if the "pitching superman" the crowd expected to see had been "reduced to the status of just a human being."

Such a transformation might have been easier to swallow had Feller been less ubiquitous off the field. But he was inescapable: in the papers, on the airwaves, on magazine racks and bookstore shelves. His autobiography, *Strikeout Story,* had been published in May with an initial print run of 50,000 copies, reportedly the largest ever for a sports book. Days before its release, during an afternoon game in Cleveland, two planes with rear banners advertising the book circled over the stadium for several innings. On the road Feller staged book signings during the day and negotiated with Hollywood studios for the movie rights to his life story at night. Fans could also read Feller's more immediate musings in his syndicated newspaper column and listen to his voice on *Baseball Today,* the weekly radio program he hosted.

So long as Feller had been mowing down batters, his business ventures had been accepted. As the losses piled up, however, a new narrative began to take hold. Some fans felt that the outside activities were distracting him from pitching, that his priorities were backward, his mind unfocused, his values corrupted. "Feller is all out for Feller first and the Indians second," one fan wrote to the *Cleveland News* in August. "True, he works plenty hard, but just as much for the furtherance of Ro-Fel, Inc., as for the Indians."

It was barnstorming that brought the anger to a boil. For two years, baseball executives had stood by while Feller transformed barnstorming into a lucrative, cutting-edge enterprise. Now, alarmed by the hurler's mounting fiscal independence and by the fear of competing for fans and players in October, they sought to rebalance the scales. In July, major-league owners voted to prohibit tours from starting until after the World Series had concluded. Players would then have thirty days to hit the circuit.

The delayed starting time infuriated Feller. "This is a democracy, isn't it?" he fumed. "We fought a war to keep this country democratic and then somebody comes along and tells a ball player how, when and where he can earn his money playing ball." His rage only intensified when the commissioner's office barred Feller from pitching in the Cuban Winter League as part of the new tour he was planning. Feeling stifled and singled out, Feller complained for weeks about the "discrimination" he faced from the baseball establishment.

It was a bridge too far for some Indians fans. They could no longer turn a blind eye to their star's perceived moneymaking fervor.

Those who believed Feller had tuckered himself out during the previous year's airborne extravaganza were dismayed at his calls for unrestricted barnstorming. Gordon Cobbledick lamented Feller's "loose-lip habit that imperils him to say things that were better left unsaid. His personal public relations are atrocious. He has exerted no effort to make friends." The boos that once had trickled from the rafters now poured down like a flood. One season after captivating Cleveland with his assault on the strikeout record, Feller found himself the unlikely "target of a city-wide bombardment of criticism and abuse."

In mid-August, Bill Veeck arranged a meeting with his beleaguered ace. Despite being cooped up in the Cleveland Clinic, the Indians owner was attuned to the mood on the streets. As he told reporters, "You can walk into any building in town and ask the first 20 people you meet: 'What's wrong with Feller?' Every one of them will say, 'He's worried about making money in October when he should be concerned about winning games right now.' Now, that diagnosis may be wrong. It may be unfair. But it's what people think."

From his hospital bed, Veeck centered their discussion not on whether Feller should curtail his off-field activities but on his being more sensitive to how the public perceived them. It was becoming clear that, in many fans' minds, the earnest country flamethrower enshrined in Feller's just-published autobiography was being replaced by a cold corporate entity, greedy and self-absorbed. It hardly mattered that Feller's on-field decline—despite his injury, he led the American League once again in 1947 in wins, strikeouts, and total innings—had been exaggerated. The moment he lost control of his personal narrative was the moment his grip on the baseball-minded public started to loosen.

Veeck could counsel Feller from his hospital bed, but he couldn't be around the club to ease Doby's transition in late July and August. During that crucial period, with his foremost supporter physically absent, loneliness hung like a weighted stone around Doby's neck, causing him to sink further and further into himself.

Sometimes, late at night, Doby would call Jackie Robinson. The two talked about the challenges of keeping their cool while being bombarded with racist invective. "Jackie got all the publicity for putting up with it (racial slurs)," Doby later stated. "But it was the same thing I had to deal with. He was first, but the crap I took was just as bad. Nobody said, 'We're gonna be nice to the second Black.'" Through these candid conversations, Doby felt, the two "kept each other from giving up."

Robinson recognized the importance of Doby's signing. "I'm glad to know that another Negro player is in the majors," he wrote. "I'm no longer in there by myself. I no longer will have the feeling that if I don't make good it will kill the chances of other Negro players."

Even so, their situations differed in key ways. At twenty-eight, Robinson was five years older than Doby. He'd been in the national spotlight since his football years at UCLA. There'd been an eighteen-month buildup from his signing to his debut at Ebbets Field. Doby, in contrast, was unknown to nearly everyone in white baseball. He'd journeyed literally overnight from the Negro Leagues to the majors. Whereas Robinson became an immediate staple of the Dodgers' lineup, Doby turned into what Wendell Smith called a "two o'clock player," someone who took batting practice in mid-afternoon and then "returned to the dungeon we sometimes call a dugout." By playing, Robinson gained the begrudging respect of the white baseball establishment; by sitting, Doby raised doubts about the readiness of everyone else in the Negro Leagues.

In some ways, the bench was territory more foreign to Doby than an all-white clubhouse, which he'd known in high school. "What I want more than anything else right now . . . is to convince myself that I can hit this big league pitching," Doby told *The Washington Post* in late July 1947. But he couldn't do that if he saw it so infrequently. In his first two days with the Indians, Doby had come to bat five times; over the season's remaining three months, he would log just twenty-eight more plate appearances. Unable to concentrate or settle into a groove, Doby pressed at the plate. "I was a frightened, lonely kid and I missed wild swings at pitches I couldn't have reached with a ten-foot pole," he later recalled. *The Baltimore Afro-American* reported that Doby's "failure to hit in the pinch-hitter roles has him down in the dumps, and he admits that he longs for the Newark Eagles."

In late July, Boudreau stationed Doby in the outfield during warm-ups but never explained his rationale for doing so. In fact, following the All-Star break, the Indians manager seldom said anything to Doby beyond "Hello, Larry." With reporters, too, Boudreau kept his lips pursed, changing the subject whenever questions arose about his plans for the rookie. In Doby's eyes, Boudreau exerted minimal effort in helping him feel accepted. "There was really no reason for me to be so isolated," Doby stated five decades later. "I think that if you're managing a ball club, you're supposed to know your people. I think if you're the manager, you should be making your people comfortable."

At first, Louis Jones accompanied Doby when the team was on the road, but his presence irked some players. Since rooming with a white player was neither practical nor socially accepted at the time, for the final two months Doby bunked by himself, sometimes at the same hotel as everyone else, other times at segregated establishments.

Not everyone on the Indians was standoffish. On Doby's first train ride with the team, Joe Gordon had saddled into the empty seat next to him for a chat. A man of many talents—he was a pilot, a musician, an acrobat, an outdoorsman—Gordon, at thirty-two, was secure enough to befriend Doby without reservation. "Gordon would always sit with me [in the dugout] and we'd talk baseball," Doby remembered. "That was all I knew and all he knew. We talked like any white players." Bob Lemon, Jim Hegan, and Bill McKechnie also were supportive.

Regardless, as the summer waned, Doby continued to feel his separation everywhere: in batting practice, where players excluded him from impromptu chitchat; in the dugout, where teammates staged what sportswriter A. S. "Doc" Young called "an iceberg act, allowing him more space on the bench than any player in the history of the game"; in opposing ballparks, where fans and bench jockeys hurled every racial slur imaginable his way. "My biggest adjustment was learning how to live with [white people] all over again," Doby said in a 1960 talk with *Sport* magazine. "Now, I'd meet you," Doby continued, "and you'd say to me, 'Larry, I'm not anti. I'm for you a hundred percent.' But I've got to wonder, and I'd say to myself, 'Does this guy really mean it?' . . . So I'd go back to the hotel room at night and I'd keep saying to myself, 'Is he, or isn't he?' And then I had to go out and play baseball the next day. A lot of my baseball was left right back there in the room at night, thinking to myself, 'What's wrong with me? Why am I different? Why can't they accept me like anybody else?' This never occurred to me until you people made it occur. You made me sensitive to this type of skin."

After the Indians' final game of the season, on September 28, Doby stopped by coach Bill McKechnie's locker. The two had forged a tentative bond that summer. McKechnie's soothing, broad-minded manner had put the guarded rookie at ease. While McKechnie recognized Doby's potential, few others had. In his three months in the majors, Doby had logged just five hits for a piddling .156 average. He'd looked anxious at the plate, unsteady in the field. "The guy'll never be a ball player," fans across Cleveland concluded.

Fully prepared to hear that he was being released at the end of the season, Doby asked his coach: "Will you tell me frankly, Mr. McKechnie, whether you think I have a chance to become a major league ball player?"

McKechnie answered bluntly but kindly. "Larry, you have a fine chance, but you'll have to get rid of some bad habits you picked up in Newark. That wild, desperation swing at any pitch near the plate may have been a crowd pleaser there, but it won't help you in the majors. You have youth, a strong arm, speed, power, and quick reactions . . . However, I don't believe you can make the grade at second base. Your best bet is the outfield, where you can capitalize on your speed." Even with McKechnie's encouragement, there was still no guarantee that Doby would wind up back on the Indians the next season.

While it's unknown if Doby spoke with Veeck before departing for the off-season, the Indians owner would concede weeks later that his integration strategy had been unsound. "Rickey was smarter than I was on that," Veeck said. "I tried to bring [Doby] along too fast." The dispiriting results led him to conclude that the gap between the Negro and the major leagues was wider than he'd assumed.

After Doby joined the Indians, three more Black players came to the majors in 1947. Joining Jackie Robinson in Brooklyn in late August had been Dan Bankhead, a pitcher from the Memphis Red Sox of the Negro American League, who'd yielded eight runs in the ten innings he threw for the Dodgers. Following Veeck's lead, and hoping to boost attendance, the St. Louis Browns had added two players directly to their roster from the Kansas City Monarchs, Hank Thompson and Willard Brown, only to release them before the season's end. A pattern was established: If Black players didn't excel right away, they were exiled to the bench or cut loose altogether. Only Jackie Robinson had flourished, winning the inaugural Rookie of the Year award while spurring the Dodgers to within one game of a World Series championship.

That off-season, no major-league owner, Veeck and Rickey included, signed any players from the Negro Leagues. It seemed that as long as Jackie Robinson appeared singular in the eyes of the white baseball establishment, the larger project of integration would remain precarious, vulnerable, by no means a settled matter.

18

Fever

On September 28, the same day that Doby asked McKechnie about his future, Bill Veeck and Lou Boudreau huddled in the owner's office at Cleveland's Municipal Stadium.

Over the past few months, as the Indians stagnated, Boudreau had felt the uncertainty of his future weighing like "an actual physical burden" upon his shoulders. So desperate was Boudreau to elevate the team's standing that, in late July, he wrested the pitch-calling duties away from catcher Jim Hegan, flashing signals from his position at shortstop for Hegan to relay to the mound. It was a strategy that pleased no one. The pitching staff grumbled; Hegan groused that Boudreau had made him "appear dumb" to bolster his own chances of remaining at the team helm; and Veeck, far from being impressed, frowned on Boudreau's player management.

On the season's last day, the tension erupted to the surface. According to one account, Veeck offered Boudreau $50,000 to cede his managerial post and stick to shortstopping. Boudreau stubbornly insisted that if he couldn't manage, he wouldn't play. Harsh words passed between them, some of "a most personal nature," Franklin Lewis reported. Finally, Boudreau stormed out, his fate undecided.

The Indians dropped the game 1-0 to the Detroit Tigers. Hurrying to his office at the far end of the clubhouse afterward, Boudreau tore off his uniform and scattered his socks and jersey about the floor. Forgoing a shower, he changed into his street clothes and then whisked the scattered books and papers off his desk. Reporters who stopped by later for a chat found his normally tidy office deserted and in shambles.

Halfway between Yankee Stadium in the Bronx and Ebbets Field in Brooklyn was Toots Shor's Restaurant in midtown Manhattan, a watering hole for the athletically inclined that had established itself as the heart of New York City's buzzy, boozy sports scene. During the 1947 World Series, an interborough clash between the Yankees and Dodgers, members of the baseball establishment, everyone from executives to reporters, attended games in the afternoon and then hopped taxis or subways bound for Toots Shor's afterward. Shor, a thickset bouncer-turned-saloonkeeper who believed jocks and those associated with them were "a naturally superior class of men," would slap his guests on the back as they strutted in, affectionately referring to the most distinguished among them as "crumbums."

Normally, Veeck, no stranger to Toots Shor's, would have been in the thick of the World Series revelry, but more pressing matters occupied his mind. One night, amid the postgame hubbub, Veeck cornered each Cleveland sportswriter to solicit opinions on a secretive plot—a trade with the St. Louis Browns that hinged on a shortstop swap: Boudreau for Vern Stephens, a three-time all-star presumably with no aspirations to manage. Veeck wanted to know if he could pull off such a trade without provoking unrest in Cleveland.

The answer, Veeck soon learned, was no. After details leaked in a Chicago newspaper, Cleveland writers decided to break their silence collectively. BOUDREAU THROUGH WITH INDIANS blared the front page of the *Cleveland News* on October 3, 1947, somewhat prematurely, since Veeck's negotiations with the Browns were ongoing. Nevertheless, the news shot across northern Ohio in a flash. In every corner of Cleveland, from living rooms to hospital wards, dive bars to high-end clubs, irate fans whipped themselves into a mutinous fury. Public opinion against Veeck, one writer later asserted, "was aroused more feverishly than it had been by any event since the enactment of Prohibition."

The first telegram to reach Veeck in New York City was sent by a minister. It read: "If Boudreau doesn't return to Cleveland, don't you bother to return either." An unbroken string of callers, less restrained by their vocations, soon tied up the phone line in his hotel room, fuming at the thought of exiling their beloved shortstop to the baseball limbo known as the Browns. As columnist Ed McAuley argued, if Veeck were to trade Bob Feller, "he might stab some of the [Indians] fans in their judgments. If he trades Boudreau, he will stab many of the fans in their hearts."

For the first time since he'd limped into Cleveland, the tide was turning against Veeck. The Indians' faithful had gone along with fireworks and integration and everything else the youthful owner had proposed, but now a line had been crossed. Veeck found himself in a position similar to the one Feller had faced that season. He'd failed to anticipate the public reaction to his business dealings, and as a result, according to columnist Franklin Lewis, "all the good he had compiled in more than a year of wooing the Ohio citizenry" was in danger of becoming undone.

As the wires and calls accumulated, Veeck took stock of his transgression. He discussed the matter with his friend Alvin "Bud" Silverman, a political reporter for *The Plain Dealer*, who convinced Veeck that the optics of remaining in New York City, flitting back and forth between World Series games and Toots Shor's, were terrible. If Veeck hoped to stop the fan uprising in its tracks, he would need to fly back to Cleveland as soon as possible.

* * *

On October 4, the day after the Boudreau news broke, Veeck and
Silverman sat through six frames of the fifth game of the World Series and then hopped into a cab idling outside Ebbets Field. It was,
Silverman claimed, the first time that Veeck had ever left a baseball
game early, and he couldn't stand not knowing the outcome. Rolling down his window, Veeck hollered "What's happening now?" to
anyone who appeared to be listening to the radio along the way to
the airport.

Their flight landed in Cleveland around eight. As the plane tax-
ied to a halt, a group of people slipped past airport security and rushed
onto the runway. As soon as Veeck emerged, cries of "Keep Boudreau,
Bill!" arose. He smiled broadly while descending the portable stairs
on elbow-length metal crutches. On the tarmac, one man grasped
Veeck's arm and begged, "Please don't sell Boudreau. You'll hurt the
Indians."

"Now, look," Veeck responded, "do you really think I, of all
people, would want to hurt the Indians? The only thing I want to do
is win the pennant."

"Trade someone else, then," another bystander yelled.

For ten minutes, the runway became an open-air forum where
Indians fans hashed out their differences face-to-face with the team's
owner. Emotions flared, yet Veeck remained calm. He listened and
explained, acquiesced and pushed back, defusing each complaint
with the same question: "Are you willing to trust my judgment as to
the best way to build a pennant winner?"

Afterward, he and Silverman set off for the Theatrical Grill, an
elegant if slightly disreputable jazz club popular with dignitaries and
mobsters alike. Outside its red-and-white façade, Veeck announced
his presence to the weekend revelers prowling Short Vincent, a
crooked bend of an avenue jam-packed with bars, nightclubs, and
burlesque joints. After conducting another open-air forum there,
he hobbled up Euclid Avenue toward Playhouse Square, trailed by
scores of pedestrians. Out of open car windows passengers shouted

"Don't sell Boudreau!" Encircling him at every stoplight were knots of people, curious and angry, caught up in a day-old fever that was breaking across Cleveland. "Bill," one remarked, "if you sell Boudreau, you'll have to put in twice as many firecrackers to attract half as many people." Their voices blended together in a communal wail. Propped up on crutches, Veeck exposed himself nakedly to the criticism.

Over the next few hours, an Indians employee drove Veeck to a local radio station for an impromptu interview, then to the lively scene at 105th Street and Euclid, then to the posh streetcar suburb of Shaker Heights. Soon, the evening dragged on and the crowds dispersed, but Veeck kept at it, roaming the city's bars and backstreets, not willing to call it a night until he'd stumbled upon seemingly everyone who happened to be awake and outdoors. By dawn, Veeck, sleepless, was on a plane back to New York City to catch the rest of the World Series.

In the end, the trade with the St. Louis Browns fell through, and since Veeck refused to peddle Boudreau to a contending club in the American League, his other options were limited. In late November 1947, after another contentious negotiating session, Boudreau signed a new two-year contract as player-manager, albeit with the caveat that Veeck would have the sole power to fill the rest of the team's coaching ranks. "For the first time in the history of baseball," Franklin Lewis wrote of the ordeal, "a player has been hoisted up on a community pedestal and the man who pays him has been told, 'Leave him right there, Bub.'"

In 1947, the Indians had inched up from sixth to fourth place, winning twelve more games than the previous year while setting another franchise record by drawing more than 1.5 million fans. But the pennant never had been within their reach, and nothing suggested it'd be any nearer in 1948. The question remained: How, with a shallow pitching staff and inexpert outfielders, could the Indians take the next step?

The team's failure to contend bore into Veeck like a virus. He'd already sacrificed so much for the Indians. He'd grown apart from his wife, Eleanor, who'd visited him only once in Cleveland. Neither she nor their children had been bedside following the amputation of his right foot. Every morning he woke early to soak his sore stump in the tub. The pain was persistent but he pushed through it, refusing to moderate his frantic pace, despite pleas from his doctors. Once again that winter, he would drive hundreds of miles weekly to speak before whichever audiences he could rustle up, no matter how small.

It was an all-encompassing pursuit, an obsession. "This game is my life. You have no conception how I feel about it," Veeck told columnist Ed McAuley late in 1947. "Even if you owned a ball club, there would be several things you would consider more important than winning the pennant. To me, nothing on this earth is more important than winning the pennant."

His own fever had yet to break. And if the Indians didn't advance to the World Series soon enough, it might consume him completely.

19

The Final Duel

The year 1947 was Satchel Paige's twenty-first season in professional baseball. Many of his peers had hung up their spikes; others, like Josh Gibson, had passed away. Regardless, quitting never crossed his mind, and so once again he pitched all through the Midwest and up and down the East Coast, in Detroit and Philadelphia, St. Louis and Newark. Despite being dubbed the "miraculous 'Ol Man River' of baseball" by *The Pittsburgh Courier* that summer, Paige still held out hope for a shot at the majors. The Brooklyn Dodgers, it was clear, had no interest in signing Paige, but perhaps the Cleveland Indians might. Paige had crossed paths with Bill Veeck often enough to know that the Indians owner held him in high esteem. So when he caught word that the Indians had signed Larry Doby, he dashed off a telegram to Veeck: "Is it time for me to come?"

Veeck's response was enigmatic, a door left slightly ajar: "All things in due time."

In the weeks after Doby's signing, Paige looked on as the St. Louis Browns signed his Kansas City Monarchs teammates Hank Thompson and Willard Brown. But the transaction that must have hit hardest was the Dodgers' signing of Dan Bankhead, a rangy twenty-seven-year-old fireballer. To give white audiences a sense of Bankhead's abilities, Memphis Red Sox owner B. B. Martin asserted that the newly inked pitcher "is a faster man than Satchel Paige." The words drove home an uncomfortable reality: Though still the bar by which Negro League pitchers were measured, Paige now was being bypassed by younger iterations of himself. Bankhead's debut for the Dodgers on August 26, 1947, laid to rest any hope Paige might have had that he'd become the first Black pitcher in Major League Baseball that century.

In October, weeks after the Monarchs had finished a disappointing second in the Negro American League, Paige married his longtime girlfriend, Lahoma. Days later, in Los Angeles, they put their honeymoon on hold. Bob Feller was coming to town. Whatever disagreements the pitchers had had last year were behind them. They had a rivalry to resume.

On October 8, two days after the New York Yankees defeated the Brooklyn Dodgers in the 1947 Major League World Series, Feller kicked off his latest barnstorming tour in Atlanta. Over the following week, his assembled troupe of major leaguers flew across the country's southern half, touching down in cities like New Orleans, Memphis, and Dallas. Because Feller feared running afoul of Jim Crow ordinances, he scheduled games at each stop against makeshift local teams of white major- and minor-league players.

As the head of Ro-Fel, Inc., Feller once again presided over the entire undertaking, starting each game, coordinating travel arrangements, and fretting over every last detail, down to the number of baseballs lost daily in batting practice. Though some of the trappings were similar—the rented DC-3 plane, the star-stocked roster, the itinerary spanning thousands of miles—the spark that had ignited the previous year's production was missing. The crowds had thinned, partly because Feller lacked a commensurate rival to face off against, and partly because the Black fans who'd swelled the stands to root for Paige's squad last October were absent.

It was only when Feller's barnstorming squad reached California, eight games into the tour, that they were to compete against the all-Black Kansas City Royals. Even then, Feller and Paige weren't scheduled to square off right away. At Los Angeles's Wrigley Field, the site of so many showdowns between the two pitchers, Feller was supposed to match up first against Dan Bankhead, perhaps as the start of a new rivalry, an insurance plan for when the fortysomething Paige aged out of baseball. Miscommunication, however, left Bankhead stranded in Memphis. Luckily, a ready-to-go replacement was on hand.

Shortly before eight o'clock on October 15, as 15,000 fans settled into their seats, Paige embarked on his latest slow walk to the mound. In the eleven years since their first encounter, Feller's face had shed its baby fat; Paige's had grown lined. They'd dueled through a depression, then a war, and now into an era of tentative integration. Both had since matured into master craftsmen who were just as likely to deceive hitters as blow them away. That evening, they threw four innings apiece. Paige struck out seven to Feller's two, allowed two hits to Feller's four. It was clear that Paige was the superior pitcher, even though the run he yielded on a pair of singles and a sacrifice fly saddled him with the loss.

He wouldn't have to wait long for a rematch. Four days later at the same ballpark, Paige fanned eight over five scoreless frames. Feller managed just two strikeouts while surrendering a run. That Feller's squad eked out a comeback victory after Paige had departed was immaterial. With fifteen strikeouts over nine total innings, Paige left little doubt about which pitcher had won that year's showdown.

Afterward, the two went their separate ways. Feller and his crew flew south to entertain fans across Mexico. Paige stayed put in Los Angeles. Another white barnstorming squad had come to town, this one fronted by Ewell Blackwell, a rail-thin sidearmer for the Cincinnati Reds who'd led the majors with twenty-two wins that season. The last week of October they matched up twice. Paige hurled nine total innings without allowing an earned run, setting down fourteen batters on strikes in the process. Blackwell, despite being seventeen years Paige's junior, couldn't keep up. He, too, went nine innings, but permitted four runs while striking out twelve. Paige's team won both contests.

The results reached Feller in Mexico City, as did news stories declaring that Paige, in his two-week residency at Wrigley Field, had outpitched the best the American and National Leagues had to offer. The headlines sparked an idea in Feller's mind. He'd be back in the States by the beginning of November. There was time still to schedule another game before the thirty-day barnstorming window closed.

On October 26, Feller issued a challenge to Paige via wire: one last duel before winter, only this time the two of them would hurl a full nine innings without relief.

Paige accepted. It was appealing in many ways. Reporters could play it up as a mano-a-mano clash between two pitchers who'd never gone the distance against each other. Fans who'd otherwise shifted their attention to football would turn back to baseball. And Feller and Paige could score one final paycheck.

The game was scheduled for Sunday, November 2. In the days leading up to it, Paige scanned the sports pages with amusement. But then, little by little, his mood soured. He bristled at Feller's playful insinuation that Paige's age would deter him from throwing a complete nine. He listened as reporters who'd praised him not even a week before voiced similar sentiments. Their words cut deep, puncturing Paige in his most sensitive spots. The press had always known what he was capable of. It was time to show them once again. "Then they wouldn't be thinking I was through," Paige reasoned, "too old to stand up to the major leaguers."

On game day, Paige chain-smoked cigarettes all the way to the stadium. During warm-ups, not even his customary deadpan demeanor could mask how worked up he was. Just before the first batter, Harry "Peanuts" Lowrey, stepped into the box, Paige reared back and blazed one last fastball down the middle. It smacked loudly into the catcher's glove—a warning shot to everyone in the opposing dugout.

All afternoon long Paige toyed with the white batters before him. A lifetime of honing his craft made up for however much speed he'd lost. He was like an aging boxer who, though his knockout punch had dulled, stayed on his feet through cunning and smarts, dancing and circling around his flustered opponents. Even batters who could see through his tricks were mostly helpless to do anything about them. Only four men rapped base hits off Paige, and none of them advanced beyond second.

Feller, meanwhile, was tuckered out from a month spent rambling across the country and into Mexico. Paige's squad jumped on him early, knocking in a run on three straight hits in the first, and then another in the second on catcher Joe Greene's home run. A series of infield errors permitted four more runners to cross home over the next two innings. Rather than signaling for relief, Feller took his lumps while going the distance.

What had been publicized as a nine-inning pitching duel ended up as an 8-0 blowout. Feller finished with five strikeouts; Paige wound up with fifteen, the most against a lineup of major-league batters since Feller had struck out eighteen Detroit Tigers on the last day of the 1938 season. Over five games in Los Angeles—three against Feller, two against Blackwell—Paige had racked up an astonishing forty-four strikeouts in twenty-seven innings.

For Feller, there was a cruel irony to how the last month had played out. He'd burned up so much goodwill defending his right to make money barnstorming only to find that there'd been so little to make. The previous season's tour had seemed to herald a new era of corporate barnstorming, with Feller as the foremost CEO, poised to reap rewards for years to come. But what he took as a beginning turned out to be an end. His 1947 tour reportedly finished thousands of dollars in the red, forcing Feller to cover the loss. "Last year we drew as many in the first ten days of our trip as we did in the entire tour this fall," he stated in reference to the tour's disappointing box-office numbers and in frustration at having had to start the tour after the World Series. "People were still baseball-minded when we started last year. Now they are thinking about football." Even the 9,145 fans that showed up for the complete-game showdown on November 2 were less than half of what a typical Feller-Paige matchup had drawn over the past few years. But beyond football's rising popularity, there were deeper reasons at play, which sportswriter John Sickels laid out in his biography of Feller: With major-league integration under way, however tentatively, the lure of Black-versus-white matchups had begun to wane. And for the first time in 1947, the World Series had been televised, bringing professional baseball directly into living rooms and saloons for people who rarely saw it.

A year after his country-spanning tour had boosted his earnings to a level that no other player had reached, Feller's dream of barnstorming moguldom faded away.

In the hours after his final duel with Feller, Paige lingered in the clubhouse, sipping a beer while his teammates showered, dressed, and departed. His body ached all over: his feet, his stomach, his right arm.

As the clubhouse emptied out, Paige pulled off his uniform and readied himself for the showers. An attendant, while handing him a towel, asked why no major-league team had nabbed him yet. Paige told him what he'd told everyone else: because his price was too high. It was a line he'd repeated for years, but in truth, he was searching for any road into the majors he could find.

Year after year, Paige had proven that he wasn't a one-dimensional pitcher, a stereotype, a showman, and now, an icon of the past too old to compete with the idols of the present. Even with barnstorming on the wane and with professional baseball undergoing seismic changes, his own narrative stubbornly refused to wrap up.

PART III

FRENZY

20

If I Can Stick with This Team

Two pitches. That was all Larry Doby needed to signal that the 1948 season would be different.

It was March 3, the third day of spring training in Tucson, Arizona. Lou Boudreau, desperate to make good in what he knew could be his final shot as manager, divvied up the Indians' roster into an A squad of likely starters and a B squad of everyone else: rookies, journeymen, and benchwarmers. That afternoon, they faced off in front of 1,400 fans scattered through Randolph Park. A strong wind was blowing in from the south, and the snowcapped mountains ringing the ballpark attested to the unseasonably frigid weather that had chilled the Sonoran Desert.

The contest itself was meaningless. Neither Boudreau nor Feller participated, and since no umpire squatted behind home plate, each batter simply swung away until he logged a hit or an out. Per usual, Doby watched from the bench. He was the backup to the outfielders on the B squad, the lowest rung on the team ladder. It wasn't until the final inning that he was summoned for pinch-hitting duties.

Relief pitcher Ed Klieman was on the mound. His first pitch sailed in hard and high, the exact sort of bait that Doby would have swung at last year. This time, practicing newfound discipline, he let it pass by.

Klieman burned the next one down the middle. The ball jumped off Doby's bat and soared upward through the fierce headwind, clear over the wall in right field. The majesty of the home run astonished the Indians owner, who was seated among the fans. "I don't think we have six men on the squad that can hit a ball that far," Bill Veeck said.

Boudreau agreed. When asked if anyone had made an impression on him in those opening days, he didn't hesitate in naming Doby. Boudreau had watched him fly around the outfield during batting practice, hauling in long drives near the adobe fence. He'd marveled, too, at the strength and accuracy of Doby's throwing arm, especially for someone who'd played the infield his entire life. There was, one reporter paraphrased Boudreau as saying, as much difference "between the Doby of today and the frightened kid who joined the club in Chicago last summer as there is between Bob Feller and the greenest of the rookie pitchers."

The previous season, the Cleveland Indians and New York Giants had set up their spring training camps in Tucson and Phoenix, respectively. The arid desert climate and cloudless skies would have been impetus enough for any major-league team to leave Florida for Arizona, but Veeck had additional reasons for doing so: a desire to stick close to his family's ranch in the surrounding foothills, and to escape the segregated facilities at ballparks across the South. Undoubtedly, he was aware of the abuse and humiliation Jackie Robinson had suffered in Daytona Beach during his first spring training with the Brooklyn Dodgers organization, which had spurred Branch Rickey to uproot his franchise's preseason operations first to Cuba in 1947 and then to the Dominican Republic in 1948. But as Veeck and Doby would soon learn, the racial climate in Arizona was hardly friendlier than Florida's.

For the white ballplayers who descended there in March, Tucson was a frontier boomtown oozing with Old West charm, nowhere more so than at the Santa Rita Hotel, the six-story institution where the Indians stayed. Nick Hall, the hotel's hefty manager, ruled the rambling structure like a cattle baron, greeting the incoming players with a full-throated "Howdy," a horse whip sometimes in hand. At night, rodeo-circuit riders and cowboys from nearby ranches would mosey in for drinks at the hotel bar, their leather heels clacking on the hotel floors. Joining them were the Indians players, some decked out in the Stetson hats and boots they'd purchased upon arrival, along with the casts of whatever Hollywood westerns were being filmed in the area.

Spring training in Tucson was, according to sportswriter Hal Lebovitz, a "time of closeness, when players really got to know each other." They dined together for breakfast and dinner; they rode the bus together to and from Randolph Park; they drank together in the evening. There were minor inconveniences, to be sure. Bob Feller groused about not being able to work up a sweat in the dry desert air; others suffered through nosebleeds and chapped skin, along with an ever-present fear of scorpions burrowing into their spikes. But those were small prices to pay for the bonding sessions that would sustain them through the arduous season ahead.

As the team's lone Black player, Doby was excluded from such camaraderie. After practice, while everyone piled into the team bus, catcher Jim Hegan recalled catching fleeting glimpses through the windows of Doby outside the gates of Randolph Park, waiting alone, sometimes for up to an hour, for the Black family with whom he bunked to pick him up.

Unlike his teammates, Doby couldn't revel in Tucson's laid-back cowboy culture. So many of the places his teammates frequented and the activities they took for granted were off-limits to Doby. "It was a difficult place for African Americans," remembered Jim "Mudcat" Grant, who later played six seasons for the Indians. "If you didn't read [in the newspapers] where you could go into a restaurant, you didn't go into those restaurants. You went to African American restaurants."

Because hotel owners believed, according to one newspaper account, that "the presence of a colored player would hurt business," Indians executives had been forced to find separate accommodations for Doby. He ended up staying in a three-bedroom, ranch-style adobe house owned by Chester Willis, the head of dry-cleaning production at a company that serviced the Santa Rita Hotel. In the off-season the Indians had let go of Louis Jones, so Doby bunked at the Willis household by himself, along with Willis's wife, Lucille, and their children. *Cleveland Press* columnist Franklin Lewis referred to Doby that spring as "a six-hour ball player per day, an 18-hour Jim Crow personality the rest of the time."

Dolores Townsend, the family's oldest daughter, remembered Doby as "polite, quiet, studious, and focused." He was guarded and mostly silent during the first few days, opening up little by little as he got more comfortable. In particular, Doby confided in Lucille, a soothing listener who'd moved from Dallas years earlier and knew how it felt to be in unfamiliar settings. She talked to Doby about being a long way from home, and he'd reciprocate by telling her about his homesickness, his struggles in the field, even the slurs he'd heard from the stands.

On top of this, Doby was locked in a fierce competition on the field. The Indians had opened spring training with eight outfielders battling for five roster spots. Despite his strong start, everyone assumed that Doby's chances of securing one were nil. He was so inexperienced that he'd passed the off-season in New Jersey borrowing books from his local library with titles like *How to Play the Outfield*. Rather than burdening Doby with learning an entirely new position in the majors, Indians officials had planned to option him to the minors, where he could stumble his way toward competency without invoking the wrath of the Indians' impatient fan base.

Teaching him the outfield ropes in Tucson was none other than the franchise's most renowned alumnus. Tris Speaker had come to Cleveland from Boston in 1916; four years later, as the team's player-manager, he'd propelled the Indians to their first and only World Series championship. The chance to apprentice under the man widely regarded as the greatest defensive center fielder of baseball's deadball era would have thrilled any young trainee, but Doby had cause for concern.

Speaker hailed from Hubbard, Texas, the same hometown as Hiram Wesley Evans, the former imperial wizard of the Ku Klux Klan, and he wore his ornery Lone Star pride on his sleeve. According to biographer Timothy M. Gay, one of Speaker's preferred pastimes later in life consisted of "hectoring any Northerner within earshot" about the so-called War between the States, his roaring Texas twang drowning out all counterarguments.

But somehow, a relationship that seemed destined to fail blossomed from the start. Decades in professional baseball had rendered Speaker a shrewd judge of talent, and in Doby he recognized it in abundance—raw, unmolded, yet as undeniable as the desert sun. "I've never seen a young ball player with such a high potential," Speaker later said. "I used to dream of that kind of rookie when I was managing the Indians." Doby already possessed the skills necessary to thrive on the grass: speed, hair-trigger instincts, and the strongest throwing arm on the team. So together the two of them worked diligently on preparing Doby for his transition from the infield to the outfield.

One afternoon in early March, Bob Feller remained on the field at Randolph Park after practice. There was no one in the stands, no coaches on the sidelines. His teammates already had decamped for the clubhouse. Their day was done, but Feller's was just beginning. He'd cycled through the usual team drills, and now it was time to move on to his self-designed training routine. As always, Feller undertook it alone.

Over the next hour or so, he sprinted back and forth from the foul pole in left field to the flagpole in center field; he jogged around the park; he did squats, knee bends, and stretches; and then he finished with a final round of wind sprints. It was a familiar yet still incongruous sight: the only untouchable man on the Indians' roster pushing himself like an endangered rookie.

Over the winter, Veeck had signed Feller to a contract with the same base pay as the previous season but with stricter bonus clauses. For him to earn as much as he had in 1947 (roughly $87,000), the Indians would have to break their attendance record for the third year running. It was reported during spring training that a national magazine had tried fruitlessly to entice Cleveland sportswriters to write an article entitled, "Is Bob Feller Getting Too Big for His Britches?" Feller, however, seemed considerably less focused on moneymaking ventures than he had the previous spring. His radio show had ended, and in interviews, he came across as newly reluctant to talk about Ro-Fel, Inc., later claiming that he planned to junk his company soon.

For the first time, Feller was entering a season in need of a fresh start, as much with the fans as on the mound. He would turn thirty years old in 1948. A few gray hairs had started to sprout around his temples. His career, it seemed, was nearer the end than the beginning, and if he didn't pitch his way to a pennant soon, he might never do so.

Unlike the season before, when his stifled emotions had tightened him up, Doby now channeled them into his performance in spring training, punishing the ball with unbottled fury. Pretty soon, Boudreau remembered, "base hits flew off his bat, his power was more controlled, his judgment noticeably better." On the base paths his speed enabled him to take risks that other players wouldn't dream of. Coach Oscar Melillo recalled one such incident: "Brother, that Doby—whoosh! Run? That guy doesn't run. He simply takes off!

He went from first to third on a single to center and when I saw him rounding second I said to myself, 'That's all. He's a dead pigeon now.' Right in front of the shortstop—and I'm not kiddin'—he left his feet. He had his hands out in front of him, just like a kid diving off a pier. I'll swear he never touched the ground until he landed on third base. Sure he beat the throw." Another time, Doby raced to the outfield fence to track down a towering fly ball. Harry Grabiner, the Indians vice president, pronounced on the spot: "There's the best outfielder in camp right now."

Still, Doby continued to be plagued with what sportswriter Ed McAuley called a "vague understandable dread of 'doing the wrong thing.'" In one game, outfielder Hank Edwards smacked a home run with Doby on base; rather than waiting at the plate to congratulate him, Doby hustled to the dugout, unsure if Edwards would want to be seen shaking his hand in public.

It didn't help that nearly everywhere the Indians traveled, Doby was shunted to separate lodgings. In Los Angeles, he boarded at the Watkins Hotel, a Westside Black establishment, while his teammates stayed at the stately Biltmore. Spud Goldstein, the Indians traveling secretary, claimed that the Biltmore refused to accommodate Doby, but a clerk at the hotel told a reporter that that wasn't the case, that in fact two Black guests were staying at the hotel as they spoke. When Goldstein was reached for a follow-up statement, he "appeared hesitant, evasive and discourteous, refusing to commit himself."

The worst for Doby came when the Indians and New York Giants embarked together on a cross-country tour to close out spring training, competing against each other first in Phoenix and Albuquerque before striking out for Texas. Around three in the morning on Friday, April 9, their train chugged into Lubbock, pulling over in the railyard so that the players onboard could sleep till sunrise.

The contrast between Feller and Doby was never starker than in Lubbock. Upon waking up, Feller was chauffeured to Sports Center,

the city's premier sporting goods store. Earlier, the Lubbock superintendent of schools had announced that any student who wanted
to see the ballplayers in action would receive an excused absence,
which enabled hundreds of boys to queue up outside the shop, several of them having waited there since dawn. For an hour Feller
signed equipment and fielded questions, donating the proceeds to
the American Legion Junior Baseball League. Afterward, he sat
down for radio interviews, then caught up with his Indians teammates at the air-conditioned Hilton Hotel downtown.

Doby, in contrast, had to fend for himself. Unable to join his
teammates at the Hilton or even to hail a cab, he was forced to walk
to the ballpark in his street clothes. Once there, he roamed around
the park's perimeter, doing whatever he could to convince skeptical
gate attendants he played for the Indians. No one believed him until
an Indians official showed up to affirm his story.

By game time, allegedly the largest crowd ever to witness a
game in West Texas turned out, roughly 8,000 strong in a park built
for little more than half that number. Fans jammed the aisles and
spilled onto the field, huddling fifteen deep from foul line to foul
line. Boudreau must have looked at the thin rope that separated the
masses from his outfielders and flinched. After batting practice,
Doby never left the dugout. There was a strong suspicion, one columnist wrote, "that [Boudreau] was acting to protect Doby from any
further indignity."

The next morning, the team's train rolled into Oklahoma City.
Franklin Lewis of the *Cleveland Press* caught up with Doby there
before that afternoon's game. Amid blustery winds that swirled dust
across the dilapidated ballpark, the soft-spoken Doby, who normally
submitted to interviews with as much enthusiasm as a patient settling into a dentist's chair, unburdened himself about the misery of
the past month.

"It's been a rough spring," he began. "Oh, maybe rough isn't the right word. But it's been lonely, believe me. I've been lonesome, though I wasn't surprised. I expected to be."

Doby continued, "In Tucson, I lived alone, but with nice people. Then on the road I've been living in colored hotels when we stopped over night. It's really been an experience for me. You know, I don't understand how some of these people feel and act in the South. I surely don't."

At one point, Doby told Lewis, "Whatever has happened has been worth everything to me, for what I've learned . . . And if I can just make the big leagues, if I can stick with this team . . ." His voice trailed off.

The Indians played two games in Oklahoma City. During the second contest, there were scattered boos when Doby was inserted as a pinch-hitter in the fifth inning. But then, according to one report, "the crowd of 11,401 fans began to applaud him as he stood at the plate." His subsequent run-scoring single padded the Indians 12-4 victory. Afterward, the Indians and Giants swung north to Kansas, then east through Kentucky and Indiana before wrapping up the spring with a pair of contests at Cleveland's Municipal Stadium. A verdict had yet to be rendered in the Indians' eight-sided outfield battle. Everything would come down to the final weekend series.

In the first game, on April 17, Boudreau started Pat Seerey in right field. A rotund slugger who hit the ball hard but rarely—at age twenty-four, he'd already led the American League in strikeouts three times—Seerey looked defenseless at the plate, whiffing three straight times. Doby took over for Seerey the next day. The crowd greeted him with a thunderous ovation, which they repeated after each of his successes: an opposite-field double, a single, a walk, a stolen base.

With so much on the line that season, Boudreau was in no mood to take risks, and there was none greater than taking a player who'd looked overmatched the previous season and switching him to an entirely new position. In the end, however, Boudreau simply couldn't justify handing his most tantalizing prospect an express ticket to the minors. Not only would Doby stick with the Indians, but Boudreau would name him the team's Opening Day starter in right field.

The same weekend the Indians returned to Cleveland, Doby reunited with his wife, Helyn. She'd been pregnant when he'd departed for spring training but had suffered a miscarriage during his seven weeks away. "Realizing the spot Doby was in," sportswriter A. S. "Doc" Young reported, "[Helyn] kept it a secret until Saturday [April 17] when she flew to Cleveland from Paterson, New Jersey." As a result, what should've been a time of triumph turned into one of tragedy. Weathering Jim Crow, loneliness, and seemingly insurmountable odds, Doby had clawed his way onto the Indians' roster, only to be blindsided as soon as the battle was won.

He carried the sadness with him into the start of the season.

All winter long Bill Veeck had been on the move, sitting for interviews, giving speeches, and flooding the airwaves with novelty "singing commercials" whose Indians-themed jingles wormed into listeners' minds. Before the season's first game, his front office mailed out 35,000 ticket applications to regular customers, dispersed 7,000 posters for local businesses to hang in their windows, supplied downtown shops with picture displays of various players, and pasted WEL-COME INDIANS signs on streetcars, taxis, and poles across the city. The result was the largest Opening Day turnout in baseball history—more than 73,000 fans piled to the rafters, shattering the previous record by almost 20,000.

To the relief of Indians fans, Feller resembled his old self that afternoon, surrendering a mere two hits in a complete-game shutout. Unfortunately, Doby also resembled the player they remembered from the previous season. Fans rooted for him unreservedly each time he came to bat, but it did no good. Doby struck out twice, grounded out twice, and muffed a low line drive in right field. One unnamed player told Franklin Lewis that Doby was so tense "that every time I passed him on the bench I could hear him hum."

After the game, Boudreau, a can of orange juice in hand, kicked his feet up on his desk and told Doc Young, "I wouldn't want you to print this without Doby's okay—but, he has been worried the last few days—and, you can't have two things on your mind and play this game." Boudreau was referring to the miscarriage, but his statement just as easily could've applied to the challenges Doby once again would face as the lone Black player in the American League.

Either way, it was going to be another long, trying season.

21

Under the Knife, Beyond the Axe

After their Opening Day victory against the St. Louis Browns, the Indians skipped to Detroit for a weekend series against the Tigers, then continued on to Chicago and St. Louis for contests against the White Sox and Browns. Back in Cleveland on April 30, after having won each of their first six games, Joe Gordon and Eddie Robinson settled into a taxi together. Casually, as if stating a fact, Gordon said, "Eddie, we're going to win the pennant."

Bill Veeck, too, sensed it in his bones, a vague yet expectant feeling that this would be the year. True, the Indians' outfield was still unsettled and the starting rotation thin, but in his third season as owner, Veeck finally seemed to be working with a roster that could match his ambitions.

That didn't mean he planned to tamp down on stadium theatrics. On the contrary, everything he did that summer would be bigger, louder, more fan-friendly than before. On evenings and weekends, Veeck shot off thousands of dollars' worth of fireworks while four different bands blared tunes through the stands. In an attempt to attract veterans who'd started families since returning stateside, Veeck converted the space beneath the right-field grandstand

into a nursery. During games, parents could pass their toddlers along to trained supervisors who herded them into playpens painted with zoo animals and strewn with swings, sandboxes, and alphabet blocks.

The team's operating expenses ballooned to such an extent that if the Indians didn't draw at least one million customers, they'd sink into the red. Veeck wasn't concerned. With 182,862 fans packing the lakefront stadium in the team's first three games alone in 1948, Veeck had set his sights on much grander numbers.

His more immediate concern was a familiar one. A long winter of hustling once more had aggravated his right leg, and now, two weeks into the season, Veeck could no longer wave off the pain. Another operation was forthcoming. Reporters who caught up with him in the days beforehand glimpsed something seldom seen: Veeck was tired. "I certainly hope it takes this time," he told them. "Maybe I'll be able to wear a leg the day we celebrate winning the pennant."

On May 4, 1948, surgeons shaved another inch off his right leg below the knee. An extended stay at the Cleveland Clinic followed, which perhaps wasn't the worst outcome. As one writer observed, Veeck "never looks so healthy as when he's in the hospital." Besides, with the way the young season was unfolding, it was to his benefit to rest up early so that he could be present for the charge late.

In the season's opening weeks, Larry Doby seemed at war with himself. In the Indians' second game, in front of a sizable crowd at Detroit's home opener, Doby walloped his first major-league home run deep into the upper deck of Tiger Stadium; innings later, on a dead run in right field, he crossed his gloved hand in front of him and snatched a screaming liner from the air. Two days later, at the same ballpark, Doby struck out five times in one afternoon, tying a single-game record.

Learning to play the outfield in real time exposed Doby to

ridicule and criticism. At the beginning of May, he committed four errors over a two-day home stand that resulted in the Indians' first two losses of the season. The Cleveland crowds that had cheered him only a week earlier now showered him with boos. To some, his missteps seemed more psychological than physical. "Larry Doby has everything it takes to become one of major league baseball's brightest stars—except the unalterable belief that he has what it takes," asserted Doc Young in the *Call & Post*, adding: "Larry's biggest battle is not with Indian teammates, opposing pitchers, and hostile fans. His biggest battle is to be fought in the cells of his brain." It was in the heat of the moment, *Cleveland News* columnist Ed McAuley argued, when Doby really shined. "When [Doby] acts only by instinct, when he races deep into the corner, he shows the trademark of true greatness. But when he has time to set himself for a play—when he has time to remember that he is his race's only representative in the American League and every eye in the park is on him—he has almost an even prospect of looking foolish."

Opposing players and bleacher bums continued to spew racist invective his way. On May 4 at Philadelphia's Shibe Park, shouts of "Porter, carry my bags!" and "Shoeshine boy, shine my shoes!" streamed from the Athletics' dugout throughout the game. The taunts and insults became so nasty over the summer that Veeck would implore Will Harridge, the president of the American League, to issue a statement against extreme bench jockeying.

To reporters in the Black press, Doby expressed a "keen desire for a colored player on the team as a companion, or even a sports writer with whom he could confide, and talk with on personal problems when off the field." Road games were particularly taxing. Facing each night alone while his teammates hit the town and bunked together remained a constant struggle. "It's a loneliness where you're glad when the next day comes," Doby explained. "Because you know you're back in the ballpark. The best time was the time on the field."

The field, however, proved an uncertain sanctuary. Weeks of inconsistent play led Boudreau to conclude that Doby might benefit from a stint in the minors after all. A month into the season, all major-league teams would have to trim their rosters to twenty-five players, which provided the Indians manager with an excuse to send Doby down.

In early May, Boudreau tasked Hank Greenberg, whom Veeck had lured to the Indians in the off-season, with broaching the subject with Doby. Even though he'd clubbed twenty-five home runs the previous year for the Pittsburgh Pirates, Greenberg had chosen to transition into the Indians' front office rather than play another season in 1948. While he'd sensed greatness in Doby during spring training, Greenberg had nonetheless offered to bet Veeck that the inexperienced outfielder would likely spend much of the season in the minors.

Now, in the dugout before a road game against the Washington Senators, Greenberg attempted to ease into that very discussion, inquiring whether it would break Doby's spirit if the Indians farmed him out for the summer. Normally taciturn around team executives, Doby responded frankly, telling Greenberg point-blank that nothing was going to break his spirit, that he knew he could play in the majors, and if it wasn't that season, it'd be the next.

Greenberg went on to ask if Doby believed he'd ever be able to hit .300 in the majors.

After pondering the question, Doby said, per Greenberg's recollection: "Mr. Greenberg, I hate to say this for fear that I'll sound as if I'm popping off, but from what I've seen of the pitching in this league so far, I'd say that I ought to hit about .315."

Greenberg admired the conviction and guts behind the answers, evidently enough for him to walk away with his mind changed. Just a few days later, he'd tell Arthur Daley of *The New York Times* that Doby "is gonna be a helluva ballplayer. He's inexperienced and erratic right now but he can run and throw and hit. My, what power!"

Doby, Greenberg declared, was "better now than Jackie Robinson was at this time last spring."

Boudreau's mind would soon change, too. On May 8, at Griffith Stadium against the Senators, he reinserted Doby into the lineup after having parked him on the bench for two games. Doby responded by driving a pitch into dead center that caromed off a loudspeaker perched atop the thirty-five-foot outfield wall. Just a day earlier, Boudreau had asked the umpiring crew what would happen should a batted ball strike those speakers. "Nobody is going to hit a ball that far," they'd assured him with a laugh. But Doby did, and in the ensuing confusion after the baseball tumbled back onto the field, the umpires ruled it still live. "With the speed of a meteor" Doby whirled around the bases, skidding headfirst into home to complete perhaps the longest inside-the-park home run imaginable.

Afterward, the Indians traveled overnight to Boston, where Doby played both ends of a doubleheader the next day. He knocked in an insurance run in the tenth inning of the opener and swatted a game-tying home run deep into the center-field bleachers at Fenway Park in the nightcap as the Indians swept. Later, Boudreau phoned Veeck at the Cleveland Clinic. "I thought," Boudreau reportedly told him, "that we'd be farming out Doby. But I've changed my mind. The way he has been going, we have to keep him." Sportswriters who'd been skeptical of Doby's chances now paid him the highest compliment a player could receive in Cleveland. "If Doby can face and conquer [his weaknesses]," Ed McAuley wrote, "the Indians have the greatest youngster to join the squad since Bob Feller came waddling from the furrows of Iowa."

As the mid-May deadline approached, Boudreau's gut cautioned him against demoting Doby. "With his speed and power, there is no telling how much Doby can do," he reasoned, "and we want to find out," mistakes and all.

For the second time in a month, Doby dodged the axe.

* * *

23

Pandemonium

The summer unfurled in fits and starts for Larry Doby. His spot on the Indians' roster finally secure, he still struggled to stay on the field. A weeks-long slump in late May led to a weeks-long benching in early June. When Boudreau reinserted him in the starting lineup, on June 17, it was not in right but in center field, a position better suited to Doby's explosive speed but yet another he'd have to learn on the fly in Cleveland's spacious outfield.

Rather than shrinking from the challenge, Doby met it with hard-nosed fury. Over the next ten days, a span which saw his batting average rise from .250 to .286, he plowed into walls, slashed triples, and tore around the bases so uninhibitedly that the severe ankle sprain he suffered on June 27 seemed almost inevitable.

For two weeks Doby nursed the injury, out of the lineup but still in Boudreau's thoughts. Since the start of the season, Boudreau had chosen to sit Doby against left-handed pitchers and to bench him altogether during slumps. But those rounds of outfield musical chairs were coming to an end. "Doby was always surprising us by looking like the best of the bunch [of outfielders] just when we were about to decide he needed further experience," Boudreau explained

In the season's opening months, a strange phenomenon took place in Cleveland. Before games, Indians loyalists filled the lakefront stadium to the brim, settling in sections so high they must've been able to glimpse the smoky freighters plowing across Lake Erie. Once the action got under way, they proceeded to boo the hometown players at the slightest mistake, interpreting every bobble, passed ball, and burned base runner as a portentous sign. Even though the Indians stuck close to first place, fans knew from experience not to trust in a club that promised the world in May. "The Cleveland fan," one writer claimed, "has been disappointed so often by the Indians that in his moments of wildest exultation he seems to be waiting apprehensively for the roof to fall in." So they shielded themselves behind jeers, wearing their cynicism on their sleeves. They booed in blowouts and in nail-biters, with the Indians ahead or behind. No one on the roster was immune, not even Boudreau, the player they'd saved and who in turn rewarded their loyalty by hitting close to .400 through May. One afternoon, Gordon Cobbledick wrote, they booed the Indians manager "not in a sudden spontaneous upwelling of disapproval for a specific overt act, but sullenly and ill-temperedly," as if it were simply his turn.

Despite their skeptical posture, fans continued to turn out in astonishing numbers, spellbound by the Indians' early-season success and the owner's ceaseless, leg-endangering quest to convince every hard-bitten resident that a new era of Cleveland baseball was dawning. Being marooned on a hospital bed didn't curb Veeck's ambitions. For weeks, he spread the word that he wanted to shatter the single-game major-league attendance record—81,841 paid customers—during a Sunday doubleheader on May 23 against the franchise that held it, the New York Yankees. The record, he declared, "belongs in the largest baseball arena, right here in Cleveland. We can do it if our friends within a radius of 200 miles will assist us." They did, gobbling up tickets and packing the scores of special trains and buses coming from Buffalo, Detroit, Dayton, and beyond.

Right before game time, the skies opened up and a cold rain drenched the jacketed masses, deterring just enough people that the Indians fell short of the record. Veeck listened over the radio in a panic. Fearful that 78,000 fans would be sent away soaked and miserable, he ducked out of his hospital room and then sped away in a cab to the lakefront. Wheeled up to the press box, the Indians owner swaddled himself in a blanket and surveyed the action, keeping a microphone on hand so that he could announce refunds for everyone should the first game be cut short.

Luckily, it never came to that. The downpour slowed, and Bob Feller was able to take the mound by game time. After only a few warm-up tosses, Feller knew: He didn't have it that day. It was becoming a familiar feeling. Feller told the *Cleveland Press* that he'd won his first two starts of the season with less stuff than he'd ever had.

That afternoon the Indians spotted Feller a four-run lead, but Joe DiMaggio single-handedly erased it by knocking a pair of sputtering fastballs over the fences. Weeks later, DiMaggio would say aloud what many players were whispering among themselves: "This year Bob Feller is just another pitcher, not the old Feller . . . He's trying to kid us with sliders. He used to blow that hard one past us all day but that's a thing of the past."

Figuring out what ailed Feller, Gordon Cobbledick claimed, became "the one truly vital issue" in Cleveland. The usual suspects were rounded up: He was distracted, stretched too thin, invested more in business than pennants, not fully recovered from his injury, just plain worn out. Whatever the case might have been, Feller bore the brunt of the fans' ire. From late May to late June, he endured five consecutive defeats, dropping his record to an unseemly 5-7. Soon, reporters began to pepper the Indians manager with a previously unthinkable question: Would the Indians be better off if Feller didn't pitch? Boudreau wouldn't hear of it. "We'll sink or swim with Feller," he stated, adding: "If Bob can't win, we're finished as far as the pennant race is concerned."

Veeck, who'd been discharged from the Cleveland Clinic in late May, decided to intervene. On June 17, he huddled one-on-one with his ace. The next day, Feller made a begrudging announcement: "There has been a lot of agitation to get me to concentrate on pitching exclusively . . . I still don't think there's anything to get alarmed about, but I've decided to dispense with all outside activities just to satisfy those people who think I'm hurting myself and the team." For the first time since returning from the war, Feller would have no barnstorming tour to plan, no planes or stadiums to book, no deals to cut with Satchel Paige. Feller the corporation had been suspended until Feller the pitcher could regain his form.

Feller's losing streak, which began the day the Indians had attempted to set the single-game attendance record, was snapped the afternoon they succeeded in doing so. On June 20, during a Father's Day doubleheader against the Philadelphia Athletics, 82,781 boisterous fans sprawled in the aisles, perched on ledges, clustered on concrete runways, and crowded behind the outfield fences at Municipal Stadium. At one point, Veeck hobbled on crutches from the press box to the field level to announce the record personally into the public-address microphone. Round after round of applause trailed the bareheaded owner through the stands. Feller nearly spoiled the mood, falling behind 3-0 through five innings, but the Indians rallied with four runs in the seventh, punctuated by a go-ahead RBI single from Doby.

Feller's winless month brought the shallowness of the Indians' pitching rotation into focus. Bob Lemon had gotten off to a fast start, as had rookie southpaw Gene Bearden, the knuckleballer whom Veeck had traded for two winters before. But with the Yankees and Athletics hot on the Indians' heels and with the Red Sox recovering from their listless spring, it seemed certain that more arms would be needed to stave them off through the summer.

Already, Veeck had placed some chancy bets. In the off-season, he'd purchased the contract of Russ Christopher, a toothpick-thin

sinkerballer whose health was in decline. Then, at the June trading deadline, Veeck forked over a whopping $100,000 to the St. Louis Browns for Sam Zoldak, a run-of-the-mill starter who was nobody's idea of a savior. All the while, Veeck kept searching. He scoured the waiver lists, combed the minors, and, in his own words, "investigated prospects from Mexico to Hawaii." The scrap heap was bare. To prevent the Indians from succumbing to their customary late-summer swoon, he'd need to place larger, riskier bets.

Like a gambler with nothing to lose, Veeck prepared to go all in.

22

Enter Paige

Two weeks into the 1948 season, Bill Veeck had named Abe Saperstein as special representative to the Indians, tasked with creating a scouting program that, as *The Chicago Defender* put it, could "siphon young Negro ball players" into the franchise's farm system. No longer would players like Doby jump straight from the Negro Leagues to the majors. Instead, they'd sprout up through the minors, on affiliates like the Wilkes-Barre Barons, which was integrated in June with the first player Saperstein recommended, a Black Canadian outfielder named Fred Thomas.

In late June, Saperstein took in an Indians game alongside Veeck, watching as the bullpen surrendered run after run. Veeck wrung his hands at the unreliability of the team's relievers. Starved for pitching help and bereft of options, Veeck listened afterward as Saperstein, an employee charged with recruiting prospects, recommended an icon of the past.

Signing Satchel Paige was an idea Veeck had toyed with since purchasing the Indians, always finding some reason to stop short. Months earlier, during spring training, he'd told *Call & Post* columnist A. S. "Doc" Young that while he believed Paige could thrive

in the majors, his salary demands would be too steep. Nevertheless, over the following days, Veeck mulled the idea over again. He spoke with Paige's barnstorming rival, Bob Feller. Then he phoned Saperstein and instructed him to bring Paige to Cleveland for a tryout.

Not wanting to incite a media firestorm, Veeck wrapped his plan in secrecy, which he ended up breaking himself. When Young stopped by his office for a chat late in June, Veeck blurted out: "I'm going to sign Satchel Paige." Floored by the bombshell, Young could only laugh. "It had never occurred to me," he later wrote, "that *any-one* would give a major league break to this fabled, deserving, old pitcher."

One thing was clear: Veeck wasn't summoning Paige to Cleveland as a means of atoning for baseball's sins. The Indians were in urgent need of someone who could stabilize the bullpen and start games whenever necessary over the season's second half. It wasn't Paige the icon Veeck was after. Paige the pitcher, he believed, would be enough.

After his autumn exploits against Bob Feller had failed to yield a major-league offer for the second straight season, Paige realized what owners must have been thinking. "They was thinkin'," he later said, "that when I was with Chattanooga [as a rookie in 1926], Larry Doby wasn't bawn [Doby was actually two years old at that time]." No level of mastery could compensate for what was forever lost to Paige: youth. Still, he had his name and he had his arm and everyone assumed he would "die with his spikes on" anyway, so in 1948 he carried on once more, pitching into the twilight, rustling up fans and funds in ballparks big and small.

Appropriately, it was while barnstorming that Paige got word of the tryout in Cleveland. Relief washed over him. Paige later told author William Price Fox that upon returning home, he and his wife, Lahoma, "whooped and hollered and started dancing and we didn't

stop until we danced through every room in the house and were out onto the porch."

A year after Paige had wired Veeck a telegram asking if it was time for him to come, it finally was.

On the morning of July 6, Lou Boudreau awoke to the clanging of his bedside phone. The Indians had split a doubleheader the day before, sending 60,000 fans home disappointed after Feller, in a relief appearance, had coughed up the lead late in the second game. Boudreau had stewed at the stadium until past midnight, and now, groggy and sore, he listened with mild irritation as Veeck beckoned him back to appraise some anonymous pitcher.

Expecting to encounter a peach-fuzzed kid, Boudreau instead found himself face-to-face with an unmistakable baseball elder, dark-skinned, mustachioed, and "built like a pencil." In earlier discussions with the Indians owner, Boudreau had made his lack of interest in Paige clear, but now here was the pitcher before him, and as with any Veeckian undertaking, Boudreau had no choice but to roll with it.

For Paige, the stakes couldn't have been higher. That morning's tryout was a lifeline. The Negro Leagues were faltering; the barnstorming well was running dry. According to Buck Leonard, one of Paige's contemporaries, in the years after Jackie Robinson's debut with the Dodgers "we couldn't even draw flies." Everything now would depend on how convincingly Paige pitched in front of the Indians' gathered brain trust and the layered rings of vacant seats at Municipal Stadium.

Rather than playing it safe, Paige leaned into what had worked for him his entire career. After some warm-up tosses and an aborted jog around the field, he folded a handkerchief, then instructed Boudreau to place it wherever he wanted on home plate. Boudreau chose the inside corner; Paige fired pitch after pitch over it. Boudreau slid it to the other side; the same results ensued.

Finally, Boudreau grabbed a bat and dug in. Paige fed him every pitch in his arsenal, "a couple Bee balls and one of the old Troubles and all [Boudreau] did was watch them go by. When I whipped in my old Stinger, I don't even think he saw it," he recalled. Boudreau popped a few flies and slapped some grounders, then threw down his bat and implored Veeck to sign him. "Now I can believe some of the tall stories they tell about [Paige's] pitching," Boudreau said afterward.

Paige, however, wasn't within earshot of Veeck and Boudreau's discussion. For several long minutes, he stood alone in the middle of baseball's largest arena, sweat dripping from his face. Silence enveloped him, a stark contrast to the cheers that customarily accompanied his pitching. For all he knew the men huddled by the dugout, jawing and gesturing his way, were discussing the quickest means of getting him back to Kansas City. Instead, they called him to the clubhouse. Veeck hobbled over not only to tell Paige that a contract would be drawn up, but also to express his regret that this day hadn't come sooner.

The news that the Indians had signed Paige shook the majors like an earthquake. "As far as I'm concerned," journalist Tom Meany proclaimed, "the signing of Satchel Paige to a Cleveland contract is far more interesting than was the news when Branch Rickey broke baseball's color line." Embedded in Paige were more than twenty years of experience in the Negro Leagues, along with the pride of a generation that had toiled in the shadows of a segregated league that had never opened up to them. If Jackie Robinson and Larry Doby succeeded, the major leagues could spin a positive story, claiming a pair of forward-thinking executives had given these twentysomething athletes on the upswing of their careers an opportunity to prove their worthiness on and off the field. But if Paige, at age forty-two, fulfilled Veeck's aims, it would further underline the prejudice that had barred him and his peers for so long. It would tear down

the scaffolding upon which arguments of Black inferiority had been constructed.

The Sporting News, channeling the sentiment of the baseball establishment, reacted with defensive fury. "Veeck has gone too far in his quest of publicity," its publisher, J. G. Taylor Spink, fumed, adding: "To sign a hurler at Paige's age is to demean the standards of baseball in the big circuits. Further complicating the situation is the suspicion that if Satchel were white, he would not have drawn a second thought from Veeck." The Indians owner vehemently denied the charges. "I signed Paige because I think he can help us," Veeck contended. "We don't need publicity, we need help on the field." The money he invested underscored his sincerity. To Saperstein and Monarchs owner Tom Baird, Veeck reportedly cut checks for $15,000 apiece. Of his negotiations with the Indians, Baird said, "Everything was above board and [Veeck] didn't pull a Rickey on us." To Paige, Veeck paid the ultimate respect. For years Paige had insisted he wouldn't take a pay cut to pitch in the majors, and the Indians owner respected that vow, offering the pitcher a total of $25,000 for the season's final three months, nearly as much as the combined salaries of the three other Black players in the league.

Paige took the scrutiny in stride. Even though he, like Doby, had bypassed the minor leagues, there was little chance of Paige coming down with the jitters. "I'm starting my major league career with one thing in my favor, anyway," he told reporters. "I won't be afraid of anybody I see in that batter's box. I've been around too long for that."

His debut came a mere two days after his signing, on July 9 in Cleveland. That night, Bob Lemon, drained and overworked, coughed up four runs in as many frames. At the start of the fifth inning, the bullpen gate swung open and Paige—dressed in black spikes and knee-high striped stirrups, a long-sleeved mesh shirt under his cream-colored uniform and a gold chain around his neck—began his long, slow journey to the mound. The oldest rookie in

major-league history, he walked as he always had: languidly, stoically, his face a cipher. According to one writer, he trod across the field "like a man on his way to the chiropodist to get his bunions pared."

Some 35,000 fans rose to their feet, screaming and hollering at the top of their lungs. It seemed, Paige recalled, "like they never was so happy to see anyone in their life."

By the mound Boudreau and Joe Gordon stood side by side, sensing the historic weight of the occasion. "Somebody ought to say something to him," the Indians manager suggested.

"Like what?" Gordon asked.

"Anything. Just to take the pressure off. You can think of something."

"*I* can think of something?" Gordon shot back. "*You're* the manager."

Tongue-tied, Boudreau clapped his throwing hand against his glove. "Okay, Satch!" he exclaimed, handing him the ball.

Photographers swarmed in a half-circle scrum around the mound. Paige glared into their lenses with his mouth agape, waiting for the umpires to shoo them away, but they stayed there throughout his warm-ups. His ungainly windup, which A. S. "Doc" Young described as "a baffling combination of legs, arms, and the aforementioned large feet," induced peals of laughter from the crowd as flashbulbs popped and cameramen crawled over one another for better angles.

The first Browns batter to dig in was Chuck Stevens, who'd faced Paige the previous November in Los Angeles as a member of Bob Feller's squad. Their paths had crossed a handful of times on the barnstorming trail, where Stevens had hit him surprisingly hard. That evening, the advantage was Stevens's. Paige was lost in the moment. "I wasn't nervous exactly, but I was as close to that feeling as I could be," he remembered.

Stevens stood still as the first pitch sailed in wide, then he laced the second into left field for a single. The boisterous crowd quieted

down; Boudreau kicked anxiously at the infield dirt. While everyone braced for the worst, Paige felt his nerves dissipate. He found himself in a familiar spot: on a mound, in a stadium he'd first pitched in fifteen years before. It was the same game he'd known for decades, no different than in the Negro Leagues. It didn't matter what uniform he wore. It was time to show major-league audiences just how seriously he took his craft.

From then on, according to *The Plain Dealer*, Paige "put most of his wares on display." After his first-pitch ball to Stevens, Paige didn't toss another outside the strike zone until six batters later. Bench jockeys tried to snap his concentration, riding him so hard the home plate umpire had to issue a warning to the opposing dugout, but Paige paid them no mind. Surrendering just two singles in two innings, he flummoxed Browns batters with speed, curves, bloopers, and everything in between. His famed hesitation pitch fooled left fielder Whitey Platt so utterly that the bat flew from his hands mid-swing and rolled halfway up the third-base line. Appropriately, Paige's major-league debut concluded with a crowd-pleasing flourish. When Browns shortstop Eddie Pellagrini popped a routine fly to left at the end of the sixth inning, Paige strode off the mound on contact, making it halfway to the dugout before the catch had been made, never once looking back.

He was everything Veeck knew him to be: skilled, captivating, and, most of all, himself. It was clear that Paige wasn't going to temper his personality or alter his style just because his path had finally crossed over into the majors. The implicit rules and regulations that bound Robinson and Doby in emotional straitjackets wouldn't similarly confine him. As he would explain time and time again: "I'm Satchel . . . I do as I do."

There was a certain poetic justice to Paige's breaking into the majors on the same team as Bob Feller. Feller had banked on Paige's drawing power to launch Ro-Fel, Inc.; Paige, in turn, had used the

tours to showcase his undiminished ability to bewilder white batters. While Feller's corporate dreams took flight, Paige's major-league aspirations remained grounded. Fittingly, his entry came about partially because Feller had faltered in the season's first half. Had Feller pitched to form, perhaps Veeck wouldn't have felt such urgency to bolster the Indians' pitching ranks. Feller's swoon, in a sense, facilitated Paige's rise.

By the time Paige arrived in Cleveland, Feller was in more than a swoon: He was in free fall. The precipitating event was his selection to the All-Star Game—an unlikely nod for someone with a paltry record of nine wins and ten losses. Believing his inclusion had to do more with nostalgia than merit, Feller, in coordination with Veeck and Boudreau, withdrew his name from the roster, the second year in a row he'd done so (Feller had skipped the previous year's contest on account of injury).

Not even the jeers he'd withstood all season could have prepared Feller for the gale-force blowback that would follow. Because proceeds of the All-Star Game funneled into the newly established player pension fund, which would provide a cushion for those who earned less in their careers than what Feller made in a season, there was a sense of betrayal and anger among ballplayers that a pitcher who never thought twice about barnstorming in the off-season couldn't drag himself to Sportsman's Park to throw an inning or two in solidarity with his less prosperous peers.

In the run-up to the All-Star Game in St. Louis, this sentiment reached a boiling point. "An anti-Bob Feller bloc—growing stronger than the anti-Truman group ever did among the Democrats—is sweeping the baseball people assembled here," wrote Hy Hurwitz of *The Boston Globe*. There was, another reporter claimed, "a lot of jealousy of Bob Feller" among players—"jealousy not only of his position, his income, and his prestige, but also of his independence."

The same independence that rankled executives and fans now alienated Feller from his peers, who had already begun to let loose

with pent-up complaints. "You can see Feller by appointment only," they joked among themselves, adding that Feller considered it "a large favor to grant a leisurely hello" to anyone outside his orbit. "Feller is in for a rough time," Boston Red Sox catcher Birdie Tebbetts predicted. "He's going to get the silent treatment from all the players around and he'll get booed all over the circuit." One writer went so far as to suggest that league officials, in honor of Feller, should erect a statue of a ballplayer "with one hand outstretched for money and the other hand at the throat of a figure which would be labeled Goodwill for Baseball, Integrity and Fair Play."

Despite Veeck's attempts to deflect blame from Feller, the furor didn't die down in the season's second half. Everywhere the Indians traveled, crowds heckled Feller with an intensity usually reserved for their team's bitterest rivals. "No player in the history of the major leagues," Boudreau wrote, "ever was booed more savagely, more persistently, more noisily, and with less justification, than was Bob Feller in the summer of 1948." Opposing players weren't any quicker to forgive. Bobby Doerr, the Red Sox's mild-mannered second baseman, speculated that Feller's unpopularity among players "may knock the Indians out of the pennant race" because opponents now would be extra-motivated to topple him from his lofty perch.

To reporters who asked if the booing bothered him, Feller snapped: "What do you think I am, a rookie?" Away from the field, however, his mood turned sour. Normally an inveterate consumer of news, Feller now tossed out the daily editions unread. What's more, rumors were spreading that his wife, Virginia, was suffering from an undisclosed disease. While giving birth to their second son late in 1947, Virginia had lost an alarming amount of blood, requiring a transfusion. In a mistake that could've cost her life, doctors injected her with a blood type incompatible with her own. A lengthy recovery followed, during which she became addicted to barbiturates and amphetamines. When she came home to their new twenty-seven-acre estate in Gates Mills, an eastern suburb of Cleveland, her moods

and sleep patterns became irregular. Sometimes, she'd pad around at all hours of the night, forcing Feller to steal away to another room to catch a few hours of precious rest. Frequently he'd show up to the stadium on game days drained, preoccupied, and braced for a hostile reception.

As fans soured on Feller, they became entranced by Paige. It was nowhere more evident than after the All-Star break on July 14, when the Indians and the Dodgers squared off against each other in a charity contest in which each of the major leagues' four Black players (Paige, Doby, Robinson, and Campanella) competed. Roughly 40 percent of the 65,000 spectators who showed up at Municipal Stadium that night were Black; it was estimated that one out of every six Black residents in Cleveland was in attendance. Unsurprisingly, Paige seized the spotlight. Coming on in relief, he struck out the side in the sixth on just thirteen pitches, then made quick work of the Dodgers the following inning. The single he legged out in his lone at-bat sent the boisterous crowd into a revelry.

Immediately afterward, the Indians traveled to Philadelphia for a four-game series against the Athletics, a club that stood a mere half-game behind the first-place Indians. Thrilled by the possibility of seeing Paige in action, fans started lining up at Shibe Park as early as nine in the morning on July 15. By the time the gates opened at five, a swirling mob, eager to scoop up any unreserved seats, ringed the park's cathedral-like exterior. Women fainted; parents hoisted children above their heads to avoid being stampeded. "If they had been giving away gold mines, or autographed baseballs, the crush couldn't have been worse," said the *Cleveland Press*.

Inside, the atmosphere was electric. A mere glimpse of Paige was enough to elicit full-throated cheers from the sellout crowd. In contrast, every time Feller poked his head out of the dugout, chants of "Crybaby!" and "Boo, Feller!" rippled through the stands. Over some seats behind the first-base line a group of fans had draped

a five-foot banner that read: SEND HIM BACK TO THE FARM, BOU-
DREAU. FELLER IS A QUITTER.

Spectators got what they wanted in the sixth inning of the second game. Indians starter Bob Lemon suffered a minor head injury,
Boudreau gestured to the bullpen, and out walked Paige to raptur-
ous applause. He wasn't nearly as effective that evening as during his
debut. Entrusted with a lead, Paige blew it by giving up a two-run
homer in the seventh. Ken Keltner and Larry Doby bailed him out
by launching bombs of their own over the next two innings. Paige
coasted to the finish with no further damage, reaching a milestone
that was his alone: the first Black pitcher to notch a win in the major
leagues.

The following day it was Feller's turn on the mound. In contrast
to Paige's calm demeanor, Feller "gave the appearance of a young
fellow whose emotions and reactions have been frozen by continuing
and increasing hostility." He didn't even make it through the first
inning. Battered for five runs, Feller logged just a single out before
Boudreau gave him the hook. In the clubhouse afterward, he sat in
a daze. "They hit good curve balls," he muttered. "Curve balls that
were just like they rolled off a table. I can't understand it." It was
Feller's eleventh loss of the season, matching his total from 1947.

Boudreau knew something had to change. After the game,
he made an unexpected announcement: Feller would move to the
bullpen for the Indians' subsequent series against the Washington
Senators. Taking his place in the rotation would be Satchel Paige.

Even though Boudreau later would reverse the decision, his instincts revealed a deeper truth: Seemingly overnight, the face of the
Indians' rotation had changed. Over the following month, crowds
would boo Feller with a fervor inversely proportionate to their cheers
for Paige, whose sudden emergence from the Negro Leagues pro-
voked a mania unseen among fans since Feller's sudden emergence
from the Iowa cornfields twelve years earlier.

while announcing that, following the All-Star break, Doby would be the team's everyday center fielder.

The Indians closed out the season's first half with a record of forty-five wins and twenty-eight losses, just barely good enough for first place. Buoyed by Doby's return and Satchel Paige's arrival, the team came out strong in the second half, then fell into a familiar pattern. Beginning on July 20, the Indians dropped eight of their next ten games, tumbling from first to third, tied with the New York Yankees and behind the Philadelphia Athletics and the first-place Boston Red Sox.

One incident came to symbolize the swoon. In the eighth inning of a game against the Philadelphia Athletics on July 28, the Indians were clinging to a one-run lead. The Athletics, in a last-ditch charge, put two runners on base. Coming on in relief of Bob Lemon, Indians pitcher Russ Christopher retired first baseman Rudy York, and then whipped an underhanded sinker to Athletics third baseman Don White, who popped a shallow fly to left-center. Hollering for the ball all the way was left fielder Dale Mitchell, but Doby, unable to hear his teammate's calls, cut off Mitchell's more leisurely route. He then blinded himself upon looking up into the midday sun. The ball, blurring into the light, ticked off Doby's glove, then clipped the bill of his cap—a humiliating error made all the worse when both runners streaked across the plate.

In the clubhouse following the Indians' 4-3 loss, Doby slouched on a stool, mute and immobile amid the usual whirl of postgame activity: teammates showering and rummaging through lockers, steam and cigarette smoke clouding the air. Bill McKechnie sat down next to him. Though seemingly paralyzed by regret, Doby opened up to the coach who'd gained his trust: "I didn't hear anybody call for the ball . . . I just wanted to catch it and I would have, too, if I hadn't lost it in the sun."

McKechnie's response was measured yet pointed, a challenge for the season's final two months. "Larry," he said softly, "now we'll find out whether or not you're the kind of big leaguer all of us have said you'd be. Personally, I'm betting you'll make it."

After tough losses in Cleveland, Doby no longer had to face the nights alone. In 1948, he and his wife lodged with Arthur "Choker" Grant, a Negro Leaguer-turned-sanitation worker whom Doby had befriended at the Great Lakes Naval Training Station. According to Olympic hurdler Harrison Dillard, Grant "seemed to know everybody and everything in [Cleveland's] Black community." Anita Jackson, Grant's oldest daughter, concurred: "Everybody looked toward him as a father-figure. He was always giving advice and helping out when he could."

Many of the city's most prominent Black residents would stop by his three-story house on Parmelee Avenue periodically, everyone from Cleveland Browns fullback Marion Motley to Perry B. Jackson, the first Black judge in Ohio, to Jesse Owens, who used to stage mock-races on the front lawn with Grant's children. The Cleveland Heights neighborhood was populated with Black professionals: doctors, teachers, and small-business owners. And it was this network of support that Doby could rely on to lift his spirits. "People were very accepting of [Doby]," Jackson said. "They loved him."

Doby's relationship with Veeck also deepened over the summer. Out of the hospital, the Indians owner kept a watchful eye over Doby. "[Veeck] always seemed to know when things were bad, if things were getting to me," Doby told sportswriter Claire Smith decades later. "He'd call up and say: 'Let's go out. Let's get something to eat.'" On the road, the two would meet up after games in unlikely locales for a major-league owner to frequent. "[Veeck] loved jazz and we would go wherever we could find a jazz club," Doby remembered. "He'd be the only white face, but he didn't care." They would sit there together, eating dinner and listening to music, enjoying each other's company. "To me," Doby said, "[Veeck] was in every sense color blind. And I always knew he was there for me." Veeck reciprocated the sentiment: "I want to tell you this: I have two sons and if they grow up to be as nice as Larry [Doby], I'll be very happy," he told a Paterson reporter in 1948.

That same warm bond never developed between Doby and his new roommate on the road. Since joining the Indians, Doby had pined for someone he could commune with after away games. Satchel Paige wasn't that teammate. The two men straddled opposing ends of a generational divide, temperamentally and philosophically at odds. Seventeen years apart in age, they'd cut their teeth during different eras in the Negro Leagues, and now faced differing pressures and expectations in the majors.

As someone who'd broken into the American League as a youthful pioneer burdened with assimilating into a white league with minimal disruption, Doby shouldered a round-the-clock obligation to appear dignified, composed, and nonthreatening. In interviews he minded his words so as not to come across as militant or improper. On the field he silently stomached slurs and players spitting tobacco juice on him despite wanting to "tear apart" the people doing so. Once, late in 1948, he almost did. After a fan in St. Louis made a vulgar crack about his wife, Doby picked up a bat and set off toward him, consumed with rage he could no longer stifle. If several teammates hadn't pulled Doby back, he could have jeopardized not only his career but possibly baseball integration as a whole.

As someone who'd broken into the American League as an elderly legend whose lofty reputation preceded him, Paige could act and speak in ways inconceivable to Doby. There was no indication that Veeck had pulled Paige aside and discussed the implicit rules he was expected to follow—or that such a talk would've made a difference. Governed by his own sense of time and decorum, he missed trains and curfews, steered clear of the ballpark when storm clouds hovered overhead, ditched team hotels for Black boardinghouses, and sometimes eschewed the team bus for chauffeured Cadillacs. Eventually, a frustrated Boudreau handed Paige a team schedule and warned: "I'm going to ask you for this every day, Satch. If you're ever without it, it'll be an automatic $100 fine."

While some in the Black press wrung their hands at Paige's mercurial tendencies, white reporters jockeyed for quotes and musings, the more colorful the better. A month-long newspaper series on Paige's life written from his perspective proved so popular that its chapters were slapped together and rushed into bookstores. Solving the supposed mystery of Paige's age turned into a national obsession that summer, with estimates ranging from late thirties to late fifties. Some claimed to have seen Paige pitch in 1920, others as far back as 1910. A master at generating publicity, Paige played along by dangling a $500 reward to anyone who could dredge up a scrap of paper that proved he'd pitched before 1927. One amateur sleuth took him up on it, tracking down a box score from 1926 with Paige's name in it. "I musta slept a year somewhere," Paige said, dumbfounded.

Paige's introductory experiences with the Indians were markedly different from Doby's. Far from giving him the silent treatment, his new teammates took to him instantly. "Satchel was a delight from the time he joined the team," Eddie Robinson said. "He was funny. He said funny things. Of course, Doby had broken the ice, but Satchel was well accepted." They reveled in his witticisms and wordplay, his willingness to take a ribbing and dish it right back, his amusing nicknames that ranged from "Bob Rapid" for Bob Feller, to "Mister Lou" for Lou Boudreau, to "Burrhead" for Bill Veeck.

These actions, among others, were often more than Doby could bear. "[Paige] was a character and he enjoyed being perceived that way," Doby later asserted. "He'd come into the clubhouse and clown around, and did some Amos 'n' Andy stuff. I didn't think it was right—at least, it wasn't right for me." Sensitive to white perceptions of Negro League players as clowns or showmen, Doby would walk out whenever Paige unspooled a yarn that left his listeners in stitches. He worried that Paige's use of humor to win over new teammates along with his laxness about team rules and regulations presented obstacles to gaining the respect that Black pioneers of Doby's generation sought in the majors. "In my opinion, he only added to racism," Doby said of Paige. "He encouraged the black stereotype of the times. He made people laugh. He came from the Stepin Fetchit era and played that role. I resented it. . . . I believed in carrying myself with pride, to seek respect and speak with some of the intelligence I was born with."

What Doby seemed to miss was the pride that Paige carried himself with, too, albeit in a manner that his new roommate failed to appreciate. Paige, biographer Larry Tye wrote, had always thrived "by playing to whites' expectations of blacks . . . then exceeding and defying them." Certainly, Paige was adept at amusing crowds and teammates. But he was also single-minded about mowing down batters as soon as innings started. When asked by a reporter from *The Plain Dealer* why he didn't ham it up more on the mound, Paige snapped: "This pitchin's a serious business with me—it's been that for 21 years."

Even so, Doby never stopped trying to convince Paige to amend his ways. "Look, Satch," he'd say, "you're not barnstorming now. You're in the big league and you gotta act like a big-leaguer. If you don't, I'll—I'll . . ."

"You'll what, Doby boy?" Paige asked.

"I don't know . . . But you gotta stop clownin' around. You gotta act like a big-leaguer."

Divided off the field, they were in harmony on it. The combination of Paige on the mound and Doby in center field proved tremendously effective. In a pennant race certain to go down to the wire, their superior play over the season's final months gave the Indians a competitive boost no other team in the American League had tried to match.

On August 1, Lou Boudreau, sore and sweat-drenched, plopped down in his office swivel chair. Though the Indians had just swept a Sunday doubleheader against the Red Sox, his mind wasn't at ease.

"Now we've got to win Tuesday night," he muttered. "That's the big one."

Four teams—the Red Sox, Yankees, Athletics, and Indians—had clustered at the top of the American League standings, with little daylight between them. Boudreau knew his pitching staff was gassed; Feller, for one, hadn't completed a game in nearly a month. The moment called for creativity, and Boudreau supplied it by tapping Paige as his surprise starter.

A mad dash for tickets commenced. "Look, I had 800 tickets for this game. They were moving like molasses," one licensed agent at the Mayflower Hotel in Akron said. "Then it's announced that Paige will pitch. In 22 minutes—count 'em if you'd like—in just 22 minutes I sold out the 800. I sent for another 700. People lined up outside the place. By noon Monday those were gone . . . So I hurried to Cleveland Monday night. They gave me what they could, 600 tickets. They were gone inside half an hour. We've sold 2200 tickets for this game right here in Akron. Well, since they said Paige is gonna pitch, that is."

Just before game time, on Tuesday, August 3, Indians coach Muddy Ruel glanced up from the dugout at the noisy mass of humanity squeezing into standing-room-only sections and traipsing up to the nosebleed seats. "Say," Ruel remarked to Paige, "some people are coming into this park. I'll bet we'll have 55,000."

"We'll do 70,000," Paige responded without bothering to look up.

For once, Paige was underestimating. In fact, more than 72,000 people elbowed their way into the stadium—the largest-ever crowd for a night game in Cleveland. A carnival-like atmosphere took hold. Franklin Lewis reported that one unnamed player for the opposing Washington Senators "wore false blackface on the bench. The attention of the umpires was called to the alleged comedian, but they overlooked the gag." It was further evidence that no matter how capably Paige had thrown from the bullpen, the degrading clown-pitcher image refused to die. His first major-league start was yet another chance to bury it.

He almost didn't. In the opening inning, Paige walked the second batter he faced, then the third—a startling sequence for a pitcher with legendary control. The next man up, outfielder Bud Stewart, blasted a triple to left-center, plating both runners. Panicked, Boudreau rushed to the mound. Paige shrugged. "Don't worry none," he said. "That ol' control ain't gonna be missing anymore. You just leave me in there."

As if flicking a switch, Paige regained his command. For the rest of the evening, the Senators would eke out just one more run against Paige, who departed after the seventh inning with a 4-3 lead that the Indians subsequently held.

It was a win Veeck had wanted as badly as Boudreau, not just to nudge the Indians into first place, but to force his outspoken critics—those who'd accused him of sullying league standards by signing Paige—to eat their words. When asked afterward about Paige's performance, Veeck deadpanned: "I don't think Satch embarrassed us."

The Indians won eight of their first nine games in August, then dropped three of the next four. By the time Boudreau summoned Paige to start again, on August 13 against the White Sox in Chicago, the Indians had slipped a half-game behind the Philadelphia Athletics. Once more, it would fall on Paige to pitch them into first.

That afternoon, Veeck and Indians publicist Bob Fishel hailed a cab from downtown Chicago, expecting to arrive at Comiskey Park well before the start of the game. Ninety minutes later, they found themselves stuck in such immovable gridlock that cops were encouraging drivers to double-park and walk to the ballpark. Abandoning the taxi, Veeck and Fishel were swept up in the onrushing masses. Even though reserved seats had been sold out in advance, no one turned back. Fans pushed and scraped and clawed their way forward, determined to see Paige somehow, ticket or no ticket.

All around Comiskey Park, thousands of fans smashed together in impenetrable blocks. Extra police officers were summoned for crowd control; more than a dozen people had to be whisked to hospitals for injuries suffered in the crush. Luckily, an eagle-eyed White Sox employee spotted Veeck's bare head and sent down someone to escort him inside. There, he begged team owner Grace Comiskey to take action. "Why don't you just let them in before they break the fences down?" Veeck reportedly pleaded.

It was too late. At one gate, the mob pressed forward so forcefully that the turnstile was wrenched right from the floor. Waves of people surged past the overwhelmed attendants. Soon, Veeck wrote, "there was not a place in the park that was not covered by human, sweating flesh." Many ticket holders, having finally muscled their way inside, found their seats already filled by freeloaders who refused to budge. Inundated with complaints, several ushers chose to hide rather than deal with the angry customers. Officials estimated the crowd size at 51,013, a nighttime attendance record at Comiskey Park, though Veeck believed that tens of thousands more had packed in, despite the stadium's official capacity being only 50,000.

Moments before the Indians took the field, Veeck sought out Paige, urging him to show the packed house exactly what he was capable of. For Paige, being back in Chicago—the nerve center of the Negro Leagues, a city chock-full of memories—was likely its own motivation. It was the same park he'd pitched in at the annual East-West All-Star Game, and many of the same fans who'd seen him mow down lineups of Negro League stars had now refused to let turnstiles or ushers stand in the way of their watching Paige do the same against major-league batters.

He didn't disappoint. All evening long, Paige threw loose and easy, spotting pitches precisely where he wanted them. After White Sox third baseman Luke Appling slapped a single in the first inning,

Paige didn't allow another base runner until the fifth. The game was a tight and tense scoreless pitching duel until Larry Doby tripled in the top of the fifth, then trotted home on a sacrifice fly. It was the only run Paige would need. Backed by a crowd that thrilled to his every delivery, Paige went the distance for the first time that year, allowing five singles and no walks in a 5-0 shutout win.

Afterward, Veeck ducked down to the clubhouse, where Paige was soaking his arm in scalding water. Grinning at the Indians owner, he quipped: "I kept 'em from running us both out of town."

They were men cut from the same cloth—inimitable in style, eccentric in character, and dogged in principle. After seasons of circling each other, they'd come together exactly when both had needed a boost. Until then, none of the stars in the Indians' lineup had so fully meshed with the owner's theatrical sensibility, had so effortlessly melded swagger with skill, spectacle with supremacy. Even though Veeck had seen him throw numerous times through the years, Paige's mastery during his first month in the majors had left him breathless. "He's done more, much more, than my fondest hopes. He's still one of the best pitchers in baseball and he has more than earned what I am paying him," Veeck said.

The two smiled at each other now from across the clubhouse, a friendship born of mutual respect and admiration blossoming between them. "Never in doubt, Burrhead," Paige assured him.

The following week, the Indians could do no wrong. They swept the White Sox, then the Browns. Even Feller got in on the action, tossing his first complete game since the All-Star break. To cap it off, three Indians starters—Bob Lemon, Gene Bearden, and Sam Zoldak—threw three straight shutouts. One more would tie the American League record for consecutive scoreless games, and it was Paige's turn in the rotation next.

On August 20, pandemonium broke out again on the streets of Cleveland. It was a Friday night, the Indians stood alone in first place, and Paige was set to start. By game time, more than 78,000 people—a new nighttime attendance record for a major-league contest—spilled into the aisles of Municipal Stadium. "If they say Old Satch is the greatest drawing card in the history of baseball, they're just reciting the plain, mathematical truth," wrote Ed McAuley, adding: "Bob Feller in his prime never possessed such magnetism. Neither did Babe Ruth. Neither does Ted Williams. The old boy from Mobile . . . has captured the imagination of the country's baseball fans as has no other competitor." In Paige's first three starts, an astounding 201,829 fans had turned out, with thousands more being denied entry at the gates. He was a sensation, the talk of the circuit, someone who, according to *The Chicago Defender,* rendered moot the long-standing fears among major-league moguls that attendance would fall and white spectators would boycott games should integration happen. Instead, the surge in Black and white fans alike was toppling records wherever Paige pitched.

That evening, he'd need help in extending the Indians' scoreless streak; his roommate would provide it. Throughout the game, every time Paige waded into trouble, Doby rescued him. It was true in the fourth inning, when Paige walked White Sox first baseman Tony Lupien, then surrendered a single to Luke Appling. Fielding the ball on a hop, Doby gunned a throw to third that beat the sliding Lupien by a hair, extinguishing the threat. In the bottom half of that inning, following a pair of singles by Boudreau and Ken Keltner, Doby laced his own single to center, driving home Boudreau for the game's first and only run.

The White Sox nearly knotted it three frames later when slugger Pat Seerey, who'd been traded by the Indians to the White Sox in June, rapped a towering fly that appeared certain to soar into the seats. Sprinting to the wall, stretching his glove high over his head, Doby pulled the ball back into play. It was the exact sort of catch that Boudreau doubtlessly had in mind when he'd shifted Doby to center field.

The game ended in a narrow 1-0 victory that was as much Doby's as Paige's. Never before had a pair of Black teammates joined forces so wholly and decisively—on the mound, in the field, at the plate—in a major-league win. An editorial in Cleveland's largest newspaper, *The Plain Dealer*, called it a "triumph of racial tolerance."

Afterward, Veeck dashed off a telegram to *Sporting News* publisher J. G. Taylor Spink, the foremost critic of Paige's signing: "Paige pitching—No runs, three hits. He definitely is in line for Sporting News' 'Rookie of the Year' award. Regards." In the clubhouse, Paige sipped a beer while the press gathered around. "Five or six years ago I was twice as good," he told them, chiding the baseball establishment, gently yet pointedly, for barring him in his prime. One reporter quipped that he looked like a shoo-in for the top-rookie prize. Paige grinned. "You may be right, man," he said, "but 22 years is a long time to be a rookie."

It was a long time, too, to wait for the storybook chapter in the major leagues that had been denied to Paige since his youth. Now, in his middle age, it was being written at the precise moment that Feller was struggling to balance wins with losses. If the Indians were to complete their run to the World Series, *Washington Post* columnist Shirley Povich wrote, it would be because Paige had "taken up much of the slack occasioned by Bob Feller's poor season." It would be Paige, Povich argued, "winning the pennant for Cleveland in a year when Bob Feller, supposedly greatest of them all, couldn't."

24

The Gingerbread Men

For Bill Veeck, the days were long and the nights even longer in the summer of 1948. As his nocturnal headquarters, Veeck chose a newly opened restaurant in the up-and-coming suburb of Shaker Heights called Gruber's. Bill Gruber, the son of co-owner Max Gruber, described the eatery as "classic French-American, very classy. Bill Veeck was the only guy allowed in without a tie." The menu was a mélange of urbane dishes, from oysters Rockefeller to calf livers to sauerkraut balls, the Gruber family's own concoction. Wooden casks stuffed with live lobsters were stacked up five feet tall in the kitchen. To encourage wine consumption, beer was priced at the outrageous sum of one dollar per bottle.

Many nights, Veeck gathered there alongside a cast of sportswriters and socialites who called themselves "The Jolly Set." Newspaper columnist and charter member Winsor French characterized them as a "small but carefree group who refused to let life's darker problems get in the way of fun." As the ringleader, Veeck, according to French, entertained "in a fashion reminiscent of Versailles": popping bottles of sparkling burgundy, dressing up for costume parties, and leading spirited games of charades. Sometimes Veeck

would hoist fellow diners on his shoulders and parade them around the restaurant, or snip feathers from women's hats and then send a dozen feather-free replacements to their doorsteps later on. With an expense account of around $100,000 annually, Veeck snatched checks and stuffed waiters' pockets, dropping money "like a sailor just ashore."

At closing time The Jolly Set dispersed, but Veeck carried on, slipping seamlessly from high to low society. In the heart of Cleveland, a handful of watering holes kept the lights burning until sunrise. Bouncing between the Alhambra Tavern, the Ten-Eleven Club, the Theatrical Grill, and various neon-lit joints along seedy Short Vincent, Veeck rubbed elbows with the racketeers, insomniacs, gamblers, and entertainers who prowled the streets while the rest of the city slumbered—everyone from northern Ohio's most notorious gangster, Shondor Birns, to the taxi drivers who made Veeck a perennial guest of honor at their Yellow Cab Co.'s safety awards banquet. Some thought it unseemly, wrote Gordon Cobbledick, "for a man in his position to be seen so often in the late spots, in the company of such characters as shared his reluctance to go to sleep until all other fun-producing resources had been exhausted. His reply was that he liked that kind of people and did anyone wish to make something of it?"

There was seemingly no time for sleep. Veeck logged endless hours at the office and on the road, communed with fans late into the night, soaked his damaged leg in a tub while paging through books ranging from bestsellers to dense histories in the early morning, and then went right back to answering letters and making calls before anyone else had shown up at the team offices. "He was the only man I knew who could drink a case of sparkling burgundy and still look as if he hadn't taken a drink," Hank Greenberg claimed. "He could work for twenty hours a day, sleep for four hours, and his generator would be recharged, his eyes would be bright."

All summer long, Veeck raced around the clock, the nursery

rhyme from childhood echoing in his mind: *Run run as fast as you can. You can't catch me, I'm the Gingerbread Man.* There were thousands of people like him spread across northern Ohio, forged in the Depression and scarred by the war, reeling from nearly two decades of hardship and sacrifice. Veeck gave those residents reason to let loose, to believe that lean times had come to an end, that Cleveland had emerged stronger than before, a city booming with industry, sports, and vice, flush with income and idealism for the first time in decades. In the words of one theater manager, Veeck blasted everyone "out of their easy chairs and got them into the habit of going downtown for their recreation." Restaurants overflowed; nightclubs swung until dawn. Game-day trains and buses spilled passengers onto the shores of Lake Erie. It was a frenzy, what Cobbledick called the "greatest demonstration of mass hysteria in the history of commercial sport." Seemingly everything Veeck had promised upon arrival in Cleveland—victory and fireworks, attendance records and inclusion, an entire civic reawakening spurred on by baseball—was coming to pass, and he couldn't bear to miss even a minute of it.

The center of it all was the Indians' success. Almost every roster move Veeck had—or hadn't—made over the past few years was bearing fruit all at once. He'd heeded the concerns of Cleveland fans about off-loading Boudreau, and the beleaguered player-manager responded with an MVP season in which he batted .355 and, as Ted Williams later wrote, "did everything for the Indians but drive the bus." Veeck had signed off on the plan to convert Bob Lemon from a utility player to a pitcher, and Lemon rewarded his confidence with twenty wins by mid-September. Veeck had requested southpaw Gene Bearden as part of a trade with the Yankees two off-seasons ago, and the rookie knuckleballer burst out of nowhere in 1948 to make his own run at twenty wins.

None of it would've mattered had Veeck not also integrated the team's roster. He'd rolled the dice on Satchel Paige, and the pitch-

er's six wins carried the Indians through what had usually been the franchise's rockiest stretch of the season. After rushing Larry Doby onto the Indians' roster, Veeck gave him something that few Negro League players who struggled in their transitions would receive: time and room to make mistakes while learning on the job. His faith in Doby paid off with the center fielder he'd been pining for since purchasing the club. "If we win the pennant this year," Veeck declared, "a lot of the credit will be due to the great improvement of Doby."

As the Indians thrived, Clevelanders responded with an enthusiasm that rivaled Veeck's own. Since April, attendance records had continuously fallen, and in the season's final month, Veeck broke the one he coveted the most. In a city of just under a million residents, the Indians smashed the Yankees' single-season mark of 2.2 million total customers by drawing a stunning 2.6 million, though some contended at least a million more attendees had gone uncounted.

The bond between fan and owner had become indissoluble. Never satisfied, Veeck sought ways to strengthen it further. One presented itself in September. Throughout the summer, the Indians had held various "nights" to honor individual players and shower them with gifts. It'd been suggested that Veeck deserved a night of his own. A Clevelander who wrote a letter to the editor in the *Cleveland Press* had a different idea. Joe Earley, a twenty-six-year-old Army veteran and security guard, proposed that the Indians stage a night instead "for good old Joe Earley, an average guy who has also done a lot for Cleveland." After all, he paid his rent on time and plunked down whatever extra cash remained at local businesses and Indians games. If anyone deserved a ceremony, Earley concluded, it was him.

The perfect promotion had fallen into Veeck's lap. What better way to show that he'd kept his word on giving the Indians back to the fans than with a "night to end all nights" for a stand-in for the common fan?

"Good Old Joe Earley Night" took place on September 28. The first 20,000 women to arrive at the lakefront stadium were greeted with an orchid flown in overnight from Hawaii. Veeck kicked off the pregame festivities with some stunts that hearkened back to his Milwaukee roots. Calling out seat numbers, he summoned fans onto the field. Prizes awaited them at home plate, each more absurd than the next: a keg of nails, a pair of squirming rabbits, a cake of ice, pigs, stepladders, a goat, a cow, and a swaybacked horse. At one point, a crateful of chickens busted open and the flock burst forth "like they were beating out a bunt."

When it came to Joe Earley and his wife, it seemed for a moment that the gags would cease. Deadpan, Veeck told the lucky couple that they would walk away that night with a new house and a new car, after which a truck bearing a wooden outhouse and then a busted-up Model T roared into the open.

Just when it looked like the whole night might devolve into a farce, a shiny yellow convertible lined with red upholstery motored onto the field, trailed by a truck overflowing with appliances and luxury goods that were still tough to come by three years after the war. Veeck read off each item one by one for the Earleys: a television set, a washing machine, a refrigerator, a dishwasher, a radio-phonograph console, a luggage set, a new wardrobe, and the convertible itself among others.

The scene was a microcosm of his tenure in Cleveland. The stadium was packed. The fans were laughing and cheering. The groundskeepers were scrambling every which way to corral the loose livestock. And in the eye of the amiable turmoil stood Veeck, a man who bore the scars of the decade's first half and the emergent look and attitude of the second, heaping hope and gifts on fans who for so long had been starved of them. Together, their moment had come. Now all they needed was the pennant.

*   *   *

For several years before and after World War II, Bob Feller and Satchel Paige faced each other in off-season barnstorming contests.

(Bettmann / Getty Images)

In 1946, at age thirty-two, with his war-injured leg wrapped in a cast, Bill Veeck bought the Cleveland Indians.

(Bettmann / Getty Images)

Bill Veeck meets Larry Doby for the first time on July 5, 1947, mere
hours before Doby's first game with the Cleveland Indians.

(Sporting News / *Getty Images)*

Larry Doby and Jackie Robinson, the first two Black players in Major League Baseball in the twentieth century.

(Sporting News / *Getty Images*)

Satchel Paige and Larry Doby, a pair of Indians teammates who gelled on the field but not always off it.

(Sporting News / *Getty Images*)

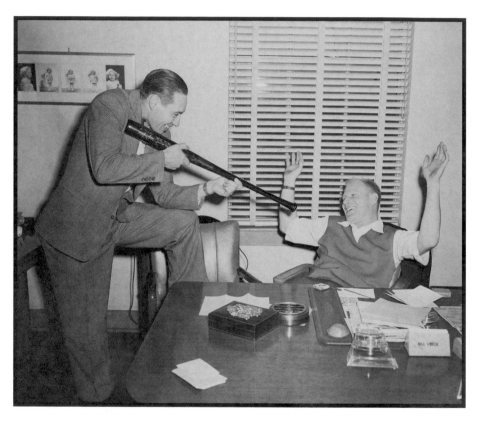

After returning from World War II, Bob Feller hustled hard to make up the money he lost, including in contract negotiations with Bill Veeck.

(Bettmann / Getty Images)

Bill Veeck took a risk when signing the fortysomething Satchel Paige to the Indians in 1948. Their friendship endured for decades afterward.

(Bettmann / Getty Images)

The mere sight of Paige, right, walking slowly onto the field was enough to whip major-league crowds into a frenzy in 1948.

(George Silk, The LIFE Picture Collection / Getty Images)

Indians player-manager Lou Boudreau and Bob Feller pose before the opening game of the 1948 World Series.

(Bettmann / Getty Images)

Satchel Paige warms up on the mound for his first, and last, World Series appearance, as Lou Boudreau looks on.

Steve Gromek and Larry Doby hug in the clubhouse after the fourth game of the 1948 World Series.

The pennant, as always, remained elusive. In the season's final month, the Indians, Yankees, Red Sox, and Athletics scrambled for it, neck and neck, nosing forward, then staggering back. To one writer, the race resembled "a steeplechase in which the horses had been thoroughly doped with gin in the paddock. No club was able to keep in a straight line for more than twenty feet." While Satchel Paige's month-long heroics had helped thrust the Indians into the lead, they soon stumbled, dropping eight of eleven games late in August to fall into third place. Players in opposing dugouts curled their thumbs and forefingers around their throats in a "choke" sign. By Labor Day weekend, the Indians had fallen four and a half games off the pace set by the Red Sox. "We're out," Cleveland sportswriters concluded, having written this story before.

A comeback would require extraordinary efforts. Over the team's final twenty-four games, Doby and Feller, alongside Boudreau and knuckleballer Gene Bearden, would provide them. All summer long, Boudreau had trusted his gut on the roster. He'd stuck with Doby after coming "within a hairsbreadth" of farming him out; he'd preserved Feller's spot in the starting rotation after seemingly the entire country had turned on him. Now, both players would help spur the Indians back into the race.

In late July, Boudreau had declared: "We'll win the pennant, but Feller will have to return to form." It'd seemed hopeless at the time. But as if in answer to a prayer, Feller turned back the clock just as the autumn breezes had begun to blow. Standing on the rubber, squeezing the ball in his fist, his eyes twitching and blinking involuntarily, he again resembled the hurler of old, right down to his explosive speed.

Evidence that Feller had reverted to form was rife: His win-loss record climbed above .500; he logged his first double-digit strikeout game in more than a year; and his tone in interviews took on its customarily blunt edge. "I've got it back," Feller asserted when asked what had changed. Veeck agreed: "Why, we'd have had won it by now if Feller had pitched the first four months of the season as he has the past four weeks." In eight starts in September, Feller allowed a mere nine earned runs, never once suffering a loss. Having booed him throughout the warm-weather months, Cleveland crowds now cheered the pitcher as if he were a wayward son who'd finally come home.

There was another, more secretive way Feller aided the Indians. He'd come back from the war with a three-foot-long telescope, the same one he'd peered through while standing guard on the USS *Alabama*. It served a different purpose now. Twenty of the Indians' final twenty-three games took place in their home stadium, largely against clubs lagging in the standings. To stage a comeback, the Indians would need to sweep the likes of the Browns and Senators, and pray for missteps along the Red Sox's and Yankees' paths. The latter result they couldn't control, but to boost their chances of the former, they would rely on a covert plan.

When the Indians came to bat, an idle member of the team—sometimes Feller or Bob Lemon—stationed himself in the manual scoreboard beyond center field, training the crosshairs of the mounted telescope on the opposing team's catcher, hundreds of feet away. So powerful was the military-grade instrument that Lemon told Russell Schneider, the sportswriter who broke the story of the Indians' espionage decades later, that he could see the grime underneath catchers' fingernails as they flashed signals to the mound. Indians batters knew to cast their gaze toward the scoreboard, where one of the groundskeepers would relay the signal to them through various gestures that they mixed up regularly to avoid arousing suspicion.

Sign-swiping and scoreboard espionage, practices as old as the game itself, had to be stealthy to be effective. So many clubs attempted such theft in that era that paranoia seeped into dugouts. Pitchers like Johnny Sain of the Boston Braves developed coded languages to thwart opposing teams' efforts. Sometimes Sain would show the face of his glove to his catcher to indicate that the next pitch would be the opposite of what the catcher called for. Other times, Sain would call the pitches himself through such gestures as picking up and dropping the resin bag. There were stakes to these rounds of one-upmanship. A spy who misread signals could put a hitter in danger. Someone primed for a curveball might be slow to react when a fastball buzzed toward his chin instead. Not every batter on the Indians elected to glance at the scoreboard, but enough did to give the offense a boost in the season's frantic final month.

Feller, for his part, professed no guilt about supplying and manning the scope. "Hey, all's fair in love and war, and when you're trying to win a pennant," he later told Schneider. Holing up on the darkened side of the scoreboard might have seemed out of step with the morally upstanding values embedded in Feller's identity, but over the past few seasons Feller had shown himself to be a more complicated figure than his prewar persona had suggested. Besides, it'd been eight years since the Indians had come this close to a pennant. If they blew it now, Feller might never get another chance.

As soon as Feller gained momentum, Satchel Paige lost his. Winning his first three starts proved the high-water mark for Paige's half-season stint. He won just one more start after that—a 10-1 drubbing of the Washington Senators on August 30—before falling cold. His and Feller's fates seemed intertwined that season; it appeared that one couldn't rise without the other falling. Feller didn't lose a game in September; Paige didn't win one. Soon, Boudreau relegated him to the bullpen. There, the pitcher who'd stirred the nation only weeks earlier became more spectator than participant during the race's nail-biting last leg.

Larry Doby picked up the slack. He charged into September in the midst of a twenty-one-game hitting streak. Immediately after it was snapped, Doby strung together another twelve-game streak. Not even a severely sprained thumb could break his stride. Whatever skepticism Indians fans harbored toward him mostly melted away. Now, an Associated Press story claimed, "they cheer his every move. They applaud every time he gathers in a fly ball. They raise the roof when he connects with a long one. They even cheer when he strikes out." Tris Speaker, Doby's outfield mentor, marveled at his pupil's rapid progress: "[Doby] has made more improvement with one season of experience than many outfielders have made after two or three years in the minors." It was Doby's determination to master his unfamiliar position that Veeck admired most: "[Doby] still makes mistakes, but only because he is young and does not have the experience yet. But he is quick to learn. Tell him something once and he never forgets. He never makes the same mistake twice."

The season's final weeks saw Doby deliver a slew of timely hits. The most dramatic came on September 19. In the first game of an afternoon doubleheader, Doby stepped to the plate with one on and one out in the ninth inning, the Indians and Athletics all knotted up at 3. The sellout crowd of 75,382—a number that marked the ninth time the Indians had drawn better than 70,000 fans in 1948—trained one eye on Doby and the other on the scoreboard, which showed the league-leading Red Sox similarly tied with the Tigers and the second-place Yankees tied with the Browns.

Doby took the first pitch for a ball, fouled off the next, then watched another zip by wide. A slow curve followed, catnip for the coiled batter. He whiffed at it with the same rash abandon that had plagued him the previous season. Shaking it off, he swung just as hard at the ensuing offering. This time, the ball sprang from his bat "as though it were shot out of a cannon," landing among the spectators bunched behind the fence in left-center. The swelling applause was likely heard clear across Lake Erie. It was a sound that was replicated twice afterward when panels on the manual scoreboard were swapped: Detroit 4, Boston 3; and St. Louis 8, New York 6.

Day by day, the Indians were chipping away at the lead. They'd won thirteen of their first fifteen post–Labor Day games, and Boudreau was quick to give credit where it was due. "Without Doby," he said in late September, "we would not be fighting for the pennant. We probably would have been in fourth place."

The Indians and Red Sox faced each other just once in September, on the 22nd. It was an emotional game for reasons unrelated to the pennant. Nine days earlier, Don Black, the Indians pitcher who'd revived his career through sobriety, had collapsed on the field while swinging at a pitch during a game he started, suffering a sudden, life-threatening cerebral hemorrhage. To help pay for Black's medical expenses, Veeck announced that the Indians would donate the gate receipts for their game against the Red Sox to their hospitalized teammate. That night, nearly 77,000 fans poured into Municipal Stadium. Under the lights, Feller held Boston batters hitless until the sixth inning. He went on to pick up a 5-2 win, while Black scooped up $40,380. "[Feller] showed me more in this game than at any other time this year," Boudreau said afterward. "He was the greatest pitcher in the world in the first five innings."

Two days later, an unprecedented situation had developed: Three teams—the Indians, Red Sox, and Yankees—were bunched atop the American League standings with identical records. The remaining seven games would decide the winner. Taking no chances, Boudreau narrowed his pitching rotation to Feller, Lemon, and Bearden.

On Friday, September 24, the Indians traveled to Detroit for a three-game series against the Tigers. The first start fell to Bob Lemon, who was running on empty after having amassed a team-leading twenty wins. Worn down and unused to starting so frequently, Lemon had dropped from 190 pounds in the spring to 158 in the fall. Periodically throughout the summer, he'd had to tighten his belt an extra loop to keep his pants from sagging to his knees. That afternoon, the Tigers hung four runs on him, just enough to defeat the Indians by a 4-3 margin. Gene Bearden avenged the loss the next day while picking up his seventeenth win of the season, and then Feller closed out the series on Sunday by pitching the Indians into sole possession of first place with a one-run, nine-strikeout performance.

Back in Cleveland, Boudreau decided to skip Lemon's turn in the rotation and hand the ball to Bearden, whose pitching arm appeared fresher than ever. He spun a shutout against the White Sox on September 28. The following afternoon Feller, like Bearden, took the mound on two days' rest. His arm was sore, his velocity down, his curves unbent. But though White Sox batters tagged Feller for ten hits, they failed to string them together in a timely fashion. Through grit and guile Feller escaped with a 5-2 win, his nineteenth overall.

Following losses by the Yankees and Red Sox, the Indians entered the season's final weekend with a two-game lead. To ensure that they advanced to the franchise's first World Series in twenty-eight years, all they needed to do was win two of three games against the fifth-place Detroit Tigers at home. One writer mused that if the Indians were to blow the race now, railroads across Ohio would have to cease operation to clear all the people who'd thrown themselves across the tracks.

Lemon shouldered the assignment in the opening game. His strength appeared to have returned. Going into the ninth, he carried a one-run lead. Then it all went wrong. An infield single, an error, a walk, another walk, and Lemon was done for the day. Three runners crossed the plate as reliever Russ Christopher took over for him. In the clubhouse afterward, Lemon wept.

The Indians quelled the drama the following afternoon when Bearden floated one knuckleball after another past the flat-footed Tigers for his second shutout in a row. He was aided in his efforts by Doby, who banged a leadoff double off the wall in the fourth inning to ignite a five-run onslaught. In September, just when the Indians had needed him the most, Doby had ripped through league pitching at a torrid pace, nudging his season batting average above the .300 mark, nearly double what it'd been the previous season.

That same day, the Red Sox defeated the Yankees, dropping them from contention. Boston now trailed Cleveland by one game. If the Red Sox and Indians wound up tied atop the American League, there would be a one-game, winner-take-all showdown in Boston for the pennant. To avert that scenario, the Indians turned to Feller, who hadn't lost a game in five weeks. A win on the last day of the season could recast his turbulent summer as yet another arduous hero's journey he'd had to undergo. For the arc of Feller's career to bend upward once more, all he had to do was shut down the Tigers.

October 3 was a cold and blustery day in Cleveland. Feller could tell before the game even started: He didn't have it. His right arm had been worn down from months of overuse. Johnny Lipon, the Tigers' leadoff batter, whacked the first pitch Feller threw into left field for a single. It was going to be that kind of afternoon.

After surviving the first two innings, Feller broke down in the third, yielding a walk, a single, a double, and then an intentional walk to Pat Mullins to bring up left fielder Dick Wakefield with the bases loaded. Feller tried to sneak a fastball by him, but Wakefield blooped a short fly down the third-base line. The ball sailed over the fingers of Ken Keltner's outstretched glove by mere inches. With three runs in, Boudreau walked to the mound and patted Feller on the butt. Not a word passed between them as Feller retreated to the dugout.

Veeck watched the game from the press box, "pacing like a caged lion and shaking from the effects of weather and baseball, both unpleasant." With Feller out and Tigers ace Hal Newhouser in top form on the mound, Veeck and the nearly 75,000 shivering fans in the stands turned their attention instead to the scoreboard, which showed the Red Sox building a commanding lead over the Yankees. After the final scores were posted, Veeck slunk off to a solitary corner of the stadium and stared into the distance. Despite winning nineteen of their final twenty-four games, the Indians had fallen one victory short of clinching the pennant outright. They would have to travel to Boston for a one-game tiebreaker against the Red Sox the next day.

That night, at Cleveland's Union Terminal, the police cleared a path for the glum-faced Indians to board. Boston was a twelve-hour train ride away. For Feller, it felt longer than any trip he'd ever taken. "I tossed the whole night," he later told Hal Lebovitz. "I was wishing I could pitch again the next day to make up for it."

The dawn broke brilliantly across the New England countryside on October 4. One by one, Winsor French wrote, the Indians filed into the dining car, looking "like youngsters getting ready for school. Everyone ate enormous breakfasts, everyone was smiling, even Bob Feller." The night had passed like any other. There'd been cards, beer, and dice. Bearden had shot craps, Lemon and Ken Keltner had downed a few too many.

Despite its being Lemon's turn in the rotation, Boudreau went with his gut. In the Indians' clubhouse following Feller's loss, he'd named Bearden as the starter for the one-game, winner-take-all showdown. It was a controversial move. Not only would Bearden pitch a mere two days after his previous start, but he'd do so in Fenway Park, where left-handed pitchers faced a distinct disadvantage. Towering over left field was the Green Monster, a high wall for the Red Sox's right-handed trio of Vern Stephens, Dom DiMaggio, and Bobby Doerr to take aim at. Only two visiting southpaws had gone the distance at Fenway that year: Lou Brissie of the Philadelphia Athletics and Bearden himself. Securing his fifth win in a row and twentieth overall would be a steep task for the rookie knuckleballer.

Red Sox manager Joe McCarthy also went with his gut, bypassing the consensus choice, left-hander Mel Parnell, for an aging journeyman named Denny Galehouse who'd been knocking around the American League since 1934, often as a back-of-the-rotation starter on break-even clubs. In spite of decades of wear on his right arm,

Galehouse still could stifle a lineup when necessary, as the Indians knew all too well. In late July, he'd held them to a mere two hits over eight and two-thirds innings. Playing a hunch, McCarthy gambled that Galehouse's sliders and slow curves would keep the ball in the park on an afternoon when the blowing breezes favored the batters.

It proved a costly bet. In the opening frame, Boudreau slammed the fourth pitch he saw into the screen above the Green Monster. Three innings later, Ken Keltner broke the game wide open with a three-run shot. While Doby contributed a pair of doubles, the day belonged to Boudreau and Bearden. The Indians manager reached base five times in as many plate appearances, capping his MVP season with two homers, two singles, and a walk, which more than vindicated the fans who'd turned out by the thousands on Cleveland streets the previous October to dissuade Veeck from trading the team's most popular player.

Bearden, meanwhile, pitched that afternoon with what Boudreau later called "the nonchalance of a veteran in a meaningless exhibition," sneaking sips of brandy between innings to calm his nerves. His knuckler was wilder than usual, darting and fluttering against the fierce headwind. Jim Hegan called for the pitch by resting his glove on his knee, fearful that the Red Sox might try to steal his signals. Despite Bearden's wildness, Hegan covered his knee for most of the game. Defying the odds, Bearden went the distance for an 8-3 victory. It was his fourth win in ten days, each one a complete game.

In a box along the third-base line, underdressed as always in the raw weather, Veeck had "yipped and yowled and yammered like a common fan" from the first pitch to the final out. As soon as the game was over, he vaulted the railing, busted across the infield, and shouldered his way into the center of the celebration. Tears welled up in his eyes.

The Indians disappeared down the runway and into the club-house. A mob converged on Bearden, ripping apart his uniform, pulling his hair, and pounding his back. One reporter made note of how strange it was "that Feller was not the hero of their pennant triumph." He'd had his chance to clinch it for the Indians, but now "he sat quietly and almost sadly in the background while two other kid pitchers, Lefty Gene Bearden and Sophomore Bob Lemon, took all of the bows."

Nearly trampled in the scrum, Doby sought refuge on a nearby rubbing table, where he soaked in the scene from a distance, a grin on his face. One reporter approached Satchel Paige for his thoughts. "Phew, man, that was the golrammest baseball stretch Ah have seen," he replied. "And remember, I've seen a lot more baseball than anybody in this here room, believe me."

The celebration carried over to a banquet hall at Boston's Kenmore Hotel, where the Indians were staying. Veeck spared no expense. Awaiting the team were platters overflowing with roast beef, lobster, and chicken a la king. Buckets of champagne dotted the floor.

According to one report in the *New York Amsterdam News,* as the festivities got under way, a few players noticed that Doby and Paige hadn't shown up. Nearly every member of the Indians set off to find them. It turned out that the two were in their room, perhaps uncertain about whether their presences would have been welcome. Their teammates coaxed Doby and Paige out and then escorted them to the party.

25

The Photo

The next morning, on October 5, Bob Feller, clad in a gray uniform and green sweatshirt, sprinted from home plate to the center-field wall at Braves Field, where the Indians would face the Boston Braves, winner of the pennant in the National League, in the World Series the following day. Soon, one by one, his teammates staggered onto the diamond. They looked, Lou Boudreau wrote, "as though they had just marched all the way from Cleveland without so much as an hour's rest." Trainer Lefty Weisman had to pass out numbers for the steam bath so that the stewed players could take turns soaking the alcohol out of their systems.

Feller hadn't attended the party at the Kenmore Hotel the previous evening. He'd missed the effusive toasts, the off-key sing-alongs, the fistfight that had broken out over unsettled gambling debts. While others swilled champagne until four in the morning, Feller had slept. Now, stone-cold sober, he galloped across the outfield, fell to his knees for push-ups, and kicked his legs high "like an overzealous chorus girl," punishing himself as if it were spring training all over again.

"This chance has been a long time coming," he remarked to

reporters after his workout. "I certainly don't want to muff it now. I was afraid the damage had been done Sunday by Detroit. You don't always get a second opportunity."

A few weeks shy of his thirtieth birthday, fourteen years since he and his father had motored to St. Louis to watch the Cardinals face the Tigers in the 1934 World Series, Feller would take to the mound the next day as the Indians' starting pitcher in the opening game of the 1948 World Series. This was the last dream of his boyhood unfulfilled—as well as his next shot at reverting his narrative to its storybook form.

Drama had defined the Indians' season, right down to its sudden-death conclusion. For their World Series opponent, the Boston Braves, the opposite had been true. Their summer had been workmanlike and efficient, more of a conveyor belt than a roller coaster. They'd plodded toward the National League pennant at a metronomic clip, never too fast, never too slow. At midseason they'd clocked in at 46-31, then went 45-31 the rest of the way. The team strung together no winning streak longer than eight games, no losing streak longer than four. Having climbed to the top of the standings in mid-June, the Braves relinquished their lead just once thereafter— and then only for a day.

They were too steady to command the nation's attention, too colorless to capture its heart. Their offense put teams away not with daring base running or soaring moon shots but with what Franklin Lewis characterized as "earth-shattering bunts and mighty one-base blows." The unfussy style of baseball the club practiced lulled opponents into a false sense of security. "They wait around until you boot a ball or make a wild throw, and then you're cooked," one rival manager said. Brooklyn Dodgers shortstop Pee Wee Reese remembered some afternoons when it seemed as if his club was beating the Braves' brains out and then, somehow, "you walk into the clubhouse and discover the Braves just beat you."

It'd been thirty-four years since the Braves had advanced to the World Series, the longest postseason drought in the majors. During those decades, the team was an afterthought, terminally insolvent and forever outshone by the Red Sox, Boston's favored franchise. Then, in 1944, a trio of construction magnates known as the "Three Little Steam Shovels" took the team's reins and laid down plans for a revival. Pragmatic, industrious, and flush with cash, they gave dingy Braves Field an overdue makeover, snagged managerial mastermind Billy Southworth, and wheeled and dealed their way into contention.

In 1944, the Braves had finished forty games behind the St. Louis Cardinals and dead last in the majors in attendance; now, four years later, they'd led the National League in wins and increased their spectatorship nearly sevenfold. Even so, few baseball scribes gave them much of a shot against the Indians. And that suited the Braves just fine. After all, these were the same writers who, according to third baseman Bob Elliott, had "laughed us off most of the summer—even while we stayed in first place. No one figured we had the stuff."

If the Braves were to pull off an upset, they'd have to match the Indians' formidable starting rotation. They boasted a pair of aces capable of doing just that: Johnny Sain, a curveball artist from Arkansas; and Warren Spahn, a southpaw from Buffalo, New York. Southworth had relied on this duo to close out the season as the National League pennant race tightened. Starting on September 6, Sain and Spahn had started eleven of the Braves' next fifteen games, with Sain going 5-1 and Spahn 4-1. A sports editor from *The Boston Post* wrote some memorable light verse that imagined the Braves' ideal four-day schedule as consisting of a start by Spahn, a start by Sain, and then two subsequent days of rain.

In the stretch drive the strategy had worked to a tee. There was no reason to assume it'd be any different in the World Series.

So much publicity was centered on Feller and his belated arrival into the postseason, but there was another member of the Indians whose

World Series debut was, if anything, even more overdue. Years before Feller left the farm, Dizzy Dean had declared that if Satchel Paige were to join the Cardinals' rotation, they'd have the pennant sewn up by midseason. In the ensuing decade and a half, Paige competed twice in the Negro League World Series, most recently in 1946 against Larry Doby, with whom he now shared the honor of being the first Black American Leaguers to advance to the Major League World Series. But before he could fulfill what he referred to as a "life ambition" long denied him, Paige would suffer one final indignity.

On the morning of the opening game, as Paige approached the players' gate, a security guard refused to let him pass.

"I'm a player," Paige insisted.

"Whadda ya play?" the guard shot back. "The trombone?"

There was nothing Paige could do. He'd already made up his mind to return to the hotel when one of his teammates strolled by. He affirmed that Paige belonged; the guard chose to believe him. Paige was both livid and bemused as he walked to the clubhouse. "Can you imagine that?" he asked. "That fellow musta thought I was Jackie Robinson, for he said I was too young to be Satchel Paige."

After the game, it would be the same story. Dressed in street clothes, Paige would ask a guard for directions to the team bus. "No busses. That way to a street car," the guard would reply, presumably never considering that the man before him was a member of the Indians.

The bus, it turned out, was idling outside. Paige would find it on his own.

Hours before the first pitch on October 6, a nor'easter howled down the Atlantic Coast, then veered out to sea. By noon, a gray mat of clouds covered Boston. Strong winds gusted off the Charles River, chilling the fans who poured out of the trolleys looping by Braves Field. Inside the park, there was plenty to warm them in the lead-up to the opening game. Baseball stuntman Jackie Price snagged liners while dangling upside down from the outfield fence; a three-piece band known as The Troubadours blew peppy tunes; and hungry attendees queued up for a distinctly New England ballpark lunch of fried clams.

In the clubhouse, Johnny Sain, the Braves' starting pitcher for the opening game, bit into an enormous hunk of tobacco. It bulged in his cheek like a golf ball. Steadily that afternoon he would chew it, pitch by pitch, inning upon inning, exercising his jaw more on the field than he ever did off it.

To many, he was known as "Silent Jawn," someone who answered writers' questions in clipped statements but otherwise remained "as quiet as an Ipswich clam." In each of the past three seasons, Sain had tallied twenty wins, something no other pitcher in the majors had done, not even the one Sain was preparing to square off against in perhaps the most anticipated pitching duel of the year. With a 19-15 record in 1948, Feller had fallen short of the twenty-win mark for the first time in a full season since he was a teenager.

Beforehand, the two right-handers had posed for photos together. At ease among the cameras, Feller flashed his customary boyish grin—dimples, pearly white teeth, and all. In contrast, Sain, clad in a tan suit jacket several sizes bigger than his burly frame, appeared stiff, dour, seemingly unable to mask the bad blood that ran between them. In 1946, Feller had lured Sain onto his barnstorming squad with fast talk of easy money. Sain had done his duty, mopping up games that Feller, the headliner, had started. In the end, he'd gone home to Arkansas with what he believed to be a smaller-than-expected check. Some speculated whether Sain now carried that grudge into their first major-league showdown.

During warm-ups, Sain took note of the frigid breeze blowing plateward. Calling over Bill Salkeld, his catcher, Sain explained that he wanted his curveball to break above, not below, batters' knees, which would entice them to swing for the fences. The countervailing wind, Sain trusted, would hamper the balls' upward trajectories,

knocking soaring drives safely into outfielders' gloves. In the opening inning, Sain put the strategy to the test. He baited batters with
fastballs outside the zone, then snapped curves high across the plate.
The results were promising. All three Indians batters hit lazy flies to
the outfield grass.

While Sain seemed sharp, Feller looked unbeatable. "No man
ever walked into a World Series game looking more like a no-hit
pitcher than Feller did in the early innings," wrote columnist Red
Smith. On the high mound at Braves Field, the Indians ace seamlessly blended the two halves of his career: prewar-Feller's intimidation and speed coupled with postwar-Feller's maturity and control.
The Braves didn't lay a finger on Feller until the fifth, when outfielder
Marv Rickert shot a single to right. Even then, it seemed so unlikely that Feller would yield another hit that fans began praying for
a premature dusk, since a game that commenced in daylight couldn't
continue under the lights. "If Sain can pitch until dark," one Bosto-
nian argued, "we can settle for a tie."

For a while, that seemed a likely outcome. Neither pitcher ceded
an inch. Feller's fastball was blazing; Sain's curves were bending. *The
Sporting News* dubbed Sain "the man with a thousand curves," and
each one—overhand, sidearm, from the hip—was finding the plate.
Forty thousand spectators held their breaths. In the Boston Common, thousands more crowded around the one hundred television sets
propped up on six-foot-tall wooden stands and fitted with specially
constructed shadow boxes to block out sunlight. In taverns and department stores, patrons stared at blurry, black-and-white screens, trans-
fixed by a pitching duel that was living up to the hype. Since the airing
of the last World Series—the first to be shown on TV—the number
of television sets across the country had almost quadrupled, from
150,000 to 550,000, according to one report in *The Sporting News*,
making this matchup likely the most watched in the sport's history.

Seven innings flew by without a runner on either team advanc-
ing beyond second base. Leading off the eighth for the Braves was

catcher Bill Salkeld. Feller fired a fastball for a first-pitch strike. Then his control deserted him. Four straight balls passed by inside; Salkeld never lifted the bat from his shoulder. In to pinch-run for the lumbering Salkeld was Phil Masi, who scurried to second when the following batter laid down a sacrifice bunt. That brought up second baseman Eddie Stanky, a fiery pest with a penchant for timely hits. Boudreau wanted nothing to do with him. Over Feller's protests, Boudreau ordered an intentional walk of Stanky to set up a potential double play with the pitcher due up next. Sain, however, spoiled the plan by lining out to right on Feller's first pitch.

With two on and two out, Braves right fielder Tommy Holmes dug into the batter's box. Masi took a wide, presumptuous lead off second. From the shortstop position, Boudreau cupped his glove over his left knee—a covert signal to Feller. Months earlier, during spring training, the two had fine-tuned a wily pickoff play. Upon glimpsing Boudreau's signal, Feller would turn his back to the runner on second base, then count slowly to three in his head, at which point he'd whirl around and fire a bullet to the bag in one motion, trusting that Boudreau would be there to receive it. During the season, the Indians had caught eight runners napping with this method.

Gunning now for a ninth, Feller counted while Boudreau broke for the bag. No sooner did the ball smack into his glove than Boudreau swiped it high across Masi's arm as he dove headfirst into second. Photos would later show Masi's fingertips to be several inches from the bag when Boudreau tagged him. It was clear as day: Masi was out. But in umpire Bill Stewart's judgment, Masi had slid under the tag.

Normally before games, Boudreau would alert umpires of the Indians' timed pickoff play, making sure they'd be ready for it when a runner reached second. This time, however, he'd been unable to shake free of Braves manager Billy Southworth for a moment alone with the officiating crew. As a result, Stewart, a National League umpire, had been as oblivious as Masi to what was coming. On the field, Boudreau and Feller howled in protest but to no avail. The inning would carry on.

To end it, Feller would have to dispatch Holmes, a natural-born hitter and perhaps the Braves' most popular player. Treading cautiously, Feller threw the first pitch inside. Holmes fouled off the next one. In hopes of running the count to 1-2, Feller attempted to sneak a shoulder-high fastball past Holmes, but his aim was off. The ball zoomed in belt-high instead, square into Holmes's sweet spot. He smacked a low line drive down the third-base line, past the reach of Ken Keltner. Off and running with the crack of the bat, Masi barreled around third and never stopped until his foot stomped on home plate. On only their second hit, the Braves had scored the game's lone run.

There would be no comeback for the Indians. Sain, the wad of tobacco still swollen in his cheek, worked around a two-base error in the ninth as calmly "as if he were watching the sunset in his native Arkansas hills," preserving the Braves' 1-0 victory. Afterward, in the clubhouse, photographers tried everything to coax a smile out of Sain. He refused. "If a couple of breaks had gone the other way," Sain told them, "you'd be in the other room taking pictures of Feller. The game was too close to smile."

In that other room, Feller stood before his locker, struggling to process the loss. "It seems every time I walk a man it beats me," he muttered. As photographers pointed their cameras at him, Feller attempted a smile, but what formed instead was "a pathetic sort of grimace. He gritted his teeth and lifted his eyebrows to clear away the tears of a heartbreaking defeat." For only the second time in World Series history, a pitcher had lost a complete game in which he'd allowed just two hits.

It wasn't over for Feller. Surely, before the series concluded, he would start another game. At the very least, there would be one more chance to rewrite the narrative of his trying season. Time, however, was running short.

* * *

The second game pitted Bob Lemon against Warren Spahn, another pitchers' duel. This one, though, seemed dull in comparison. To writer Grantland Rice, it seeped forward "with the speed of half-frozen molasses."

The Braves struck first, scoring an early run on an error and a pair of singles before the Indians cut the rally short by executing the same pickoff play they'd tried the day before. The umpire's immediate signaling of "out" was a promising sign that Lemon wouldn't suffer the same fate as Feller that afternoon. After Joe Gordon tied the score with an RBI single in the fourth, Larry Doby drove him home two batters later with a base hit to right. The lead was enough for Lemon. Unlike in September, when he'd sputtered late in games, Lemon gained strength as the innings dragged on, coasting to a 4-1 victory.

There was no time to celebrate. The World Series was to be played over seven consecutive days, two games in Boston, three in Cleveland, then two more in Boston, with no rest in between. The third game would start in less than twenty hours, hundreds of miles away. Players from both clubs showered, stuffed clothes into their trunks, and dashed to Boston's South Station. The Braves caught their train on time, but the Indians sat around for two hours, downing oyster stew and checking their watches anxiously for their train.

In Cleveland, the anxiety ran just as high. It was the moment the city had been waiting for all summer long. In June, the Indians had had to install an extra operator at their switchboard just to inform callers that World Series tickets wouldn't be available until late September, and then only if the Indians qualified for the postseason. The day before tickets finally went on sale, fans eager to mail in their applications snarled up traffic for blocks around post offices. Cleveland police reported that in some areas the gridlock "was bigger than the Easter parade jam." More than a million requests poured in, so many that Veeck had been forced to send out an emergency call for workers to sort through the sacks of letters that littered the office floors.

The night before the third game, it rained hard in Cleveland, a cold, drenching downpour. The ticketless fans who'd queued up for the one-dollar bleacher seats that would go on sale at ten the next morning weren't deterred. Some laid down ponchos and blankets on the wet pavement and tried to doze until sunrise; others forked over fifty cents to roving vendors for empty beer cartons to squat on.

By the morning of October 8, thousands of Clevelanders were huddled downtown around Public Square and Union Terminal to welcome the Indians home for the first time since before they'd clinched the pennant. Team flags and colorful bunting hung from shop awnings along Euclid and Prospect Avenues. Sound trucks blared music; hawkers peddled everything from squeaking rubber dolls to orchids. But the celebration never hit its climax. Because the Indians' train pulled into the station hours behind schedule, the players had no time to revel in the reception. They arrived to the stadium so late that Boudreau had to hustle onto the field in his street clothes when the umpires summoned both managers for a pregame discussion.

As the rain continued to fall, a sellout crowd never materialized. Just over 70,000 fans braved the elements—impressive by any standards except for Cleveland's. Luckily, the skies cleared by game time. Groundskeepers rolled the tarp off the field and eight bands decked in festive uniforms gathered around home plate for a joint rendition of the national anthem, after which planes roared overhead, fireworks exploded, and miniature American flags strung to parachutes dropped to the ground.

Bill Veeck supervised everything himself. While attendees bundled up in their overcoats and furs, Veeck roamed hatless and coatless—his white sports shirt open so widely at the neck that it was likened to a "very low cut gown"—from the field-level boxes to the far reaches of the upper deck just to ensure that those fans seated at the rim of the stadium had a view of the diamond as satisfactory as their view of Lake Erie. Out-of-town journalists learned quickly not to question whether Veeck's ceaseless activity was advisable for someone who'd endured three major surgeries in two years. "[Veeck] walks with a limp," one writer noted, "and if you give him a smile of sympathy, you won't get a second press pass from him."

It was Gene Bearden's turn on the mound, and being on baseball's biggest stage didn't break the southpaw's hot streak. In nine innings he threw just eighty-five pitches, most of them knuckleballs that Braves batters swung through. They scratched out a mere five hits, only one of which went for extra bases. The Indians, with five hits of their own, did little better, though they managed to push two runners past home plate for the game's sole runs.

The 2-1 series advantage the Indians now enjoyed gave Boudreau room for creativity. Rather than matching the Braves ace-for-ace in the fourth game, he came up with a different plan. "Gentlemen," Boudreau reportedly announced in the clubhouse after Bearden's victory, "I'm not pitching Feller tomorrow." If Sain pitched as dominantly as he had in the opening contest, the Indians risked wasting another brilliant Feller performance. But if they somehow managed to crack Sain's curveballs, then the Indians would have Feller rested and ready to close out the championship in the fifth game.

To start the fourth game, Boudreau chose twenty-eight-year-old pitcher Steve Gromek, a so-called spare part in the Indians' rotation. During the war, Gromek had seemed an ace in the making. The Michigan native won nineteen games in 1945 but then fell back to earth as soon as major-league rosters repopulated with players lost to the service. His first two postwar seasons, in which he'd managed just eight total wins against twenty losses, proved so disastrous that Gromek had been the only member of the Indians whose pay Veeck had slashed in 1948. There'd been doubt during spring training about whether Gromek would make the roster at all. Regardless, he'd performed respectably that summer, winding up with a 9-3 record and a sub-3.00 ERA. Now, unexpectedly, a full three weeks since Gromek's last start, the pivotal game of the World Series was his.

Veeck established his World Series headquarters at the Hollenden Hotel in downtown Cleveland, where he entertained more than seven hundred writers and notable figures from across the country. No matter if they were small-town scribblers or Hollywood celebrities, Veeck treated them like visiting royalty. Limousines idled outside to chauffeur them to and from the stadium or anywhere else they desired to go. In the ballroom-turned-cafeteria, a bustling team of waiters and bartenders whipped up whatever guests might want, whether sandwiches or sirloins, beer or champagne. Abbott and Costello amused diners by ripping through their "Who's on First?" routine while luminaries ranging from Bob Hope to Rogers Hornsby to Ohio governor Thomas Herbert flitted in and out of the action. At one point, Toots Shor, in town from New York City, pulled a hundred dollars from his pocket and told Veeck he'd like to buy a drink. Unhesitatingly, Veeck tore the bill to shreds and slipped the pieces under Shor's plate. What difference would Shor's money have made to someone already on the hook for an astronomical tab?

By the start of the fourth game, on October 9, a dense and delirious crowd had wedged into Cleveland's lakefront stadium, more than 82,000 fans in total, shattering the single-game World Series record. Celebrities filled the reserved boxes—Abbott and Costello, George Raft, and Bob Hope, among others. Seated among the crowd, too, was another familiar figure. Effa Manley had flown to Cleveland before the third game. Upon arrival, she'd found the city's Black hotels overflowing with guests eager to see Doby and Paige in action. The only room she could procure was a closet-like space with a shared bathroom.

Word of her predicament spread to heavyweight boxing champion Joe Louis, who'd become so enamored of the Indians that he'd wired Doby for tickets late in the season. Louis and Manley had crossed paths before, most notably during the second game of the Negro League World Series in 1946, when Louis had thrown out the ceremonial first pitch at Newark's Ruppert Stadium. Now, out of respect for Manley, Louis vacated his suite at the Majestic Hotel so that she could stay there while he bunked with friends.

The fervor of Cleveland's Black fans for the player she'd sold to the Indians fifteen months earlier must have stirred up mixed emotions in Manley. As she told *The Sporting News*, she believed that fate had made her "a sort of agent in this vital, this very involved situation having to do with the Negro in the major leagues. And the effort to solve the complex problems of social mixing in the American pastime." At the same time, she was dismayed at how quickly loyalties had shifted, and true to form, she didn't bite her tongue. "Negro fans are acting like d— fools and the press [meaning the Negro press] is not trying to educate them," she'd fumed to *The Chicago Defender* in September. "The Negro fans have deserted the Negro teams because a few players get 'four cents' more and the white teams have put their stamp of approval on them."

She spoke from experience. Selling Doby had plunged the Newark Eagles into a tailspin. After his departure, Manley claimed, "the incentive was gone, the players operated with a sense of doom for Negro baseball." Attendance in Newark plummeted from 120,000 fans in 1946, to 57,000 in 1947, to 32,000 in 1948. The situation became so dire that Manley and her husband planned to disband the Eagles in the off-season, which some saw as a fatal blow to the Negro Leagues. "When a team like the Newark Eagles, with plenty of money behind it, is the first to cry 'quits,' it looks bad—very bad," a *Pittsburgh Courier* columnist lamented.

For now, Manley settled in to watch the player she'd nurtured lead the Indians' offensive attack. Doby, who sported a .364 average so far in the World Series, had been the only player to have hit safely in each game. One *Boston Globe* reporter characterized Doby as "a free and lethal swinger. When he misses, he is a perfect replica of an electric fan. But when he connects—the ball becomes a blur across the topography." He'd hit Johnny Sain hard in the first game, though it'd resulted in a mere single. The thunderous ovation that Doby received during the announcement of the starting lineups before game four suggested that the sold-out crowd anticipated more from him that afternoon.

Working on just two days' rest, Sain came out "as cold as the biting wind which blew for the benefit of the batters." His second pitch was roped up the middle for a leadoff single by Indians left fielder Dale Mitchell, who jogged home two batters later on an RBI double by Boudreau. Sain settled into a groove immediately afterward, retiring six of the next seven batters. By the time Doby, in his second at-bat, stepped to the plate in the third inning with two outs and no one on base, Sain had reverted fully to form.

Presumably to keep Doby guessing, Sain greeted him with a surprise offering: a sidearm fastball right over the middle. It was too good for Doby to pass up. He took a fearsome, full-bodied cut, his whirling momentum nearly twisting him around. The bottom of his bat nipped the top of the ball, caroming it foul off the catcher's leg. Eighty-two thousand fans groaned in unison.

Working quickly, Sain came back with a slow curve high and outside, seemingly a tougher pitch to handle than the last. It fooled Doby, rendering him unable to lash at it with his customary fury. Nevertheless, he recovered just in time to meet the ball squarely and forcefully. It rocketed off his bat and arced upward into the cloudless sky. Twice that year he'd launched similarly majestic and timely shots, once during the first scrimmage game of spring training in Tucson, and once off the loudspeakers at Griffith Stadium in Washington, D.C. Both home runs had been crucial to Doby's—and the Indians'—fate, helping persuade the team's skeptical management to give him time and space to find his bearings in the majors. Now, on baseball's biggest stage, in the swing game of the World Series, Doby's season came full circle.

As the ball soared beyond the sign that read 380 FEET on the wire fence in right field, Doby trotted around the bases at such a brisk pace that his teammates poked fun at him afterward. "That crowd scare you, Larry?" Ken Keltner would ask amid laughter. And on some level, maybe it did. Since the morning he'd shown up suddenly in the Indians' clubhouse, he'd had to worry that one misstep, one misinterpreted phrase, one innocuous gesture could derail his season, turn the masses against him, cast him out of the majors, sink integration in baseball altogether. Doby ran around the bases like a man who hadn't been able to let his guard down for a second, not even when an entire city was screaming his name in rapture.

The home run saved Gromek from wasting what would turn out to be the start of a lifetime. The Braves would cut into the Indians' lead with a solo home run by outfielder Marv Rickert, but it seemed that every other time Gromek wandered into trouble, Doby was there to right the course. In the sixth, Doby tracked down a screaming line drive that shortstop Alvin Dark hit deep to center. Two innings later, Tommy Holmes whacked one even deeper. In the soggy outfield grass Doby slipped while turning around and then appeared to lose the ball momentarily in the sun. But this one wouldn't conk him on the head. While sprinting at full speed toward the fence, his back partially turned, Doby plucked the ball from the air just before it fell for extra bases. The crowd rose to its feet for another ovation.

There would be no comeback for the Braves. Though Sain surrendered just one further hit after Doby's home run, the Braves' offense failed to support him. In the ninth Gromek set down the side to seal the 2-1 win. Immediately afterward, he raced to the dugout with hardly a trace of emotion on his face. After descending into the privacy of the clubhouse, however, Gromek ripped off his hat and started whooping and hollering like "a high school hero."

As the postgame celebration got under way, Gromek wrapped his arms around the neck of the player whose home run had provided the margin of victory. Doby in turn squeezed Gromek's waist so tightly that Gromek thought for a second his ribs might break. News photographers captured the moment. The pictures they snapped ran in newspapers across the country the following day. They showed two men, one white, one Black, locked in a cheek-to-cheek embrace, Gromek laughing, Doby grinning, their eyes nearly shut in ecstasy—a rare sight in a sport and a nation that remained mostly segregated at the tail end of the century's first half.

For Marjorie McKenzie of *The Pittsburgh Courier*, the photos were "the best race relations plug the general public has been treated to since the war." Their chief message, she argued, was acceptance, perhaps an unexpected one from a league that once had policed the color line with unyielding rigor. But here were two unlikely players who'd brought their club within a game of winning the World Series expressing themselves spontaneously and unequivocally, neither self-conscious in front of the cameras nor discreet with the emotions passing between them. Such an image, McKenzie wrote, was "capable of washing away, with equal skill, long pent-up hatred in the hearts of men and the beginnings of confusion in the minds of small boys."

For Doby, the image struck a more personal chord. "It was such a scuffle for me," he would tell biographer Joseph Thomas Moore decades later, "after being involved in all that segregation, going through all I had to go through, until that picture. The picture finally showed a moment of a man showing his feelings for me."

An hour or so after the game, thousands of fans were still milling around the gates outside Municipal Stadium. When Doby emerged in his street clothes, they cheered. They whistled. They gave him one final ovation as he left the ballpark.

26

Fever Dreams

Boudreau's gamble had paid off. The Indians had squeaked past Sain without burning a top-line starter. Now they would have three shots at clinching the championship in as many days: one in Cleveland, two in Boston. Not that anyone in Cleveland expected the series to shift back to Beantown. Hours before the fifth game, on Sunday, October 10, several Indians players arrived at Municipal Stadium carrying no more luggage than the combs in their back pockets. So complete was Cleveland's confidence that, one reporter joked, gamblers were offering bets not on whether the Indians would win but whether Bob Feller would pitch a no-hitter. When asked who would pitch for the Indians in the sixth game, Boudreau replied: "Nobody."

The stage was set. Everything had fallen into place. It was Feller's destiny to close out the World Series in front of a hometown crowd. A victory that afternoon would be the culmination of a dream that had commenced on the diamond he and his father had carved into the family farm. Even the two heartbreaking losses Feller had suffered over the past week now could be recast in this new narrative as setbacks that made this particular game all the more dramatically satisfying.

The city stood ready to explode. The foul weather had broken. By the time the first fleet of buses and passenger trains shuttling fans from all over Ohio pulled into Cleveland, the sun shone overhead. Bumper-to-bumper traffic brought all roads leading to the stadium to a standstill. Bars and restaurants that usually closed on Sunday flung open their doors around lunchtime. Though state laws prohibited them from selling beer on Sunday with an alcohol content greater than 3.2 percent, owners looked the other way when customers smuggled in refreshments of their own. Those with no interest in drinking tiptoed in regardless with the same sheepish question: "How much does it cost to watch the game by television?" Across Cleveland public televisions were besieged by swarms of squinting viewers. The six TV sets erected in the Central Armory building downtown attracted hundreds of ticketless fans. For everyone else, there were improvised scoreboards that popped up in unlikely places and phone numbers that provided callers with live updates. Unlucky workers toiling on weekend shifts could hope to listen in on portable radios. A few factories went so far as to hook up their public-address systems directly to the broadcast.

During the previous game, it'd seemed that not another soul could've squeezed into Cleveland's Municipal Stadium, but somehow thousands more managed to cram in that afternoon. They stood on partitions, perched on rafters, clustered dozens deep behind fences, and spilled across runways and aisles. Hardly a speck of open space was left unfilled.

Bill Veeck himself sprawled out on a newspaper spread across the concrete runway. Next to him in an aisle seat was his eleven-year-old son, Will, who'd made the trip up from Tucson.

Packed shoulder to shoulder around them were more people than Veeck likely could've imagined the first time he'd glimpsed the mammoth lakefront stadium—some 86,288 fans in total, by far the largest crowd ever to attend a major-league baseball game, more spectators than had watched the first two contests at Braves Field combined. It was seemingly everything he'd been building toward since purchasing the club.

"Isn't this great, Will?" Veeck asked, eager to share the moment with his son. "Did you ever see such a tremendous crowd? Did you ever in your life see anything like this?"

Whether because of his lack of interest in baseball or because distance had loosened their familial bond, Will responded: "How come you couldn't have been a scientist or something I could have been proud of?" It was a crushing question, a pin stuck straight through his father's puffed-up chest.

There was another problem that afternoon: Bob Feller didn't have it. Catcher Jim Hegan sensed as much when Braves leadoff batter Tommy Holmes clipped an inside fastball off the handle of his bat. Rather than squirting foul, the ball carried on a line to the outfield grass. Hitters, Hegan said afterward, "don't do that to Feller when he's right." The next batter, Alvin Dark, legged out a rolling dribbler down the third base line, and suddenly, before the first out, Feller already had surrendered as many hits as in his previous start.

Any hope of escaping unscathed was dashed when Bob Elliott, the reigning National League MVP, swatted a sluggish offering over the right-field fence. It was a mood-killing blow, ice water dumped on a freshly lit fire. With one swing, the Braves, who'd encountered such trouble putting men on base that one writer claimed they'd looked like "so many Venus di Milos" at the plate, had equaled their run total for the entire series.

Nevertheless, Boudreau resisted giving his ace a swift hook. He'd declared during the season's first half that the Indians would sink or swim with Feller. This game would be no different. Despite the deficit, fans showered the pitcher with support, desperately and feverishly begging Feller to snap out of it, to regain his command, to realize the dream they all had invested in.

Over the next few innings Feller weaved in and out of trouble,

yielding only a solo shot by Elliott, his second homer of the afternoon. In the fourth, the Indians' offense came alive. Following an
RBI single by outfielder Walt Judnich, Hegan blasted a three-run
bomb that propelled the Indians to a 5-4 lead and injected hope into
the frenzied masses. The contest had been reset; they were back on
script. Now, if this game were to mirror the season, Feller would
recover precisely when his team needed him most.

It wasn't to be. Fussing and fidgeting, Feller tried frantically
to pull himself together. He pawed at the dirt, blew on his right
hand, hitched his pants, and wiped his fingers across his jersey.
Nothing worked. He gave up a game-tying home run in the sixth,
then fell apart in the seventh. Tommy Holmes once again led off
with a single, Alvin Dark sacrificed him to second, and outfielder
Earl Torgeson drove him home. Boudreau threw up his hands. He'd
stuck with Feller for as long as he could. But there would be no storybook ending. Feller's day was through.

Wasting no time, Feller strode briskly toward the dugout, "as
if he just felt a great thirst and had to have a drink of water." He
was a picture of despair, his shoulders slumped, his gaze vacant, his
head "hung like a turkey" at Thanksgiving. "At that moment,"
observed sportswriter Joe Williams, "you felt that if it were within
[Feller's] power he'd gladly give up a sizable hunk of his opulent
earnings to get his name into the records as the winner of a World
Series game."

At the start of the afternoon, such an outcome had seemed pre-
determined. Feller, however, had missed his cue. He'd lost the narrative.

From the Indians' bullpen, Satchel Paige had watched the game with
apprehension. Because of how well the Indians' starters had thrown
during the first four games, none had required relief. As a result,
Paige, who'd waited more than two decades to pitch in the Major
League World Series, had remained on the bench. In the fifth game,

his fate yet again was inversely tied to Feller's. If Paige were to fulfill his ambition, Feller would have to fail in his own. "I guess deep down," Paige admitted, "I was pulling against my own team."

It'd been a frustrating week for Paige. In Boston, he'd bided his time in the bullpen, chatting with fans, smoking cigarettes, and nibbling on a hot dog bought for him by a spectator. So dominant was Feller in the opening contest that no reliever so much as removed his jacket. In the second game, Bob Lemon skirted into trouble often enough for Boudreau to put his bullpen on notice. Paige leapt to his feet, eager for his shot. Much to his chagrin, Lemon quelled the offensive attacks by himself.

During game three in Cleveland, Bearden had retired Braves batters with such efficiency that Boudreau again never glanced at the bullpen. Afterward, Paige was hopeful that his manager would finger him as the starter for the fourth game. When Steve Gromek was named instead, he put his best face forward. "I guess old Satch is a relief man now," Paige told reporters. But deep down, he was crestfallen.

Surprisingly, Gromek, too, went the distance. With his chances dwindling, desperation took hold. Cornering Boudreau, Paige offered forth his services. Boudreau said nothing. His mind had already been made up. Feller would start the fifth game.

That afternoon, Paige's emotions ricocheted from one extreme to another. As Feller muddled through the opening frames, Paige sat expectantly in the bullpen, waiting for the call. But then, when the Indians stormed back into the lead, he abandoned hope. His opportunity had passed and, as he later wrote, "all I could do was ask myself, 'Why?' It was the same why I used to ask myself when I couldn't get into the major leagues. There never was an answer."

After Feller allowed a leadoff single in the seventh, Boudreau signaled for Ed Klieman, Russ Christopher, and Paige to start warming up. The three relievers threw while Feller got roughed up. Finally, the call came. But it wasn't for Paige. Boudreau waved in Klieman to stop the Braves from adding to their 6-5 advantage. Klieman, however, couldn't buy an out. He walked the first batter, surrendered a two-run single to the next, then walked the following. Once more, Boudreau signaled to the bullpen—this time for Christopher. Though the emaciated sidearmer had been the Indians' most effective stopper during the regular season, he, too, had nothing that afternoon. Two batters came up; two lined pitches into right for RBI singles. And just like that, a tight game morphed into a 10-5 blowout.

All afternoon long, the restless crowd had rooted for Feller to realize his long-deferred dream, but now, with the contest suddenly out of reach, they sought solace in witnessing Paige's instead. Little by little, scattered chants began to ripple through the stands, building slowly but persistently into a collective plea that proved impossible for Boudreau to ignore: "Put in Satch! Let's have Paige! Put him in, Lou!"

Almost exactly three months after Paige's major-league debut, the bullpen gate swung open and onto the field stepped a gangly figure who walked across the field "with the drowsy ease of a man who has just gotten up from an enormous dinner," in the words of sportswriter Bob Considine. The ovation when the public-address announcer called out Paige's name was deafening. Cheering among the masses was boxer Joe Louis. "No man can say what another man may be thinking about," Louis later wrote, "but as 'Satch' toed the rubber for that first pitch, I like to think that he murmured to himself: 'At last.'"

Unlike every other pitcher that afternoon, Paige would run into less trouble with batters than with home plate umpire George Barr, who halted the proceedings at several points to instruct Paige, who most likely had appeared in more ball games than everyone else on the field combined, on not throwing spitballs and on his pitching form in general. Per usual, Paige blocked out the distractions, including a questionably called balk, and focused on the job at hand. Within no time Warren Spahn lifted a sacrifice fly to center, Holmes grounded to short, and an inning that neither Klieman nor Christopher could complete had ended. So too had Paige's participation in the World Series.

Short as it was, the stint was a muddy reflection of Paige's odyssey to the majors. For days he'd waited and waited for a call that came too late for him to make a larger mark. Still, he'd endured. "I'd been in a World Series," he later wrote. No other Black pitcher could say as much.

There was no time to wallow in the clubhouse after the game. The Indians' train to Boston was scheduled to depart at 5:40 P.M., which left the players less than two hours to pull together luggage for a trip they hadn't expected to take.

An entourage of friends and family who'd journeyed from as far away as California to watch Feller close out the World Series met up with him afterward. Unbeknownst to Feller, they'd reserved a handful of tables at a high-end Cleveland restaurant for a victory celebration. Those plans were quickly scrapped following the loss. Instead of champagne, they sipped coffee on the way to Cleveland Union Terminal.

There, a fanatical mob of more than 10,000 fans "hailed and farewelled" the Indians off to Boston, lining each side of the concourse "from the far end clear down to Gate 22 beneath the mural." Some banged on cowbells, others hollered encouraging words at the players who wormed through the narrow lanes that police officers carved out for them.

Wanting nothing to do with the crowds, Feller and his wife, Virginia, snuck in through a back entrance, rode down a freight elevator, and scurried onto the train. They sat facing each other in a compartment as the railcars rattled east under the dim light of a waxing half-moon. In his hands Feller held the Sunday paper, but he couldn't read a line. The defeat had stunned him into silence, and

Virginia later wrote that she couldn't think of anything that might offer him comfort. For hours, not a word passed between them.

In his second autobiography, Feller would write, "To lose that last game of the year, lose the opening game of the World Series on a controversial play and then get knocked out in the seventh inning of what could have been the final game added up to a heavy load." In the stillness of his compartment, Feller must have felt the weight of it all at once. "I had been to the heights," he concluded, "and now I was in the depths."

It was Lemon's turn in the rotation for the sixth game, and there was cause for concern. Since his previous outing, he'd come down not only with a cold but with a sore arm as well. Wringing nine more innings out of it would require emergency maintenance. On the train he swaddled himself in heating pads, then splayed out across a trainer's table at Braves Field the next morning while Lefty Weisman limbered up his muscles sufficiently enough for Lemon to be able to take the mound by game time.

That afternoon, thanks to Lemon's sinkerball, the Braves' bats fell dormant again. With the score knotted at 1 in the sixth inning, Indians second baseman Joe Gordon snapped the tie with a smash deep into the left-field seats against Braves pitcher Bill Voiselle. Two more runs would follow, providing a 4-1 lead for the Indians. Some 40,000 hushed Braves fans sensed that the end was near.

Or perhaps not. Five outs short of the championship, Lemon lost steam. A single, a double, and a walk loaded the bases for the Braves in the eighth. Suddenly, Boudreau had a decision to make. Handing the ball to Feller was an option—that afternoon the Braves had trotted out Warren Spahn, who'd thrown almost as many innings as Feller in the previous game—but Boudreau once again resolved to press his luck with Bearden, even though he was slated as the Indians' probable seventh-game starter. But with the World Series on the line, this was no time for thinking ahead. Besides, Bearden had been on such a tear—in his last five starts, all complete-game victories, he'd allowed a mere four earned runs over forty-five innings—that even if his knuckleball was flat that afternoon, it seemed that fate would intervene should he stray into trouble.

The first two batters would put this belief to the test. Pinch-hitter Clint Conatser blasted Bearden's initial offering, a floating knuckler that hung high over the plate, almost four hundred feet to center. Anywhere else in the ballpark and it would've been gone. But outfielder Thurman Tucker, whom Boudreau had started in center while shifting Doby to right field, snagged it while slamming into the wall. Two pitches later, Phil Masi popped one far to left. For a second, it appeared certain the drive would land in the bleachers, but whatever divine fortune had fueled Bearden's charmed season kept it in the park. The ball banged off the fence, then ricocheted to left fielder Dale Mitchell in time for him to hold the tying runner on third.

The lead had been whittled down to 4-3. One more run, Boudreau reasoned, and he'd bring in Feller. But he didn't tell that to Bearden as he stalked to the mound. "Okay, Gene," Boudreau said instead. "Keep chucking. You'll stop 'em. And if you don't, you'll pitch tomorrow anyway." Buoyed by the pep talk, Bearden went on to retire the following batter, then finish off the Braves in the ninth. Unlike when the Indians had defeated the Red Sox, the celebration on the field was muted. Exhaustion, emotional as well as physical, sank in immediately after the final out had been made.

In the clubhouse a swarm of players buzzed around Bearden, planting kisses on his cheeks, pawing at his uniform, and hailing him once more as the savior of the Indians' season. Far from the revelry, in a distant corner, Feller undressed in silence. In the eyes of one reporter, he "stood almost forlorn, smiling bravely and a bit self-consciously, as he sadly-gladly watched his beaming teammates celebrate with gay abandon." It was as if, a United Press article surmised, Feller deliberately was setting himself apart from his teammates "in penance for three times letting them down in these last mad two weeks. It lent an edge of sadness to this noisy jubilee and you knew that Feller would have given almost anything to be standing in Bearden's shoes." There was a certain irony to the scene: The pitcher who'd always seemed destined to steer the Indians to a championship had become an overlooked figure by the time it finally happened.

The player most sensitive to exclusion homed in on Feller. For so long, Larry Doby had been the one sitting by himself on the train or on the bench. The sting he'd felt when certain players had refused to shake his hand during his first day with the Indians had stayed with him, and now Doby did what he no doubt wished every teammate had done for him: He walked over to Feller and stuck out his hand. "There were a lot of things—apology, brief happiness, and earnest congratulations—in Feller's eyes at that moment," observed one writer. "He in turn reached out with an eager hand which once fired the fastest pitch in baseball and lighted that somber corner with his smile."

And with that handshake came a passing of sorts. Since his first start on the Indians a dozen years earlier, Feller's life story had been cast as the prototypical baseball origin story. As early as 1941, *Look* magazine had predicted that the Feller farm in Van Meter, Iowa— the red barn in particular where he'd first started throwing with his father—would become "a shrine one of these days. Folks will turn off the main highway to gape at it. A uniformed attendant will guide visitors about its wonders, and twice a day a spieler will deliver a talk on the great man who got his start behind it."

But now Doby had carved out a competing storybook origin story of his own, one that had taken him from jittery benchwarmer straight out of the Negro Leagues to indispensable star without whom the Indians wouldn't have succeeded. Though a mere five years separated them in age, the two teammates at that moment, clasping hands, represented different yet overlapping generations:

Feller the quintessence of a long lineage of major-league stars, and Doby the harbinger of a more racially and narratively diverse league.

Statistics alone couldn't measure Doby's impact. Perhaps the most telling sign was that in the days following his club's loss, Braves owner Lou Perini declared that he intended to open spring training next year with a delegation of Black players vying for spots in the Boston lineup. The edge that Doby had given the Indians in such a closely contested World Series—he'd led Indians starters with a .318 batting average—was not one Perini could afford to surrender any longer. An article published months later in *Ebony* magazine entitled "The Future of Negroes in Big League Baseball" stated that while Jackie Robinson had "pioneered in the majors garnering honors as 'Rookie Of The Year,' probably Doby has been an even more important factor in sending club owners into the chase for Negro talent."

During a season in which Robinson, who'd shown up overweight at spring training after attending multiple off-season banquets, got off to such a sluggish start that Branch Rickey had placed him on waivers in June—a pointed rebuke that Robinson would shrug off while finishing the summer strong—there was a sense that Doby's horizons appeared more limitless than his fellow pioneer's. His unlikely success had flown in the face of proclamations, including one from the teammate whose hand he'd just clasped, that no one in the Negro Leagues could measure up to major-league standards. More than shattering stereotypes, it had demonstrated unequivocally, as *Ebony* concluded, "that a Negro player, given the right opportunity, encouragement and direction, can attain baseball heights."

No one seemed more surprised by this twist of fate than Doby himself. On the train ride back to Cleveland, he mused, "Two years ago, when I was in the Negro League, if anyone had told me I'd be playing for the champions of the world some day, I'd have started yelling for his keeper to take him back where he came from." But there he was, the first Black player, alongside Satchel Paige, to earn a World Series ring in the majors.

Veeck, for one, believed that Doby hadn't yet come close to tapping his full potential. He predicted that Doby was "going to be as good, or better, than Stan Musial," the St. Louis Cardinals outfielder who collected his third Most Valuable Player award in 1948. *The Sporting News* went further than that. In a piece that alternated praise with condescending pleas for Doby to maintain his exemplary behavior, their editorial board proclaimed: "Doby occupies the position that just a year ago was filled by [Jackie] Robinson."

"Now he is," the editorial continued, "the major league baseball bellwether of the entire Negro race."

Following the sixth game, Bill Veeck relayed an order to team officials: buy up all the champagne and sparkling burgundy the Kenmore Hotel had in stock. At Boston's South Station, in preparation for the overnight journey back to Cleveland, the train's dining car was loaded up with some thirty cases of "happiness hop." As soon as Veeck stepped foot inside the car, hours after the game, the players and their wives stood up and applauded.

It was a rare moment of calm for an owner who had been running on fumes for weeks. A series of incidents had cast a shadow over Veeck's postseason. In late September, Harry Grabiner, his partner in purchasing the Indians and now a club vice president, had suffered a stroke in the team offices and lapsed into a coma. Grabiner would pass away toward the end of October. And then there'd been Veeck's oldest son's pointed question during game five, along with the understanding that a divorce from his wife was likely imminent.

Now, however, in the dining car of a train chugging west across New England, Veeck drowned everything in a shower of champagne and burgundy, spraying streams of bubbly liquid at players and their wives until late into the night. At one point, Johnny Berardino, a bit player who doubled as a bit actor in the off-season, jumped up on a table and recited a soliloquy from *Mutiny on the Bounty*. Every few seconds his teammates hollered, "Look out! Another wave on the way!" while they doused him in alcohol. By sunrise, as the revelers stumbled back into the dining car for breakfast, champagne continued to drip down on them from the ceiling.

They steamed into Cleveland with their clothes stained purple and their eyes streaked red. Awaiting the team were 15,000 shrieking fans jammed into Union Terminal, along with a caravan of convertibles outside. To make themselves presentable, players pulled off their soiled shirts and buttoned their overcoats to the neck.

Veeck, Boudreau and his wife, and Cleveland mayor Thomas A. Burke piled into the lead car. Behind a marching band blaring "Hail, Hail, the Gang's All Here," the motorcade nudged into a narrow lane continually under threat of being overrun by a "happy, howling knot of humanity." There were roughly 100,000 people in Cleveland's Public Square, another 100,000 or so were sprawled up the parade route to University Circle. Confetti, rolls of toilet paper, torn-out pages from telephone books, and ticker tape rained down from office windows. Firecrackers exploded; horns blared. Every so often, spectators burst through the police line and sprinted alongside Veeck, begging for a handshake.

The triumph extended to corners of the city that hadn't shared in the Indians' previous championship twenty-eight years earlier. "Veeck made the Indians a real American team—the only one in the inappropriately named American League," the *Call & Post*, Cleveland's largest Black newspaper, had declared earlier. "Because of Veeck, Larry Doby and Satch Paige have been given the opportunity of demonstrating to America what happens when it takes off its color-conscious glasses. Negro Cleveland is 100 percent behind this man Veeck and his Indians. For the first time in American League history the Indians are OUR Team, without quiggle or qualification."

By parade's end, the backseat of Veeck's convertible was a pool of scrap paper. "This is a day I'll never forget," the Indians owner said with a grin as he struggled to extricate his submerged legs. Around him, the crowds dispersed, the mayor departed, and the press scurried away to file their stories. Hopping off their convertibles, the players waved goodbye and departed with their families. Veeck, however, found himself with nowhere to go and no one to go with. For once, there were no phone calls to make, no speeches to deliver, no business to tend to at the office. It was too early to head to Gruber's or to the neon-lit clubs along Short Vincent. After weeks of nonstop activity during which the goal that the last few years of his life had been dedicated to finally came to pass, Veeck returned to his apartment alone.

There, he sat by himself in the cold October sunlight. Thoughts that he'd kept at bay through years of constant motion flooded into his mind all at once: his distant family, his comatose business associate, his failing marriage, the physical and emotional toll he'd paid to arrive at this very spot.

"I'd had it all," Veeck later wrote, "everything I'd hoped for when I came to Cleveland. Everything and more." The championship was his, as were the attendance records and the love of an entire city. At last his fever had broken. He'd stopped running. And the moment he did so, a realization, as clear as the autumn day, came to him: "I had never been more lonely in my life."

EPILOGUE

The promise of 1948 wasn't kept.

Following the World Series, Doby returned to Paterson. More than 10,000 residents and a banner that read WELCOME HOME, LARRY DOBY. PATERSON IS PROUD OF YOU greeted him. Doby paraded through the downtown streets in a convertible. On the baseball diamond at Eastside High School, in front of family and acquaintances like Effa Manley, the mayor of Paterson declared: "We are not only here to pay tribute to Larry's achievements in baseball, but we also want to tell him how proud we are to have such a good, regular, clean-cut and capable young man representing our city in the major leagues."

Months later, when Doby and his wife, Helyn, decided to sink his championship spoils into a house, he would discover that all the pomp and high-minded rhetoric opened few doors. Some sellers, upon learning of Doby's interest in their properties, bumped up their asking prices. Others refused to show their houses altogether. One told Doby point-blank that he wouldn't sell to him because "you are a Negro and my neighbors would object." A World Series championship hadn't reversed long-ingrained attitudes. "I honestly feel more of a hero in Cleveland than here in my own hometown," Doby said in January 1949.

In Cleveland, too, the hero's sheen would wear off fast. When Doby reported to spring training in 1949, he found Tucson's Santa Rita Hotel still off-limits to Black players. In Texarkana, during the Indians' whistle-stop tour through the South before the start of the season, Doby, Satchel Paige, and Minnie Minoso, another player the Indians had signed from the Negro Leagues, had to walk to the ballpark already dressed in their uniforms, since no taxis would transport them and officials had informed them beforehand that the clubhouse would remain segregated, leaving them nowhere to change. In the outfield, fans pelted Doby with bottles, forcing Boudreau to pull him for his own safety. "The clock turned back," Doby would later say about such stops.

Tensions in the Indians' clubhouse lingered into the next decade. Bill Robinson, who served as the club's assistant traveling secretary in the early fifties, remembered that between games of a doubleheader, when sandwiches and hot dogs were made available, "there were certain ballplayers who wouldn't eat if there was something [Doby] might've touched." In some cities on the road, Doby continued to room in different hotels from the white players for years.

There were problems, too, in integrated accommodations. Once, while eating with a pair of white teammates in a hotel dining room, Doby struggled to flag down the waiter. When his party complained, the manager ordered the waiter to serve Doby. Rather than doing so, he peeled off his jacket, dropped it to the floor, and walked off the job.

By and large, white sportswriters deemed Doby moody, sullen, and thin-skinned—an introverted loner lost in his head. Certain team officials thought similarly. "The guy's fighting himself all the time, and this game should be easy for him," remarked Al Lopez, who replaced Boudreau as the Indians manager in 1951. But few made the effort to understand the conditions he was forced to live under through his thirteen-year tenure in the majors. There were times, remembered Jim "Mudcat" Grant, who once roomed with Doby on the Indians, when the burdens, slights, and abuses accumulated to such a degree that Doby would scream out in frustration. "To play baseball is one thing," Doby said in 1958. "To live with the problems you have, knowing you're not getting equality, it has a tendency to affect your baseball if you're the kind that's bothered by it. I was. I had a lot of sleepless nights."

Doby led the American League twice in home runs, competed in seven All-Star Games, and spearheaded another Indians run to the World Series in 1954, where they lost to the New York Giants. Nonetheless, there was a widespread sense that because of everything he faced as a pioneer and had to grapple with internally and externally throughout his entire career, Doby ultimately failed to reach the heights that many had predicted after his 1948 season. Veeck would say as much in his autobiography: "If Larry had come up just a little later, when things were just a little better, he might very well have become one of the greatest players of all time."

Jackie Robinson would be inducted into baseball's Hall of Fame during his first year of eligibility; Doby would wait four decades for his call to come. The Indians wouldn't retire Doby's number until 1994, thirty-five years after his last major-league game; every major-league organization would retire Jackie Robinson's number in 1997. Each year on April 15, Major League Baseball celebrates Jackie Robinson Day; though Doby continues to be lauded in certain circles, especially in Cleveland, he has faded from memory in others.

Contrary to the prediction of Boston Braves owner Lou Perini, the Indians' 1948 championship did not cause clubs to scour the Negro Leagues in search of the next Doby. By the time the 1949 season opened, the Indians and Dodgers remained the lone integrated major-league franchises.

Being an outlier didn't bother Veeck. On the contrary, he extended his inclusive policies beyond the field, hiring Black security guards, vendors, janitors, groundskeepers, ushers, and musicians. After local track-and-field star Harrison Dillard won two gold medals at the 1948 Olympics, Veeck phoned him out of the blue with an offer to join the team's front office. A member of the NAACP, Veeck posed with Doby and Paige for a nationally distributed recruitment poster. In speeches, he railed against residential segregation.

While Veeck doubled down, other owners stood pat. As late as 1950, Black players were nowhere to be found in the American League outside Cleveland. "The scurrying after Negro players in [the American League] was restrained to a point which would have thrilled any card-carrying member of the White Citizens Council," Veeck later asserted. The Yankees fielded all-white lineups until 1955, the Detroit Tigers until 1958. The Red Sox held out until the bitter end, refusing to promote a Black player until 1959, Doby's last year in the league.

Despite having witnessed Doby's transformation from a timid infielder to a hard-hitting outfielder without whom a pennant wouldn't have been possible, Bob Feller told *Ebony* magazine after the 1948 World Series that he didn't anticipate a sudden influx of Negro League talent into the majors because, in his mind, "there are few Negro ball players who can make the grade." Equally improbably, he asserted that "baseball today has no politics in playing. There is no discrimination against anybody, foreign-born or Negro. Either you have it or you don't. If players have the ability, they'll make the grade. I think that more clubs will open to Negroes in the coming years—once there is more available talent."

Later in life, Feller would be recognized as someone whose barnstorming tours had proven crucial in showing blinkered white audiences just how good Black players were. Because of his contributions, former Negro League players invited him annually to their Negro Baseball League Reunion in Kentucky, which Feller relished attending. Even so, he seemingly continued to view racial matters through the prism of his own life story, which sometimes blinded him to the barriers that grit, hard work, and self-reliance alone couldn't topple. Even while acknowledging that he'd heard and was aware of racial prejudice, Feller would tell former Major League Baseball commissioner Fay Vincent nearly six decades later: "I think your ability should get you the job, period. And if you can't do it with your ability, go learn how to do this. I know it's difficult, and if somebody was asking me . . . what would you do if you were black, I say, 'I don't know, probably the same thing I do if I were white, go to work.'"

Following the 1948 season, Feller would appear in the All-Star Game just once more. He tossed a record-tying third no-hitter in 1951, the last season in which he won more than twenty games. Three years later, in 1954, when the Indians again advanced to the World Series, Feller, at age thirty-five, had lost his spot at the top of the rotation. The Giants beat the Indians in four straight games. Feller, who was slated to start the fourth game, was skipped over instead. He would start only fifteen games over his final two seasons in the majors before retiring in 1956 with 266 career wins, none of which came in the postseason.

Satchel Paige would never pitch in the postseason again either, which remained a sore subject for the rest of his life. "Why wasn't I good enough to start in the World Series (1948)?" Paige fumed to the *Cleveland Press* in 1971. "I won five of six games starting that year and I saved seven games relieving and I was the last pitcher to pitch in the World Series. I had to follow Bob Feller (in relief) when he was losing 12-0 or something like that. They started men in the bullpen ahead of me, men who couldn't stay on the mound two minutes."

Paige had held out hope for a return trip to the World Series in 1949, a year in which he'd pledged to win twenty games, but injuries and ineffectiveness limited him to four. As soon as Veeck sold the team in the off-season, Paige found himself out of work. He hit the barnstorming trail in 1950, then resurfaced in the majors the following season after Veeck bought the St. Louis Browns. For three years, Paige reinvented himself once more as one of the league's most valuable relievers. While waiting to enter games, he sometimes lounged in a rocking chair that Veeck had placed in the bullpen for Paige's comfort and the crowd's amusement. In 1953, at age forty-seven, Paige became the oldest player ever selected to the All-Star Game, a record that still stands. That same year, Veeck unloaded the Browns, and with them went Paige. Despite the crowds he drew and the games he saved, no other owner would give him a chance.

On September 25, 1965, twelve years after the Browns had cut him, fourteen months after the passage of the Civil Rights Act of 1964, and one month after the passage of the Voting Rights Act, Paige would throw one last time in the major leagues. Charlie Finley, owner of the cash-strapped Kansas City Athletics and a Veeck acolyte, cooked up a scheme to boost attendance. When Finley asked the fifty-nine-year-old Paige if he might be able to throw three innings for his club, the geriatric hurler replied: "That depends. How many times a day?"

Even though little was expected of him, Paige shocked the baseball establishment by blowing through the Boston Red Sox lineup in just twenty-eight pitches. Outside of a Carl Yastrzemski double, no other batter would get a hit off him. When Paige was removed in the fourth inning with a 1-0 lead, Finley cut the stadium lights, fans waved lighters above their heads, and the public-address announcer led a rousing sing-along of "The Old Gray Mare."

Retirement was a foreign concept to Paige. Into his sixties, he continued to roam the country's back roads, living off the legend he'd fashioned for himself. "There's bound to be people," Paige wrote in his autobiography, "who'll want a man who's done what I've done, who's got that big name like Ol' Satch. And until they want me, I'll just keep pitching—maybe forever."

"Forever" was not a word associated with the Bill Veeck era in Cleveland. Though he ended up sticking around for an encore with the Indians, Veeck would find that the first fine careless rapture could never, even a year removed, be recaptured.

The 1949 season was a long, sobering hangover. Lou Boudreau's batting average plunged south of the .300 mark. Gene Bearden's win total didn't even crack double digits. By mid-June, the Indians were barely breaking even. After a second-half surge fell short, Veeck commemorated the club's elimination from the pennant race as only he knew how: with one last bit of showmanship. Before the opening game of the final homestand, Veeck lowered the previous year's pennant from the flagpole in center, laid it to rest in a casket, then drove it around the stadium in a horse-drawn hearse. In front of a cardboard gravestone that read 1948 CHAMPS, as a trumpeter played "Taps," Veeck buried the flag beyond the outfield fence.

It was a funeral as much for the Indians' season-long reign as for Veeck's entire three-and-a-half-year tenure in Cleveland. By then, his wife, Eleanor, had filed for divorce. To pay for the proceedings and to establish trust funds for his three children, Veeck sold the Indians shortly after the 1949 World Series concluded.

The year after Veeck departed, attendance in Cleveland dipped below the two-million mark. Six seasons later, the Indians drew fewer than a million fans, second worst in the American League. For as long as the Indians played in Municipal Stadium, until 1993, the team would never match the crowds Veeck had attracted. Without him, the stadium reverted to its previous status as a white elephant sprawled across the shores of Lake Erie, its bands of empty seats a reminder of rosier times. Only when the Indians moved into a new ballpark downtown, exorcising the ghost of Veeck, did they clear three million in attendance for a season.

Cleveland, too, began a slow but inexorable decline. Little by little, families fled the city for the suburbs. The downtown, which had swung until dawn when Veeck bustled through its streets, hollowed out. The Hollenden Hotel closed; the bars along Short Vincent went dark. Deindustrialization shuttered factories across northern Ohio and elsewhere in the Rust Belt. Racial tensions came to a head as discrimination, overcrowding, and dilapidated housing persisted. In 1966, riots broke out in the heavily segregated Hough neighborhood on the east side of Cleveland. At several points after Veeck's departure, the Cuyahoga River, steeped in industrial waste, caught fire. In the streets and on the water, Cleveland was burning.

In the ensuing decades, many Clevelanders would look back at those initial postwar years as the city's apex, a time when civic pride, economic strength, and athletic triumph converged, a time of fun, fireworks, and championships incited by a curiously attired baseball owner. By 1998, the fiftieth anniversary of the Indians' World Series victory, Cleveland had shed half its population.

Veeck chased the magic of 1948 for the rest of his life. At every stop along his subsequent journey, he cribbed from the same playbook: speeches, promotions, urgency, trades, innovation, dissidence, tirelessness, hope. In 1951, as owner of the cellar-dwelling St. Louis Browns, Veeck enraged baseball purists once more when he sent Eddie Gaedel, a little person, to the plate with a toy bat in his hands. Eight years later, as the head of the Chicago White Sox, Veeck came closest to recapturing his success in Cleveland. While establishing the attendance record at Comiskey Park, he watched his "Go-Go Sox" storm to the pennant, only to fall in six games to the Los Angeles Dodgers in the World Series. Along the way, there were experiments galore, some fruitful, some not: exploding scoreboards, names on the backs of players' uniforms, and games where fans managed the team from the grandstands, among others.

During his second stint as owner of the White Sox, Veeck would stage a reunion of sorts. After the team got off to a rocky start in 1978, he replaced pitcher-turned-manager Bob Lemon with one of his old Indians teammates: Larry Doby. The second Black player to break into the majors, Doby now became the second Black manager, behind Frank Robinson, whom the Indians had hired as their skipper three years earlier.

Once more, Veeck thrusted Doby into the action midseason. This time, however, Doby wouldn't be afforded a learning curve. The team's fortunes failed to improve, and Veeck would be forced to relieve Doby of his duties at the end of the season. Nevertheless, their friendship endured. "I lost my father when I was 8 and I always said that I would've liked my father to be like Bill Veeck," Doby said in 1997, eleven years after Veeck's death. "He's the kind of person I would put all the faith in the world in, a person I trusted," Doby continued. "I know one thing: It would have been hard to have been successful if I hadn't had a person like him."

Veeck exited the baseball scene decades ago, but traces of his fingerprints are everywhere, in each stadium giveaway, postgame fireworks show, and creative burst of pregame hijinks. The Veeckian spirit lives on, too, in every athletic underdog, visionary, rabble-rouser, and iconoclast. It's no coincidence that his autobiography— like Paige's before him—ends with an evocation of immortality. "Sometime, somewhere, there will be a club no one really wants," Veeck wrote. "And then Ole Will will come wandering along to laugh some more. *Look for me under the arc-lights, boys. I'll be back.*"

ACKNOWLEDGMENTS

I am grateful for everyone who took time to speak with me, including: Robert Alden, Dave Anderson, Mark Aubrey, Laureen Beach, Bobby Brown, Bob DiBiasio, Gene Budig, Leonard S. Coleman, Jr., Janie Culos, Paul Dickson, Harrison Dillard, Larry Doby, Jr., Bob Dolgan, Raymond Doswell, Morris Eckhouse, Carl Erskine, Anne Feller, Steven Feller, Dave Ferriss, Ned Garver, Maguerite Goodson, Judy Gordon, John J. Grabowski, Jim "Mudcat" Grant, Carl Gromek, Bill Gruber, Arnold Hano, Samuel Hynes, Jerry Izenberg, Anita Jackson, Al Kachadurian, Fred Krehbiel, Don Larsen, Larry Lester, Stephanie Liscio, Scott H. Longert, Bill Madden, Ellen Maggs, William J. Marshall, Joseph Thomas Moore, Leonard N. Moore, Louis Moore, Hal Naragon, James E. Odenkirk, Michael D. Roberts, Bill Robinson, Su Schaffer, Carl Scheib, Chuck Stevens, John Thorn, Dolores Townsend, David Vaught, Gregory Veeck, Mayra Veeck, Gay Vernon, Jed Weisman, Pat Williams. Special thanks go to Eddie Robinson, the only surviving member of the 1948 Cleveland Indians, who invited me into his home and answered my questions with candor and good humor.

Several people made my stay in Cleveland enjoyable and fruitful. Two subject librarians, Mark Moore and Terry Metter, at the Cleveland Public Library were welcoming and guiding presences as I spent weeks scrolling through roll after roll of microfilm. Terry has also quickly responded to every request I've subsequently made for newspaper articles that I'm missing. Jeremy Feador, a team historian for the Cleveland Indians, granted me access to archival material at Progressive Field and helped out with contacts and tips. Thanks also to Kristan Schiller and Sarah Jaquay for their helpful advice and tips, and to Dorothy Perelman for helping me find an apartment.

Writing a book in New York City would have been much harder were it not for the Allen Room at the New York Public Library. Heartfelt thanks to Melanie Locay for granting me access to this bookish space, along with the NYPL's considerable resources. At the Giamatti Research Center at the National Baseball Hall of Fame in Cooperstown, Cassidy Lent and Katherine Walden were helpful in helping me find exactly what I needed. For always keeping me busy with freelance work while I researched and wrote, I'm grateful to the production department at the Random House Publishing Group.

Jerel Merical and Wayne Lacox generously led me on a tour of Van Meter, Iowa, which included a stroll through the barnyard where Bob Feller first practiced with his father. We searched for Oak View Park, the diamond that Feller and his father carved into the wheat field, but it's been lost to time. The staff at the USS *Alabama* Battleship Memorial Park in Mobile, Alabama, patiently walked me through Feller's old haunts and what his duties entailed. Rebecca Brown also mailed me her self-published oral-history compilation of the sailors who served on the USS *Alabama, The "Mighty A" and the Men Who Made Her Mighty*, which proved to be a tremendous resource.

While this book delves into the lives of four figures from the Cleveland Indians, it's by no means intended to be a biography of any of them. Each of the four main characters in this book has already received at least one full-length biographical treatment, and I'd be remiss not to call out the ones that most deeply influenced and filled in holes for my project: *Larry Doby: The Struggle of the American League's First Black Player* by Joseph Thomas Moore; *Bob Feller: Ace of the Greatest Generation* by John Sickels; *Bill Veeck: Baseball's Greatest Maverick* by Paul Dickson; *"If You Were Only White": The Life of Leroy "Satchel" Paige* by Donald Spivey; and *Satchel: The Life and Times of an American Legend* by Larry Tye. In addition, Russell Schneider's *The Boys of the Summer of '48: The Golden Anniversary of the World Champion Cleveland Indians* is a tremendous feat of reporting and just a great read on the many players who made up the Indians championship roster.

My unending gratitude goes to everyone who read early chapters or drafts of the manuscript and gave notes: Vince Guerrieri, Dave Jordan, Jeff Katz, Louis Moore, Miriam Parker, John Thorn, and Mark Tavani, among others. Thanks as well to Matthew Silverman for his fact-checking work.

Peter Steinberg believed that I could write a book and stood by while that idea was severely put to the test. Noah Eaker acquired the project and shepherded it through its early stages. William Boggess did an outstanding job of taking the raw mess of material that I'd turned over to him and shaping it into something shorter, structured, and more coherent. Zachary Wagman then took control and offered several helpful structural suggestions. Thanks also go out to the entire team at Flatiron Books in art, design, production, and publicity.

It was a long journey from start to finish, and I wouldn't have made it without my family. I offer my eternal gratitude to my parents, Jerome and Renee; to the Baima family, Kate, Joe, Olivia, and Ethan; and to the Epplin-Rincker family, Rachel, Thomas, Nathan, and Michael. Special thanks are also in order for David, Elaine, Miriam, Ben, Nora, and Jake. Finally, my entire heart goes to Beth Parker, without whose love and support I'd have been lost. I could live a thousand lifetimes and still be in your debt.

NOTES

INTRODUCTION

2   *"sat, stood, stooped"*: Associated Press, "201,829 See Satch in Three Games," *The Marion Star*, August 21, 1948, 12, Newspapers.com.

2   *"Baseball sure has changed"*: Charles Heaton, "Satch Says He's Gettin' in Shape," *The Plain Dealer*, August 21, 1948, 12.

2–3 *"a phenomenon the like"*: Gordon Cobbledick, "Bill Veeck—Baseball's Greatest Showman," *Sport*, September 1948, 56.

3   *"the customers at the end"*: Ed Fitzgerald, "Lou Boudreau—Last of the Boy Managers?" *Sport*, July 1948, 58.

3   *In the tents that he'd*: Alvin Silverman, "400 Ohio Mayors Say Bill Veeck Bats 1.000," *The Plain Dealer*, August 21, 1948, 1, 14.

4   *"the greatest drawing card"*: Ed McAuley, "'Satchel's Fables' Has Baseball World Standing in Line for Shutout Tour," *Cleveland News*, August 21, 1948.

5   *"This thing has gone"*: Frank Gibbons, "Paige+Doby=0 for White Sox, 78,382 for Veeck," *Cleveland Press*, August 21, 1948.

5   *"It's Paige. The guy"*: Henry Andrews, "Paigeing Mr. Spink: Another Telegram Goes Out from Veeck's Office," *Cleveland Press*, August 21, 1948.

6   *"the most serious of workmen"*: Jim Schlemmer, "80,403 See Paige Blank White Sox, 1–0," *Akron Beacon Journal*, August 21, 1948, 10–11, Newspapers.com.

6   *Paige pitched around*: For more on Paige's pitch count from this game, see

Ed Bang, "Between You and Me: Ninety-Two Pitches a Game—That's Real Pitching!" *Cleveland News*, August 23, 1948.

6   *"This was undoubtedly the first":* Schlemmer, "80,403 See Paige."

6–7   *Paige would later call it:* Satchel Paige, as told to David Lipman, *Maybe I'll Pitch Forever: A Great Baseball Player Tells the Hilarious Story Behind the Legend* (Lincoln, NE: Bison Books, 1993), 214.

7   *"triumph of racial tolerance":* Editorial, "Triumph of Tolerance," *The Plain Dealer*, August 22, 1948, 21.

1. THE DUEL

11   *No player had ever:* For more on Feller's ascension to the major leagues, see Donald Honig, *Baseball America: The Heroes of the Game and the Times of Their Glory* (New York: Barnes & Noble, 1997), 210–12; and Donald Honig *The Greatest Pitchers of All Time* (New York: Crown, 1988), 87–88.

12   *"the greatest major league pitching":* Gordon Cobbledick, "17-Year-Old Indian Rookie Strikes Out 15, Within One of Record; Wins First Start," *The Plain Dealer*, August 23, 1936, 1.

12   *The mayor awarded him:* Leighton Housh, "Herring Talks as Van Meter Honors Hero," *Des Moines Register*, October 6, 1936, 7, Newspapers.com.

12   *In the decades before television:* For more on barnstorming's origins, see Jules Tygiel, *Baseball's Great Experiment: Jackie Robinson and His Legacy* (New York: Oxford University Press, 1983), 26.

13   *His father, Bill, snatched:* Sec Taylor, "Feller, Satchel Paige Foes Tonight," *Des Moines Register*, October 7, 1936, 5A.

13   *"It was just a continuous scuffle":* John Holway, *Black Diamonds: Life in the Negro Leagues from the Men Who Lived It* (Stadium Books, 1991), 162.

14   *"the way I had to keep":* John Holway, *Voices from the Great Black Baseball Leagues, Revised Edition* (New York: Da Capo Press, 1992), 162.

14   *that first glimpse of Paige:* The description of Paige's slow walk to the mound is based on two sources: Robert Peterson, *Only the Ball Was White: A History of Legendary Black Players and All-Black Professional Teams* (New York: Oxford University Press, 1970), 129; and Donald Spivey, *"If You Were Only White": The Life of Leroy "Satchel" Paige* (Columbia, MO: University of Missouri Press, 2012), 75.

14–15   *would hum as it zipped past:* For more on the humming sound Paige's fastball supposedly made, see Spivey, *"If You Were,"* 45.

15   *"I ain't no clown":* Leroy (Satchel) Paige as told to Hal Lebovitz, "Satchel Paige's Own Story: 'Let's Talk About My Feet,'" *Cleveland News*, July 27, 1948.

15 *"almost every night":* Marguerite Goodson, phone interview with author, August 26, 2016.

15 *"he didn't get to do":* Ibid.

15 *he hung a wire loop:* Kyle Crichton, "High School Hero," *Collier's,* March 6, 1937, 22.

16 *Bill strung lights through:* Bob Feller, with Burton Rocks, *Bob Feller's Little Black Book of Baseball Wisdom* (Lincolnwood, IL: Contemporary Books, 2001), 9. See also David Vaught, *The Farmers' Game: Baseball in Rural America* (Baltimore: Johns Hopkins Press, 2012), 93.

16 *Bill could sense a rare:* J. Roy Stockton, "Bob Feller—Storybook Ball Player," *Saturday Evening Post,* February 20, 1937, 12.

16 *Building the baseball diamond:* Donald Honig referred to the diamond that Bill Feller carved into his farmland as an "act of faith." Honig, *Baseball America,* 210.

16 *"People would drive":* Marguerite Goodson, phone interview with author, August 26, 2016.

17 *"I can do that":* Bob Feller, with Bill Gilbert, *Now Pitching, Bob Feller: A Baseball Memoir* (New York: Citadel Press, 2002), 18.

17 *"it got so the high school":* Crichton, "High School Hero," 22–23.

17 *"His fastball":* Russell Schneider, *The Cleveland Indians Encyclopedia* (Champaign, IL: Sports Publishing LLC, 2001), 375.

17 *"Gentlemen, I've found the greatest":* Franklin Lewis, *The Cleveland Indians* (Kent, OH: Kent State University Press, 2006), 190.

18 *there seemed to be little more:* Bob Feller, "My Own Story," *Cleveland Press,* August 23, 1937.

18 *"Who in the hell":* Tom Meany, *Baseball's Greatest Players* (New York: Grosset & Dunlap, 1953), 74.

18 *"They're not gonna get":* Ibid.

19 *"clay pigeon in a shooting":* Feller, with Gilbert, *Now Pitching,* 20.

19 *"The kid's a natural":* "'A Natural', Dizzy's Tribute to Feller," *Cleveland News,* July 7, 1936.

19 *"The best pitcher I have":* Ibid.

19 *"You're on your way":* Bob Feller, *Strikeout Story,* (New York: Bantam Books, 1948), 24.

20 *"like a white streak":* O. K. Armstrong, "Young Feller," *The Plain Dealer,* March 7, 1937, 6.

20 *wolfed down salt:* Feller, *Strikeout Story,* 38.

20   *"Feller's magical feat":* Franklin Lewis, "Tribe Ballyhoos Feller's Appearances as League Welcomes Customer Bait," *Cleveland Press,* August 25, 1936.

20   *"Thought I'd come in":* Feller, *Strikeout Story,* 42.

21   *"a picture of their wives":* Bob Ray, "The Sports X-Ray," *Los Angeles Times,* September 15, 1936, 12, ProQuest Historical Newspapers.

21   *"What are you going to do":* Stuart Bell, "Feller Explains His Record Strikeout Creed," *Cleveland Press,* September 14, 1936, 18.

21   *the American Dream writ large:* For a larger consideration of how Feller represented the American Dream, see Ron Briley, "'Do Not Go Gently into That Good Night: Race, the Baseball Establishment, and the Retirements of Bob Feller and Jackie Robinson." In Joseph Dorinson and Joram Warmund, eds., *Jackie Robinson: Race, Sports, and the American Dream* (New York: Routledge, 2006).

21   *They poured funds into:* The idea of major-league clubs preferring to maximize white talent rather than seeking a competitive edge by breaking the color line drawn from Neil J. Sullivan, "Baseball and Race: The Limits of Competition," *The Journal of Negro History,* vol. 83, no. 3 (Summer 1998), 168–77.

22   *"I carried so many satchels":* Gordon Cobbledick, "Old Satch: He's Really Got It," *Sport,* December 1948, 35. This is the most common story of how Paige earned the nickname "Satchel," though Paige biographer Larry Tye notes that Paige himself told contradictory tales about where the nickname came from. See Larry Tye, *Satchel: The Life and Times of an American Legend* (New York: Random House, 2006), 9–10.

22   *Paige first learned the game:* Tye, *Satchel,* 12.

22   *"all that wild-a'-loose":* Richard Donovan, "The Fabulous Satchel Paige," *Collier's,* May 30, 1953, 68.

23   *study batters' knees:* Paige, *Pitch Forever,* 26. For more on Paige's adolescent training, see Tye, *Satchel,* 17–18; and Spivey, *"If You Were,"* 35–36.

23   *passed a hat through the stands:* Donn Rogosin, *Invisible Men: Life in Baseball's Negro Leagues* (New York: Atheneum, 1983), 44.

23   *knock down rows of soda:* Tye, *Satchel,* 27.

23   *"I said to myself":* Satchel Paige, as Told to William Dismukes, "My Greatest Thrill!: 'Satch' Struck Out Josh Gibson for Biggest Thrill," *Pittsburgh Courier,* May 8, 1943, 19.

24   *He had strong, agile:* Quincy Trouppe, *20 Years Too Soon: Prelude to Major-League Integrated Baseball* (Los Angeles: S and S Enterprises, 1977), 103.

24   *His fastball became:* Sportswriter Joe Posnanski writes of Paige's nicknames

for his fastball in: Joe Posnanski, *The Soul of Baseball: A Road Trip Through Buck O'Neil's America* (New York: William Morrow, 2007), 130.

24   *"You know how sometimes":* Hal Bock, "Paige Liked to Fan First Man, Irvin Remembers," *The Courier-Journal (Louisville),* June 8, 1982, B8, Newspapers.com.

24   *Occasionally, against bush-league:* For more on Paige's bravado and showmanship, see Spivey, *"If You Were,"* xxii.

24   *"You gotta live":* Al Wolf, "Sportraits," *Los Angeles Times,* February 1, 1954, C2.

24   *"If there was a place":* A. S. (Doc) Young, "An 'Old Man' Makes Baseball History," *Ebony,* March 1969, 124.

25   *Landis laid down strict regulations:* Larry Lester, "Can You Read, Judge Landis?" *Black Ball: A Negro Leagues Journal,* 1, No. 2 (Fall 2008): 60. See also Rogosin, *Invisible Men,* 183–84.

25   *"Most of us didn't believe":* Ralph Kiner, with Danny Peary, *Baseball Forever: Reflections on 60 Years in the Game* (Chicago: Triumph Books, 2004), 71.

26   *"The well-publicized exploits":* Tygiel, *Baseball's Great Experiment,* 27.

26   *"DiMaggio All We Hoped":* Donovan, "Fabulous Satchel Paige," 78.

26   *"If they could hit Satchel":* Holway, *Great Black Baseball Leagues,* 238.

26   *A twenty-year-old office boy:* Bill Veeck, with Ed Linn, *Veeck—As in Wreck: The Chaotic Career of Baseball's Incorrigible Maverick* (Chicago: The University of Chicago Press, 2001), 182.

26   *"'Heck,' he drawled":* Tim Cohane, "The Ancient Satchel," *Look,* April 7, 1953, 66.

27   *By 1935, as many as:* Mark Metcalf, "Organized Baseball's Night Birth," *Baseball Research Journal,* SABR, 45, no. 2 (Fall 2016). Accessed October 10, 2019, at https://sabr.org/research/organized-baseball-s-night-birth.

27   *"who undoubtedly would be":* Taylor, "Feller, Satchel Paige Foes," 5-A.

28   *The next batter up:* Leighton Housh, "Feller Stars in Exhibition Game," *Des Moines Register,* October 8, 1936, 5-A.

28   *"The pitches served up by":* Ibid.

28   *Feller walked away:* John Sickels, *Bob Feller: Ace of the Greatest Generation* (Washington, D.C.: Potomac Books, 2004), 54.

2. LEARNING TO BE ALONE

In this chapter, Joseph Thomas Moore's book *Larry Doby: The Struggle of the American League's First Black Player* (Mineola, NY: Dover Publications, Inc.) provided valuable background material on Larry Doby's childhood.

29   *staked a reputation:* Associated Press, "Former Coach Recalls Doby Was
     'Natural,'" *The Morning Call*, July 8, 1947, 12, Newspapers.com.

29   *"looking for his daddy":* Associated Negro Press, "Doby Says Lou Boudreau's
     Patience Was Chief Factor in His '48 Success," *The Baltimore Afro-American*,
     December 4, 1948, 8, ProQuest Historical Newspapers.

30   *The town's miles of bridle paths:* Karl P. Abbott, *Open for the Season* (New
     York: Doubleday & Co., 1950), 181.

30   *"the establishment with trained":* Ibid., 183.

30   *Black workers were expected:* Lindsay Crawford, Ashley Guinn, McKenzie
     Kubly, Lindsay Maybin, Patricia Shandor, Santi Thompson, and Louis Ven-
     ters, "The Camden African-American Heritage Project" (2006). Books and
     Manuscripts. 2, https://scholarcommons.sc.edu/pubhist_books/

30   *David Doby toiled:* Details in this paragraph drawn from Joseph Thomas
     Moore, *Larry Doby: The Struggle of the American League's First Black Player*
     (Mineola, NY: Dover Publications, Inc.), 6.

31   *roads remained unpaved:* Crawford et al., "Camden African-American,"
     73–74.

31   *On occasion during Doby's:* The horse-drawn carriage episode and the idea
     of white-gloved racism in Camden derived from two sources: Moore,
     Larry Doby, 7–8; and Ira Berkow, "He Crossed Color Barrier, But in
     Another's Shadow," *The New York Times*, February 23, 1997, 1, Archive
     .nytimes.com.

31   *Augusta Brooks scrubbed clothes:* Moore, *Larry Doby*, 8–9.

31   *so long as he swept:* Sean Horgan, "S.C. Native Was Baseball Trailblazer,"
     The Sun News, April 1, 2006.

31   *wore out two brooms:* Horgan, "S.C. Native."

31   *"That kid was just a natural":* Jake Penland, "Doby Succeeded Father at
     First," *The Plain Dealer*, July 8, 1947, 14.

31   *Doby sometimes would ride:* Fay Vincent, *The Only Game in Town: Baseball
     Stars of the 1930s and 1940s Talk About the Game They Loved* (New York:
     Simon & Schuster, 2006), 172. See also Moore, *Larry Doby*, 10–11.

32   *barefoot next to a pie pan:* Amy Nutt, "He Refused to Hate," *Arizona Repub-
     lic*, July 7, 1997, D8, Newspapers.com.

32   *he'd enrolled in the Mather:* Crawford et al., "Camden African-American,"
     57–59. For more on this period, see also Moore, *Larry Doby*, 9–12.

32   *It was, Doby would later:* Moore, *Larry Doby*, 10.

32   *The change came by request:* Ibid., 11.

32   *clustering in Paterson:* Karel M. Waer, "The Negro in the History of Paterson, New Jersey." Unpublished college research paper, May 1969, 42. Accessed at the Newark Public Library on November 14, 2016. Anita Flynn,
"Being a Negro in Paterson." Unpublished research paper, 1947. Accessed at
the Newark Public Library on November 14, 2016.

33   *Of the roughly three:* Al Kachadurian claimed that in his and Doby's graduating class of three hundred, there were only two other Black students. Al
Kachadurian, personal interview with the author, August 16, 2016.

33   *Strapping on a brown leather:* For a larger discussion of high school foot-
ball in New Jersey during this time, see Hank Gola, *City of Champions: An
American Story of Leather Helmets, Iron Wills, and the High School Kids from
Jersey Who Won It All.* (Brooklyn: Tatra Press, 2018).

33   *Often, opposing players would purposefully:* Moore, *Larry Doby,* 17.

33   *"I never saw him lose":* Al Kachadurian, personal interview with the author,
August 16, 2016.

34   *"school hero, always one":* "Larry Doby: First to Break the Line in American
League; Never Realized How Much Discrimination There Was Until He
Served in US Navy," *Boston Globe,* June 14, 1964, A6

34   *"the important thing is that":* Vincent, *Only Game,* 174

34   *"My mother would take the bus":* Nutt, "He Refused to Hate," D8.

34   *"I had been alone":* Moore, *Larry Doby,* 16.

34   *Soon, Doby began timing:* Dave Anderson, "Sports of the Times: A Pioneer's
Hall of Fame Wife," *The New York Times,* July 26, 2001, D-2, *New York
Times* Articles Archive.

34   *"Everybody looked at him with":* Sam Lacy, "Girls Behind the Guys," *The
Baltimore Afro-American,* April 5, 1952, 22H, ProQuest Historical Newspapers.

35   *By the time he graduated:* A. S. "Doc" Young, "Is Larry Doby the New Tris
Speaker?" *Sport,* March 1949, 93.

35   *"known from Cape May":* Charles Dexter, "Larry Doby's War with Himself,"
Sport, April 1953, 57.

35   *"he was pure speed":* Kachadurian, interview with the author.

35   *"a St. Bernard":* Doc Goldstein, "Eastside Cagemen Batter Ramsey, Central
Quintet Loses," *Paterson Evening News,* January 8, 1941, 17, Newspapers.com.

35   *"We thought we were playing":* Joe Gootter, "Sportograms: A Comfort to Any
Ball Club, Is Eastside's Mr. Doby," *Paterson Evening News,* December 11,
1941, 40.

35   *Doby broke the conference record:* Art McMahon, "The Sportsman's Corner," *The Herald-News* (Passaic), May 4, 1942, 16.

35   *"saw in Larry a devotion":* Margery Miller, "Larry Chose the Diamond," *The Christian Science Monitor,* March 10, 1949, 13, ProQuest Historical Newspapers.

35   *"Doby, who has played everything":* Doc Goldstein, "Doby Called Greatest Baseball Player in Eastside's History," *Paterson Evening News,* June 23, 1941, 17.

35   *"When ever that ball":* Ibid.

36   *"the greatest athlete to ever":* Hardy Whritenour, "Doby, Eastside High Star, Honored at Testimonial," *Paterson Evening News,* February 20, 1942, 23.

36   *"nervously fidgeting in his chair":* Ibid.

36   *"You could see the potential":* Al Kachadurian, interview with Hank Gola. Accessed on Gola's website on February 10, 2019: https://www.hankgola.com/city-of-champions.

36   *he never aspired:* Vincent, *Only Game,* 175.

37   *"The first two or three days":* Holway, *Black Diamonds,* 126.

37   *"overnight sensation":* "Eagles to Meet Chicago at Ruppert Stadium Sunday," *New York Age,* August 15, 1942, 11, ProQuest Historical Newspapers.

37   *Doby played under an alias:* Moore, *Larry Doby,* 20.

3. THE STORYBOOK BALLPLAYERS

39   *"Babe Ruth made his big-league":* "Sport: Baseball: New Season," *Time,* April 19, 1937, 25.

39   *"[Feller] has captured the imagination":* Ed McAuley, "Slapnicka Aims Feller's Fastball at Million-Dollar Mark," *Cleveland News,* February 19, 1937.

39   *Just as Ruth, with his towering:* For more on Babe Ruth as the hero of the Jazz Age, see Warren I. Susman, *Culture as History: The Transformation of American Society in the Twentieth Century* (New York: Pantheon Books, 1973). 141–47.

40   *"I never knew of another case":* J. Roy Stockton, *Saturday Evening Post,* "Storybook Ball Player," 12.

40   *Mythmaking was second nature:* For more on sportswriters and mythmaking in the early half of the twentieth century, see Mark Inabinett, *Grantland Rice and His Heroes: The Sportswriter as Mythmaker in the 1920s* (Knoxville: University of Tennessee Press, 1994).

40   *"Other boys in their teens":* William C. Utley, "Country Boy's Dream Comes

True: Bob Feller, at 17, Left the Iowa Cornfields to Stand Big League Sluggers on Their Ears; He's New Idol of Youth," *Fayette County Leader*, May 13, 1937, 6, Newspapers.com.

40   *"the American boy in the"*: "A Jolly Good Feller," *Baseball Magazine*, February 1946, 292.

40   *"He hasn't acquired any air"*: Stuart Bell, "Feller to Eat Ice Cream—Free; Takes Buildup Ordeal Calmly Unspoiled by Fans' Adulation," *Cleveland Press*, April 14, 1937.

41   *"I don't smoke or drink"*: Associated Press, "Bob Feller Gives Boy Scouts Advice on Their Birthday," *Chicago Tribune*, February 14, 1937, 35, Newspapers.com.

41   *His life story, a narrative:* The idea of Bill Feller as a shrewd businessman who was skilled in constructing narratives about his son's origin story was deeply informed by two sources: David Vaught, phone interview with the author, May 18, 2016, and Vaught, *The Farmers' Game*, 76–103.

41   *"Barring misfortunes which"*: McAuley, "Slapnicka Aims Feller's Fireball." John Sickels noted that Feller's contract was the highest ever for a rookie in: Sickels, *Bob Feller*, 59.

41   *NBC Radio aired:* Broadcast of Feller's high school graduation ceremony accessed from the archives of the Paley Center for Media in New York City on July 12, 2016.

42   *"hiking his left leg high"*: Franklin Lewis, "Latest Evolution in Bob's Pitching Style Means More Triumphs, Fewer Strikeouts," *Cleveland Press*, August 17, 1940.

42   *Feller stocked a file cabinet:* Mark McLemore, *"Look* Examines Bob Feller," *Look*, April 22, 1941, 20.

42   *"When he first came up"*: Bob Dolgan, phone interview with the author, March 23, 2016.

42   *"an epileptic snake"*: Dom DiMaggio, with Bill Gilbert, *Real Grass, Real Heroes: Baseball's Historic 1941 Season* (New York: Zebra Books, 1990), 53.

43   *"unquestionably the idol"*: St. Clair McKelway, "Bob Feller: Baseball Idol Devotes Himself to Care and Worship of His Right Arm, *Life*, May 12, 1941, 51.

43   *"They started talking about me"*: Paige, *Pitch Forever*, 95.

43   *"subject of a baseball saga"*: Wendell Smith, "Smitty's Sports Spurts: Ole Satch'," *Pittsburgh Courier*, September 13, 1941, 17, ProQuest Historical Newspapers.

43   *"I was living"*: Dick Young, "Boston?" *Daily News*, February 10, 1971, p. C26, Newspapers.com.

44   *"He was terminally unpredictable":* As quoted in William A. Young, *J. L. Wilkinson and the Kansas City Monarchs: Trailblazers in Black Baseball* (Jefferson, NC: McFarland & Company, 2016), 106.

45   *"Paige was a very intelligent man":* As quoted in Cal Fussman, *After Jackie: Pride, Prejudice, and Baseball's Forgotten Heroes: An Oral History* (New York, ESPN Books, 2007), 44.

45   *"many whites saw Fetchit's screen character":* Mel Watkins, *Stepin Fetchit: The Life and Times of Lincoln Perry* (New York: Pantheon, 2005), 157.

45   *White spectators who'd:* There are numerous sources that explore the subversiveness of Paige's persona. Larry Tye, for one, writes, "[Paige] knew whites would love his caricature, the way they did Step's, playing as it did to their stereotype of the happy-go-lucky colored coot. He knew, too, that his slow-motion stroll offered the ideal setup for his supersonic delivery." Tye also explores how Paige used humor to engage white players and fans, and then his talent to dazzle them. See Tye, *Satchel,* 190–91. Daniel A. Nathan explored how Black athletes like Paige had to negotiate ways to appeal to white audiences without selling out their own racial identity. See Daniel A. Nathan, "Satchel Paige, the Baltimore Black Sox and the Politics of Remembrance," in Leslie A. Heaphy, ed., *Satchel Paige and Company: Essays on the Kansas City Monarchs, Their Greatest Star and the Negro Leagues,* (Jefferson, NC: McFarland & Company, 2007), 18–19. For more on how Paige upended expectations among white fans, see Gordon Cobbledick, "Old Satch: He's Really Got It," *Sport,* December 1948, 33–34. For more on Lincoln Perry and his Stepin Fetchit character, see Watkins, *Stepin Fetchit.*

45   *"Highest salaried man":* Ed R. Harris, "The King Can Do No Wrong," *Philadelphia Tribune,* April 11, 1935, 9.

46   *Paige searched for:* Paige, *Pitch Forever,* 127.

46   *Paige froze at the peak:* Ibid., 135.

46   *"second childhood":* Tim Cohane, "The Ancient Satchel," *Look,* 68.

46   *"to see a Negro baseball game":* Fay Young, "The Stuff Is Here: Past-Present-Future," *Chicago Defender,* September 20, 1941, 22.

47   *"NEGRO HURLER EARNS MORE":* "Negro Hurler Earns More Money Yearly Than Feller," *Adams County Independent,* October 16, 1941, 4, Newspaper.com.

47   *"Fellerian":* Ted Shane, "Chocolate Rube Waddell," *Saturday Evening Post,* July 27, 1940, 81.

47 *"I thought they would be harder":* "Bobby Feller Shades Satchel Paige in St. Louis Mound Duel," *New York Amsterdam Star-News,* October 11, 1941, 17.

47 *the game was called:* "Monarchs in 5-2 Win Over Frigidaire," *Dayton Journal,* October 7, 1941, 9, Newspapers.com.

47 *"Whadda you expect":* Bob Frame, "What Feller Thinks of Paige And Paige Thinks of Feller," *The Dayton Herald,* October 7, 1941, 14.

48 *"[Paige] can really throw":* Ibid.

48 *fell short of the threshold:* The notion that Paige didn't unleash his fastball often enough was shared by others. After the game in St. Louis, a writer for the *Globe-Democrat* criticized Paige for "trying to slip curveballs past big-league hitters after getting them down in the count, 0–2." As quoted in Timothy M. Gay, *Satch, Dizzy & Rapid Robert: The Wild Saga of Interracial Baseball Before Jackie Robinson* (New York: Simon & Schuster, 2006), 184.

49 *"I ain't had three days'":* Edward W. Cochrane, "Satchel Paige Hurls in 134 Games in Season," *The Dispatch* (Moline, IL), July 25, 1941, 25, Newspapers .com.

49 *"We don't get no babying":* Bob Considine, "On the Line with Considine," *The Washington Post,* July 22, 1941, 18, ProQuest Historical Newspapers.

4. THE GINGERBREAD MAN

50 *Milwaukee had been among:* Ernie Mehl, "A New Owner for Milwaukee Brewers Soon May Be Found," *The Kansas City Star,* June 22, 1941, 15, GenealogyBank.

51 *Hank Greenberg, the Detroit Tigers' slugger:* Hank Greenberg, "Unforgettable Bill Veeck," *Reader's Digest,* July 1986.

51 *"to carry everybody along":* Ed Linn, "Lou Boudreau—The Boy Manager Grows Up," *Sport,* May 1957, 58.

51 Run, run as fast: Veeck, *As in Wreck,* 206.

51 *"I certainly couldn't do":* Warren Brown, *The Chicago Cubs* (New York: G. P. Putnam's Sons, 1946), 80.

51 *Both he and Wrigley:* Several sources informed the following paragraphs on William Wrigley and Bill Veeck, Sr., including: Peter Golenbock, *Wrigleyville: A Magical History Tour of the Chicago Cubs* (New York: St. Martin's Press, 1996); Glenn Stout, *The Cubs: The Complete Story of Chicago Cubs Baseball* (Boston: Houghton Mifflin Harcourt, 2007); Roberts Ehrgott, *Mr. Wrigley's Ball Club: Chicago & the Cubs During the Jazz Age* (Lincoln:

University of Nebraska Press, 2013); and Paul Dickson, *Bill Veeck: Baseball's Greatest Maverick* (New York: Walker Books, 2012).

52   *While many owners feared:* Dickson, *Bill Veeck*, 27–28.

52   *In 1929, they shattered:* Ehrgott, *Mr. Wrigley's Ball Club*, 51.

52   *"You look at that money":* Veeck, *As in Wreck*, 24.

53   *Veeck felt like a burden:* Fred Krehbiel, phone interview with author, January 12, 2017.

53   *"The joy ride was over":* Howard Preston, "Indians Sold to Veeck," *Cleveland News*, June 22, 1946, 7.

54   *"a restless young man":* Charlie Grimm, with Ed Prell, *Jolly Cholly's Story: Grimm's Baseball Tales* (Notre Dame, IN: Diamond Communications, 1983), 140.

54   *Whenever Veeck brought up:* Veeck, *As in Wreck*, 45.

54   *"parson telling the faithful":* Robert M. Yoder and James S. Kearns, "Boy Magnate," *Saturday Evening Post*, August 28, 1943. 81.

54   *covering more ground:* Stoney McGlynn, "The Sports Parade," *Milwaukee Sentinel*, July 27, 1941, B3, GenealogyBank.

55   *"What's the idea?":* Sam Levy, "Sport Shirt Bill, Who Brightened up Brewers, Now Fashioning a Winning Style for Spring," *The Sporting News*, October 30, 1941, 5, Paper of Record.

55   *"The meat always looks":* Davis J. Walsh, "Veeck Turns Baseball into Big Business at Milwaukee," *The Dispatch* (Moline, IL), August 3, 1943, 8, Newspapers.com.

55   *"any Hippodrome stuff":* Jesse Berrett, "Diamonds for Sale: Promoting Baseball During the Great Depression," *Baseball History 4: An Annual of Original Baseball Research*, ed. Peter Levine (Wesport, CT: Meckler, 1991), 53.

56   *"Curiosity is the spice":* John C. Hoffman, "Squirrel Night at the Brewers," *Esquire*, September 1943, 141.

56   *Sometimes, a beer keg:* Ibid., 140.

56   *"What we are trying to do":* Bill Veeck, with Ed Linn, *The Hustler's Handbook* (Chicago: Ivan R. Dee, 2009), 19.

56   *"He has no patience":* Hoffman, "Squirrel Night," 141.

56   *"Who is on the team today?":* Ibid.

56   *The only time Veeck seemed:* Sam Levy, "Veeck Eats Only After Victory; Mrs. Grimm Good Fan; Al Todd Is Doing Well," *The Milwaukee Journal*, May 6, 1942, 27, GenealogyBank.

57   *"Bill Veeck won't let us down":* Levy, "Sport Shirt Bill," 5.

5. TWO SIDES OF THE NAVY

58 *Feller's mind went blank:* Feller recounts how he learned of the attacks on Pearl Harbor during his drive to Chicago in: Feller, *Now Pitching, Bob Feller,* 115.

58 *Feller had mulled over:* John P. Leacacos, "Talk with Tunney Is Hint Feller Will Be in Navy Blue Soon," *The Plain Dealer,* December 5, 1941, 1.

58 *Tunney reportedly had told:* Gordon Cobbledick, "Feller Joins Navy, Trains at Norfolk," *The Plain Dealer,* December 10, 1941, 1.

59 *His enlistment ceremony was broadcast:* For more on this ceremony, see William B. Mead, *Baseball Goes to War: Stars Don Khakis, 4-Fs Vie for Pennant* (Washington D.C.: Broadcast Interview Source, Inc., 1998), 32.

59 *"With all the kids":* Gordon Cobbledick, "Feller Joins Navy, Trains at Norfolk," *The Plain Dealer,* December 10, 1941, 1.

59 *"empty lot in a blackout":* John Kieran, "Sports of the Times: The Muster Roll at Cleveland," *The New York Times,* July 7, 1942, 24.

60 *"animated recruiting poster":* Gordon Cobbledick, "Plain Dealing: Cochrane Declines to Name Starting Pitcher for All-Star Game Here," *The Plain Dealer,* July 1, 1942, 18.

60 *She would finally get:* Feller, *Strikeout Story,* 209–10.

60 *It'd been his father's wish:* Tommy Devine, "Feller's Wedding Fulfills Dad's Wish," *Des Moines Register,* January 17, 1943, 13.

61 *Nothing, he sensed:* Details in this paragraph drawn from Feller, *Now Pitching,* 118.

61 *Doby transferred in the spring:* Moore, *Larry Doby,* 24.

61 *"We were all on the same train":* Vincent, *Only Game,* 177.

61 *"the first time that segregation":* Ibid., 178. See also Moore, *Larry Doby,* 24–25.

62 *"It was a shock":* As quoted in Jerry Malloy, "Black Bluejackets," *The National Pastime* 4, no. 2 (Winter 1985), 73.

62 *They were allowed to enlist again:* Paul Stillwell, ed., *The Golden Thirteen: Recollections of the First Black Naval Officers* (Annapolis, MD: Naval Institute Press, 1993), xviii. See also Arnold Rampersad, *Jackie Robinson: A Biography* (New York: Alfred A. Knopf, 1997), 90.

62 *"I thought the Navy at times":* Clark Clifford, with Richard C. Holbrooke, *Counsel to the President: A Memoir* (New York: Anchor Books, 1992), 209.

62 *"as outsiders, excluded":* Bernard C. Nalty, *Long Passage to Korea: Black Sailors and the Integration of the U.S. Navy* (Washington, D.C.: Naval Historical Center, Department of the Navy, 2003), 21.

62   *"Camp Smalls' duty"*: John Wilhelm, "Negro Makes Quality Sailor, Navy Discovers," *Chicago Tribune*, August 16, 1942, Newspapers.com.

63   *having to sing spirituals*: Robert J. Schneller, Jr., *Breaking the Color Barrier: The U.S. Naval Academy's First Black Midshipmen and the Struggle for Racial Equality* (New York: NYU Press, 2005), 153. See also Moore, *Larry Doby*, 25; and Malloy, "Black Bluejackets," 73.

63   *"I don't ever recall"*: A. S. "Doc" Young, "Is Larry Doby the New Tris Speaker?" *Sport*, March 1949, 92.

63   *"you could throw a baseball"*: Steven R. Bullock, *Playing for Their Nation: Baseball and the American Military During World War II* (Lincoln, NE: University of Nebraska Press, 2004), 78.

63   *racking up an astonishing*: Robert Elias, *The Empire Strikes Out: How Baseball Sold U.S. Foreign Policy and Promoted the American Way Abroad* (New York: The New Press, 2010), 147.

63   *"one of the best"*: Bob Meyer, "Mikan, Leg Still Sore, Will Face Ohio State," *Des Moines Tribune*, February 24, 1944, 20, Newspapers.com.

63   *with Doby netting*: Joe Gootter, "Sportograms: Larry Goes Great at Great Lakes," *Paterson Evening News*, March 1, 1944, 14, Newspapers.com.

64   *"We hit the deck"*: Ibid.

64   *"I wanted to find out"*: Dexter, "Larry Doby's War," 58.

65   *"This is a crying shame"*: Jackie Robinson, *Baseball Has Done It*, (Brooklyn: Ig Publishing, 2005), 70.

65   *"if I was still managing"*: Dexter, "Larry Doby's War," 58.

65   *Because of his athletic prowess*: Moore, *Larry Doby*, 25.

6. NO GENTLEMAN

In addition to the sources cited below, Paul Dickson's book *Bill Veeck: Baseball's Greatest Maverick* (New York: Walker Books, 2012) provided valuable background information on Bill Veeck's pursuit of the Philadelphia Phillies.

67   *Veeck developed a deeper*: Veeck, *As in Wreck*, 182.

67   *"surprising knowledge of outstanding"*: Cleveland Jackson, "Indian Owner Would Hire Qualified Negro Players," *Call & Post*, July 27, 1946, 9B.

67   *Veeck wandered into the colored section*: This incident recounted in Veeck, *As in Wreck*, 177–78.

68   *"I have always had a strong feeling"*: Ibid., 171.

68   *Veeck had hosted Paige*: For more on these games, see Dickson, *Bill Veeck*, 58–59, 71.

68   *"Negro athletes are supposed"*: Stu Keate, "Sports Shots: Abe's back in Town," *The Vancouver Daily Province*, January 16, 1942, 26, Newspapers.com.

69   *"an individual proposition"*: Ibid.

69   *"The only thing blocking"*: Jim Murray, "Baseball and America: Browns Owner Was a Hardball Patriot," *The Park Record* (Park City, UT), January 30, 1986, 39, Newspapers.com.

69   *Intrepid columnists like:* For more on how Black writers challenged the segregated status quo, see Tygiel, *Baseball's Great Experiment*, 37–41.

70   *"There is no law"*: Editorial, "No Good from Raising Race Issue," *The Sporting News*, August 6, 1942, 4.

70   *an old quote from Leo Durocher:* Buster Miller, "Time Out . . ." *New York Age*, July 25, 1942, 11.

70   *"Negroes are not barred"*: Fay Young, "Through the Years: Judge Landis' Decision—Bosh!" *The Chicago Defender*, July 25, 1942, 20. Paul Dickson offers a more detailed account of this incident with Durocher and Landis that informed my own telling. See Dickson, *Bill Veeck*, 76–77. See also Moore, *Larry Doby*, 21.

70   *"take up Landis' challenge"*: Young, "Judge Landis' Decision—Bosh!" *Chicago Defender*, 20.

71   *some historians would cast:* David M. Jordan, Larry R. Gerlach, and John P. Rossi, "A Baseball Myth Exploded: Bill Veeck and the 1943 Sale of the Phillies," *National Pastime*, 18 (1998), 3–13.

71   *"I always will believe Landis"*: Shirley Povich, "Negro Has Found Real Democracy in Baseball," *The Washington Post*, May 10, 1953, C1.

72   *Almost 40 percent:* Richard L. Pifer, *A City at War: Milwaukee Labor During World War II* (Madison: Wisconsin Historical Society Press, 2002), 11.

72   *"We're bringing baseball into tune"*: John Detmer, "Brewers Play Morning Game," *Rockford Morning Star*, May 8, 1943, 10, Newspapers.com.

72   *swing-shift workers were greeted:* For a fuller account of morning baseball, see Dickson, *Bill Veeck*, 84–85.

72   *"Billy Veeck,"* Esquire *crowed:* Hoffman, "Squirrel Night," 53.

72   *"one of the loneliest stretches"*: Yoder and Kearns, "Boy Magnate," 19.

72   *former boxing champion Barney Ross:* Dave Condon. *The Go-Go Chicago White Sox* (Chicago: Coward-McCann, 1960), 27.

73   *"I'm the guy"*: Stoney McGlynn, "The Sports Parade," *Milwaukee Sentinel*, November 28, 1943, B3, GenealogyBank.com.

73   *Veeck bounded out:* Grimm, *Jolly Cholly's*, 154.

73 *"seemed sudden":* R. G. Lynch, "Maybe I'm Wrong: Bill Veeck Just Decided the Time Had Come," *The Milwaukee Journal,* November 28, 1943, 39, GenealogyBank.com.

73 *Declining all commissions:* Dickson, *Bill Veeck,* 88–89.

7. TALES FROM THE SOUTH PACIFIC

74 *Men talked of waves:* Rebecca Bundy Brown and Heidi Bundy Brown, eds., *The "Mighty A" and the Men Who Made Her Mighty: Sea Stories from USS Alabama BB-60 "The Mighty A"—Remembrances of Things Past by the Men Who Made Her Mighty* (Self-published, 1999), 5.

74 *One blustery night:* Feller, *Strikeout Story,* 211–12. See also Sickels, *Bob Feller,* 122–23.

75 *They downed cup after cup:* Bundy, *The "Mighty A,"* 65.

75 *some pressed pennies:* Ibid., 26.

75 *twenty-piece, Glenn Miller–style:* Ibid., 80.

75 Casablanca *was shown:* Ibid., 19.

75 *Feller kept in shape:* Bullock, *Playing for Their Nation,* 118.

75 *"I was lucky":* "Jolly Good Feller," 291.

75 *Once, a game was disrupted:* Eugene Kinkead, "That Was the War: Wild Pigs and Mr. Feller," *The New Yorker,* May 11, 1946, 84–88, Newyorker.com /archive.

76 *a plane on a suicide mission:* Bundy, *The "Mighty A,"* 65.

76 *"saw an opportunity":* Harold J. Goldberg, *D-Day in the Pacific: The Battle of Saipan* (Bloomington, IN: Indiana University Press, 2007), 4.

76 *another plane swooped down:* Barrett Tillman, *Clash of the Carriers: The True Story of the Marianas Turkey Shoot in World War II* (New York: NAL Hardcover, 2005), 167.

77 *"the most exciting 13 hours":* Feller, *Strikeout Story,* 213.

77 *Feller listened to the World Series:* In January 1945, Feller told *The Sporting News:* "On our ship we heard the World's Series by short wave when we were a lot of miles from home. You can't imagine the thrill it gave us." Royal Broughman, "Feller, Back from War, Says 'Keep Game Going,'" *The Sporting News,* January 18, 1945, 5, Paper of Record.

77 *more than 60 percent:* Bill Gilbert, *They Also Served: Baseball and the Home Front, 1941–1945* (New York: Crown Publishers, Inc., 1992), 113.

77 *the lofty goals Feller:* Virginia Feller, as told to Hal Lebovitz, "He's My Feller!" *Baseball Digest,* (May 1952), 94.

78   *And soon he had an inkling:* In several interviews, Feller talked about con-
      ceiving of his grand barnstorming tour with Satchel Paige while on board
      the *Alabama.* In *After Jackie,* Feller said: "The racial rivalry tour came to me
      when I was aboard the battleship *Alabama* during WWII: the best blacks
      against the best whites across country." In an interview with William Mar-
      shall, Feller said: "I had it all laid out . . . I knew what I was going to do and
      I knew the people personally that I was going to have get the black clubs
      together—the Kansas City operator, Mr. Wilkinson and Satchel Paige and
      many others that I wanted to oppose us." Fussman, *After Jackie,* p. 41. See
      also William Marshall, *Baseball's Pivotal Era 1945–1951* (Lexington: The
      University of Kentucky Press, 1999), 341.

78   *"like running across thirty":* John Monks, Jr., *A Ribbon and a Star: The Action-
      Filled Account of the Third Marines at Bougainville* (New York: Pyramid
      Books, 1966), 40.

78   *"Jungle rot," it was called:* Peter Schrijvers, *Bloody Pacific: American Soldiers at
      War with Japan* (New York: Palgrave Macmillan, 2010), 118.

78   *Veeck shuttled in and out:* Dickson, *Bill Veeck,* 99.

78   *"Get that Imperial":* Bill Veeck, as told to S/Sgt Dick Hannah, "Pfc. Veeck
      Back with Title to Bougainville 'Finds,'" *The Sporting News,* November 2,
      1944, 11, Paper of Record.

78   *he tracked the team's:* Ibid.

79   *he suffered a grave injury:* Dickson, *Bill Veeck,* 99.

79   *"an albatross":* Veeck, *As in Wreck,* 373.

79   *"tears filled his eyes":* "Caught on the Fly: Tributes Choke Up Veeck," *The
      Sporting News,* December 21, 1944, 16, Paper of Record.

79   *"the great time of my life":* Veeck, *As in Wreck,* 80.

79   *Veeck would spend:* For more on Veeck's injuries and his extended hospital
      stay in 1945, see Dickson, *Bill Veeck,* 102–03.

79   *His wife, Eleanor, did not:* Ibid., 106–07.

80   *Eleanor had to nail rugs:* Ellen Maggs, phone interview with the author, May
      25, 2016.

80   *To the idle sailors:* Samuel Hynes, phone interview with the author, June 24,
      2016.

80   *There were water taxis:* "Mogmog Island at Ulithi in the Marianas," accessed
      on January 10, 2017, from: http://navy.memorieshop.com/Adair/Cruise
      -Book/Mogmog.html.

80   *After herding the native residents:* Ralph J. Donahue, *Ready on the Right: A*

True Story of a Naturalist Seabee on the Islands of Kodiak, Unalask, and Others (Whitefish, MT: Kessinger Publishing, 2010), 139.

81 *linked together all the empty:* John Marx, "Mog Mog Memories," *The Dispatch* (Moline, Illinois), September 14, 1996, B1, Newspapers.com.

81 *whether he was leading calisthenics:* Moore, *Larry Doby,* 26.

81 *"seemed a pastoral":* Samuel Hynes, *Flights of Passage: Recollections of a World War II Aviator* (New York: Penguin Books, 2003) 178.

82 *Because home plate was a mere:* Harrington E. Crissey, Jr., *Athletes Away: A Selective Look at Professional Baseball Players in the Navy During World War II* (Sharon Hills, PA: Archway Press, Inc., 1984), 47–48.

82 *the relatively relaxed attitude:* About segregation in the Ulithi Atoll, Samuel Hynes told me, "You have to realize that if you're on an island that's 1,500 feet in diameter, segregation is not really possible." Samuel Hynes, phone interview with the author, June 24, 2016.

82 *"Many nights," Vernon told:* Rich Westcott, *Mickey: The Gentleman First Baseman* (Philadelphia: Camino Books, Inc., 2005), 78.

83 *"Baseball and malted milks":* Brougham, "Feller, Back from War," 5.

83 *Though he wasn't slated:* Sickels, *Bob Feller,* 128.

83 *"Oh, young man":* Mead, *Baseball Goes to War,* 225.

83 *"another V-Day":* Ed McAuley, "Cleveland Gives Stirring Welcome to Stellar Feller; Bob's Fast Ball Adds Blazing Climax to Festivities," *The Sporting News,* August 30, 1945, 5, Paper of Record.

83 *"In welcoming Bob Feller home":* Ad for the Higbee Company, *The Plain Dealer,* August 24, 1945, 11.

84 *"had outgrown his role":* Roelif Loveland, "Cleveland Will Welcome Hero Bob Feller Back to Stadium Tonight," *The Plain Dealer,* August 24, 1945, 1.

84 *"has been places—dangerous":* Ibid.

84 *so many fans phoned:* "Bob Sets Another Record; Calls Wreck Tribe's PBX," *The Sporting News,* August 30, 1945, 5, Paper of Record.

84 *In a downtown hotel:* Mead, *Baseball Goes to War,* 226.

84 *"how splendid it was":* Roelif Loveland, "46,477 See Feller Fan 12 to Win," *The Plain Dealer,* August 25, 1945, 1, 3.

85 *"We lost several years":* Franklin Lewis, "Feller Asks Barnstorming Permit of Czar: Heavy Taxes Cause Plea to Be Made," *The Dayton Herald,* September 6, 1945, 24, Newspapers.com.

85 *On October 2, 1945, more than 22,000 fans:* Associated Negro Press, "22,000

See Paige Outpitch Bob Feller in Coast Tilt," *The Baltimore Afro-American*, October 13, 1945, 23, ProQuest Historical Newspapers.

86 *"a typical football player":* Vincent X. Flaherty, "Feller Doubts Robinson Future: Claims Negro Weak Against Major Hurling," *Akron Beacon Journal*, October 27, 1945, 12, Newspapers.com.

86 *"He let you know":* Marguerite Goodson, phone interview with author, August 26, 2016.

86 *"All of the Negro ball players":* Flaherty, "Feller Doubts Robinson," 12.

87 *"Are we going home?":* The story of how Doby heard of the signing of Jackie Robinson is recounted in: Dexter, "Larry Doby's War," 58.

87 *A tingling sensation:* Larry Doby told sportswriter Bill Madden: "When I heard the news of Jackie's signing, I knew then I had a chance to play major league baseball . . . I'll never forget the tingling sensation I felt inside." Bill Madden, *1954: The Year Willie Mays and the First Generation of Black Superstars Changed Major League Baseball Forever* (Boston: Da Capo Press, 2014), 148–49.

87 *"I forgot about going back":* Moore, *Larry Doby*, 29.

8. THE CROSSROADS

91 *"Any club that":* Paige, as Told to William Dismukes, "My Greatest Thrill!: *Pittsburgh Courier*, 19.

92 *"Bangin' around the way I was":* Donovan, "Fabulous Satchel Paige," 66.

92 *Now, in Kansas City, he laid down:* For more on Satchel Paige settling down in Kansas City and professing his loyalty to J. L. Wilkinson and the Kansas City Monarchs, see Tye, *Satchel*, 166.

92 *"Once a baseball gypsy":* Wendell Smith, "The Sports Beat: Wilkinson's a Credit to Baseball," *Pittsburgh Courier*, June 9, 1945, 12, ProQuest Historical Newspapers.

92 *"who can tell what the bull":* Braven Dyer, "The Sports Parade," *Los Angeles Times*, September 30, 1945, 21, Newspapers.com.

92 *"Mr. It" in sports:* Wendell Smith, "Smitty's Sport Spurts: Ole Satch,'" *Pittsburgh Courier*, September 13, 1941, 17.

93 *"They'd have to offer me":* Associated Press, "Signing of Negroes Can't Be Worked Out, Says Paige," *The Washington Post*, August, 7, 1942, 24.

93 *With his star power, he'd:* For more on the ways that Paige fought segregation, see Tye, *Satchel*, 191–92.

93 *"I see in* The Courier": Wendell Smith, "The Sports Beat: Satchel Takes Pen in Hand . . ." *Pittsburgh Courier,* May 12, 1945, 17, ProQuest Historical Newspapers.

94 *"the sun is setting":* Smith, "Ole Satch'," 17.

94 *He also later admitted:* Tye, *Satchel,* 200.

94 *"They didn't make a mistake":* Gene Friedman, "Satchel Paige, Perhaps Greatest of All Pitchers, Hails Robinson Signing," *Nevada State Journal,* October 26, 1945, 12.

94 *"I'd been the guy":* Paige, *Pitch Forever,* 173.

94 *"He's no Satchel Paige":* Ibid.

95 *For a quarter-century, Rickey had:* The descriptions of Branch Rickey and his persona were influenced by Tygiel, *Baseball's Great Experiment,* 48–58.

95 *"Cave of the Winds":* Arnold Rampersad, *Jackie Robinson: A Biography* (New York: Alfred A. Knopf, 1997), 121.

95 *"Black skin . . . black skin":* Murray Polner, *Branch Rickey: A Biography,* Revised Edition (Jefferson, NC: McFarland & Company, 2007), 38.

95 *But Rickey was not motivated solely:* For more on Rickey's reasoning, see Marshall, *Baseball's Pivotal Era,* 122–23.

96 *"the greatest untapped reservoir":* Harold Parrott, *The Lords of Baseball: A Wry Look at a Side of the Game the Fan Seldom Sees—The Front Office* (New York: Praeger Publishers, 1976), 187.

96 *Rickey, in contrast, tiptoed toward*: For more on Rickey's integration strategy, see Tygiel, *Baseball's Great Experiment,* 55–57.

96 *"Branch Rickey was innovative":* Tygiel, *Baseball's Great Experiment,* 55.

9. EFFA MANLEY'S DILEMMA

97 *"He is some basketball player":* Letter from Effa Manley to Monte Irvin, January 28, 1946. Accessed from the Newark Eagles collection at the Newark Public Library on May 5, 2016.

98 *a scout had approached Irvin:* For more on this incident, see Monte Irvin, with James A. Riley, *Nice Guys Finish First: The Autobiography of Monte Irvin* (New York: Carroll & Graf Publishers, 1996), 103.

98 *"I believe more Major League teams":* Letter from Effa Manley to Monte Irvin, February 9, 1946. Accessed from the Newark Eagles collection at the Newark Public Library on May 5, 2016.

98 *"I have not had the courtesy":* Letter from Effa Manley to Larry Doby, March

19, 1946. Accessed from the Newark Eagles collection at the Newark Public Library on May 5, 2016.

99   *looks were deceiving:* For more on the two sides of Effa Manley, see: James Overmyer, *Queen of the Negro Leagues: Effa Manley and the Newark Eagles* (Lanham, MD: Scarecrow Press, 1998), 3–4.

99   *"runs a man's business":* Lem Graves, Jr., "From the Press Box: Introducing Our Daughter," *Norfolk Journal and Guide,* July 26, 1941, 12, ProQuest Historical Newspapers.

99   *Effa learned to negotiate:* Overmyer, *Queen,* 7.

99   *"[Effa] would take the subway":* Shakeia Taylor, "Effa Manley's Hidden Life: The Only Woman in the National Baseball Hall of Fame Had a Fascinating—and Confusing—Past," *SB Nation,* April 30, 2020, https://www.sbnation.com/2020/4/30/21238190/effa-manley-hall-of-fame-negro-league-newark-eagles.

100 *Theaters shuttled Black customers:* Brad R. Tuttle, *How Newark Became Newark: The Rise, Fall, and Rebirth of an American City* (New Brunswick, NJ: Rutgers University Press, 2009), 149.

100 *"something we possessed":* Amiri Baraka, *The Autobiography of LeRoi Jones* (New York: Freundlich Books, 1984), 43.

100 *she summoned the offending party:* Holway, *Black Diamonds,* 162.

101 *"You are my ball players":* Ibid.

101 *While Abe Manley reveled:* Effa Manley and Leon Herbert Hardwick, *Negro Baseball . . . Before Integration* (Haworth, NJ: St. Johann Press, 2006), 53.

101 *"My husband manages and travels":* Donovan, "Between You and Me," [New York] *Daily News,* December 30, 1940.

101 *"the proper place for women":* As quoted in Neil Lanctot, *Negro League Baseball: The Rise and Fall of a Black Institution* (Philadelphia: University of Pennsylvania Press, 2004), 86.

101 *"in seven languages":* Graves, "Introducing Our Daughter," 12.

101 *In between innings, she often raised:* Lawrence Hogan, James Overmyer, and James DiClerico, "Baseball as Black Comfortability: Negro Professional Baseball in New Jersey in the Era of the Color Line," paper delivered on June 11, 1991, at the Third Annual Cooperstown Symposium on Baseball and American Culture. Accessed at the Newark Public Library on May 5, 2016.

101 *Appalled at reports of violence:* Monte Irvin, with Phil Pepe, *Few and Chosen: Defining Negro Leagues Greatness* (Chicago: Triumph Books, 2007), 178.

102   *a million calls:* Letter from Effa Manley to Abe Manley, April 5, 1946, accessed from the Newark Eagles collection at the Newark Public Library on May 5, 2016.

102   *"racial treachery of the rankest":* Manley, *Negro Baseball,* 72.

102   *"I think we look positively stupid":* Letter from Effa Manley to Ed Gottlieb, April 16, 1946, accessed from the Newark Eagles collection at the Newark Public Library on May 5, 2016.

102   *"We have so many boys":* Letter from Effa Manley to Abe Manley, April 5, 1946, accessed from the Newark Eagles collection at the Newark Public Library on May 5, 2016.

102   *"In continuing in the baseball":* Letter to Raleigh "Biz" Mackey, February 24, 1946, accessed from the Newark Eagles collection at the Newark Public Library on May 5, 2016.

10. THE DEAL IS CLOSED

103   *a piece of bone:* "Bill Veeck in Cast Again," *The Sporting News,* March 21, 1946, 18, Paper of Record.

103   *"I felt there was something":* Veeck, *As in Wreck,* 373.

104   *Baseball was where:* Preston, "Indians Sold," 1, 7.

104   *he tossed some outfits:* J. G. Taylor Spink, "Looping the Loops: A Stiff Workout—Or a Talk with Bill Veeck," *The Sporting News,* July 10, 1946, 8.

104   *As soon as Veeck resolved:* Veeck, *As in Wreck,* 82–83.

104   *Veeck and Grabiner huddled:* Herman Goldstein, "Indians Appeal to Bill Veeck as Very Good Buy," *Cleveland News,* June 20, 1946.

105   *"ore mountains, towering smokestacks":* L. H. Robbins, "A Century and a Half for Cleveland," *The New York Times Magazine,* May 26, 1946, 51, Archive .nytimes.com.

105   *That year, more than 550,000:* Leonard N. Moore, *Carl B. Stokes and the Rise of Black Political Power* (Urbana: University of Illinois Press, 2002), 18.

105   *Production boomed:* W. Dennis Keating, Norman Krumholz, and David C. Perry, *Cleveland: A Metropolitan Reader* (Kent, OH: The Kent State University Press, 1995), 42.

105   *the mood on the street:* George E. Condon, *Cleveland: The Best Kept Secret* (New York: Doubleday, 1967), 280.

105   *For days Veeck sidled:* In a 1976 interview, Veeck claimed never to sit in the backseat of taxis, always the front. See Bob Sudyk, "Baseball's Barnum Hasn't Changed," *Cleveland Press,* June 4, 1976.

105   *To Veeck's astonishment:* Bill Veeck with Gordon Cobbledick, "So You Want to Run a Ball Club?" *Saturday Evening Post,* April 23, 1949, 141. See also Dickson, *Bill Veeck,* 109.

106   *"It occurred to me":* Veeck with Cobbledick, "So You Want," 141

106   *local titans of industry:* Lewis, *Cleveland Indians,* 153.

106   *The late 1920s:* For more on Cleveland in this period, see John J. Grabowski, *Sports in Cleveland: An Illustrated History* (Bloomington, IN: University of Indiana Press, 1992), 48. See also Philip Suchma, "From the Best of Times to the Worst of Times: Professional Sport and Urban Decline in a Tale of Two Clevelands: 1945–1978," (The Ohio State University: unpublished dissertation, 2005), 33.

107   *"Always, in Cleveland,":* Shirley Povich: "This Morning: Springtime in Cleveland—It's Grand!" *The Washington Post,* May 5, 1941, 18, ProQuest Historical Newspapers.

108   *"Where would I get that kind":* "Veeck Scoffs at Reports He's Trying to Buy Tribe," *The Sporting News,* June 5, 1946, 4, Paper of Record.

109   *His infected right leg:* Goldstein, "Indians Appeal."

109   *capsules of cologne:* Veeck, *As in Wreck,* 90.

109   *then rang up Bob Hope:* Milton Yelsky, "Veeck, Who Held First Baseball job at 11, Bids to Better Dunn's Time," *The Plain Dealer,* June 23, 1946, 1-C, 3-C.

109   *"made a strange appearance":* Associated Press, "Indians Sale Completed; Veeck New President; Boudreau Status Not Clear," *The Boston Globe,* June 23, 1946, 32, Newspapers.com.

109   *Exhaustion and the worsening infection:* Ed McAuley, "Anniversary Tribute— from a Fat Man on the Aisle," *Cleveland News,* June 22, 1948.

110   *"baseball is baseball":* Spink, "A Stiff Workout," 8.

110   *"has got to be fun":* Preston, "Indians Sold," 1-C, 3-C.

110   *"Gentlemen, the deal":* Ed McAuley, "Veeck Buys Indians, Fans Cheer Change," *The Sporting News,* July 3, 1946, 5, Paper of Record.

110   *"visibly shaken":* Alex Zirin, "Bill Veeck Plans 'New Deal' Here," *The Plain Dealer,* June 23, 1946, 1-C.

110   *His entrance elicited:* McAuley, "Veeck Buys Indians," 5.

110   *"I suppose you gentlemen":* McAuley, "Anniversary Tribute."

110   *"Hell, I never sat in a box":* Associated Press, "Veeck Syndicate Buys Indians; Price Estimated at $1,750,000," *New York Herald Tribune,* June 23, 1946, A1.

111   *even the umpires:* Zirin, "Bill Veeck Plans," 1-C.

111 *crowd sentiment was unreservedly:* Editorial, "Bill Veeck in Face-Lifting Job at Cleveland," *The Sporting News,* July 3, 1946, 10, Paper of Record.

111 *Starting in the upper reaches:* Henry Andrews, "The Common Touch: Bill Veeck, Tribe's New Boss, Sweats Out Twin Bill with 'His Fans,'" *Cleveland Press,* June 24, 1946, 13.

111 *After walking about for hours:* Ibid.

11. EXPLODING THE FIREWORKS

112 *One of the first things to go:* Greenberg, "Unforgettable Bill Veeck."

112 *"We know how many":* Franklin Lewis, "Veeck Finds Fan with Century Note Who Prefers Sun," *Cleveland Press,* June 25, 1946, 22.

112 *"Veeck's immediate and close":* Ibid.

113 *"I shouldn't want anybody to get":* Ed McAuley, "Swing Band Added Starter for Indians," *Cleveland News,* July 22, 1946.

113 *a canvas tepee crowned:* Ed McAuley, "'Twas Corn, Pure Corn—But Try It Again," *Cleveland News,* July 23, 1946.

113 *"I want the whole works":* Shirley Povich, "This Morning with Shirley Povich," *The Washington Post,* July 29, 1946, 8. Povich claimed that Veeck shot off these fireworks before a game against the Washington Senators, but those games were all played during the day. The *Cleveland Press,* in contrast, mentioned on July 23 that Veeck intended to shoot off a half-hour's worth of fireworks in ten minutes.

113 *"a scattering of aerial bombs":* George Scofield, "All This and Victory Too— Veeck Sideshow Wows 'Em," *The Plain Dealer,* July 24, 1946, 1, 6.

113 *"three brilliantly lighted airplanes":* Ibid.

114 *"To me," she later wrote:* Feller, "He's My Feller!" 93.

114 *"blazing Bobby Feller":* Associated Press, "Bob Feller Shows Signs of Slipping," *Lansing State Journal,* April 27, 1946, 10, Newspapers.com.

114 *an average of 10.5 per game:* Ed McAuley, "Keltner Climbs, Gromek Glistens— Boudreau Grins," *The Sporting News,* May 23, 1946, 11, Paper of Record.

115 *On game days, he began:* "Feller Reveals That Best Games Come After Off-days," *The Sporting News,* May 23, 1946, 14, Paper of Record.

115 *"Sorry I cannot accept":* Alfonso Flores, "Pasquel Urges 'Good Neighbor' Policy in Game," *The Sporting News,* March 21, 1946, 7, Paper of Record.

115 *"Because I don't do business":* Walter L. Johns, "Feller Is Real 'Triple Threat,'" *Palladium-Item* (Richmond, IN), March 31, 1946, 11, Newspapers.com.

115 *"What good would [Pasquel's] money":* Ibid.

116 *pulled in more than $20,000:* Shirley Povich, "This Morning with Shirley Povich," *The Washington Post,* July 30, 1946, 8. *The Washington Post* put the figure at $25,000 while the *Cleveland News* put it at around $20,000.

116 *what he perceived as its central purpose:* Vincent, *Only Game,* 49.

116 *the Orson Welles:* Ned Mills, "Bob Feller Looking into Future; Hopes to Be Big League Manager, Owner after Retiring," *Lancaster Eagle-Gazette,* July 25, 1946, 14, Newspapers.com. For more on the planning of Feller's 1946 tour, see Gay, *Satch, Dizzy & Rapid Robert,* 201–02.

116 *"I had a lot of faith":* Feller, "He's My Feller!" 96.

116 *In interviews he laid out:* "Chandler Opposes Feller Tonight as Yanks Play Indians at Stadium," *The New York Times,* July 11, 1946, 15, Archive.nytimes .com.

117 *Does Satchel Paige still:* Veeck, *As in Wreck,* 183.

117 *He sensed that such a signing:* Ibid., 175.

117 *"The only way I know":* Veeck with Cobbledick, "So You Want," 33.

117 *Ten days into his tenure:* Ed McAuley, "Veeck Wears 'Em Out—Even His Cast Yells 'Uncle,'" *Cleveland News,* July 2, 1946.

118 *"Only a few of Veeck's close friends":* Franklin Lewis, "Veeck Made Sale of Baseball Here His First Duty," *Cleveland Press,* October 30, 1946.

118 *"I'm going to lose this thing":* Ed McAuley, "Good Luck, Bill—Your Fans Are with You," *Cleveland News,* November 1, 1946.

118 *"We've all been through this terrible":* Danny Peary, ed., *We Played the Game: 65 Players Remember Baseball's Greatest Era, 1947–1964* (New York: Hyperion, 1994), 9.

119 *people like fire trucks:* Frank Gibbons, "Bob Attacks Own Mark as Part of 'Weisman Night,'" *Cleveland Press,* August 13, 1946.

119 *If the action lagged:* For more on Max Patkin's antics, see Marshall, *Baseball's Pivotal Era,* 174–75; and Dickson, *Bill Veeck,* 113.

119 *"a travesty on serious baseball":* Ed McAuley, "Traffic Commissioner Blecke, We Apologize," *Cleveland News,* August 29, 1946, 14.

119 *"There are times when":* Ted Williams, "Ted Williams Says: Boudreau Has Characteristics of Barnum and Billy Rose," *The Boston Globe,* August 26, 1946, 8, Newspapers.com.

119 *"did they spell your name":* Max Patkin, and Stan Hochman, *The Clown Prince of Baseball* (Waco, TX: WRS Publishing, 1994), 39.

119 *"as if he were a magician":* Gordon Cobbledick, "Plain Dealing," *The Plain Dealer,* August 6, 1946, 14.

119 *"It is doubtful":* Feller, *Strikeout Story,* 232.

120 *Veeck could do nothing more:* "500,000 Attracted by 'Magnet' Veeck," *The Plain Dealer,* August 5, 1946, 16.

120 *"I'm going to pitch all I can":* Gayle Hayes, "Feller Pledges 30 Victories, Strikeout Mark," *The Des Moines Register,* August 2, 1946, 13, Newspapers.com.

120 *Veeck, for one, embraced:* Veeck, *As in Wreck,* 103.

120 *"Feller does not look quite":* Sec Taylor, "Sittin' In with the Athletes," *The Des Moines Register,* August 8, 1946, 13, Newspapers.com.

121 *Senators owner Clark Griffith cooked up:* Feller recounts Griffith's stunt and his reaction to it in: Feller, *Now Pitching,* 129.

121 *He'd shipped in a lumiline chronograph:* George Zielke, "Feller Fires Ball at 98.6 Miles-an-Hour Rate . . . in Army Speed Test," *The Sporting News,* August 28, 1946, 5, Paper of Record.

121 *Feller saw the speed test:* For more on Feller's hardening attitude toward owners in reference to Griffith's speed test in particular, see Sickels, *Bob Feller,* 143–44.

121 *"The main reason I incorporated":* Ed McAuley, "'Feller Corporation Just for Sideline,' Says Bob," *The Sporting News,* May 14, 1947, 4, Paper of Record.

122 *"the personification of":* Shirley Povich, "This Morning with Shirley Povich," *The Washington Post,* July 12, 1948, 10.

122 *"I don't think I could":* Ed McAuley, "Deacons' Job in Wigwam to Make Darts Go Straight," *The Sporting News,* October 9, 1946, 21, Paper of Record.

12. OPPOSITE DIRECTIONS

123 *"At the Grand Hotel":* Baraka, *LeRoi Jones,* 43.

123 *At times, groups would peel:* Bill Handleman, "When Eagles Soared," *Asbury Park Press,* March 6, 1994, H7, Newspapers.com.

123 *a compact version of Harlem:* Tuttle, *How Newark,* p. 149.

124 *"Those were special times":* Handleman, "When Eagles," H7.

124 *The Eagles, he recalled:* Vincent, *Only Game,* 177.

124 *The players lodged:* Ken Davidoff, "Newark Eagles Helped Spirits Soar," *Asbury Park Press,* July 6, 1997, H2, Newspapers.com.

124 *He stood stiff and deep:* Franklin Lewis, "Big League Chance Awes Larry Doby as He Joins Tribe," *Cleveland Press,* July 5, 1947.

124 *Trusting his snap reflexes:* Lester Bromberg, "Doby Credits Study in Earning Steady Job," *The Sporting News,* October 27, 1948, 5, Paper of Record.

124 *"high knee-action":* Shirley Povich, "That Doby Boy Well on His Way to Greatness," *The Washington Post,* June 26, 1949, 1-C.

124 *"I think Larry is":* Henry C. Schwartz, "In the Sports Cauldron," *Paterson Evening News,* August 10 ,1946, 14, Newspapers.com.

124 *It was rumored that Clyde:* Wendell Smith, "The Sports Beat: Cleveland Signed Doby in Nick of Time," *Pittsburgh Courier,* July 12, 1947, 14, ProQuest Historical Newspapers.

125 *"Larry was the reason":* Schwartz, "In the Sports Cauldron."

125 *"Mr. Rickey, I hope you're not":* As quoted in Overmyer, *Queen,* 190.

125 *"there were several men on":* Effa Manley letter to J. B. Martin, October 17, 1946, accessed from the Newark Eagles files at the Newark Public Library on May 5, 2016.

125 *she attempted to forge:* Ibid. For the 20 percent number, see Alfred M. Martin and Alfred T. Martin, *The Negro Leagues in New Jersey: A History* (Jefferson, NC: McFarland & Company, 2008), 20.

126 *"Adding machines, comptometers":* "All-Stars Suffer Humiliating Loss to Eagles, 31–4," *Trenton Evening Times,* July 5, 1946, 19, Genealogybank.com.

127 *"greatest attraction in Negro baseball":* "Paige to Appear with Newark Nine," *Asbury Park Press,* August 5, 1946, 10, Newspapers.com.

127 *"whipping his throwing arm":* "Eagles, Cubans Dunn Field Foes Tomorrow Night," *Trenton Evening Times,* August 9, 1946, 20, Genealogybank.com.

127 *"to nurse a hope":* Skipper Patrick, "Satchel Paige Still Exhibits Blinding Speed," *The News and Courier* (Charleston), September 6, 1946, 6, Genealogybank.com.

128 *During an East Coast swing:* "Sporting Comment," *Kansas City Star,* July 19, 1946, 17, Genealogybank.com.

128 *retiring the first nine batters:* "Negro League Teams Split Double Header," *Muncie Evening Press,* August 31, 1946, 10, Newspapers.com.

128 *"Eighteen thousand in the stands":* Patrick, "Blinding Speed," 6.

128 *"Bob Feller and that [barnstorming] series":* Fay Young, "Through the Years," *The Chicago Defender,* September 7, 1946, 11, ProQuest Historical Newspapers.

129 *"show that he too":* Lacy, "Girls Behind the Guys," 22H.

129 *They exchanged vows:* Moore, *Larry Doby,* 33.

129 *"bragging about what he was":* Dan Burley, "Satchel Paige Twirls Master Ball in Classic," *New York Amsterdam News,* September 21, 1946, 1, 25, ProQuest Historical Newspapers.

129 *"proved his right to the distinction":* Ibid.

129 *In the second game:* Details of this game from "Doby Hits Homer in Second Game; Eagles Win 7-4," *New Journal and Guide,* September 28, 1946, 12.

130 *"At that point," wrote Monarchs first baseman:* Buck O'Neil, with Steve Wulf and David Conrads, *I Was Right on Time: My Journey from the Negro Leagues to the Majors* (New York: Simon & Schuster, 1996), 179.

131 *Roy Campanella, who'd just wrapped:* Roy Campanella, *It's Good to Be Alive* (Boston: Little, Brown, 1959), 128.

13. HEAD-TO-HEAD

In addition to the sources cited below, Timothy Gay's book *Satch, Dizzy, & Rapid Robert: The Wild Saga of Interracial Baseball Before Jackie Robinson* (New York: Simon & Schuster, 2006) provided valuable background information on barnstorming in general and Bob Feller's 1946 tour in particular.

132 *Streetcars and buses:* "Conciliators Meet Again Today with Union, Company," *Pittsburgh Post-Gazette,* October 1, 1946, 1–2, Newspapers.com.

132 *newspaper ads urged residents:* Ad for the Duquesne Power Company in *Pittsburgh Post-Gazette,* October 1, 1946, 3.

132 *not even a fourth:* Burton Hawkins, "Bob Feller's $150,000 Pitch," *Saturday Evening Post,* April 19, 1947, 170. See also Gay, *Satch, Dizzy & Rapid Robert,* 228.

133 *"uproariously funny":* Ed Linn, "Immortal Hanger-on," *Sport,* August 1956, 21–23.

133 *Even Bill Veeck, though supportive:* Alvin Silverman, "The Inside of the News in Cleveland," *The Plain Dealer,* October 6, 1946, 19.

133 *The owners of the Boston:* Feller, *Now Pitching,* 138. See also Sickels, *Bob Feller,* 150–51; and Gay, *Satch, Dizzy & Rapid Robert,* 222.

133 *"We want the best players":* Tom Baird letter to Effa Manley from September 2, 1946, accessed from the Newark Eagles files at the Newark Public Library on May 5, 2016.

134 *"The deal gives Feller":* Joe Gootter, "Sportograms: Bulldog's Bite May Be Worse Than His Bite," *Paterson Evening News,* October 3, 1946, 72, Newspapers.com.

134 *many of the 10,000 fans:* "Feller's All-Stars Whitewash Satchel Paige's Nine, 5-0; Lead in Series 2-1," *Call & Post,* October 5, 1946, 9B, ProQuest Historical Newspapers.

134   *"Negro fans will support"*: Cleveland Jackson, "Headline Action," *Call & Post*, October 26, 1946, 8B.

134   *"a roar of pride rose"*: "Feller's All-Stars Whitewash," 9B.

134   *When a languorous curve:* Ibid.

135   *On Sunday, October 6, a massive crowd:* Haskel Cole, "27,462 See Satch's Team Beat Feller's," *Pittsburgh Courier*, October 12, 1946, 13, ProQuest Historical Newspapers.

135   *"were loaded to such an extent"*: Dan Burley, "'Confidentially Yours': Inside Football from the Huddle," *New York Amsterdam News*, October 12, 1946, 12, ProQuest Historical Newspapers. See also Gay, *Satch, Dizzy & Rapid Robert*, 232.

135   *Burley estimated:* Burley, "Inside Football from the Huddle," 12.

135   *"The duel between Paige and Feller"*: "Paige's All-Stars Rout Feller's, 4–0," *The New York Times*, October 7, 1946, 25, Archive.nytimes.com.

136   *"Satchel made his case"*: O'Neil, *Right on Time*, 180.

136   *"You can bet on one thing"*: United Press, "Feller and Paige Exchange Orchids," *Detroit Free Press*, October 7, 1946, 14, Newspapers.com.

136   *"It's nice to collect"*: Dave Lewis, "Once Over Lightly," *Long Beach Independent*, October 25, 1946, 19–20, Newspapers.com.

137   *At some point, Brewer:* Holway, *Black Diamonds*, 23.

137   *After confronting Feller:* Fay Young, "Through the Years," *The Chicago Defender*, November 9, 1946, 11, ProQuest Historical Newspapers.

137   *He was to start a game:* Hawkins, "$150,000 Pitch," 170.

137   *"I'd like to ask you"*: Steve George, "250,000 See Feller-Paige Teams Play," *The Sporting News*, October 30, 1946, 9, Paper of Record.

138   *"Not even Jackie Robinson"*: Ibid.

138   *"the most astonishing commitments"*: Cleveland Jackson, "Headline Action: Bobby Feller Blasts Negro Baseball Players," *Call & Post*, November 2, 1946, 8B.

138   *"You have to be a relative"*: As quoted in Holway, *Black Diamonds*, 71.

138   *Still, from a modern perspective:* For a longer consideration of Feller and his attitude toward race that informed my own telling, see Sickels, *Bob Feller*, 159–61.

139   *"by the Dixie riff-raff"*: John Jasper, "They Said He'd Never Make Good," *The Baltimore Afro-American*, July 12, 1947, M4, ProQuest Historical Newspapers.

139 *"even though it was black against white"*: O'Neil, *Right on Time*, 180.

139 *"I had more money"*: As quoted in Holway, *Black Diamonds*, 126.

139 *"[Paige and I] never talked about"*: Fussman, *After Jackie*, 41.

140 *"If the magnates"*: Dan Daniel, "Low Series Share to Bring Scale Demand," *The Sporting News*, October 23, 1946, 1–2, Paper of Record.

140 *In the end, Feller's earnings:* John B. Old, "Feller's Bonanza Tops Ruth's Richest 'Take': Tour Hikes '46 Income to $175,000," *The Sporting News*, November 6, 1946, 1, 2, Paper of Record.

14. HANDS AND KNEES

141 *Unable to stand, he crawled:* Editorial, "Veeck Again Shows His Gameness," *The Sporting News*, November 13, 1946, 12, Paper of Record.

141 *In the examination room:* Ibid.

141 *Every corner was littered:* Frank Gibbons, "Leg Amputated, Veeck in Good Condition," *Cleveland Press*, November 1, 1946.

142 *"in more hospitals than"*: Lewis, "Veeck Made Sale."

142 *"How did those picks go"*: Frank Gibbons, "The Incredible Bill Veeck: Ether to Phone in Four Hours," *Cleveland Press*, November 2, 1946.

142 *he found a bedridden Veeck:* Pat Williams, with Michael Weinreb, *Marketing Your Dreams: Business and Life Lessons from Bill Veeck, Baseball's Marketing Genius* (Champaign, IL: Sports Publishing, Inc., 2000), 261.

142 *So many bouquets:* Ed McAuley, "'Finish Three Positions Ahead of Bucs and Bing,' Hope Plea," *The Sporting News*, November 20, 1946, 8, Paper of Record.

142 *"I said there would be changes"*: Ed Prell, "You Can't Stop Veeck," *Sport*, January 1, 1947, accessed on December 15, 2015 at www.sportthemagazine.com.

142 *A truck was needed:* Cobbledick, "Greatest Showman," 57.

142 *"cocky grin"*: Vince Johnson, "Bill Veeck Beams with Pleasure as Artificial Right Leg Is Fitted," *Pittsburgh Post-Gazette*, January 23, 1947, 14, Newspapers.com.

143 *"Depends on how big"*: Ibid.

143 *Veeck sent out invitations:* Ed McAuley, "Tribe Outfielder Chase, Leading to Florida, Gives Veeck Busy Days and Sleepless Nights," *The Sporting News*, February 5, 1947, 5, Paper of Record.

143 *He danced waltzes and rumbas:* "Veeck Has Own Ideas on Rumba," *Akron Beacon Journal*, January 29, 1947, 10, Newspapers.com.

143 *blood started to trickle:* Bob Dolgan, "Making a Splash, Bill Veeck, Baseball's

Ultimate Showman, Turned the Sleepy Indians into Champions—and a Box Office Smash—During his Brief Tenure," *The Plain Dealer*, June 28, 1998. See also Dickson, *Bill Veeck*, 120.

143 *"and the blood, in drying"*: Veeck, *As in Wreck*, 374.

143 *"ripping pains tore"*: Lewis, *Cleveland Indians*, 243.

143 *"I'm very happy Bob Feller"*: Warren Brown, "Quote and Unquote: Dizzy Trout's Pitching Secret: 'Nobody Likes to Hit a Man Who Wears Glasses,'" *The Sporting News*, February 19, 1947, 5, Paper of Record.

144 *an agreement between:* Hawkins, "$150,000 Pitch," 25.

144 *Feller came to the talks:* Ed Fitzgerald, "Feller Incorporated," *Sport*, June 1947, 67.

144 *"something like $25,000 more"*: Ed McAuley, "Feller to Cop $80,000-Plus as New Pay King," *The Sporting News*, January 15, 1947, 1, Paper of Record.

144 *"I'm willing to gamble"*: Ed McAuley, "Feller Aims at Ruth Pay Record for '47," *The Sporting News*, January 8, 1947, 8, Paper of Record.

144 *The next morning at ten:* Walter L. Johns, "Writer Takes You into Business Office of Ball Club as Feller Signs Contract for All-Time High Salary," *The Star Press* (Muncie, IN), January 27, 1947, 7, Newspapers.com.

144 *"give us five minutes, please"*: Associated Press, "Feller Signs with Indians for Price Said to Be Higher Than $80,000 Paid 'Babe,'" *Wilkes-Barre Times Leader*, January 21, 1947, 13, Newspapers.com.

144 *"[This contract] is the biggest"*: Associated Press, "Baseball's Top Salary for Bob Feller," *Des Moines Tribune*, January 21, 1947, 12, Newspapers.com.

145 *"Well, he owns it"*: Ibid.

145 *"I come to you"*: Cobbledick, "Greatest Showman," 55.

145 *Despite having more than doubled:* Hal Lebovitz, "Watch the Indians' Farm System Grow," *Cleveland News*, May 14, 1947.

145 *"I'm not the kind"*: Ed McAuley, "Veeck Plans to Win While Waiting for Future," *Cleveland News*, October 17, 1946.

146 *If Veeck hoped to match:* Dickson, *Bill Veeck*, 117.

146 *"for the exclusive"*: "For Rent Sign on 'Managers' Graveyard' in Cleveland," *The Sporting News*, August 20, 1942, 4, Paper of Record.

147 *"runs like a dray"*: Kyle Crichton, "Lou Boudreau—Civic Project," *Baseball Digest*, August 1948, 5.

147 *Too often, in Veeck's mind:* Veeck, *As in Wreck*, 97.

147 *"If I am relieved"*: Lou Boudreau, with Ed Fitzgerald, *Player-Manager* (Boston: Little, Brown and Company, 1949), 79.

147   *aware of the resentment:* Stanley Frank, "They're Just Wild About Boudreau," *Saturday Evening Post,* September 4, 1948, 23.

149   *There, they bobbed:* Ed Rumill, "Cleveland's Ace Southpaw, Gene Bearden," *Baseball Magazine,* September 1948, 329.

149   *"Bearden holds [the ball]":* J. G. Taylor Spink, "Looping the Loops: A Butterfly Chase with Bearden," *The Sporting News,* October 13, 1948, 4, Paper of Record.

149   *If Black stuck with:* Shirley Povich, "This Morning with Shirley Povich," *The Washington Post,* May 5, 1947, 8, ProQuest Historical Newspapers.

150   *In desperation, manager Billy Herman:* Crissey, Jr., *Athletes Away,* 59. See also Al Stump, "Pop Lemon's Boy," *Sport,* June 1950, 82.

150   *Lemon seemed incapable of throwing:* Stump, "Pop Lemon's Boy," 82.

150   *"Any pitch of mine":* Bob Lemon, as told to Al Stump, "I Learned to PITCH in the Majors," *Sport,* May 1953.

150   *"bet a nickel":* Tom Meany, *Baseball's Greatest Pitchers* (New York: A. S. Barnes & Co., 1951), 154.

150   *"How about pitching":* Stump, "Pop Lemon's Boy," 82.

150   *"I knew as much about pitching":* Lemon, as told to Stump, "I Learned to PITCH."

150   *"From now on you're":* Stump, "Pop Lemon's Boy," 82.

151   *"not only failed":* McAuley, "Tribe Outfielder Chase," *The Sporting News,* February 5, 1947, 5, Paper of Record.

151   *"I would like for you":* Alvin Silverman, "Bill Veeck Makes Big Hit with Ohio's Lawmakers," *The Plain Dealer,* February 27, 1947, 4.

151   *"slowly and carefully":* Veeck, *As in Wreck,* 175.

151   *"purchase a qualified":* Cleveland Jackson, "Indian Owner Would Hire Qualified Negro Players," *Call & Post,* July 27, 1946, 9B. See also Stephanie M. Liscio, *Integrating Cleveland Baseball: Media Activism, the Integration of the Indians and the Demise of the Negro League Buckeyes* (Jefferson, NC: McFarland & Company, 2010), 114.

152   *a joint steering committee:* For further discussion of the report, see Tygiel, *Baseball's Great Experiment,* 80–86, and Marshall, *Baseball's Pivotal Era,* 134–35. A full draft of the "Joint Major League Steering Committee, Report to Commissioner of Baseball, A. B. Chandler, August 27, 1946" can be found in Thomas W. Zeiler, *Jackie Robinson and Race in America: A Brief History with Documents* (New York: Bedford/St. Martin's, 2013).

152   *The following month, a Black man:* Fay Young, "Through the Years: Wonders

Never Cease!" *The Chicago Defender,* July 12, 1947, 20, ProQuest Historical Newspapers.

152 *"had two special strikes":* Lena Horne and Richard Schickel, *Lena* (New York: Doubleday, 1965), 83.

153 *"If Jackie Robinson does come up":* Polner, *Branch Rickey,* 174.

153 *"self-policing":* For more on this topic, see: Veeck, William Louis, Interview by William J. Marshall, Febuary 23, 1977. Lexington: Louie B. Nunn Center for Oral History, University of Kentucky Libraries. See also Tygiel, *Baseball's Great Experiment,* 161–63.

153 *What's more, Veeck believed:* Veeck, *As in Wreck,* 175.

153 *Over the past few decades:* Grabowski, *Sports in Cleveland,* 41.

153 *The Cuyahoga River, which split:* Moore, *Carl B. Stokes,* 10.

153 *"the first American city":* "Cleveland: Most Democratic City in U.S.," *Ebony,* September 1950, 43–45. See also Liscio, *Integrating Cleveland Baseball,* 4–5.

154 *"the most democratic city":* "Cleveland: Most Democratic City in U.S.," 43–45.

154 *Improbably, the Buckeyes:* Suchma, "From the Best," 88.

15. THE PROMISE

155 *"a black Don Quixote":* Jackie Robinson, as told to Alfred Duckett, *I Never Had It Made: An Autobiography of Jackie Robinson* (New York: Ecco, 1995), 68.

155 *"had to walk a straight":* A. S. "Doc" Young, *Great Negro Baseball Stars and How They Made the Major Leagues* (New York: A. S. Barnes, 1953), 10.

155 *"In the clubhouse Robinson":* Jimmy Cannon, "Lynch Mobs Don't Always Wear Hoods," *Boston Herald,* May 15, 1947, 27.

156 *The Eagles ran away:* Several newspapers at the time misidentified the location of this game, claiming it was played in Hartford, not Stamford. For a write-up of the contest, see "Newark Eagles Trounce Yankees," *Stamford Advocate,* May 5, 1947, 11, Genealogybank.com.

156 *"a vigor that fairly":* Manley, *Negro Baseball Before Integration,* 93.

157 *"The personal health":* "Heavy Stickmen Eye '47 Pennant for Champ Newark Club," *New York Amsterdam News,* April 5, 1947, 13, ProQuest Historical Newspapers.

157 *as fans became increasingly captivated:* Manley, *Negro Baseball Before Integration,* 94.

157 *"separate the club coffers":* Frank Gibbons, "Boudreau Asks Veeck for New Outfield Strength," *Cleveland Press,* May 28, 1947.

157 *But Dandridge, according to Veeck biographer:* Dickson, *Bill Veeck*, 122–23.

157 *Veeck also reached out:* Veeck, *As in Wreck,* 175.

158 *"[Doby] can play in":* Bill Veeck, with Gordon Cobbledick, "So You Want," 144.

158 *"is a fine prospect":* Hal Lebovitz, "Cleveland Infielder Needs Two Years in Minor Leagues," *Cleveland News,* August 15, 1947.

158 *"are many excellent athletes":* Ibid.

158 *"I'm not going to sign":* Smith, "Cleveland Signed Doby," 14.

159 *"too much pressure":* Al Dunmore, "Cleveland Owner Kept His Word," *Pittsburgh Courier,* July 12, 1947, 14. See also Tygiel, *Baseball's Great Experiment,* 213.

159 *"One afternoon when the team":* Smith, "Cleveland Signed Doby," 14.

159 *Over the phone, he told Doby:* Doby recalled this phone call with Roy Campanella in an interview with William J. Marshall. See Doby, Lawrence E. Interview by William J. Marshall, November 15, 1979. Lexington: Louie B. Nunn Center for Oral History, University of Kentucky Libraries.

159 *"It certainly would be good":* Smith, "Cleveland Signed Doby," 14.

160 *Late in June:* Doby talked about attending this Yankees game with Louis Jones in interviews with Fay Vincent and William J. Marshall. See Vincent, *Only Game,* 179; and Doby, interview by William J. Marshall.

160 *Jones likely didn't know:* Dan Feitlowitz, "Doby All-Round High School Star; Hit .358 in Puerto Rico Last Winter," *The Sporting News,* July 16, 1947, 4, Paper of Record.

160 *"There's nothing down there":* Cleveland Jackson, "Believe Newark Star Headed for Indians," *Call & Post,* July 5, 1947, 1A.

160 *The Eagles racked up:* "Baltimore Elite Giants Trip Eagles in Dunn Field Clash," *Trenton Evening Times,* June 27, 1947, 26.

160 *Before leaving, he pulled Doby:* Doby, interview by William J. Marshall. See also Moore, *Larry Doby,* 42.

16. A NEW AND STRANGE WORLD

161 *Veeck cut right to:* Manley, *Negro Baseball Before Integration,* 74.

161 *Veeck, for his part:* Jackson, "Hire Qualified Negro Players," 9B.

161 *"Mr. Veeck, you know":* Manley, *Negro Baseball Before Integration,* 74.

162 *"Oh, Effa, we can't":* Ibid.

162 *Ultimately, mindful of:* In his autobiography, Veeck would later claim that Effa Manley offered to throw in Monte Irvin for an additional $1,000,

which he rejected. Manley and some in the Black press offered differing accounts. *The Pittsburgh Courier,* for example, would report that "Veeck sought both Doby and Irvin, but Effa Manley . . . felt that the loss of both of these stars would wreck her team." See Dunmore, "Cleveland Owner," 14. See also Veeck, *As in Wreck,* 176.

162 *"It may be":* Associated Press, "Baseball Men Mum on Signing by Veeck of Negro Player," *The Marion Star,* July 4, 1947, 14, Newspapers.com.

162 *It was 5:30 in the morning:* "Doby Roused from Sleep to Hear News of Signing," *The Baltimore Afro-American,* July 12, 1947, 13. See also Moore, *Larry Doby,* 42.

162 *"Larry," she reportedly said:* Sam Lacy, "Larry Doby: He's One of the Key Figures in Cleveland Indians' Pennant Drive," *The Baltimore Afro-American,* August 14, 1948, B5, ProQuest Historical Newspapers.

162 *Doby was speechless:* "Doby Sure He'll Click as First Negro in A.L.," *Newark Star-Ledger,* July 3, 1947, 1, 10, Genealogybank.com.

163 *"wore nothing more than":* Lacy, "Indians' Pennant Drive," B5.

163 *"I don't think any man":* United Press, "Expect Doby to Join Cleveland Saturday," *Des Moines Tribune,* July 3, 1947, 12, Newspapers.com.

163 *"[Jackie] Robinson has proved":* Associated Press, "Scramble on for Negro Stars, Reports Veeck," *Newark Star-Ledger,* July 5, 1947, 6, Genealogybank .com.

163 *Doby was going to be a star:* Lou Boudreau, with Russell Schneider, *Covering All the Bases* (Champaign, IL: Sagamore Publishing, 1993), 95. See also Moore, *Larry Doby,* 45.

163 *careers on farm clubs:* Tygiel, *Baseball's Great Experiment,* 215.

163 *"a routine baseball purchase":* Frank Gibbons, "Larry Doby to Report at Chicago" *The Dayton Herald,* July 3, 1947, 12.

164 *It led the Indians' manager:* Boudreau, *Covering All the Bases,* 95.

164 *"his knuckles seemed to pop":* Franklin Lewis, "Second Newark Trip Recalls Unfond Memories," *Cleveland Press,* June 9, 1948.

164 *Racked with emotion:* Ibid.

164 *Amid sustained applause:* Franklin Lewis, "Bits and Bites of Sports Chosen and Well Chewed," *Cleveland Press,* July 7, 1947.

165 *"Larry's so nervous":* Franklin Lewis, "Big-League Chance Awes Larry Doby as He Joins Tribe," *Cleveland Press,* July 5, 1947.

165 *As the second game got under way:* Paul Jacobs, "Tribe's New Negro Player Stars in Newark Finale," *Cleveland News,* July 5, 1947, p. 6.

165 *He spoke faintly:* Lewis, "Big-League Chance."

165 *"I feel—well":* Lewis, *The Cleveland Indians*, 247.

165 *"the strangeness of his position":* Dan Burley, "Dan Burley's Confidentially Yours: Round Robin on Sports Trail," *New York Amsterdam News*, July 12, 1947, 12, ProQuest Historical Newspapers.

166 *"Lawrence, I'm Bill Veeck":* Doby, interview with William J. Marshall. This exchange between Veeck and Doby is also recounted in Dickson, *Bill Veeck*, 127–28.

166 *with discernible sincerity:* Doby spoke about being able to discern Veeck's sincerity by looking in his eyes in Vincent, *Only Game*, 181.

166 *From the taxi:* Russell Schneider, *The Boys of the Summer of '48: The Golden Anniversary of the World Champion Cleveland Indians* (Champaign, IL: Sports Publishing LLC, 1998), 84.

166 *"We're in this together":* Dickson, *Bill Veeck*, 128.

166 *"It made me relax":* Vincent, *Only Game*, 181.

166 *"half the news photographers":* Jim Schlemmer, "Cleveland Accepts Doby as Player Who May Give Them Added Strength," *Akron Beacon Journal*, July 6, 1947, 23, Newspapers.com.

166 *"His voice was so low":* Ibid.

167 *"Just remember you're only":* Jerry Liska, "Larry Doby, Negro Player with Cleveland, Strikes Out in First Official Time at Bat," *The Morning Call*, July 6, 1947, 17, Newspapers.com.

167 *"an electric tension charged":* Gordon Cobbledick, "Is Larry Doby a Bust?" *Sport*, February 1952, 8.

167 *"Not even the scuffle":* Lewis, *The Cleveland Indians*, 247.

167 *Boudreau peppered Doby:* Boudreau, *Player-Manager*, 105.

167 *Some, like Joe Gordon:* Moore, *Larry Doby*, 48. See also Bob Sudyk, "The Year the A.L. Signed Its First Black," *Cleveland Press*, November 29, 1973.

167 *"With each step the chorus":* Gordon Cobbledick, "Doby Shows Strong Arm as He Works at 2D Base," *The Plain Dealer*, July 6, 1947, 17-A, 20-A.

168 *Doby couldn't put into perspective:* Doby talked about this incident in several interviews. Notably, to William J. Marshall, he indicated that he "wasn't mature enough to put [his first day] in a different perspective until I had been there about three or four years." Marshall, *Baseball's Pivotal Era*, 144. See also Jerry Izenberg, "Doby Stood Alone When He Changed A.L.," *The Spokesman-Review* (Spokane, WA), July 8, 2007, C7, Newspapers.com.

168 *"stiff and not sure":* Cobbledick, "Doby Shows Strong Arm," 17-A, 20-A.

168 *Boudreau watched him intently:* Ed McAuley, "Will He Become an All-Star?" *St. Louis Post–Dispatch,* July 7, 1949, 45.

168 *"It took but a few short":* Cleveland Jackson, "Larry Doby Breaks into Lineup on First Day with Team; Plays at First," *Call & Post,* July 12, 1947, 1A. See also Moore, *Larry Doby,* 50.

168 *As Doby assumed:* Wendell Smith, "Wendell Smith's Sports Beat: Trouble Brewing at West Virginia?" *Pittsburgh Courier,* November 15, 1947, 13, Pro-Quest Historical Newspapers.

168 *"I didn't hear a sound":* Bob Sudyk, "Forgotten Pioneer," *Hartford Courant,* April 3, 1987, D12.

169 *"like a bullet":* Fay Young, "48,000 Hail Doby at First for Indians," *The Chicago Defender,* July 12, 1947, 1, ProQuest Historical Newspapers.

169 *With the count even:* Jerry Liska, "Nervous Doby Fans in Tribe Debut," *Miami Herald,* July 6, 1947, 3-C.

169 *He and Jones were driven:* Moore, *Larry Doby,* 52.

169 *"didn't bother me":* Doby, interview by William J. Marshall.

17. CLOSED RANKS

170 *Across the city's South Side:* Jackson, "Larry Doby Breaks," 1A. See also Moore, *Larry Doby,* 53.

171 *"Don't worry about it":* Eddie Robinson, with C. Paul Rogers III, *Lucky Me: My Sixty-Five Years in Baseball* (Dallas: Southern Methodist University Press, 2011), 48.

171 *integration triggered historically:* For more on this point, see Robert F. Burk, *Much More Than a Game: Players, Owners, & American Baseball Since 1921* (Chapel Hill: The University of North Carolina Press, 2001), 61.

171 *"Well, we're going to get":* Eddie Robinson, interview with the author, February 19, 2016.

171 *there were more than twelve thousand:* David E. Kaiser, *Epic Season: The 1948 American League Pennant Race* (Amherst: University of Massachusetts Press, 1998), 4.

172 *"I'm a Texan boy":* Robinson, interview with the author.

172 *Robinson reportedly told Boudreau:* Boudreau, *Covering All the Bases,* 96.

172 *"who might've wanted":* Anthony J. Connor, *Voices from Cooperstown: Baseball's Hall of Famers Tell It Like It Was* (New York: Galahad Books, 1998), 214.

172 *"We were Southerners":* Kirby Higbe, with Martin Peter Quigley, *The High Hard One,* (Lincoln: University of Nebraska Press, 1998), 104.

172 *"didn't make any difference"*: As quoted in Moore, *Larry Doby*, 68.

172 *"Any white guy who might"*: As quoted in Fussman, *After Jackie*, 88.

172 *Eddie Robinson chipped some mud:* McAuley, "Will He Become."

173 *Robinson flatly refused:* Eddie Robinson claims that it was Lou Boudreau, not Spud Goldstein, who approached him about his glove. Boudreau disputed this account, affirming in his second autobiography that Goldstein was the one who asked Robinson for his glove. See Boudreau, *Covering All the Bases*, 96.

173 *"You can quit"*: Robinson, interview with the author.

173 *As the game started, Robinson sat:* Robinson told me that he "might've been crying" while he sat alone in the locker room. Robinson, interview with the author.

173 *"I understand why you quit"*: Robinson, *Lucky Me*, 49.

173 *As he walked by, several:* Robinson, interview with the author.

173 *"The unfortunate aspect"*: Gordon Cobbledick, "Plain Dealing: Robinson, Only Indian with Chance to Become Needed Power Hitter, Deserves Thorough Trial," *The Plain Dealer*, July 10, 1947, 15.

174 *"at the expense of Eddie"*: Ed McAuley, "Predicts Victory for National League," *Cleveland News*, July 8, 1947.

174 *"a big league baseball player"*: Ibid.

174 *"likely will be in major league"*: "Jethroe Is Eyed by Tribe," *Cleveland Press*, July 9, 1947.

174 *"snorting and claiming"*: Jim Schlemmer, "Jim Schlemmer," *Akron Beacon Journal*, July 10, 1947, 28, Newspapers.com.

174 *"The Negroes holler 'discrimination'"*: Editorial, "Once Again, That Negro Question," *The Sporting News*, July 16, 1947, 16, Paper of Record.

175 *"[Doby's] going to get"*: Frank Gibbons, "Doby to Play First Base Against Mack (A's) Here," *Cleveland Press*, July 7, 1947.

175 *"I intended to play [Doby]"*: Frank Gibbons, "Feller to Hurl, Doby on Doubtful List Tonight," *Cleveland Press*, July 10, 1947.

175 *"We don't like to take"*: Associated Press, "Veeck Welcomes Doby; Start 'Up to Boudreau,'" *Cleveland News*, July 5, 1947.

175 *It was later revealed:* Moore, *Larry Doby*, 58.

175 *"You would have to be an idiot"*: Franklin Lewis, "A Quiet Evening in San Francisco; Bum Rap for Doby," *Cleveland Press*, July 12, 1947.

176 *he'd shed seven pounds:* Hy Engel, "Starring a Habit with Larry Doby," *PM*, July 30, 1947, accessed from the Larry Doby file at the A. Bartlett Giamatti Library in the National Baseball Hall of Fame.

176 *aren't a half-dozen promising*: Ed McAuley, "Doby Is Being Groomed for Outfield Post," *Cleveland News*, July 25, 1947, 16.

176 One package contained mounds: Veeck's son Mike mentioned this package in Fussman, *After Jackie*, 17.

176 *Often shirtless, he'd swat:* Hal Lebovitz, "Swing Session: Veeck Tests Leg in Batting Practice," *Cleveland News*, June 28, 1947. For more on the footraces, see Patkin, *Clown Prince*, 45.

176 *"I've got no one but myself"*: "Veeck Enters Clinic Hospital," *The Plain Dealer*, July 23, 1947, 15.

176 *"This one was rougher"*: "Indians Items: Veeck to See Indians Face A's Tonight," *Cleveland Press*, August 26, 1947.

177 *"Feller was sort of in"*: Scott Eyman, "The Second," *The Plain Dealer Magazine*, April 10, 1983, 19.

177 *"I paid very little attention"*: Vincent, *Only Game*, 51.

177 *"swinging at a flea"*: Gordon Cobbledick, "Gordon's Two Homeruns Give Indians 5-4 Victory; Feller Fans 12," *The Plain Dealer*, June 14, 1947, 14.

177 *Losing his balance:* Linn, "Immortal Hanger-on," 23.

177 *For a minute or so:* Ed McAuley, "Let's Standardize Those Mounds Before Someone Breaks a Leg," *Cleveland News*, June 14, 1947.

178 *"ice pick stabs"*: Frank Gibbons, "Feller Hurt as Redskins Nip Browns," *Cleveland Press*, July 2, 1947.

178 *"If I lost it"*: Bob Feller, as told to Ken W. Purdy, "I'll Never Quit Baseball," *Look*, March 20, 1956.

178 *"The All-American Boy"*: Franklin Lewis, "Booing of Feller Strange Symphony in Soot Stadium," *Cleveland Press*, May 24, 1947.

178 *His signature pitch no longer:* Gordon Cobbledick, "Plain Dealing: Feller Must Continue to Be Most Spectacular Pitcher If He Is to Retain Drawing Power," *The Plain Dealer*, July 8, 1947, 14.

178 *"seemed to be protecting"*: Jimmy Cannon, "Feller Legend Bows to Materialism," *Baseball Digest*, January 1948, 51.

178 *"pitching superman"*: Frank Gibbons, "Heat Really Is on Tribe and Feller," *Cleveland Press*, August 19, 1947.

178 *reportedly the largest ever:* "Book Notes," *New York Herald Tribune*, April 18, 1947, 19, ProQuest Historical Newspapers.

179 *two planes with rear banners:* Jim Schlemmer, "Feller Fails in Relief Role; Senators Spank Indians, 6–3," *Akron Beacon Journal*, May 5, 1947, 15, Newspapers.com.

179   *On the road Feller staged:* Sec Taylor, "Sittin' In with the Athletes: Bob's 'Strikeout Story,'" *Des Moines Register,* April 28, 1947, 9, Newspapers.com.

179   *"Feller is all out for Feller":* Ed Bang, "Readers Rap Feller's Conceit," *Cleveland News,* August 16, 1947.

179   *"This is a democracy":* "Feller Protests Baseball Rule Curtailing Post-Season Junkets," *The New York Times,* August 2, 1947, 8, Archive.nytimes.com.

179   *Feeling stifled and singled out:* "Chandler Bars Major Leaguers from Playing Winter Baseball with Clubs in Cuban League," *New York Herald Tribune,* August 15, 1947, 18, ProQuest Historical Newspapers.

180   *"loose-lip habit":* Gordon Cobbledick, "Feller Urged to Call Off Tour Until He Regains Winning Form: Plain Dealing," *The Plain Dealer,* August 19, 1947, 17.

180   *"target of a city-wide":* Ed McAuley, "Feller, Under Fire by Tribe Fans, Will Let Arm Do All the Talking Now," *The Sporting News,* August 27, 1947, 1, Paper of Record.

180   *"You can walk into any building":* Ed McAuley, "Veeck Sees Strong Finish for 'Jolted' Feller: Bob Expected to Drop Cuba Plans," *Cleveland News,* August 18, 1947.

180   *It was becoming clear:* McAuley, "Feller, Under Fire," 1.

181   *"Jackie got all the publicity":* "Larry Doby Doesn't Mind Being 'Second Black' Again," *Jet,* July 20, 1978, 53, Google Books.

181   *"kept each other":* Jeff Prugh, "Larry Doby: He Bore the Burden, May Now Get Reward," *The Boston Globe,* May 26, 1974, 66, Newspapers.com.

181   *"I'm glad to know":* Jackie Robinson, "Jackie Robinson Says: Larry Doby Is a Good Ball Player; Glad to See Him with Cleveland," *Pittsburgh Courier,* July 12, 1947, 15, ProQuest Historical Newspapers.

181   *"two o'clock player":* Wendell Smith, "Wendell Smith's Sports Beat: . . . Before . . . He Can Do It Again," *Pittsburgh Courier,* May 1, 1948, 11. For more on the differences between Robinson's and Doby's situations, see Tygiel, *Baseball's Great Experiment,* 214.

181   *"What I want more":* "Larry Doby Slow Starting but Confident About Future," *The Washington Post,* July 27, 1947, C2.

182   *"I was a frightened":* "Larry Doby as told to Ed McAuley of the *Cleveland News,*" in Don Schiffer, ed., *My Greatest Baseball Game* (New York: A. S. Barnes, 1950), 57.

182   *"failure to hit":* Al Sweeney, "Doby Finds Pitching Smart and Baffling," *The Baltimore Afro-American,* August 2, 1947, 13, ProQuest Historical Newspapers.

182 *the Indians' manager seldom said:* A. S. "Doc" Young, "Doby to Remain in Cleveland Organization, Veeck Says," *Call & Post,* October 18, 1947, 8B.

182 *Boudreau kept his lips pursed:* Frank Gibbons, "Boudreau Will Try New Batting Order," *Cleveland Press,* July 26, 1947.

182 *"There was really no reason":* Andrew Lee Ellner, "Winning Race: Larry Doby, Cleveland, and the Integration of American League Baseball" (Harvard College: Unpublished honors thesis in history, 1997), accessed from the Larry Doby file at the National Baseball Hall of Fame in Cooperstown, New York, on November 7, 2015. Doby also divulged his frustration with Boudreau during his first season to Jerry Izenberg decades later. Jerry Izenberg, phone interview with the author, August 23, 2016.

182 *Joe Gordon had saddled:* Ed McAuley, "Doby Spikes Cut—But His Personality Pleases," *Cleveland News,* March 23, 1948.

182 *"Gordon would always sit":* Sudyk, "The Year."

183 *where players excluded him:* McAuley, "Doby Is Being Groomed," 16.

183 *"an iceberg act":* Young, "Is Larry Doby," 44

183 *"My biggest adjustment":* Ed Fitzgerald, ed., "Round Table Discussion: The Negro in American Sport," *Sport,* March 1960, 31–32.

183 *While McKechnie recognized:* Staff Special, "Will Farm Doby or Start Him Regularly," *The Plain Dealer,* March 24, 1948, 27.

183 *"The guy'll never":* Gordon Cobbledick, "Plain Dealing," *The Plain Dealer,* April 20, 1948, 18.

183 *Fully prepared to hear:* Doby mentioned his fear of being released in Dexter, "Larry Doby's War," 60.

183–84 *"Larry, you have a fine chance":* Young, *Great Negro Baseball Stars,* 55.

184 *"Rickey was smarter":* Young, "Doby to Remain," 8B. See also Moore, *Larry Doby,* 62.

184 *the larger project of integration would remain:* For a longer consideration on where integration stood in Major League Baseball at the end of 1947, see Tygiel, *Baseball's Great Experiment,* 223–26.

18. FEVER

185 *"an actual physical burden":* Boudreau, *Player-Manager,* 86.

185 *"appear dumb":* Roger Birtwell, "'Boudreau Made Me Appear Dumb to Better Own Chances,' Says Hegan," *The Boston Globe,* December 21, 1947, C27, Newspapers.com. Veeck's view on Boudreau from: Frank Gibbons, "Yanks, Bosox, Tigers Go after Boudreau," *Cleveland Press,* October 4, 1947, 1.

185 *Veeck offered Boudreau $50,000:* Ed McAuley, "Boudreau Through with Indians," *Cleveland News,* October 3, 1947, 1.

185 *"a most personal nature":* Franklin Lewis, "Harsh Words Reported in Verbal Clash Between Veeck, Boudreau," *Cleveland Press,* September 30, 1947.

186 *The Indians dropped the game:* Details in this paragraph come from two sources: "Boudreau Leaves in a Hurry," *Cleveland News,* September 29, 1947; and Lewis, "Harsh Words."

186 *"a naturally superior class":* John Bainbridge, "Toots's World," *The New Yorker,* November 11, 1950, 54, Newyorker.com/archive.

186 *Veeck cornered each Cleveland:* Lewis, *The Cleveland Indians,* 249.

187 *"was aroused more feverishly":* Fitzgerald, "Last of the Boy Managers?" 61.

187 *"If Boudreau doesn't return":* Veeck, *As in Wreck,* 153.

187 *"he might stab":* Ed McAuley, "Boudreau Should Stay, But Not as Manager," *Cleveland News,* October 8, 1947, 16.

187 *"all the good he had":* Lewis, *The Cleveland Indians,* 250.

188 *"What's happening now?":* Alvin Silverman, "Veeck Flies In, Puts Up Boudreau Sale to Fans," *The Plain Dealer,* October 5, 1947, 1.

188 *"Please don't sell Boudreau":* Ibid.

188 *"Are you willing to trust":* Ed McAuley, "Tribal Chief to Shape Deals to Cop Flag," *The Sporting News,* October 15, 1947, 13, Paper of Record.

189 *"Don't sell Boudreau!":* Silverman, "Veeck Flies In," 1.

189 *"Bill," one remarked:* Ibid.

189 *"For the first time in the history":* Franklin Lewis, "Veeck Learns His Boy Manager Isn't Mortal in Cleveland," *Cleveland Press,* October 4, 1947.

190 *Once again that winter:* Lewis, *The Cleveland Indians,* 252.

190 *"This game is my life":* Ed McAuley, "Boudreau-to-Browns Deal Still Red Hot, Decision Near on Trade, McAuley Says," *Cleveland News,* October 7, 1947, 1, 9.

19. THE FINAL DUEL

191 *"miraculous 'Ol Man River'":* "Monarchs, Grays in Two Games," *Pittsburgh Courier,* July 5, 1947, 3, ProQuest Historical Newspapers.

191 *"All things in due time":* Veeck, *As in Wreck,* 183.

192 *"is a faster man":* Associated Press, "Bankhead Confers Today with Rickey; Called 'Fastest Pitcher in Baseball,'" *Newark Star-Ledger,* August 25, 1947, 22, Newspapers.com.

192 *Because Feller feared running:* Gay, *Satch, Dizzy & Rapid Robert,* 249.

192 *Feller once again presided:* "Feller Has Gate, Not Arm, Worry on Exhibition Tour," *The Sporting News,* October 29, 1947, 21, Paper of Record.

192 *The crowds had thinned:* "Feller on Game-a-Day Schedule as Stars Average 5,000 on Jaunt," *The Sporting News,* October 22, 1947, 4.

194 *as did news stories declaring:* "Paige's Arm Stops Feller's Challenge," *Call & Post,* November 8, 1947, 9B.

194 *On October 26, Feller:* The date of Feller's wire comes from "Paige Challenges Feller to 9-Inning Duel: Top Hurlers in Hot Feud Next Sunday," *Los Angeles Sentinel,* October 30, 1947, 23, ProQuest Historical Newspapers.

194 *Reporters could play it up:* See, for example, "Feller, Paige Hook Up in Hill Duel at Wrigley," *Los Angeles Times,* November 2, 1947, 13, ProQuest Historical Newspapers. For more on the buildup to this game, see Gay, *Satch, Dizzy & Rapid Robert,* 257–58; and Spivey, *"If You Were,"* 219–20.

194 *He bristled at Feller's playful:* Sickels, *Bob Feller,* 179.

194 *"Then they wouldn't be thinking":* Paige, *Pitch Forever,* 189.

195 *Paige reared back and blazed:* Ibid., 190.

196 *"Last year we drew":* Matt Gallagher, "Late Start Dooms Tour—Feller," *The Sporting News,* November 12, 1947, 1, 2, Paper of Record.

196 *But beyond football's rising popularity:* John Sickels lays out a succinct case for why Feller's 1947 tour faltered in Sickels, *Bob Feller,* 179–80. For more on the decline of barnstorming in general, see Gay, *Satch, Dizzy, & Rapid Robert,* 259–60, 273–74, and 278–79.

196 *His body ached:* Paige, *Pitch Forever,* 191–92.

196 *but in truth, he was searching:* Ibid., 192.

20. IF I CAN STICK WITH THIS TEAM

200 *"I don't think we have":* "Indians to Shift Doby to Outfield: Larry's Hitting Wins Praise of Bill Veeck," *The Baltimore Afro-American,* March 13, 1948, 7, ProQuest Historical Newspapers.

200 *"between the Doby of today":* Ed McAuley, "Doby Surprises with Strong Outfield Bid," *Cleveland News,* March 3, 1948.

201 *Nick Hall, the hotel's:* Greg Hansen, "Spring in Tucson," *Arizona Daily Star,* February 26, 1998, 8E. See also Ellsworth Moe, "First Large Downtown Hotel Built Here 46 Years Ago," *Arizona Daily Star,* February 23, 1950, 97, Newspapers.com.

201 *Joining them were the:* Hal Lebovitz, "Hal Asks: Movie Stars and Indians?" *The Plain Dealer,* April 15, 1973, 2-C.

201 *"a time of closeness"*: Ibid.

201 *others suffered through:* Chris Cobbs, "Tucson's Lost Tribe," *The Arizona Republic,* March 8, 1992, G3.

201 *Jim Hegan recalled catching:* Hegan, James, interview by William J. Marshall. May 15, 1979, A. B. "Happy" Chandler: Desegregation of Major League Baseball Oral History Project, Louie B. Nunn Center for Oral History, University of Kentucky Libraries. See also Sam Lacy, "Indian Star Larry Doby Forced to Live Apart," *The Baltimore Afro-American,* March 12, 1949, 8, ProQuest Historical Newspapers.

201 *"It was a difficult place":* Jim Grant, phone interview with the author, February 9, 2017.

202 *"the presence of a colored player":* National Negro Publishers Association, "Larry Doby's Training Antics Impress Bill Veeck, Cleveland Indians' Prexy," *The Baltimore Afro-American,* April 3, 1948, 8, ProQuest Historical Newspapers.

202 *He ended up staying:* James E. Odenkirk, *Of Tribes and Tribulations: The Early Decades of the Cleveland Indians* (Jefferson, NC: McFarland & Company, 2015), 207. See also Moore, *Larry Doby,* 68–69.

202 *"a six-hour ball player":* Franklin Lewis, "About Larry Doby, His Thoughts and His Problems," *Cleveland Press,* April 14, 1948.

202 *Dolores Townsend, the family's:* The information in this paragraph comes from the author's phone interview with Lucille Willis's oldest child, Dolores Townsend, December 5, 2016.

202 *borrowing books from his local:* Moore, *Larry Doby,* 67.

202 *Indians officials had planned:* Staff Special, "Will Farm Doby, 27

203 *"hectoring any Northerner":* Timothy M. Gay, *Tris Speaker: The Rough-and-Tumble Life of a Baseball Legend* (Lincoln: University of Nebraska Press, 2006), 31.

203 *"I've never seen":* Shirley Povich, "That Doby Boy Well on His Way to Greatness," *The Washington Post,* June 26, 1949, C1, ProQuest Historical Newspapers.

203 *One afternoon in early March:* Details in the following two paragraphs drawn from Gordon Cobbledick, "Plain Dealing," *The Plain Dealer,* March 25, 1948, 18.

204 *to earn as much:* Harry Jones, "Feller Signs, Can Equal 1947 Earnings; Barons Tie Rockets, 6–6," *The Plain Dealer,* January 22, 1948, 16.

204 *It was reported during spring:* "Indian Items: Greenberg's Condition 'Better Than Last Year,'" *Cleveland Press,* March 11, 1948.

204   *planned to junk:* George C. Carens, "Feller Can't See Indians for Flag," *Boston Traveler*, May 10, 1948, 15.

204   *A few gray hairs:* Harold Kaese, "Feller Longs for Youthful Speed: The Ace for Whom Red Sox Prepared $150,000 Bonus, Beats Them Again," *The Boston Globe*, May 10, 1948, 11, Newspapers.com.

204   *"base hits flew":* Boudreau, *Player-Manager*, 109.

204   *"Brother, that Doby":* Ed McAuley, "A Vote Against Mixing Football and Baseball," *Cleveland News*, March 28, 1948, 10.

205   *"There's the best outfielder":* Gordon Cobbledick, "Plain Dealing," *The Plain Dealer*, March 7, 1948, 2-C.

205   *"vague understandable dread":* McAuley, "Doby Spikes Cut," 16.

205   *rather than waiting at the plate:* Ibid.

205   *"appeared hesitant, evasive":* Eddie Burbridge, "Larry Doby Segregated from Cleveland Tribe," *Los Angeles Sentinel*, March 25, 1948, 1, ProQuest Historical Newspapers.

205   *pulling over in the railyard:* "Record Crowd Expected for Giant-Indian Contest Here," *Lubbock Evening Journal*, April 9, 1948, 6, Newspapers.com.

206   *Earlier, the Lubbock superintendent:* "Bob Feller Brings Joy to Kids; Autographs Their Equipment," *Lubbock Evening Journal*, April 9, 1948, 8, Newspapers.com.

206   *Once there, he roamed:* Moore, *Larry Doby*, 72.

206   *"that [Boudreau] was acting":* Frank Gibbons, "Boudreau's Garden Experiment Fails to Produce Hits," *Cleveland Press*, April 10, 1948. Over the decades, the popular retelling of Doby's first spring training had it that the Indians traveled to Texarkana and Houston after Lubbock. However, newspaper accounts of the time show that the team went to Oklahoma City next. The Indians would play in Texarkana and Houston during their barnstorming swing through the South in 1949. Veeck and others would claim that a long home run that Doby smacked in Houston in 1948 was what convinced them to keep Doby on the Indians, but they likely mixed up a game that the Giants and Indians played in Houston on April 6, 1949. On that day, the Associated Press would report that Doby became "the second player in history to slam a ball over [Buffalo Stadium's] centerfield fence—440 feet from the plate" in Houston. See: Associated Press, "Houston Stands Full as Giants Rout Cleveland," *The Daily Oklahoman*, April 7, 1949, 27, Newspapers.com.

206   *"It's been a rough spring":* Lewis, "About Larry Doby, His Thoughts."

207   *"the crowd of 11,401 fans"*: Jim Schlemmer, "Feller Proves He's Ready for '48 Season," *Akron Beacon Journal*, April 12, 1948, 17, Newspapers.com.

207   *Boudreau was in no mood:* Boudreau, *Player-Manager*, 109.

208   *"Realizing the spot Doby"*: A. S. "Doc" Young, "Doby Opens Indians' Season in Right; Finds Pressure Great," *Call & Post*, April 24, 1948, 7B.

208   *"singing commercials"*: Vince Johnson, "Whacky Ways to Woo Fans," *The Sporting News*, March 10, 1948, 14, Paper of Record.

208   *Before the season's first game:* Herman Goldstein, "How They Do It: Tribe Beats Tom-Toms and Fans Respond," *Cleveland News*, April 26, 1948.

208   *Fans rooted for him unreservedly:* Harry Jones, "Record 73,163 See Indians Win, 4–0," *The Plain Dealer*, April 21, 1948, 1, 4.

209   *"that every time I passed"*: Franklin Lewis, "Need a Soft Touch on a Slow Boat? Ask Jack Kramer," *Cleveland Press*, April 22, 1948.

209   *"I wouldn't want you to print"*: Young, "Doby Opens," 7-B.

21. UNDER THE KNIFE, BEYOND THE AXE

210   *"Eddie, we're going to win"*: Eddie Robinson, interview with the author, February 19, 2016.

210   *Bill Veeck, too, sensed:* Veeck, *As in Wreck*, 151.

211   *The team's operating expenses:* Burton Hawkins, "Win, Lose, or Draw," *The Evening Star* (Washington, D.C.), May 8, 1948, 11, Genealogybank.com.

211   *"I certainly hope it takes"*: "Veeck Faces Operation Tomorrow," *Cleveland Press*, May 3, 1948.

211   *"never looks so healthy"*: Ed McAuley, "Talks to Some People in the Baseball News," *Cleveland News*, May 19, 1948.

211   *In the season's opening week:* For more on Doby's early-season struggles, see Tygiel, *Baseball's Great Experiment*, 237.

212   *"Larry Doby has everything"*: A. S. "Doc" Young, "Doby's Biggest Battle Is with Doby," *Call & Post*, May 8, 1948, 7B.

212   *"When [Doby] acts only"*: Ed McAuley, "Time Is Running Out for Outfield Experiment," *Cleveland News*, May 5, 1948.

212   *"Porter, carry my bags!"*: Ira Berkow, *The Corporal Was a Pitcher: The Courage of Lou Brissie* (Chicago: Triumph Books, 2009), 184.

212   *The taunts and insults:* Young, "Is Larry Doby," 47.

212   *"keen desire"*: "Doby Is Determined to Stick with Indians," *The Baltimore Afro-American*, May 15 1948, 9, ProQuest Historical Newspapers.

212 *"It's a loneliness":* Tony Grossi, "The Debt Owed to Larry Doby; Segrega-
     tion and Ignorance Couldn't Deter Black All Star," *The Plain Dealer,* July 3,
     1994, 1A.

213 *Greenberg had nonetheless offered:* Ed McAuley, "Doby Makes Eating Crow
     Popular Pastime," *Cleveland News,* May 11, 1948, 16.

213 *Doby responded frankly:* Shirley Povich, "This Morning with Shirley Po-
     vich," *The Washington Post,* October 13, 1948, 17, ProQuest Historical
     Newspapers.

213 *"Mr. Greenberg, I hate":* McAuley, "Doby Makes Eating Crow," 16.

213 *"is gonna be a helluva":* Arthur Daley, "Sports of the Times: Behind Dressing
     Room Doors," *The New York Times,* May 12, 1948, 35, Archive.nytimes.com.

214 *"Nobody is going to hit":* Herman Goldstein, "Hit 'Em a Mile and Run Say
     Ground Rules," *Cleveland News,* June 7, 1948.

214 *"With the speed of a meteor":* Harry Jones, "Doby Raps Record Homer with 2
     on," *The Plain Dealer,* May 9, 1948, C-1.

214 *"I thought," Boudreau reportedly:* McAuley, "Doby Makes Eating Crow," 16.

214 *"If Doby can face":* Ibid.

214 *"With his speed and power":* Frank Gibbons, "Keltner Eclipses Comeback by
     Feller, Doby," *Cleveland Press,* May 10, 1948.

215 *"The Cleveland fan":* Frank, "Wild About Boudreau," 90.

215 *"not in a sudden spontaneous":* Details in this paragraph drawn from Gordon
     Cobbledick, "Plain Dealing," *The Plain Dealer,* June 9, 1948, 25.

215 *"belongs in the largest":* "Veeck Again Shows His Fellow Magnates," *The
     Sporting News,* June 2, 1948, 12, Paper of Record.

216 *keeping a microphone on hand:* Shirley Povich, "This Morning with Shirley
     Povich," *The Washington Post,* May 26, 1948, 17. See also Dickson, *Bill
     Veeck,* 143.

216 *After only a few warm-up:* Bob Yonkers, "Everybody Excited but Di Maggio
     after His Greatest Exhibition of Power Hitting," *Cleveland Press,* May 24,
     1948.

216 *less stuff than:* "Keltner Day Planned; Feller Still Below Peak," *Cleveland
     Press,* April 26, 1948.

216 *"This year Bob Feller":* Shirley Povich, "This Morning with Shirley Povich,"
     The Washington Post, June 26, 1948, 11, ProQuest Historical Newspapers.

216 *"the one truly vital":* Gordon Cobbledick, "Plain Dealing," *The Plain Dealer,*
     June 13, 1948, 2-B.

216 *"We'll sink or swim":* Ed McAuley, "'We'll Sink or Swim with Feller,' Boudreau Declares, Pins Hopes of Pennant on Bob," *Cleveland News,* June 17, 1948, 1.

217 *"There has been a lot":* Frank Gibbons, "Feller Not Worried About Feller," *Cleveland Press,* June 19, 1948.

217 *the shallowness of the Indians' pitching rotation:* For a similar assessment of the Indians' pitching staff and the need to reinforce it, see Sickels, *Bob Feller,* 191–92.

218 *"investigated prospects from Mexico":* Ed McAuley, "Satchelfoot Finally Gets Brogan into Big League Door as Indian," *The Sporting News,* July 14, 1948, 11, Paper of Record.

22. ENTER PAIGE

219 *"siphon young Negro ball":* Fay Young, "Through the Years: Merit," *The Chicago Defender,* May 15, 1948, 11, ProQuest Historical Newspapers.

219 *first player Saperstein recommended:* Fay Young, "Satchel Hurls for Cleveland Indians," *The Chicago Defender,* July 17, 1948, 10, ProQuest Historical Newspapers.

219 *In late June, Saperstein:* Information in this paragraph based on interviews with Saperstein in: Al Wolf, "Sportraits," *Los Angeles Times,* February 13, 1954, B2; and Wendell Smith, "Wendell Smith's Sports Beat: Truth, Like Murder, Will 'Out,'" *New Pittsburgh Courier,* January 14, 1961, 25, ProQuest Historical Newspapers.

219 *Months earlier, during spring training:* A. S. "Doc" Young, "Veeck Says: Doby Will Be a Great Player," *Call & Post,* March 27, 1948, 6B.

220 *"It had never occurred":* A. S. "Doc" Young, "An 'Old Man' Makes Baseball History," *Ebony,* March 1969, 122.

220 *"They was thinkin'":* Richard Donovan, "'Time Ain't Gonna Mess with Me'," *Collier's,* June 13, 1953, 58.

220 *"die with his spikes on":* Wendell Smith, "Life Story of Leroy 'Satchel' Paige," undated pamphlet from 1948, accessed in the archives of the Cleveland Public Library on March 5, 2016.

220 *"whooped and hollered":* William Price Fox, *Satchel Paige's America* (Tuscaloosa: University of Alabama Press, 2005), 99.

221 *On the morning of July 6:* Details in this paragraph from two sources: Steven Goldman, "1948 and 1949 American League: Tyranicide," in Steven Goldman, ed., *It Ain't Over 'Til It's Over: The Baseball Prospectus Pennant Race Book* (New York: Basic Books, 2007), 61; and Boudreau, *Covering All the Bases,* 112.

221 *"built like a pencil"*: Maury Allen, "Satchel Withstood the Test of Time," *New York Post*, June 9, 1982.

221 *In earlier discussions*: Veeck, *As in Wreck*, 183.

221 *"we couldn't even draw flies"*: As quoted in Young, *J. L. Wilkinson*, 152.

221 *Boudreau chose the inside*: Boudreau, *Covering All the Bases*, 112–13.

222 *"a couple Bee balls"*: Fox, *Satchel Paige's America*, 101.

222 *Boudreau popped a few flies*: Veeck, *As in Wreck*, 184.

222 *"Now I can believe"*: Frank Gibbons, "Satchel Paige Signed to Pitch for Indians," *Cleveland Press*, July 7, 1948.

222 *For all he knew*: Fox, *Satchel Paige's America*, 101.

222 *Veeck hobbled over*: Paige, *Pitch Forever*, 198.

222 *"As far as I'm concerned"*: Tom Meany, "$64 Question: Paige's Age?" *The Sporting News*, July 21, 1948, 12, Paper of Record.

222 *it would further underline*: Paul Dickson makes a similar point in Dickson, *Bill Veeck*, 146, as does John Sickels in Sickels, *Bob Feller*, 157–58.

223 *"Veeck has gone too far"*: J. G. Taylor Spink, "Two Ill-Advised Moves," *The Sporting News*, July 14, 1948, 8, Paper of Record.

223 *"I signed Paige because"*: Gibbons, "Satchel Paige Signed."

223 *"Everything was above board"*: "Deals with Monarchs," *Kansas City Star*, July 7, 1948, 22.

223 *the combined salaries*: According to baseball-reference.com, Jackie Robinson made $14,000, Larry Doby $6,000, and Roy Campanella $6,500 in 1948.

223 *"I'm starting my major league"*: Ed McAuley, "'Too Late,' Says Jackie, But Satchel Thinks He's Wrong," *Cleveland News*, July 7, 1948, 10.

224 *"like a man on his way"*: Frank Gibbons, "'Stepin Pitchit' Clicks in Debut," *Cleveland Press*, July 10, 1948.

224 *"like they never was"*: Paige, *Pitch Forever*, 200.

224 *"Somebody ought to say"*: Exchange between Boudreau and Gordon from Ed Fitzgerald, "Joe Gordon: The Acrobatic Flash," *Sport*, July 1949, 92.

224 *"a baffling combination"*: Young, "An 'Old Man,'" 129. For more on the crowd's laughter, see: Gibbons, "'Stepin Pitchit' Clicks."

224 *Their paths had crossed*: Chuck Stevens, phone interview with the author, October 14, 2017. See also Tye, *Satchel*, 208.

224 *"I wasn't nervous exactly"*: Leroy (Satchel) Paige as told to Hal Lebovitz, "'Satchel' Paige Pitching," *Cleveland News*, July 24, 1948.

225 *Boudreau kicked anxiously*: Boudreau, *Player-Manager*, 164.

225 *Home plate was where:* Ed McAuley, "Life in the Majors with Satchel Paige, Part 2," *The Sporting News,* September 29, 1948, 13, Paper of Record.

225 *"put most of his wares":* Harold Sauerbrei, "Flash Bulbs Pop, But Old Satch Just Hurls in Usual Cool Manner," *The Plain Dealer,* July 10, 1948, 13.

225 *His famed hesitation pitch:* Tygiel, *Baseball's Great Experiment,* 228.

225 *When Browns shortstop Eddie:* Bob Dolgan, "Paige Played to the Crowd," *The Plain Dealer,* August 9, 1998.

225 *"I'm Satchel . . . I do":* Donovan, "'Time Ain't Gonna," 55.

226 *Believing his inclusion:* At the time, Bill Veeck claimed that he'd encouraged Feller to skip the All-Star Game in order to get some much-needed rest. Feller told a similar story in his second autobiography, but then admitted to his biographer, John Sickels, that it'd been his idea to withdraw and that Veeck had agreed to cover for him. See Sickels, *Bob Feller,* 194–95.

226 *"An anti-Bob Feller bloc":* Hy Hurwitz, "Anti-Feller Bloc Grows; Red Sox Join," *The Boston Globe,* July 13, 1948, 18, Newspapers.com.

226 *"a lot of jealousy":* Harold Kaese, "Jealousy of Feller Seen Behind Move to Force All-Star Participation," *The Boston Globe,* July 13, 1948, 18, Newspapers.com.

227 *"You can see Feller":* Oscar Fraley, "Eye on Dollar, Bob Feller Loses Sight of the Plate," *The Dispatch,* July 6, 1948, 17.

227 *"Feller is in for a rough":* Hurwitz, "Anti-Feller Bloc," 18.

227 *"with one hand outstretched":* Lawton Carver, "Feller's Refusal Said Due to Money Greed," *St. Petersburg Times,* July 14, 1948, 19, Newspapers.com.

227 *"No player in the history":* Boudreau, *Player-Manager,* 167.

227 *"may knock the Indians":* Hurwitz, "Anti-Feller Bloc," 18.

227 *"What do you think I am":* Associated Press, "Feller Ignores Boos of Fans at Philadelphia," *The Boston Globe,* July 16, 1948, 6, Newspapers.com.

227 *Normally an inveterate:* Virginia Feller, "He's My Feller!" 100.

227 *While giving birth:* Frank Deford, "Rapid Robert Can Still Bring It," *Sports Illustrated,* August 8, 2005, https://vault.si.com/vault/2005/08/08/rapid -robert-can-still-bring-it.

228 *Sometimes, she'd pad:* Feller, *Now Pitching,* 207–08.

228 *one out of every six:* A. S. "Doc" Young, "The Jackie Robinson Era," *Ebony,* November 1955, 155. See also Tygiel, *Baseball's Great Experiment,* 230.

228 *Coming on in relief:* A. S. "Doc" Young, "Dodgers-Indians Exhibition Draws 25,000 Negro Fans; Tribe Wins, 4–3," *Call & Post,* July 24, 1948, 6B.

228 *"If they had been giving"*: "Paige Wins Starting Role Against Nats by Beating A's," *Cleveland Press*, July 16, 1948.

229 SEND HIM BACK: Associated Press, "Feller Ignores Boos," 6.

229 *"gave the appearance"*: Frank Gibbons, "Double Steal, Etc. Sends Bewildered Feller to Bull Pen," *Cleveland Press*, July 17, 1948.

229 *"They hit good"*: Ibid.

229 *Feller would move:* Ibid.

23. PANDEMONIUM

230 *"Doby was always surprising"*: Ed McAuley, "Tribe Picket Line Picked for Last Half," *The Sporting News*, July 21, 1948, 9, Paper of Record.

231 *"I didn't hear anybody"*: Harry Jones, "A's Score 2 Runs on Fly Lost in Sun, Drop Tribe into 3d Place, 4–3," *The Plain Dealer*, July 29, 1948, 18.

231 *"Larry," he said softly:* Ed McAuley, "Deacon Bill to Larry: 'Now's Chance to Prove You're Big League,'" *Cleveland News*, July 29, 1948, 22.

232 *"seemed to know everybody"*: Harrison Dillard, phone interview with the author, December 6, 2016.

232 *"Everybody looked toward him"*: Anita Jackson, phone interview with the author, February 13, 2017.

232 *mock-rules:* Ibid.

232 *"People were very accepting"*: Ibid.

232 *"[Veeck] always seemed"*: Claire Smith, "A Ripple of Recognition Follows Robinson," *The New York Times*, May 2, 1997, B9, Archive.nytimes.com

232 *"[Veeck] loved jazz"*: Ibid.

232 *"To me," Doby said:* Ibid.

233 *"I want to tell you this"*: Joe Gootter, "Sportograms: Gene Goes in for the Sneer Technique," *The News* (Paterson), October 9, 1948, 18, Newspapers.com.

233 *the two men straddled:* Numerous sources have recounted the differences and disagreements between Larry Doby and Satchel Paige. The ones that most influenced my account include Tye, *Satchel*, 201–02, 214-16; Moore, *Larry Doby*, 167-72; Young, *Great Negro Baseball Stars*, 80–81.

233 *"tear apart"*: Franklin Lewis, "Doby Looks Back Without Sorrow," *Cleveland Press*, August 14, 1957.

233 *After a fan in St. Louis:* Moore, *Larry Doby*, 79.

234 *"I'm going to ask you"*: Hal Lebovitz, "The '48 Indians: One Last Hurrah," *Sport*, June 1965, 78.

234 *"I musta slept a year"*: Hal Lebovitz, "An Error Costs Satchel Paige $500; News Reader Proves He Hurled in '26," *Cleveland News*, August 23, 1948, 6.

234 *"Satchel was a delight"*: Eddie Robinson, interview with the author, February 19, 2016.

234 *his amusing nicknames*: Young, *Great Negro Baseball Stars*, 80. See also Tye, *Satchel*, 216.

234 *"[Paige] was a character"*: Ira Berkow, "He Crossed Color Barrier," 1, 30.

235 *"In my opinion he"*: Sudyk, "Forgotten Pioneer," D12.

235 *"by playing to whites' expectations"*: Tye, *Satchel*, 200.

235 *"This pitchin's a serious"*: Charles Heaton, "Startin' Is Lots Easier Than Savin', Satch Says," *The Plain Dealer*, August 4, 1948, 22.

235 *"Look, Satch," he'd say*: Cobbledick, "Old Satch," 35.

236 *"Now we've got to win"*: Harry Jones, "Tribe's Game with Nats Tonight Is Another 'Big One' to Boudreau," *The Plain Dealer*, August 3, 1948, 17.

236 *"Look, I had 800 tickets"*: Franklin Lewis, "Satchmo Provides Last 1/3 of 72,434 Record Audience," *Cleveland Press*, August 4, 1948.

236 *"Say," Ruel remarked to Paige*: Ed McAuley, "'Satch Didn't Embarrass Us'— Veeck: 72,000 Stamp 'OK' on Paige," *Cleveland News*, August 4, 1948.

236 *"wore false blackface"*: Lewis, "Satchmo Provides Last 1/3."

237 *"Don't worry none"*: Paige, *Pitch Forever*, 209.

237 *"I don't think Satch"*: McAuley, "'Satch Didn't Embarrass Us'." See also Gordon Cobbledick, "Plain Dealing," *The Plain Dealer*, August 5, 1948.

237 *immovable gridlock*: "Fans Crash Gate to See Old Satch," *Cleveland News*, August 14, 1948.

238 *"Why don't you just let"*: Bill Veeck, as told to George Vass, *The Game I'll Never Forget*, in John Kuenster, ed., *From Cobb to "Catfish": 128 Illustrated Stories from Baseball Digest* (Chicago: Rand McNally & Company, 1975), 174.

238 *Waves of people surged*: "Fans Crash Gate."

238 *"there was not a place"*: Veeck, *As in Wreck*, 187.

238 *Inundated with complaints, several ushers*: "Biggest Crowd of the Year Sees Paige," *The Baltimore Afro-American*, August 21, 1948, 7, ProQuest Historical Newspapers.

238 *Moments before the Indians took the field*: Veeck, *As in Wreck*, 187.

238 *For Paige, being back*: Paige, *Pitch Forever*, 212.

239 *"I kept 'em from"*: Vass, *The Game I'll Never Forget*, in Kuenster, *From Cobb to "Catfish,"* 174.

239   *"He's done more, much more"*: Frank Gibbons, "No One-Year Wonder, Satchel to Be Back in '49," *Cleveland Press*, August 14, 1948.

239   *"Never in doubt, Burrhead"*: Vass, *The Game I'll Never Forget*, in Kuenster, *From Cobb to "Catfish,"* 174.

240   *"If they say Old Satch"*: Ed McAuley, "'Satchel's Fables' Has Baseball World Standing in Line for Shutout Tour," *Cleveland News*, August 21, 1948.

240   *rendered moot the long-standing*: "The Ways of White Folks," *The Chicago Defender*, August 28, 1948, 14, ProQuest Historical Newspapers.

240   *Fielding the ball on a hop*: Fay Young, "Paige Is Baseball's Greatest Drawing Card," *The Chicago Defender*, August 28, 1948, 11, ProQuest Historical Newspapers.

241   *"triumph of racial"*: Editorial, "Triumph of Tolerance," *The Plain Dealer*, August 22, 1948, 21.

241   *"Paige pitching—No runs"*: Henry Andrews, "Paigeing Mr. Spink: Another Telegram Goes Out from Veeck's Office," *Cleveland Press*, August 21, 1948.

241   *"Five or six years ago"*: Frank Gibbons, "Paige + Doby = 0 for White Sox, 78,382 for Veeck," *Cleveland Press*, August 21, 1948.

241   *"You may be right, man"*: Associated Press, "201,829 See Satch," 12.

241   *"taken up much of"*: Shirley Povich, "This Morning with Shirley Povich," *The Washington Post*, August 23, 1948, 10, ProQuest Historical Newspapers.

24. THE GINGERBREAD MEN

242   *"classic French-American"*: Bill Gruber, phone interview with the author, April 10, 2016.

242   *To encourage wine consumption*: "Gruber's: Death of a First Class Act," *Cleveland Magazine*, February 1978.

242   *"small but carefree group"*: Winsor French, "A Legend from a Laundry . . . ," Winsor French and Franklin Lewis, eds., *Curtain Call* (Cleveland: The Gruber Foundation, 1952), 52. For more on Winsor French and his involvement with The Jolly Set, see James M. Wood, *Out and About with Winsor French* (Kent, OH: The Kent State University Press, 2011).

242   *"in a fashion reminiscent"*: Winsor French, "Long Last Look at Gruber's Jolly Days," *Cleveland Press*, November 5, 1960.

242–43   *Sometimes Veeck would hoist*: Ibid.

243   *"like a sailor just ashore"*: "Man with the Pink Hair," *Time*, December 5, 1949, 84.

243   *"for a man in his position"*: Cobbledick, "Baseball's Greatest Showman," 58.

243 *"He was the only man I knew":* Hank Greenberg, with Ira Berkow, *Hank Greenberg: The Story of My Life* (Chicago: Ivan R. Dee, 2009), 259.

244 *"out of their easy chairs":* Cobbledick, "Baseball's Greatest Showman," 63.

244 *"greatest demonstration":* Ibid., 55. For more on the frenzy, see Schneider, *Boys of the Summer,* xi.

244 *"did everything for the Indians":* Ted Williams, with John Underwood, *My Turn at Bat: The Story of My Life* (New York: Simon & Schuster, 1988), 167.

245 *time and room to make:* For more on Doby receiving time to fail and recover in his first two seasons, see Louis Moore, "Doby Does It! Larry Doby, Race, and American Democracy in Post-World War II America" *Journal of Sports History* 42, No. 3 (Fall 2015), 363–70.

245 *"If we win the pennant":* Harry Jones, "Team with 'Pennant Possibilities' Fulfills Boudreau's Prophecy of Flag," *The Plain Dealer,* October 5, 1948, 25.

245 *In a city of just under:* Bob Dolgan, "A Smash Hit at the Gate '48 Tribe Was No. 1 at Box Office, Too, Drawing Record 2.6 Million to Stadium," *The Plain Dealer,* August 30, 1998.

245 *"for good old Joe Earley":* Tom Carroll, "Local Scene," *Dayton Daily News,* September 26, 1948, 26, Newspapers.com.

245 *"night to end all nights":* Ibid.

246 *"like they were beating out":* Joe Collier, "'Good Old Joe' Even Beats Shmoos; Gifts Range from Cars to Chickens," *Cleveland Press,* September 29, 1948.

246 *When it came to Joe Earley and his wife:* Details in this paragraph from Veeck, *As in Wreck,* 113; and Dickson, *Bill Veeck,* 154–55.

247 *"a steeplechase":* Kyle Crichton, "The Big Series Scramble," *Collier's,* October 9, 1948, 22.

247 *Players in opposing dugouts:* Hal Lebovitz, "Summer of '48," *The Plain Dealer,* January 21, 1974, 1-D.

247 *"within a hairsbreadth":* Boudreau, *Player–Manager,* 200.

247 *"We'll win the pennant":* Ed McAuley, "Indians Fans Throw Away Hammer and Buy a Horn," *The Sporting News,* August 4, 1948, 6, Paper of Record.

247 *"I've got it back":* Franklin Lewis, "Chalk Up Feller's Return to Winning Form as Genuine," *Cleveland Press,* September 2, 1948.

248 *Lemon told Russell Schneider:* For the fully story of the Indians' espionage in 1948, see Schneider, *The Boys of the Summer of '48,* 38–42.

248 *Indians batters knew:* Ibid., 40–41.

249 *Other times, Sain would call:* Peary, ed., *We Played,* 84.

249   *"Hey, all's fair"*: Schneider, *The Boys of the Summer*, 39.

250   *"they cheer his every move"*: Associated Press, "Indian Fans Breath Easier as Elbow Injury to Popular Doby Proves to Be Only Painful," *Akron Beacon Journal*, September 27, 1948, 59, Newspapers.com.

250   *"[Doby] has made more"*: A. S. "Doc" Young, "Cold, Unbiased Figures Prove Larry Doby's Right to Be an Indian," *Call & Post*, September 25, 1948, 7B.

250   *"[Doby] still makes mistakes"*: Associated Press, "Indians Fans Breath Easier," 59.

250   *trained one eye on:* Harry Jones, "Scoreboard Is 'Three'-Ring Circus Until Doby's Clout," *The Plain Dealer*, September 20, 1948, 18.

250   *"shot out of a cannon"*: Ibid.

250–51   *"Without Doby," he said:* Associated Press, "Indian Fans Breath Easier," 59.

251   *"[Feller] showed me more"*: Joe Reichler, "Feller Back on Throne as King of Pitchers," *Iowa City Press-Citizen*, September 23, 1948, 20.

251   *he'd had to tighten his belt:* Stump, "Pop Lemon's Boy," 18.

252   *railroads across Ohio:* Ritter Collett, "The Journal of Sports," *Dayton Journal*, September 30, 1948, 19, Newspapers.com.

252   *Lemon wept:* Dick Dugan, "Triple Tie Is Possible: Cleveland-Detroit," *The Dayton Herald*, October 2, 1948, 12, Newspapers.com.

252   *In September, just when:* Moore, *Larry Doby*, 81.

253   *Johnny Lipon, the Tigers':* Harry Jones, "Indians Defeated in Final Game, Battle Boston in Play-off Today," *The Plain Dealer*, October 4, 1948, 1.

253   *Not a word passed:* Bill Bryson, "It's a Tie: Sox Versus Tribe in Boston Today," *Des Moines Register*, October 4, 1948, 11–12, Newspapers.com.

253   *"pacing like a caged lion"*: Robert J. Drake, "Fans' Pennant Whoops Dwindle to Whispers," *The Plain Dealer*, October 4, 1948, 1, 7.

253   *Veeck slunk off:* Ibid.

254   *"I tossed the whole night"*: Hal Lebovitz, "Bob Feller's Disappointment," *Sport*, October 1959, 75.

254   *"like youngsters getting ready"*: Winsor French, "Winsor French," *Cleveland Press*, October 5, 1948.

254   *Bearden had shot craps:* Terry Pluto, "The Right Choice," *Akron Beacon Journal*, August 1, 1998, 43.

255   *"the nonchalance of a veteran"*: Lou Boudreau as told to Ed McAuley of the *Cleveland News*, in Schiffer, ed., *My Greatest Baseball Game*, 27. Russell Schneider reported Bearden's brandy sips in: Schneider, *The Boys of the Summer*, 21.

255 *Jim Hegan called for:* Hal Lebovitz, "Summer of '48, Part 4," *The Plain Dealer,* January 23, 1974, 1-C–2-C.

255 *"yipped and yowled":* Red Smith, "View of Sport: The Man Who Hates Ties," *New York Herald Tribune,* October 5, 1948, 26.

255 *he vaulted the railing:* Staff Special, "Veeck Sets Record in Dash to Congratulate His Champions," *Cleveland Press,* October 5, 1948.

256 *"that Feller was not":* Carl Lundquist, "Feller to Achieve His Final Goal as Greatest Pitcher," *Cleveland Press,* October 5, 1948.

256 *Doby sought refuge:* Staff Special, "Veeck Sets Record."

256 *"Phew, man":* Clif Keane, "Indian Players Mob Boudreau; Lou, Bearden Thank Each Other," *The Boston Globe,* October 5, 1948, 20, Newspapers.com.

256 *According to one report:* Jackie Reemes, "Jackie Reemes' Reams of Sports: They Treated Doby the Right Way," *New York Amsterdam News,* October 16, 1948, 28, ProQuest Historical Newspapers.

25. THE PHOTO

257 *The next morning, on October 5:* Charles Heaton, "Feller Goes Through Strenuous Workout for Today's Series Opener," *The Plain Dealer,* October 6, 1948, 26.

257 *"as though they had just marched":* Boudreau, *Player-Manager,* 221.

257 *Trainer Lefty Weisman had:* Boudreau, *Covering All the Bases,* 129.

257 *Feller hadn't attended:* Lebovitz, "Feller's Disappointment," 75.

257 *he galloped across:* Heaton, "Feller Goes Through Strenuous," 26.

257 *"This chance has been":* Ibid.

258 *The team strung together:* "Sport: Double-Pennant Fever," *Time,* September 20, 1948, 71.

258 *"earth-shattering bunts":* Franklin Lewis, "Braves Play Dull if Winning Baseball and Scare Crowds," *Cleveland Press,* October 7, 1948.

258 *"They wait around until":* "Sport: The Annual Fever," *Time,* October 11, 1948, 57.

258 *"you walk into the clubhouse":* Lewis, "Braves Play Dull."

259 *"laughed us off":* "Bob Elliott as told to Bob Ajemian of the *Boston American,*" in Schiffer, ed., *My Greatest Baseball Game,* 63.

259 *Starting on September 6:* Bill Nowlin, ed., Mark Armour, Bob Brady, Len Levin, and Saul Wisnia, associate eds., *Spahn, Sain, and Teddy Ballgame: Boston's (almost) Perfect Summer of 1948* (Burlington, MA: Rounder Books, 2008), 149.

259 *A sports editor from* The Boston Post: Gerald V. Hern, "Braves Boast Two-Man Staff: Pitch Spahn and Sain, Then Pray for Rain," *Boston Post,* September 14, 1948.

260 *"life ambition":* Ted Smits, "Satchel Feels Miserable," *Cleveland News,* October 7, 1948.

260 *"Whadda ya play?":* Frank Gibbons, "Tribe Slices World Series Financial 'Pie' 36 Ways," *Cleveland Press,* Oct. 7, 1948.

260 *"Can you imagine that?":* "Second Game Gossip," *The Sporting News,* Oct 13, 1948, 7, 11.

260 *"No busses. That way":* Jim Schlemmer, "We'll Get 'Em!" *Akron Beacon Journal,* October 7, 1948, 47, Newspapers.com.

261 *In the clubhouse, Johnny Sain:* Sportswriter Albert Hirshberg wrote that before starts Sain would take a bite of tobacco as soon as he put on his uniform. See Albert Hirshberg, *The Braves: The Pick and the Shovel* (Boston: Waverly House, 1948), 206.

261 *"as quiet as an Ipswich":* Harold Kaese, "Now the American Leaguers Know Sain's All-Star Stunt Was No Fluke," *The Boston Globe,* October 7, 1948, 26, Newspapers.com.

261 *Some speculated whether Sain:* Ed Rumill, "Classic Opener Just Another Tough Ball Game to Cool Johnny Sain of Braves," *The Christian Science Monitor,* October 7, 1948, 11, ProQuest Historical Newspapers.

261 *Calling over Bill Salkeld:* "Johnny Sain, as told to Bob Ajemian of the *Boston American,*" in Schiffer, ed., *My Greatest Baseball Game,* 151.

262 *"No man ever walked":* Red Smith, "View of Sport: The Wrong Comedians," *New York Herald Tribune,* Oct 7, 1948, 25.

262 *"If Sain can pitch until":* Ibid.

262 *"the man with a thousand":* "Sain Victor in Opener, Feller Losing 2-Hitter," *The Sporting News,* October 13, 1948, 6, Paper of Record.

262 *In the Boston Common, thousands:* Paul F. Kneeland, "How They Operated 100 Sets on Common," *The Boston Globe,* Oct 10, 1948, 34-A, Newspapers.com.

262 *the number of television sets:* Roger Birtwell, "Television Brought Series to 7,771,000," *The Sporting News,* Oct 27, 1948, 7, Paper of Record.

263 *Upon glimpsing Boudreau's signal:* Boudreau, *Player-Manager,* 110–11.

263 *the Indians had caught eight:* Terry Pluto, "Nothing Stops Tribe," *Akron Beacon Journal,* August 2, 1998, D8.

263 *Normally, before games, Boudreau:* Ibid.

264 *The ball zoomed in belt-high:* Bob Feller, as told to Ed Fitzgerald, "Who Says I'm Finished?" *Sport,* April 1949, 19.

264 *"as if he were watching":* Ritter Collett, "The Journal of Sports," *Dayton Journal,* October 7, 1948, 21, Newspapers.com.

264 *"If a couple of breaks":* Sain, as told to Bob Ajemian of the *Boston American,"* in Schiffer, ed., *My Greatest Baseball Game,* 149.

264 *"It seems every time":* Herman Goldstein, "Haunted, Feller Says, by 'Base on Balls,'" *Cleveland News,* October 7, 1948.

264 *"a pathetic sort of grimace":* Oscar Fraley, "Hard-Luck Feller Heartbroken," *The Washington Post,* October 7, 1948, 19, ProQuest Historical Newspapers.

265 *"with the speed of half-frozen":* Grantland Rice, "Better Than 'Good' Pitching Needed to Top Bearden," *The Boston Globe,* Oct 8, 1948, 33, Newspapers.com.

265 *downing oyster stew:* Mary Van Rensselaer Thayer, "Society Columnist Sees World Series and Finds Cleveland a Town Gone Mad," *The Washington Post,* October 9, 1948, 13, ProQuest Historical Newspapers.

265 *install an extra operator:* Frank, "Wild About Boudreau," 23.

265 *"was bigger than the Easter":* Associated Press, "Fans to Get Only 2 Series Tickets to One Game," *Dayton Daily News,* Sept 28, 1948, 12, Newspapers.com.

265 *More than a million:* "Fans Apply for Million Tickets," *Cleveland Press,* September 28, 1948, 1.

266 *Some laid down ponchos:* Thayer, "Society Columnist Sees," 13.

266 *thousands of Clevelanders:* "Late Train Curtails Tribe Welcome Celebration," *Cleveland Press,* October 8, 1948.

266 *Boudreau had to hustle:* "Third Game Gossip," *The Sporting News,* October 20, 1948, 14, Paper of Record.

266 *miniature American flags:* Thayer, "Society Columnist Sees," 13.

266 *Bill Veeck supervised everything:* Al Wolf, "Gene Bearden Shuffles Style for Pitching," *Los Angeles Times,* October 9, 1948, 30, ProQuest Historical Newspapers.

266 *"very low cut gown":* John O'Donnell, "Sports Chat," *The Democrat and Leader* (Davenport, IA), October 10, 1948, 46, Newspapers.com.

267 *"[Veeck] walks with a limp":* Ibid.

267 *"Gentlemen," Boudreau reportedly announced:* Bob Dolgan, "A Racial Milestone" *The Plain Dealer,* April 26, 1998, 10-C.

267 *spare part:* Gordon Cobbledick, "Gromek, 'Spot' Hurler, Comes Through Again," *The Plain Dealer,* Oct 10, 1948, 1C.

268 *Veeck established his World Series:* Details in this paragraph from: Joe Garretson, "Cleveland Wakes Up to the Series; Umpires Take Booings to Heart," *The Cincinnati Enquirer,* Oct. 10, 1948, 26; and Dale Stevens, "Boston's Chances Not Worth Plugged Nickel Says Stevens," *Palladium-Item* (Richmond, IN), October 10, 1948, 13, Newspapers.com.

268 *Unhesitatingly, Veeck tore:* Bill Lee, "With Malice Toward None," *Hartford Courant,* October 11, 1948, 11, Newspapers.com.

268 *Joe Louis, who'd become so enamored:* Associated Press, "Sofa Pillows Employed as Louis Boxes," *The Democrat and Leader,* September 21, 1948, 13, Newspapers.com.

269 *Now, out of respect for Manley:* Manley, Effa. Interview by William J. Marshall. October 19, 1977. Lexington: Louie B. Nunn Center for Oral History, University of Kentucky Libraries.

269 *"a sort of agent":* J. G. Taylor Spink, "Looping the Loop: Doby's Play Makes the Eagles Scream," *The Sporting News,* October 20, 1948, 2, Paper of Record.

269 *"Negro fans are acting like":* Lillian Scott, "Effa Manley 'Hotter Than Horse Radish,'" *The Chicago Defender,* September 18, 1948, 11, ProQuest Historical Newspapers.

269 *"the incentive was gone":* Spink, "Doby's Play Makes," 2.

269 *"When a team like the Newark":* Jack Saunders, "The Sports: Could This Be the Beginning of the End," *Pittsburgh Courier,* September 11, 1948, 10, ProQuest Historical Newspapers.

269 *"a free and lethal":* Jerry Nason, "Indians Win, 2–1," *The Boston Globe,* October 9, 1948, 4, Newspapers.com.

270 *"as cold as the biting":* Hy Hurwitz, "Potter Surprise Choice Against Feller Today," *The Boston Globe,* Oct 10, 1948, 36, Newspapers.com.

271 *"That crowd scare you":* United Press, "Only Curve Knuckler in Majors Saves Gromek for World Series," *Akron Beacon Journal,* October 10, 1948, 1C, Newspapers.com. Doby claimed that he ran fast because he couldn't tell if the ball was going to clear the fence. See: Larry Doby, "Doby Says Indians Let Down over Trip," *The News* (Paterson), October 11, 1948, 34, Newspapers.com.

271 *While sprinting at full speed:* "Doby's Home Run Brings Indians Three Straight," *The Chicago Defender,* October 16, 1948, 13, ProQuest Historical Newspapers.

271 *"a high school hero":* Frank Gibbons, "Gromek Will Top Them All," *Baseball Digest,* March 1949, 26.

272   *Gromek thought for a second:* Schneider, *The Boys of the Summer,* 94.

272   *"the best race relations plug":* Marjorie McKenzie, "Pursuit of Democracy: Doby-Gromek Picture Treated Eyes to Sight of Equality in Action," *Pittsburgh Courier,* October 23, 1948, 16, ProQuest Historical Newspapers.

272   *"It was such a scuffle":* Moore, *Larry Doby,* 4.

272   *An hour or so after:* "Doby's Home Run Brings Indians Three Straight," *The Chicago Defender,* October 16, 1948, 13, ProQuest Historical Newspapers.

26. FEVER DREAMS

273   *carrying no more luggage:* Harry Jones, "Indians Caught Short Rushing to Make Train," *The Plain Dealer,* October 11, 1948, 22.

273   *gamblers were offering bets:* Bill Cunningham, "Braves Look Panicky; Hits Needed Badly," *Boston Herald,* October 10, 1948, 42, Genealogybank.com.

273   *Boudreau replied: "Nobody":* Ibid.

274   *Though state laws prohibited:* Joe Trimble, "Elliott Raps Pair; Tribe Leads, 3–2," *Daily News,* October 11, 1948, 69.

274   *"How much does it cost":* Si Steinhauser, "Network Chief Explains Ban on Giveaways," *Pittsburgh Press,* Oct. 13, 1948, 43.

274   *A few factories:* "Thousands Watch Indians Win by TV," *The Plain Dealer,* October 9, 1948, 4.

275   *"Isn't this great, Will?":* Veeck, *As in Wreck,* 207.

275   *"How come you couldn't have been":* Ibid.

275   *"don't do that to Feller":* Charles Heaton, "'We're on Our Way,' Declares Braves' Elliott," *The Plain Dealer,* October 11, 1948, 22.

275   *"so many Venus di Milos":* Bill Cunningham, "Series Now Alive as Braves Revive," *Boston Herald,* October 11, 1948, 16, Genealogybank.com.

275   *fans showered the pitcher:* Bob Yonkers, "Fans Understood: Most of the 86,288 at Stadium Knew Why Lou Kept Feller on Hill," *Cleveland Press,* October 11, 1948.

276   *He pawed at the dirt:* Whitey Martin, "Sharp Contrast in Walks Taken by Bob, Satchel," *The Boston Globe,* October 11, 1948, 7, Newspapers.com.

276   *"as if he just felt":* Ibid.

276   *"hung like a turkey":* Tony Cordaro, "Pay Cut for Bob?—To About $60,000," *Des Moines Tribune,* Oct. 11, 1948, 16, Newspapers.com.

276   *"At that moment," observed:* Joe Williams, "Feller Tragic Figure When Relieved in 7th Inning," *Cleveland Press,* Oct. 11, 1948.

277   *"I guess deep down":* Paige, *Pitch Forever,* 221.

277 *"I guess old Satch":* Will Cloney, "Boudreau, Indians Praise Bearden," *Boston Herald,* October 9, 1948, 9, Genealogybank.com.

277 *"all I could do":* Paige, *Pitch Forever,* 222.

278 *"Put in Satch!":* Bob Considine, "On to Boston! 86,288 See Braves Win," *San Francisco Examiner,* October 11, 1948, 23–24.

278 *"with the drowsy ease":* Ibid.

278 *"No man can say":* Joe Louis, "Brown Bomber Praises Doby's Work with Bat," *New York Age,* October 16, 1948, 15, ProQuest Historical Newspapers.

278 *who halted the proceedings:* Mark Ribowsky, *Don't Look Back: Satchel Paige in the Shadows of Baseball* (New York: Simon & Schuster, 1994), 272.

279 *"I'd been in a World Series":* Paige, *Pitch Forever,* 224.

279 *Instead of champagne:* Feller, "He's My Feller!" 101.

279 *"hailed and farewelled":* Peter B. Greenough, "Thousands at Terminal Cheer Indians Onward," *The Plain Dealer,* Oct. 11, 1948, 1, 9.

279 *The defeat had stunned:* Feller, "He's My Feller!" 101.

280 *"To lose that last game":* Feller, *Now Pitching,* 171.

280 *On the train he swaddled:* "Lemon Had Sore Arm, Says Lefty," *The Plain Dealer,* October 12, 1948, 23.

280 *but Boudreau's gut pointed him:* Boudreau, *Player-Manager,* 239. See also Schneider, *The Boys of the Summer,* 35.

281 *a floating knuckler:* Gene Bearden, "Hero or Bum? Step Right Up and Call Me 'Lucky,'" *Cleveland News,* January 1, 1949, 9. See also Schneider, *The Boys of the Summer,* 126.

281 *"Okay, Gene," Boudreau said:* Ibid.

281 *Exhaustion, emotional as well:* Boudreau, *Covering All the Bases,* 135.

281 *"stood almost forlorn":* Oscar Fraley, "Series Forgotten Man!" *Cleveland Press,* October 12, 1948.

282 *"in penance for three times":* United Press, "Over in a Corner Stood Feller as Indians Celebrate Wildly," *Dayton Journal,* Oct 12, 1948, 1.

282 *"There were a lot of things":* Fraley, "Series Forgotten Man!"

282 *"a shrine one of":* McLemore, "*Look* Examines Bob Feller," 20.

283 *Braves owner Lou Perini:* Editorial, "High Responsibility for Larry Doby," *The Sporting News,* October 27, 1948, 12. See also Mark Ribowsky, *A Complete History of the Negro Leagues: 1884 to 1955* (New York: Birch Lane Press, 1995), 305.

283 *"pioneered in the majors":* "The Future of Negroes in Big League Baseball," *Ebony,* May 1, 1949, 35. See also Tygiel, *Baseball's Great Experiment,* 243.

283 *"that a Negro player, given"*: Ibid.

283 *"Two years ago, when"*: Ed McAuley, "Boudreau Applauds Each Tribe Player," *Cleveland News*, October 12, 1948.

284 *"going to be as good"*: Frank Gibbons, "Veeck Sees Few Changes for 1949," *Cleveland Press*, October 12, 1948.

284 *"Doby occupies the position"*: "High Responsibility for Larry Doby," *The Sporting News*, October 27, 1948, 12, Paper of Record.

284 *buy up all the champagne*: Winsor French, "Veeck's '48 Indians Were Party Champions," *Cleveland Press*, October 2, 1954.

284 *As soon as Veeck stepped*: Franklin Lewis, "1948 World Series, Screened for Quick Day-After Review," *Cleveland Press*, October 12, 1948.

284 *understanding that a divorce*: Veeck later wrote that his wife, Eleanor, had initiated divorce proceedings earlier that year but had agreed to hold off until the season was over. See Veeck, *As in Wreck*, 208.

285 *"Look out! Another wave"*: French, "Veeck's '48 Indians."

285 *champagne continued to drip*: Robinson, *Lucky Me*, 69.

285 *To make themselves presentable*: DiMaggio, *Real Grass, Real Heroes*, 90.

285 *"happy, howling knot"*: "200,000 Hail Return of Champion Indians," *Cleveland News*, October 12, 1948, 1.

285 *spectators burst through*: "Fans Yell, Hurl Hail of Paper on 'The Big Parade,'" *Cleveland Press*, October 12, 1948.

285 *"Veeck made the Indians a real"*: "They're Really Our Indians," *Call & Post*, October 9, 1948, 1A, 14A.

286 *"This is a day"*: Associated Press, "200,000 Clevelanders Welcome Indians Home in Spontaneous Demonstration," *Democrat and Chronicle*, October 13, 1948, 26, Newspapers.com.

286 *"I'd had it all"*: Veeck, *As in Wreck*, 208.

286 *"I had never been more"*: Ibid.

EPILOGUE

287 *"We are not only here"*: Dan Feitlowitz, "10,000 Turn Out for Doby's Homecoming," *The Sporting News*, October 27, 1948, 5. See also, Moore, *Larry Doby*, 83–84.

287 *"you are a Negro"*: "Larry Doby Finally Gets Action in Quest for Residence," *The Baltimore Afro-American*, January 8, 1949, 5, ProQuest Historical Newspapers.

287–88 *"I honestly feel more"*: Ibid. Joseph Thomas Moore reported that Doby grew so frustrated in his attempts to purchase a house that he had to enlist the help of the mayor of Paterson. See Moore, *Larry Doby*, 2–3 and 87.

288 *In Texarkana, during the Indians':* "Indians' Tan Trio Compelled to Walk to Ball Park by Bigoted Texas Taxis," *The Baltimore Afro-American,* April 23, 1949, 8, ProQuest Historical Newspapers.

288 *In the outfield, fans pelted:* Moore, *Larry Doby*, 72–73. Moore and others claim this game took place in 1948, but the Indians and Giants did not play in Texarkana that year. The two teams traveled to Texarkana and Houston during their spring training tour in 1949.

288 *"The clock turned back":* Sudyk, "Forgotten Pioneer," D12.

288 *"there were certain ballplayers":* Bill Robinson, phone interview with the author, April 20, 2016.

288 *Once, while eating:* Cobbledick, "Is Larry Doby," 82.

288 *"The guy's fighting himself":* Bill Roeder, "Did They Expect Too Much of Larry Doby?" *Sport,* May 1958, 70.

288–89 *But few made the effort:* For more on this point, see Moore, *Larry Doby*, 98.

289 *Doby would scream out:* Jim Grant, phone interview with the author, February 9, 2017. See also Jim "Mudcat" Grant, with Tom Sabellico and Pat O'Brien, *The Black Aces: Baseball's Only African-American Twenty-Game Winners* (Chula Vista, CA: Aventine Press, 2007), 208.

289 *"To play baseball is one":* Roeder, "Did They Expect," 70.

289 *"If Larry had come up":* Veeck, *As in Wreck*, 180.

290 *Veeck phoned him out of:* Harrison Dillard, phone interview with the author, December 6, 2016.

290 *Veeck posed with Doby:* Dickson, *Bill Veeck*, 173.

290 *"The scurrying after Negro players":* Bill Veeck, with Ed Linn, "Speaking Out: They've Wrecked the American League," *Saturday Evening Post,* July 11/18, 1964, 10.

290 *"there are few Negro":* "The Future of Negroes in Big League Baseball," *Ebony,* May 1, 1949, 39.

290 *former Negro League players invited:* Sickels, *Bob Feller,* 161.

291 *"I think your ability":* Vincent, *Only Game,* 46.

291 *"Why wasn't I good enough":* Jim Braham, "Paige Ends Silence, Rips Indians," *Cleveland Press,* April 16, 1971, C1.

292 *"That depends. How many":* Mike Huber, "September 25, 1965: Satchel Paige Pitches Three Scoreless Innings at Age 59," accessed from the SABR

.org website on November 30, 2018 at: https://sabr.org/gamesproj/game/september-25-1965-satchel-paige-pitches-three-scoreless-innings-age-59.

292 *rousing sing-along:* Ibid.

292 *"There's bound to be people":* Paige, *Pitch Forever,* 285.

293 *Veeck lowered the previous year's:* For more on this stunt, see Dickson, *Bill Veeck,* 175.

294 *the city's apex:* The idea of 1948 as an apex for Cleveland was deeply influenced by John J. Grabowski's introduction to William Ganson Rose, *Cleveland: The Making of a City* (Kent, OH: Kent State University Press, 1990), v–vii; and Grabowski, *Sports in Cleveland,* 83.

295 *"I lost my father":* Mike Penner, "He Is Second Only to One," *Los Angeles Times,* July 8, 1997, C1, C5, ProQuest Historical Newspapers.

295 *traces of his fingerprints:* Numerous writers have argued for Veeck as essentially the father of the modern stadium experience. For more on this point, see Dickson, *Bill Veeck,* 1–2.

295 *"Sometime, somewhere":* Veeck, *As in Wreck,* 380.

BIBLIOGRAPHY

WEBSITES, DATABASES, AND ARCHIVES

Archive.nytimes.com

Baseballdigest.com

Baseball-Reference.com

Classic.esquire.com

CPL.org

Genealogybank.com

Kentuckyoralhistory.org

Newspapers.com

Newyorker.com/archive

NYPL.org

Paperofrecord.com

Sabr.org

I relied on a number of archives while researching this project. At the Main Library of the Cleveland Public Library system, I accessed the microfilm for the *Cleveland Press*, the *Cleveland News*, *The Plain Dealer*, and the *Call & Post*. The Sports Research Center in the same building holds a wealth of books and documents related to the Indians. The Michael Schwartz Library at Cleveland State University holds the "morgue" for the *Cleveland Press*, which includes numerous newspaper clippings helpfully catalogued by person and topic. The Newark

Eagles collection at the main branch of the Newark Public Library contains a treasure trove of materials related to the Eagles, including letters to and from Effa Manley. The New York Public Library holds bound-up physical copies of *The Sporting News* and *Sport* magazine, along with microfilm for *Look, Esquire,* and *Life* magazines. The Giamatti Research Center at the National Baseball Hall of Fame and Museum in Cooperstown, New York, keeps files of clippings for major-league players, as well as oral histories, broadcasts, and World War II–related material. The A. B. "Happy" Chandler: Desegregation of Major League Baseball Oral History Project contains interviews conducted by William J. Marshall with numerous players and executives from the immediate post–World War II era, including Larry Doby, Bob Feller, Bill Veeck, and Effa Manley.

MAGAZINE AND JOURNAL ARTICLES

Bainbridge, John, "Toots's World," *The New Yorker,* November 11, 1950. Newyorker.com/archive.

Berlage, Gai Ingham, "Effa Manley: A Major Force in Negro Baseball in the 1930s and 1940s." In *Nine: A Journal of Baseball History and Social Policy Perspectives* (Spring 1993): 163–184.

Berrett, Jesse, "Diamonds for Sale: Promoting Baseball During the Great Depression." In *Baseball History 4: An Annual of Original Baseball Research*, edited by Peter Levine, 51–61. Westport, CT: Mercker, 1991.

Boswell, Thomas, "Always Leave 'Em Laughing," *Inside Sports*, March 1981.

Boudreau, Lou, as told to Ed Fitzgerald, "Bill Veeck and Me," *Sport*, May 1949.

Cannon, Jimmy, "Feller Legend Bows to Materialism," *Baseball Digest*, January 1948.

"Cleveland: Most Democratic City in U.S.," *Ebony*, September 1950.

Cobbledick, Gordon, "Bill Veeck—Baseball's Greatest Showman," *Sport*, September 1948.

Cobbledick, Gordon, "Is Larry Doby a Bust?" *Sport*, February 1952.

Cobbledick, Gordon, "Old Satch: He's Really Got It," *Sport*, December 1948.

Cohane, Tim, "The Ancient Satchel," *Look*, April 7, 1953.

Crawford, Lindsay; Ashley Guinn, McKenzie Kubly, Lindsay Maybin, Patricia Shandor, Santi Thompson, and Louis Venters, "The Camden African-American Heritage Project" (2006). Books and Manuscripts. 2. https://scholarcommons.sc.edu/pubhist_books/.

Crichton, Kyle, "The Big Series Scramble," *Collier's*, October 9, 1948.

Crichton, Kyle, "High School Hero," *Collier's*, March 6, 1937.

Crichton, Kyle, "Lou Boudreau—Civic Project," *Baseball Digest*, August 1948.

Deford, Frank, "Rapid Robert Can Still Bring It," *Sports Illustrated*, August 8, 2005. https://vault.si.com/vault/2005/08/08/rapid-robert-can-still-bring-it.

Dempsey, Jack, "Why Bob Feller Is a Champion." *Liberty*, August 9, 1941.

Dexter, Charles, "Larry Dohy's War with Himself," *Sport*, April 1953.

Donovan, Richard, "The Fabulous Satchel Paige," *Collier's*, May 30, 1953.

Donovan, Richard, "'Time Ain't Gonna Mess with Me,'" *Collier's*, June 13, 1953.

Feller, Bob, as told to Ed Fitzgerald, "Who Says I'm Finished?" *Sport*, April 1949.

Feller, Bob, as told to Ken W. Purdy, "Baseball a Game? What a Laugh!" *Look*, February 11, 1956.

Feller, Bob, as told to Ken W. Purdy, "I'll Never Quit Baseball," *Look*, March 20, 1956.

Feller, Bob, as told to Edward Linn, "The Trouble with the Hall of Fame," *Saturday Evening Post*, January 27, 1962.

"Feller Means Business," *Newsweek*, June 2, 1947.

Feller, Virginia, as told to Hal Lebovitz, "He's My Feller!" *Baseball Digest*, May 1952.

Fitzgerald, Ed, "Feller Incorporated," *Sport*, June 1947.

Fitzgerald, Ed, "Joe Gordon: The Acrobatic Flash," *Sport*, July 1949.

Fitzgerald, Ed, "Lou Boudreau—Last of the Boy Managers?" *Sport*, July 1948.

Flaherty, Joe, "Toots Shor Among the Ruins," *Esquire*, October 1974. Classic .esquire.com.

Frank, Stanley, "Barnum of Baseball," *Liberty*, July 19, 1947.

Frank, Stanley, "The Flame Thrower." *Liberty*, August 3, 1946.

Frank, Stanley, "They're Just Wild about Boudreau," *Saturday Evening Post*, September 4, 1948.

Frank, Stanley, and Edgar Munzel, "A Visit with Bill Veeck." *Saturday Evening Post*, June 6, 1959.

"The Future of Negroes in Big League Baseball," *Ebony*, May 1, 1949.

Gibbons, Frank, "Gromek Will Top Them All," *Baseball Digest*, March 1949.

Greenberg, Hank, "Unforgettable Bill Veeck," *Reader's Digest*, July 1986.

Grody, Ray, "Baseball's No. 1 Screwball," *Look*, September 7, 1943.

Gross, Milton, "The Emancipation of Jackie Robinson," *Sport*, October 1951.

Gross, Milton, "Why They Boo Jackie Robinson," *Sport*, February 1953.

"Gruber's: Death of a First Class Act," *Cleveland Magazine*, February 1978.

Hawkins, Burton, "Bob Feller's $150,000 Pitch," *Saturday Evening Post*, April 19, 1947.

Hoffman, John C., "Squirrel Night at the Brewers," *Esquire*, September 1943.

Hogan, Lawrence, James Overmyer, and James DiClerico, "Baseball as Black Comfortability: Negro Professional Baseball in New Jersey in the Era of the Color Line," paper delivered on June 11, 1991, at the Third Annual Cooperstown Symposium on Baseball and American Culture. Accessed at the Newark Public Library.

"A Jolly Good Feller," *Baseball Magazine*, February 1946.

Jordan, David M., Larry R. Gerlach, and John P. Rossi, "A Baseball Myth Exploded: Bill Veeck and the 1943 Sale of the Phillies," *The National Pastime* 18, (1998): 3–13.

Kinkead, Eugene, "That Was the War: Wild Pigs and Mr. Feller," *The New Yorker*, May 11, 1946. Newyorker.com/archive.

"Larry Doby Doesn't Mind Being 'Second Black' Again," *Jet*, July 20, 1978. Google Books.

Lebovitz, Hal, "Bob Feller's Disappointment," *Sport*, October 1959.

Lebovitz, Hal, "The '48 Indians: One Last Hurrah." *Sport*, June 1965.

Lemon, Bob, as told to Al Stump, "I Learned to PITCH in the Majors," *Sport*, May 1953.

Lester, Larry, "Can You Read, Judge Landis?" *Black Ball: A Negro Leagues Journal* vol. 1, no. 2 (Fall 2008): 57–82.

Linn, Ed, "Immortal Hanger-on," *Sport*, August 1956.

Linn, Ed, "Lou Boudreau: The Boy Manager Grows Up," *Sport*, May 1957.

Malloy, Jerry, "Black Bluejackets," *The National Pastime* vol. 4, no. 2 (Winter 1985): 72–77. http://research.sabr.org/journals/files/SABR-National_Pastime-04-2 .pdf.

McKelway, St. Clair, "Bob Feller: Baseball Idol Devotes Himself to Care and Worship of His Right Arm," *Life*, May 12, 1941.

McLemore, Henry, "*Look* Examines Bob Feller," *Look*, April 22, 1941.

Metcalf, Mark, "Organized Baseball's Night Birth," *Baseball Research Journal*, SABR, 45, no. 2 (Fall 2016). https://sabr.org/research/organized-baseball -s-night-birth.

Moore, Louis, "Doby Does It! Larry Doby, Race, and American Democracy in Post-World War II America," *Journal of Sports History* 42, no. 3 (Fall 2015): 363–70.

Nathan, Daniel A, "Satchel Paige, the Baltimore Black Sox and the Politics of Remembrance." In *Satchel Paige and Company: Essays on the Kansas City Monarchs, Their Greatest Star and the Negro Leagues*, edited by Leslie A. Heaphy, 13–20. Jefferson, NC: McFarland & Company, 2007.

Parker, Dan, "How Democratic Is Sport?" *Sport*, September 1949.

Prell, Ed, "You Can't Stop Veeck," *Sport*, January 1, 1947. www.sportthemagazine
.com.

Reissman, Norman, "How McKechnie Makes Ballplayers." *Liberty*, July 15, 1939.

Rice, Grantland. "Reg'lar Fellers," *Sport*, September 1946.

Roeder, Bill, "Did They Expect Too Much of Larry Doby?" *Sport*, April 1958.

Rumill, Ed, "Cleveland's Ace Southpaw, Gene Bearden," *Baseball Magazine*,
September 1948.

Schuld, Fred. "Alva Bradley: Baseball's Last Purist." In *Batting Four Thousand:
Baseball in the Western Reserve*, edited by Brad Sullivan, 46–51. Cleveland,
OH: Society for American Baseball Research, 2008.

Shane, Ted, "Chocolate Rube Waddell," *Saturday Evening Post*, July 27, 1940.

"Sport: The Annual Fever," *Time*, October 11, 1948, 57.

"Sport: Baseball: New Season," *Time*, April 19, 1937.

"Sport: Double-Pennant Fever," *Time*, September 20, 1948.

"Sport: Man with the Pink Hair," *Time*, December 5, 1949.

Stockton, J. Roy, "Bob Feller—Storybook Ball Player," *Saturday Evening Post*,
February 20, 1937.

Stump, Al, "Pop Lemon's Boy," *Sport*, June 1950.

Sullivan, Neil J., "Baseball and Race: The Limits of Competition," *The Journal of
Negro History*, 83, no. 3 (Summer 1998): 168–77.

Taylor, Shakeia, "Effa Manley's Hidden Life: The Only Woman in the National
Baseball Hall of Fame Had a Fascinating—and Confusing—Past." *SB Nation*, April 30, 2020, https://www.sbnation.com/2020/4/30/21238190/effa
-manley-hall-of-fame-negro-league-newark-eagles.

Veeck, Bill, as told to Gordon Cobbledick, "Baseball and Me, Part I—The Boys I
Left Behind," *Sport*, March 1950.

Veeck, Bill, as told to Gordon Cobbledick, "Baseball and Me, Part II—I Believe
in Fireworks," *Sport*, April 1950.

Veeck, Bill, as told to Gordon Cobbledick, Part III—Am I Bad for Baseball?"
Sport, May 1950.

Veeck, Bill, with Gordon Cobbledick, "So You Want to Run a Ball Club?" *Saturday Evening Post*, April 23, 1949.

Veeck, Bill, with Ed Linn, "Speaking Out: They've Wrecked the American
League," *Saturday Evening Post*, July 11/18, 1964.

Yoder, Robert M., and James S. Kearns, "Boy Magnate," *Saturday Evening Post*,
August 28, 1943.

Young, A. S. "Doc," "Is Larry Doby the New Tris Speaker?" *Sport*, March 1949.

Young, A. S. "Doc," "The Jackie Robinson Era," *Ebony*, November 1955.

Young, A. S. "Doc," "An 'Old Man' Makes Baseball History, *Ebony*, March 1969. Google Books.

BOOKS

Aaron, Hank, and Lonnie Wheeler. *I Had a Hammer: The Hank Aaron Story*. New York: HarperCollins Publishers, 1991.

Abbott, Karl P. *Open for the Season*. New York: Doubleday & Co., 1950.

Anderson, Dave. *Pennant Races: Baseball at Its Best*. New York: Doubleday, 1994.

Baraka, Amiri. *The Autobiography of LeRoi Jones*. New York: Freundlich Books, 1984.

Barthel, Thomas. *Baseball Barnstorming and Exhibition Games, 1901–1962: A History of Off-Season Major League Play*. Jefferson, NC: McFarland & Company, 2007.

Battleship USS Alabama BB-60 Golden Anniversary History. Nashville: Turner Publishing Company, 1993.

Beck, Peggy. "Working in the Shadows of Rickey and Robinson: Bill Veeck, Larry Doby and the Advancement of Black Players in Baseball." *Cooperstown Symposium in Baseball and American Culture, 1997*. Jefferson, NC: McFarland & Company, Inc., 2000.

Berkow, Ira. *The Corporal Was a Pitcher: The Courage of Lou Brissie*. Chicago: Triumph Books, 2009.

Boudreau, Lou, with Ed Fitzgerald. *Player-Manager*. Boston: Little, Brown and Company, 1949.

Boudreau, Lou, with Russell Schneider. *Covering All the Bases*. Champaign, IL: Sagamore Publishing, 1993.

Bradlee, Jr., Ben. *The Kid: The Immortal Life of Ted Williams*. New York: Little, Brown and Company, 2013.

Branson, Douglas M. *Greatness in the Shadows: Larry Doby and the Integration of the American League*. Lincoln: University of Nebraska Press, 2016.

Briley, Ron. "Do Not Go Gently into That Good Night: Race, the Baseball Establishment, and the Retirements of Bob Feller and Jackie Robinson." In Joseph Dorinson and Joram Warmund, eds. *Jackie Robinson: Race, Sports, and the American Dream*. New York: Routledge, 2006.

Brown, Rebecca Bundy and Heidi Bundy Brown, eds. *The "Mighty A" and the Men Who Made Her Mighty: Sea Stories from USS Alabama BB-60 "The Mighty*

A"—Remembrances of Things Past by the Men Who Made Her Mighty. Self-published, 1999.

Brown, Warren. *The Chicago Cubs.* New York: G. P. Putnam's Sons, 1946.

Bryant, Howard. *The Heritage: Black Athletes, a Divided America, and the Politics of Patriotism.* Boston: Beacon Press, 2019.

Bryant, Howard. *Shut Out: A Story of Race and Baseball in Boston.* Boston: Beacon Press, 2003.

Bullock, Steven R. *Playing for Their Nation: Baseball and the American Military During World War II.* Lincoln: University of Nebraska Press, 2004.

Burk, Robert F. *Much More Than a Game: Players, Owners, & American Baseball Since 1921.* Chapel Hill: The University of North Carolina Press, 2001.

Campanella, Roy. *It's Good to Be Alive.* Boston: Little, Brown and Company, 1959.

Clifford, Clark, with Richard Holbrooke. *Counsel to the President: A Memoir.* New York: Anchor Books, 1992.

Condon, Dave. *The Go-Go Chicago White Sox.* Chicago: Coward-McCann, 1960.

Condon, George E. *Cleveland: The Best Kept Secret.* New York: Doubleday, 1967.

Connor, Anthony J. *Voices from Cooperstown: Baseball's Hall of Famers Tell It Like It Was.* New York: Galahad Books, 1998.

Crissey, Jr., Harrington E. *Athletes Away: A Selective Look at Professional Baseball Players in the Navy During World War II.* Sharon Hill, PA: Archway Press, Inc., 1984.

Crissey, Jr., Harrington E. *Teenagers, Graybeards and 4-F's, vol. 2: The American League.* Trenton, NJ: Society for American Baseball Research, 1982.

Cvornyek, Robert L. *Baseball in Newark.* Mount Pleasant, SC: Arcadia Publishing, 2003.

Daley, Arthur. *Times at Bat: A Half Century of Baseball.* New York: Random House, 1950.

Dickson, Paul. *Bill Veeck: Baseball's Greatest Maverick.* New York: Walker Books, 2012.

DiClerico, James and Barry J. Pavelec. *The Jersey Game: The History of Modern Baseball from Its Birth to the Big Leagues in the Garden State.* New Brunswick, NJ: Rutgers University Press, 1991.

DiMaggio, Dom, with Bill Gilbert. *Real Grass, Real Heroes: Baseball's Historic 1941 Season.* New York: Zebra Books, 1990.

Donahue, Ralph J. *Ready on the Right: A True Story of a Naturalist-Seabee on the Islands of Kodiak, Unalask, Adak, and Others.* Whitefish, MT: Kessinger Publishing, 2010.

Du Bois, W. E. B. *The Souls of Black Folk*. New York: Signet Classics, 2012.

Ehrgott, Roberts. *Mr. Wrigley's Ball Club: Chicago & the Cubs During the Jazz Age*. Lincoln: University of Nebraska Press, 2013.

Eig, Jonathan. *Opening Day: The Story of Jackie Robinson's First Season*. New York: Simon & Schuster, 2007.

Einstein, Charles, ed. *The Baseball Reader: Favorites from the Fireside Books of Baseball*. New York: Lippincott & Crowell, Publishers, 1980.

Elias, Robert. *Baseball and the American Dream: Race, Class, Gender, and the National Pastime*. Philadelphia: Routledge, 2001.

Elias, Robert. *The Empire Strikes Out: How Baseball Sold U.S. Foreign Policy and Promoted the American Way Abroad*. New York: The New Press, 2010.

Ellner, Andrew Lee. "Winning Race: Larry Doby, Cleveland, and the Integration of American League Baseball." Unpublished honor's thesis in History at Harvard College, 1997. Accessed from the Larry Doby HOF file at the National Baseball Hall of Fame.

Eskenazi, Gerald. *Bill Veeck: A Baseball Legend*. New York: McGraw-Hill, 1988.

Feller, Bob. *Strikeout Story*. New York: Bantam Books, 1948.

Feller, Bob, with Bill Gilbert. *Now Pitching, Bob Feller: A Baseball Memoir*. New York: Citadel Press, 2002.

Feller, Bob, with Burton Rocks. *Bob Feller's Little Black Book of Baseball Wisdom*. Lincolnwood, IL: Contemporary Books, 2001.

Flynn, Anita. "Being a Negro in Paterson." Unpublished research paper, 1947. Accessed at the Newark Public Library on November 14, 2016.

Fox, William Price. *Satchel Paige's America*. Tuscaloosa: University of Alabama Press, 2005.

Freedman, Lew. *A Summer to Remember: Bill Veeck, Lou Boudreau, Bob Feller, and the 1948 Cleveland Indians*. New York: Sports Publishing, 2014.

French, Winsor and Franklin Lewis, eds. *Curtain Call*. Cleveland: Gruber Foundation, 1952.

Fussman, Cal. *After Jackie: Pride, Prejudice, and Baseball's Forgotten Heroes: An Oral History*. New York: ESPN Books, 2007.

Gailey, Harry A. *Bougainville, 1943–1945: The Forgotten Campaign*. Lexington: The University Press of Kentucky, 1991.

Gardner, Michael R. *Harry Truman and Civil Rights: Moral Courage and Political Risks*. Carbondale: Southern Illinois University Press, 2002.

Gay, Timothy M. *Satch, Dizzy, & Rapid Robert: The Wild Saga of Interracial Baseball Before Jackie Robinson*. New York: Simon & Schuster, 2006.

Gay, Timothy M. *Tris Speaker: The Rough-and-Tumble Life of a Baseball Legend*. Lincoln: University of Nebraska Press, 2006.

Gilbert, Bill. *They Also Served: Baseball and the Home Front, 1941–1945*. New York: Crown Publishers, 1992.

Gogan, Roger. *Bluejackets of Summer: The History of the Great Lakes Naval Baseball Team 1942–1945*. Gurnee, IL: Great Lakes Sports Publishing, 2008.

Gola, Hank. *City of Champions: An American Story of Leather Helmets, Iron Wills, and the High School Kids from Jersey Who Won It All*. Brooklyn: Tatra Press, 2018.

Goldberg, Harold J. *D-Day in the Pacific: The Battle of Saipan*. Bloomington: Indiana University Press, 2007.

Goldman, Steven, ed. *It Ain't Over 'Til It's Over: The Baseball Prospectus Pennant Race Book*. New York: Basic Books, 2007.

Golenbock, Peter. *Wrigleyville: A Magical History Tour of the Chicago Cubs*. New York: St. Martin's Press, 1996.

Grabowski, John J., *Sports in Cleveland. An Illustrated History*. Bloomington: University of Indiana Press, 1992.

Grant, Jim "Mudcat," with Tom Sabellico and Pat O'Brien. *The Black Aces: Baseball's Only African-American Twenty-Game Winners*. Chula Vista, CA: Aventine Press, 2007.

Grayson, Harry. *They Played the Game: The Story of Baseball Greats*. New York: A. S. Barnes and Company, 1944.

Greenberg, Hank, with Ira Berkow. *Hank Greenberg: The Story of My Life*. Chicago: Ivan R. Dee, 2009.

Grimm, Charlie, with Ed Prell. *Jolly Cholly's Story: Grimm's Baseball Tales*. Notre Dame, IN: Diamond Communications, 1983.

Halberstam, David. *October 1964*. New York: Villard, 1994.

Halberstam, David. *Summer of '49*. New York: William Morrow, 1989.

Halberstam, David and Tate Donovan. *The Teammates: A Portrait of a Friendship*. New York: Hyperion, 2003.

Hano, Arnold. *A Day in the Bleachers*. Boston: Da Capo Press, 2004.

Heaphy, Leslie A. *The Negro Leagues: 1896–1960*. Jefferson, NC: McFarland & Company, 2003.

Heaphy, Leslie A., ed. *Satchel Paige and Company: Essays on the Kansas City Monarchs, Their Greatest Star and the Negro Leagues*. Jefferson, NC: McFarland & Company, 2007.

Higbe, Kirby and Martin Peter Quigley. *The High Hard One*. Lincoln: University of Nebraska Press, 1998.

Hillstrom, Laurie Collier. *Jackie Robinson and the Integration of Baseball (Defining Moments)*. Detroit: Omnigraphics Inc., 2013.

Hirshberg, Albert. *The Braves: The Pick and the Shovel*. Boston: Waverly House, 1948.

Holtzman, Jerome. *No Cheering in the Press Box*. New York: Henry Holt & Company, 1978.

Holway, John. *Black Diamonds: Life in the Negro Leagues from the Men Who Lived It*. New York: Stadium Books, 1991.

Holway, John. *Voices from the Great Black Baseball Leagues*. New York: Dodd, Mead & Co., 1975.

Honig, Donald. *Baseball America: The Heroes of the Game and the Times of Their Glory*. New York: Barnes & Noble, 1997.

Honig, Donald. *Baseball Between the Lines: Baseball in the '40s and '50s as Told by the Men Who Played It*. New York: Coward, McCann, & Geoghegan, 1976.

Honig, Donald. *Baseball When the Grass Was Real: Baseball from the '20s to the '40s Told by the Men Who Played It*. New York: Coward, McCann & Geoghegan, 1975.

Honig, Donald, *The Greatest Pitchers of All Time*. New York: Crown, 1988.

Horne, Lena and Richard Schickel. *Lena*. New York: Doubleday, 1965.

Hynes, Samuel. *Flights of Passage: Recollections of a World War II Aviator*. New York: Penguin Books, 2003.

Irvin, Monte, with Phil Pepe. *Few and Chosen: Defining Negro Leagues Greatness*. Chicago: Triumph Books, 2007.

Irvin, Monte, with James A. Riley. *Nice Guys Finish First: The Autobiography of Monte Irvin*. New York: Carroll & Graf Publishers, 1996.

Izenberg, Jerry. *Through My Eyes: A Sports Writer's 58-Year Journey*. Haworth, NJ: Saint Johann Press, 2009.

Kahn, Roger. *Rickey & Robinson: The True, Untold Story of the Integration of Baseball*. Emmaus, PA: Rodale Books, 2014.

Kaiser, David E. *Epic Season: The 1948 American League Pennant Race*. Amherst: University of Massachusetts Press, 1998.

Kashatus, William C. *Jackie & Campy: The Untold Story of Their Rocky Relationship and the Breaking of Baseball's Color Line*. Lincoln: University of Nebraska Press, 2014.

Keating, W. Dennis, Norman Krumholz, and David C. Perry. *Cleveland: A Metropolitan Reader*. Kent, OH: The Kent State University Press, 1995.

Kelley, Brent. *The Pastime in Turbulence: Interviews with Baseball Players of the 1940s*. Jefferson, NC: McFarland & Company, 2001.

Kiner, Ralph, with Danny Peary. *Baseball Forever: Reflections on 60 Years in the Game*. Chicago: Triumph Books, 2004.

Klima, John. *The Game Must Go On: Hank Greenberg, Pete Gray, and the Great Days of Baseball on the Home Front in WWII*. New York: Thomas Dunne Books, 2015.

Knight, Jonathan. *Classic Tribe: The 50 Greatest Games in Cleveland Indians History*. Kent, OH: Kent State University Press, 2009.

Kuenster, John, Ed., *From Cobb to "Catfish": 128 Illustrated Stories from Baseball Digest*. Chicago: Rand McNally & Company, 1975.

Kukla, Barbara J. *Swing City: Newark Nightlife, 1925–50*. Philadelphia: Temple University Press, 1991.

Lacy, Sam and Moses J. Newsom. *Fighting for Fairness: The Life Story of Hall of Fame Sportswriter Sam Lacy*. Centreville, MD: Tidewater Publishers, 1998.

Lamb, Chris. *Conspiracy of Silence: Sportswriters and the Long Campaign to Desegregate Baseball*. Lincoln: University of Nebraska Press, 2012.

Lanctot, Neil. *Campy: The Two Lives of Roy Campanella*. New York: Simon & Schuster, 2011.

Lanctot, Neil. *Negro League Baseball: The Rise and Ruin of a Black Institution*. Philadelphia: University of Pennsylvania Press, 2004.

Lebovitz, Hal. *The Best of Hal Lebovitz: Great Sportswriting from Six Decades in Cleveland*. Cleveland: Gray & Company, 2004.

Levine, Peter, ed. *Baseball History 4: An Annual of Original Baseball Research*. Westport, CT: Meckler, 1991.

Lewis, Franklin. *The Cleveland Indians*. Kent, OH: Kent State University Press, 2006.

Lingeman, Richard. *Small Town America: A Narrative History, 1620–Present*. Boston: Houghton Mifflin Company, 1980.

Liscio, Stephanie M. *Integrating Cleveland Baseball: Media Activism, the Integration of the Indians and the Demise of the Negro League Buckeyes*. Jefferson, NC: McFarland & Company, 2010.

Longert, Scott H. *No Money, No Beer, No Pennants: The Cleveland Indians and Baseball in the Great Depression*. Athens: Ohio University Press, 2016.

Lott, Arnold S. and Robert F. Sumrall. *USS Alabama (BB60)*. Annapolis, MD: Leeward Publications, 1974.

Luke, Bob. *The Most Famous Woman in Baseball: Effa Manley and the Negro Leagues*. Lincoln, NE: Potomac Books, 2011.

Macht, Norman L. *The Grand Old Man of Baseball: Connie Mack in His Final Years, 1932–1956*. Lincoln: University of Nebraska Press, 2015.

Madden, Bill. *1954: The Year Willie Mays and the First Generation of Black Superstars Changed Major League Baseball Forever*. Boston: Da Capo Press, 2014.

Manley, Effa and Leon Herbert Hardwick. Edited by Robert Cvornyek. *Negro Baseball . . . Before Integration*. Haworth, NJ: St. Johann Press, 2006.

Marshall, William. *Baseball's Pivotal Era, 1945–1951*. Lexington: The University Press of Kentucky, 1999.

Martin, Alfred M. and Alfred T. Martin. *The Negro Leagues in New Jersey: A History*. Jefferson, NC: McFarland & Company, 2008.

McGregor, Robert Kuhn. *A Calculus of Color: The Integration of Baseball's American League*. Jefferson, NC: McFarland & Company, 2015.

Mead, William B. *Baseball Goes to War: Stars Don Khakis, 4-Fs Vie for Pennant*. Washington, D.C.: Broadcast Interview Source, 1998.

Meany, Tom. *Baseball's Greatest Pitchers*. New York: A. S. Barnes & Co., 1951.

Meany, Tom. *Baseball's Greatest Players*. New York: Grosset & Dunlap, 1953.

Monks, Jr., John. *A Ribbon and a Star: The Action-Filled Account of the Third Marines at Bougainville*. New York: Pyramid Books, 1966.

Moore, Joseph Thomas. *Larry Doby: The Struggle of the American League's First Black Player*. Mineola, NY: Dover Publications, 2011.

Moore, Leonard N. *Carl B. Stokes and the Rise of Black Political Power*. Urbana: University of Illinois Press, 2002.

Nalty, Bernard C. *Long Passage to Korea: Black Sailors and the Integration of the U.S. Navy*. Washington, D.C.: Naval Historical Center, Department of the Navy, 2003.

Nichols, David, ed. *Ernie's War: The Best of Ernie Pyle's World War II Dispatches*. New York: Random House, 1986.

Nowlin, Bill, ed., Mark Armour, Bob Brady, Len Levin, and Saul Wisnia, associate eds. *Spahn, Sain, and Teddy Ballgame: Boston's (almost) Perfect Baseball Summer of 1948*. Burlington, MA: Rounder Books, 2008.

Odenkirk, James E. *Of Tribes and Tribulations: The Early Decades of the Cleveland Indians*. Jefferson, NC: McFarland & Company, 2015.

Odenkirk, James E. *Plain Dealing: A Biography of Gordon Cobbledick*. Tempe, AZ: Spider-Naps Publications, 1990.

O'Neil, Buck, and Steve Wulf and David Conrads. *I Was Right on Time: My Journey from the Negro Leagues to the Majors*. New York: Simon & Schuster, 1996.

Overmyer, James. *Queen of the Negro Leagues: Effa Manley and the Newark Eagles*. Lanham, MD: Scarecrow Press, 1998.

Paige, Leroy (Satchel), as told to David Lipman. *Maybe I'll Pitch Forever: A Great*

Baseball Player Tells the Hilarious Story Behind the Legend. Lincoln, NE: Bison Books, 1993.

Paige, Leroy Satchel and Hal Lebovitz. *Pitchin' Man: Satchel Paige's Own Story*. New York: Ishi Press International, 1948.

Parrott, Harold. *The Lords of Baseball: A Wry Look at a Side of the Game the Fan Seldom Sees—The Front Office*. New York: Praeger Publishers, 1976.

Patkin, Max and Stan Hochman. *The Clown Prince of Baseball*. Waco, TX: WRS Publishing, 1994.

Peary, Danny, ed., *We Played the Game: 65 Players Remember Baseball's Greatest Era, 1947–1964*. New York: Hyperion, 1994.

Pells, Richard H. *Radical Visions and American Dreams: Culture and Social Thought in the Depression Years*. Champaign: University of Illinois Press, 2004.

Peterson, Robert. *Only the Ball Was White: A History of Legendary Black Players and All-Black Professional Teams*. New York: Oxford University Press, 1970.

Phillips, Kimberley L. *AlabamaNorth: African-American Migrants, Community, and Working-Class Activism in Cleveland, 1915–45*. Urbana: University of Illinois Press, 1999.

Pifer, Richard L. *A City at War: Milwaukee Labor During World War II*. Madison: Wisconsin Historical Society Press, 2002,

Pluto, Terry. *The Curse of Rocky Colavito: A Loving Look at a Thirty-Year Slump*. New York: Simon & Schuster, 1994.

Polner, Murray, *Branch Rickey: A Biography, Revised Edition*. Jefferson, NC: McFarland & Company, 2007.

Posnanski, Joe. *The Soul of Baseball: A Road Trip Through Buck O'Neil's America*. New York: William Morrow, 2007.

Prager, Joshua. *The Echoing Green: The Untold Story of Bobby Thomson, Ralph Branca and the Shot Heard Round the World*. New York: Pantheon Books, 2006.

Rampersad, Arnold. *Jackie Robinson: A Biography*. New York: Alfred A. Knopf, 1997.

Reisler, Jim. *Black Writers/Black Baseball: An Anthology of Articles from Black Sportswriters Who Covered the Negro Leagues*. Jefferson, NC: McFarland & Company, 1994.

Ribowsky, Mark. *A Complete History of the Negro Leagues: 1884–1955*. New York: Birch Lane Press, 1995.

Ribowsky, Mark. *Don't Look Back: Satchel Paige in the Shadows of Baseball*. New York: Simon & Schuster, 1994.

Riley, James A. *Dandy, Day, and the Devil*. Cocoa, FL: TK Publishers, 1987.

Robinson, Eddie, with C. Paul Rogers III. *Lucky Me: My Sixty-Five Years in Baseball*. Dallas: Southern Methodist University Press, 2011.

Robinson, Jackie. Charles Dexter, ed. *Baseball Has Done It*. Brooklyn: Ig Publishing, 2005.

Robinson, Jackie, as told to Alfred Duckett. *I Never Had It Made: An Autobiography of Jackie Robinson*. New York: Ecco, 1995.

Rogosin, Donn. *Invisible Men: Life in Baseball's Negro Leagues*. New York: Atheneum, 1983.

Rose, William Ganson. *Cleveland: The Making of a City*. Kent, OH: Kent State University Press, 1990.

Rust, Art. *Get That Nigger Off the Field!: An Oral History of Black Ballplayers from the Negro Leagues to the Present*. Brooklyn, NY: Book Mail Services, 1992.

Schiffer, Don, ed. *My Greatest Baseball Game*. New York: A. S. Barnes, 1950.

Schneider, Russell. *The Boys of the Summer of '48: The Golden Anniversary of the World Champion Cleveland Indians*. Champaign, IL: Sports Publishing, 1998.

Schneider, Russell. *The Cleveland Indians Encyclopedia*. Champaign, IL: Sports Publishing, 2001.

Schneller, Jr., Robert J. *Breaking the Color Barrier: The U.S. Naval Academy's First Black Midshipmen and the Struggle for Racial Equality*. New York: NYU Press, 2005.

Schoor, Gene. *Bob Feller: Hall of Fame Strikeout Star*. Garden City, NY: Doubleday & Company, Inc., 1962.

Schrijvers, Peter. *Bloody Pacific: American Soldiers at War with Japan*. New York: Palgrave Macmillan, 2010.

Sickels, John. *Bob Feller: Ace of the Greatest Generation*. Washington, D.C.: Potomac Books, 2004.

Soderholm-Difatte, Bryan. *The Golden Era of Major League Baseball: A Time of Transition and Integration*. New York: Rowman & Littlefield Publishers, 2015.

Sokol, Jason. *All Eyes Are Upon Us: Race and Politics from Boston to Brooklyn*. New York: Basic Books, 2014.

Sokol, Jason. *There Goes My Everything: White Southerners in the Age of Civil Rights, 1945–1975*. New York: Knopf, 2006.

Spivey, Donald. *"If You Were Only White": The Life of Leroy "Satchel" Paige*. Columbia: University of Missouri Press, 2012.

Stillwell, Paul, ed. *The Golden Thirteen: Recollections of the First Black Naval Officers*. Annapolis, MD: Naval Institute Press, 1993.

Stout, Glenn. *The Cubs: The Complete Story of Chicago Cubs Baseball*. Boston: Houghton Mifflin Harcourt, 2007.

Stradling, David and Richard Stradling. *Where the River Burned: Carl Stokes and the Struggle to Save Cleveland*. Ithaca, NY: Cornell University Press, 2015.

Suchma, Philip C. "From the Best of Times to the Worst of Times: Professional Sport and Urban Decline in a Tale of Two Clevelands: 1945–1978." Unpublished dissertation: The Ohio State University, 2005.

Sullivan, Brad, ed. *Batting Four Thousand: Baseball in the Western Reserve*. Cleveland, OH: Society for American Baseball Research, 2008.

Susman, Warren I. *Culture as History: The Transformation of American Society in the Twentieth Century*. New York: Pantheon Books, 1973.

Swaine, Rick. *The Black Stars Who Made Baseball Whole: The Jackie Robinson Generation in the Major Leagues, 1947–1959*. Jefferson, NC: McFarland & Company, 2005.

Tillman, Barrett, *Clash of the Carriers: The True Story of the Marianas Turkey Shoot in World War II*. New York: NAL Hardcover, 2005.

Trouppe, Quincy, *20 Years Too Soon: Prelude to Major-League Integrated Baseball*. Los Angeles: S and S Enterprises, 1977.

Turbow, Jason and Michael Duca. *The Baseball Codes: Beanballs, Sign Stealing, and Bench Clearing Brawls, The Unwritten Rules of America's Pastime*. New York: Anchor, 2011.

Tuttle, Brad R. *How Newark Became Newark: The Rise, Fall, and Rebirth of an American City*. New Brunswick, NJ: Rutgers University Press, 2009.

Tye, Larry. *Satchel: The Life and Times of an American Legend*. New York: Random House, 2006.

Tygiel, Jules. *Baseball's Great Experiment: Jackie Robinson and His Legacy*. New York: Oxford University Press.

Tygiel, Jules. *Extra Bases: Reflections on Jackie Robinson, Race, and Baseball History*. Lincoln, NE: Bison Books, 2002.

Vaught, David. *The Farmers' Game: Baseball in Rural America*. Baltimore: Johns Hopkins University Press, 2012.

Veeck, Bill, with Ed Linn. *The Hustler's Handbook*. Chicago: Ivan R. Dee, 2009.

Veeck, Bill, with Ed Linn. *Veeck—As in Wreck: The Chaotic Career of Baseball's Incorrigible Maverick*. Chicago: The University of Chicago Press, 2001.

Vincent, Fay. *The Only Game in Town: Baseball Stars of the 1930s and 1940s Talk About the Game They Loved*. New York: Simon & Schuster, 2006.

Voigt, David Q. *America Through Baseball*. Chicago: Nelson-Hall, 1976.

Waer, Karl M. "The Negro in the History of Paterson, New Jersey." Unpublished college research paper, May 1969. Accessed in the Newark Public Library.

Watkins, Mel. *Stepin Fetchit: The Life and Times of Lincoln Perry*. New York: Pantheon, 2005.

Wees, Marshall Paul and Francis Beauchesne Thornton. *King-Doctor of Ulithi*. New York: Macmillan, 1950.

Weintraub, Robert. *The Victory Season: The End of World War II and the Birth of Baseball's Golden Age*. New York: Little, Brown and Company, 2014.

Wendel, Tim. *High Heat: The Secret History of the Fastball and the Improbable Search for the Fastest Pitcher of All Time*. Cambridge, MA: Da Capo Press, 2010.

Westcott, Rich. *Mickey Vernon: The Gentleman First Baseman*. Philadelphia: Camino Books, Inc., 2005.

White, G. Edward. *Creating the National Pastime: Baseball Transforms Itself, 1903–1953*. Princeton: Princeton University Press, 1996.

Wilkerson, Isabel. *The Warmth of Other Suns: The Epic Story of America's Great Migration*. New York: Random House, 2010.

Williams, Pat and Michael Weinreb. *Marketing Your Dreams: Business and Life Lessons from Bill Veeck, Baseball's Marketing Genius*. Champaign, IL: Sports Publishing, 2000.

Williams, Ted, with John Underwood. *My Turn at Bat: The Story of My Life*. New York: Simon & Schuster, 1988.

Winegardner, Mark. *Crooked River Burning: A Novel*. New York: Harcourt, 2001.

Wood, James M. *Out and About with Winsor French*. Kent, OH: The Kent State University Press, 2011.

Wright, Giles R. *Afro-Americans in New Jersey: A Short History*. Trenton: New Jersey Historical Commission, 1989.

Young, A. S. "Doc." *Great Negro Baseball Stars and How They Made the Major Leagues*. New York: A. S. Barnes, 1953.

Young, William A. *J. L. Wilkinson and the Kansas City Monarchs: Trailblazers in Black Baseball*. Jefferson, NC: McFarland & Company, 2016.

Zeiler, Thomas W. *Jackie Robinson and Race in America: A Brief History with Documents*. New York: Bedford/St. Martin's, 2013.

INDEX